UNCLE TOM
MANIA

To

Hedi 306

108

UNCLE TOM MANIA

SLAVERY, MINSTRELSY
AND TRANSATLANTIC CULTURE
 # IN THE 1850s

BY SARAH MEER

THE UNIVERSITY OF GEORGIA PRESS · ATHENS & LONDON

© 2005 by the University of Georgia Press
Athens, Georgia 30602
All rights reserved
Designed by Sandra Strother Hudson
Set in 10.5/14 Bertholdt Bodoni by Graphic Composition
Printed and bound by Maple-Vail
The paper in this book meets the guidelines for permanence and durability
of the Committee on Production Guidelines for Book Longevity
of the Council on Library Resources.
Printed in the United States of America
09 08 07 06 05 c 5 4 3 2 1
09 08 07 06 05 p 5 4 3 2 1

Library of Congress Cataloging-in-Publication Data
Meer, Sarah, 1969–
Uncle Tom Mania : slavery, minstrelsy, and transatlantic culture in the 1850s /
Sarah Meer
p. cm.
Includes bibliographical references and index.
ISBN 0-8203-2736-0 (alk. paper) – ISBN 0-8203-2737-9 (pbk : alk. paper)
1. Stowe, Harriet Beecher, 1811–1896. Uncle Tom's cabin. 2. Stowe, Harriet
Beecher, 1811–1896–Adaptations–History and criticism. 3. Stowe, Harriet Beecher,
1811–1896–Appreciation–Great Britain. 4. Stowe, Harriet Beecher, 1811–1896–
Appreciation–United States. 5. Stowe, Harriet Beecher, 1811–1896–Parodies,
imitations, etc. 6. Didactic fiction, American–History and criticism. 7. Stowe,
Harriet Beecher, 1811–1896–Influence. 8. Uncle Tom (Fictitious character).
9. African Americans in literature. 10. Fugitive slaves in literature. 11. Minstrel
shows–History. 12. Slavery in literature. I. Title.
PS2954.U6M44 2005
813'.6–dc22
2005008505

British Library Cataloguing-in-Publication Data available

CONTENTS

ACKNOWLEDGMENTS

I should like to thank Nottingham Trent University for employment, leave, and research expenses; the University of Cambridge for my current employment; and the Master and Fellows of Selwyn College, Cambridge, for the Keasbey Research Fellowship in American Studies during which I began this project.

The comments and suggestions of the anonymous readers for the University of Georgia Press were immensely helpful. I am also very grateful for all the help and advice I have received from the press, especially from Nancy Grayson, Jennifer L. Reichlin, and Mary M. Hill.

I should also like to thank the staff at the following libraries: the University Library at Cambridge, Nottingham Trent University's library at Clifton, the British Library, the Hallward Library at the University of Nottingham, the Literary and Philosophical Society Library in Newcastle-upon-Tyne, the Rare Books Department at Princeton University, the Library of Congress, the Harvard Theater Collection, the Harry Ransom Humanities Research Center at the University of Texas at Austin, the American Antiquarian Society, the Stowe-Day Center, and the Library Company of Philadelphia. I am especially grateful to Annette Fern at the Harvard Theatre Collection, Phillip Lapsansky at the Library Company of Philadelphia, and Nik Smith at Nottingham Trent.

I owe special thanks to those of my friends who live or have lived near these libraries and who generously offered their hospitality when I visited, especially Nicola Bown, Wendy Carter, Jean and Cyrus Chothia, John Dickinson, Liz Dickinson, Carole Dupont-Stonestreet, Sam Inglis, Judith Johnson, Walton Johnson, Anne Habiby, Barbara McCarthy, Gene McCarthy, Sangeeta Pratap, Leah Price, Melissa Pullen, Paul Stonestreet, Pam Thurschwell and family, and Tao Wang (who also gave me an unforgettable dumpling master class). I should like, in addition, to thank them for references, suggestions, and/or less tangible kinds of help, for which I also thank Carolyn Batstone, Gillian Beer, Janet Beer, Bridget Bennett, Celeste-Marie Bernier, Graham

Black, David Booth, Daphne Brooks, Nemesis Bruce, Jeanne Buntinx, Vicki Burke, Catherine Byron, Maxine Clarke, Marie-Louise Coolahan, Martin Crawford, Ahsana Dar, Hans Giesen, Oona Giesen, Heather Glen, Soraya Goga, Priyamvada Gopal, Fiona Green, Cindy Hamilton, Dave Hamilton, Lynne Hapgood, Brian Hearns, Stephen Heath, Caroline Howlett, Yasmine Janmohamed, Lee Jenkins, Melanie John, Nicole King, Denise Kohn, Olivia Lacey, John Lucas, Tim Lustig, Denise McCoskey, Susan Manning, Colin Marx, Haroon Meer, Rashid Meer, Amy Morris, Mary Morrissey, Judie Newman, Clíona O'Gallchoir, Sharon Ouditt, Kyriaki Panteleou, Jon Parkin, Monica Pearl, Alan Rice, Diane Roberts, Dominique Santos, Alinah Segobye, Mike Sewell, Clare Macdonald Shaw, Peter Smith, Neelam Srivastava, David Stack, Trudi Tate, Michael Tilby, Emily Todd, Lyndsey Traub, Nadia Valman, and Richard Yarborough.

I am especially grateful to Jean Chothia for many kinds of help; to Carole Dupont-Stonestreet for all her thoughtfulness; and to Cindy Hamilton, Judie Newman, and Michael O'Brien for reading complete drafts, for encouragement at difficult points, and for sharing some of their own work at early stages. Their generosity and insight are inspiring.

My own *Tom* mania must have tested the patience of my family, but they have never let me feel it. I remember with gratitude the encouragement of my grandmother Alice Hearns, my great-aunt Ruby Standley, my honorary grandfather A. K. M. Docrat, and my great-uncle Ismail Meer; and for her interest I thank my great-aunt Fatima Meer.

For unstinting support and assistance of every possible kind, for their apparently unflagging interest and insights—even "from the purlieus of Paddington"—I thank my parents, Maureen and Iqbal Meer. This book is for them, with love.

INTRODUCTION

UNCLE TOM WAS THERE,
IN CROCKERY,
RECEIVING
THEOLOGICAL
INSTRUCTIONS FROM
MISS EVA.

Charles Dickens, "The Lazy
Tour of Two Idle Apprentices in
Five Chapters," 1857

On 8 October 1852 half of the front page of the *Liberator*, William Lloyd Garrison's weekly abolitionist newspaper, featured items related to a single antislavery novel.[1] Harriet Beecher Stowe's *Uncle Tom's Cabin* appeared in almost every issue of the *Liberator* that year, linked to a profuse variety of texts in many genres and several languages. There were clippings from other papers, reviews, readers' poems, notices of proslavery "answers," and an account of a New York dramatization. There was also evidence of the novel's reception abroad: items about foreign editions and translations, overseas reviews, and letters to the *Times* of London.[2]

This interest was by no means confined to the antislavery press. The *Liberator*'s attention was just one small facet of what one London newspaper called "Tom-Mania," a phrase that encompassed the extraordinary public interest Stowe's book aroused on both sides of the Atlantic, its unprecedented sales, and the volume of ink spent in responding to it.[3] For a large part of 1852 and 1853 *Uncle Tom's Cabin* seemed inescapable: it was bought, discussed, imitated, and invoked on a scale hitherto unseen and previously unimaginable for a novel by an American woman, let alone a novel about slavery.

Stowe's story was also rewritten, turned into songs, plays, sketches, and even new novels, and the book inspired a vast and varied collection of *Uncle Tom* merchandise. Its imagery was transferred to paintings, puzzles, cards, board games, plates, spoons, china figurines, bronze ornaments, dolls, and

1

wallpaper.[4] *Uncle Tom* was a best-selling commodity and also many commodities, and the novel's impact was multiplied by hundreds of derivatives.

This book examines in detail the ways in which *Uncle Tom's Cabin* was rewritten—the ways in which it was, in a sense, reread—in the United States and Britain in the 1850s. It reads Stowe's novel alongside some of the products of *Tom* mania, many of them now forgotten. These products included texts asserting a variety of different positions on slavery as well as texts that sought to avoid controversy while capitalizing on Stowe's success. They demonstrate that a single text can be adapted into hundreds of forms that suit a vast spectrum of political opinions, but they also reveal the concessions and accommodations that have to be made to different genres. Any investigation of *Tom* mania needs to take account of such conditions to understand how *Uncle Tom's Cabin* contributed to the discussion of slavery in the 1850s.

This discussion was in no way confined to the United States. All over Europe *Uncle Tom's Cabin* was avidly read, translated, and talked over. But as the origin of the term "*Tom* mania" in London suggests, Britain would prove most significant in the reception and transmission of *Uncle Tom's Cabin*. As Paul Gilroy has pointed out, the slave trade created cross-Atlantic routes that have been renewed ever since for intellectual and cultural traffic. For a book about slavery these exchanges offered especially ironic resonances, but *Tom* mania had a particular relevance for the relationship between Britain and the United States.[5]

This was no small matter: in the 1850s the United States and Britain were still tightly connected economically, socially, and culturally. Businesses, churches, reform groups, and individuals in the two countries had close links.[6] The slavery question in particular formed the subject of extensive Anglo-American confrontation and cooperation—on all sides of the debate. British and American antislavery societies had for many years shared techniques, campaigns, and even personnel that provided the basis for lecture tours in the 1840s by former slaves and other abolitionists from the United States.[7] These societies not only provided part of *Uncle Tom*'s initial market in the British Isles, but also based campaigns around Stowe's novel, collecting funds in Uncle Tom Penny Offerings and circulating petitions that cited Stowe's text. They also invited Stowe to visit Britain in 1853, and her account of that trip in *Sunny Memories of Foreign Lands* called attention to her novel's popularity in Britain, which was already an absorbing topic of interest in the antislavery press.[8]

Literature's role in constituting this transatlantic world was crucial, but the relationships it set up were often fraught and troubled ones.[9] In this period the majority of books Americans read were British, and British periodicals were widely followed in the United States. By comparison, only a small number of American writers were reviewed (and even fewer published) in Britain, while certain infamous British essays decrying American literature were remembered for decades.[10] These attacks had been exacerbated by the numerous books on the United States produced by British travelers. Many of these books were regarded by Americans as vicious assaults, and several of them reinforced the charge that America was not a literary nation. Partly in reaction to this cultural defamation, American writers were themselves calling, throughout the first half of the nineteenth century, for a national literature that would finally break free of British models and reflect the particularity of the new nation (see chapter 7).

Thus it was immensely significant that *Tom* mania crossed the Atlantic. When Stowe visited Britain she toured as a famous author, reversing Charles Dickens's earlier triumph in the United States, and for once British and American reviewers were all occupied with an American book. In Britain several reviews treated *Uncle Tom's Cabin* as a major document of American society, while the British writer Barbara Bodichon used Stowe's book as a frame to help her interpret—and describe—her travels in the Southern United States. Frances Hodgson Burnett, who later migrated to Tennessee, wrote a startling account of *Uncle Tom*'s effect on her as an English child, describing how her (sympathetic) view of the Confederacy during the Civil War was partly formed by Stowe's novel (see chapters 1 and 3).

But *Uncle Tom*'s subject matter complicated the shift it caused in the cultural power of the two nations. The book's popularity renewed international antislavery alliances and forged new ones, but some American readers saw only hostility in the British reception of *Uncle Tom's Cabin*, assuming its critique of slavery was being used to reinforce anti-American prejudice. *Uncle Tom's Cabin* contributed to transatlantic enmity as well as friendship, and *Tom* mania itself came to reflect both. For some readers the British reception of *Uncle Tom's Cabin* was so important that their rewritings of the novel featured parodies of the prime players in English discussions of the text. Such books made *Uncle Tom* more than a representation, they made it a textual representative of the United States in Britain (see chapter 6).

Reduced to its basics, *Uncle Tom's Cabin* is a condemnation both of slavery and the Fugitive Slave Act of 1850, which facilitated the recapture of ex-slaves from the Northern "free" states. It uses two interlinked plots, the stories of two slaves threatened with separation from their families by the financial problems of their (relatively kind) master. Tom, a Christian, accepts his fate patiently until required to punish other slaves, whereupon he refuses, and his last owner beats him to death; while Eliza runs away, desperately carrying her child to freedom across the cracking ice of the Ohio River. In the fashion of sentimental novels, the antislavery point is reinforced by the evocation of readerly emotion not only at Eliza's rescue and Tom's sufferings but also at the premature death of Tom's child-patron Eva, whose virtues inspire her aunt to abandon racial prejudice.

This text became a prodigy of publishing history, rewriting the definition of a best-seller and triggering an apparently self-fueling explosion of publicity and international celebrity. The book was not only popular, not only expanded the midcentury concept of success, but made the slavery question marketable. The *Uncle Tom* phenomenon prefigured the scope and speed of twentieth-century mass culture and yet predated much of the technology and the marketing structures now associated with it. The *Times* understated the case emphatically in pronouncing it a "decided hit."[11]

Ironically, Stowe had been turned down by the first publishers she approached on the grounds that books about slavery did not sell.[12] But after appearing as a serial in the *National Era*, an antislavery journal based in Washington, D.C., *Uncle Tom's Cabin* was brought out by John P. Jewett on 20 March 1852. Jewett's first edition of 5,000 copies sold out within a week, and from that point onward sales were astonishing—50,000 copies within eight weeks, 200,000 by January 1853, 300,000 after the first year.[13]

These figures were exceptionally good, although the 1850s were boom years for American publishing, and other female sentimentalists were selling in huge numbers. Susan Warner's *The Wide, Wide World* sold 500,000 copies but over many years, while the figure for Maria Cummins's *The Lamplighter*—100,000 within a decade—looks modest beside Stowe's. Comparing *Uncle Tom* to the productions of the American Antislavery Society suggests how much more of an achievement this was for a book about slavery. *The Narrative of the Life of Frederick Douglass, an American Slave* took five years of promotion to sell 30,000 copies in the 1840s: its hard-won English, Irish, and Scottish readers were wooed by Douglass himself during an energetic lecture tour.[14] *Uncle Tom's Cabin* managed similar returns within weeks and made its way across the Atlantic without assistance; perhaps half a million copies had been sold (in pirated editions) in Britain and its colonies by 1853.

Thus, contrary to the commercial wisdom of the time, Stowe had made the slavery issue sell, and it sold on a huge scale not only at home but also abroad. Contemporary reviewers had several theories about this success. Many, including both abolitionists and their opponents, credited the work of previous and current antislavery activists with some of the novel's popularity.[15] The *New York Independent* suggested the "religious adaptation of the book," which "is absolutely universal in its application to all classes in all lands and at all times." William Lloyd Garrison drew attention to its emotional appeal: "We confess to the frequent moistening of our eyes, and the making of our heart grow liquid as water, and the trembling of every nerve within us, in the perusal of the incidents and scenes so vividly depicted in her pages."[16]

There may also have been more circumstantial reasons. There was the effect on Northern attitudes of the Fugitive Slave Act, which may have predisposed some readers to sympathize with Stowe, especially as the novel was written in direct response to the law. Additionally, *Uncle Tom's Cabin* shared the domestic themes and sentimental style of other American best-sellers of the 1850s. And, as Ronald Zboray has pointed out, it also benefited from the technology that had contributed to the midcentury publishing explosion: the invention of electrotyping, the spread of the railroads, stronger domestic light, and cheap corrective eyeglasses. The concentration of the reading public in the Northeast as a result of the location of rail lines may also have diminished the importance of the Southern market and made its share in the sales of Stowe's book less important.[17]

The book even gained some perverse publicity from the libel action launched by the Presbyterian minister Joel Parker. Stowe had quoted a statement of Parker's that seemed to play down the evils of slavery in the novel: he threatened her with a lawsuit for holding "me up to the public, in an odious light," and though this did not materialize, each party was respectively taken up by a rival New York newspaper, the *Independent* and the *Observer*.[18] The *Observer*'s attacks on the *Independent*, Stowe, and Henry Ward Beecher and their vigorous replies comprised an acrimonious public feud for the seven months between May and November 1852.[19]

Perhaps most important, as Joan Hedrick records, Jewett made serious efforts to promote the novel, agreeing to "employ agents every where" to sell it and even commissioning John Greenleaf Whittier to write a poem, which he then had set to music.[20] In hawking the novel Jewett made a point precisely of the fact that it was selling so well, and this strategy of marketing celebrity was so patently effective that it immediately became a standard technique.[21] Stowe's novel may have reaped the greatest benefit from emerging at the very moment that publicity on a giant scale was both becoming possible and being pursued.

For the *Liberator* part of the fascination lay in the political implications of Stowe's text. For a publication dedicated to the liberation of American slaves, the book, although it did not demand immediate emancipation, was an important ally. It must have been exhilarating, and perhaps a little galling, for long-standing abolitionists to watch *Uncle Tom's Cabin*, a novel by a newcomer to antislavery politics, bring the subject into the farthest reaches of public discourse. Yet the responses to the text were by no means homogeneous. The *Liberator* recorded a diverse set of opinions on the subject of Stowe's novel, proslavery denunciations (reprinted from other periodicals) jostling against antislavery eulogies.

The *Liberator* thus reflected another aspect of *Tom* mania: it spanned the spectrum of the debate on slavery in the 1850s. According to legend, Abraham Lincoln told Stowe that the book had started the Civil War: if so, it could have fought on both sides.[22] Reviews of Stowe's book might have been expected to vary in their enthusiasm, and a reviewer's position on slavery often determined the angle taken. But these adaptations of *Uncle Tom's Cabin* both revealed the contradictions of the original and inflated them into contrary and sometimes conflicting positions on slavery. Some played down the politics, attempting to exploit *Uncle Tom*'s popularity while avoiding controversy; others pursued an extreme at which most abolitionists balked and advocated slave insurrection. Still others adapted Stowean scenes to preach the virtues of slavery itself. And some of this activity was driven more by commerce than politics. These rewriters were seeking to replicate different aspects of the novel's career, some hoping for a part of the commercial success, some to counter its polemical impact, some to share and others to assume its perceived power.

The mania was thus fueled by the countless writers and manufacturers who attempted to hijack Stowe's creation for their own purposes. A cartoon in the French satirical magazine *Le Charivari* showed a lady bluestocking telling two bespectacled companions, "We should take advantage of the opportunity. Uncle Tom is in vogue. . . . Let us hasten and write a novel called Aunt Tom."[23] Stowe's readers were not just consumers: many, like these ladies, quickly became producers too. Different contexts and political positions resulted in *Uncle Toms* not only adapted to British and French readerships but also designed for children, for various shades of pro- and antislavery opinion, or to further the designs of everyone from radical women to misogynists.

In its turn, *Tom* mania was propagated in a number of forms that were themselves notable cultural phenomena in the 1850s. As I have indicated, the genre of the sentimental novel, to which *Uncle Tom* partly belonged, produced several best-sellers in the 1850s, but *Uncle Tom's Cabin* was also reproduced in the minstrel show and in "moral drama," both at the height of their popularity in those years, during which their commercial successes were equally remarked by contemporaries. And Stowe's book also became associated with the work of the most popular American songwriter of the mid-nineteenth century, Stephen Foster. Foster's work, like *Uncle Tom's Cabin*, would be transposed into other texts, appearing in plays, sketches, and even novels, most of which were also indebted to *Uncle Tom*.

Shaped by and encompassing all these components, the idea of *Uncle Tom's Cabin* necessarily had to become a flexible, at times indistinct, and contradictory creature, working almost in the way Foucault once described the function of an author's name, so that, say, "Marx" conjures up a constellation of texts, concepts, and associations for not all of which the author himself is strictly responsible.[24] In this case it was the title of a novel that could summon an array of competing and even conflicting interpretations. *Tom* mania quickly absorbed traditions and motifs derived from outside the novel, and they began to recur as often as elements created by Stowe herself. Examining these permutations suggests the way a number of obscure and apparently insignificant texts contributed to the attitudes associated with one famous one, just as Paul Lauter has insisted that "many, often nameless individuals" can lie behind the "great ideas" eventually attributed to a single figure.[25] *Uncle Tom's Cabin* has been restored to the canon of nineteenth-century American literature only relatively recently—consideration is also due to the miasma of texts and products by which it was soon surrounded for its contemporaries.

Recent work on other writers who have been much dramatized or absorbed into popular culture has highlighted the relationship between consumption and production in this process. Martin Baker and Roger Sarbin called *The Last of the Mohicans*, another much-adapted American text, a "hollow vessel," redeployed by generations of rewriters for their own purposes.[26] And yet Patsy Stoneman observes in relation to the Brontë sisters that each adaptation or interpretation is also in part a reading of the original: "Every writer (or painter or film-maker) is also a reader who transforms previous texts into new shapes."[27] Meanings accrue to a novel partly because of the ways in which it has been read, and some of the idea of *"Uncle Tom's Cabin,"* in its own culture and ours, was created by those who reviewed it, dramatized it, or borrowed its name or imagery to construct something else. The plethora of tie-ins and spin-offs helped make the novel a ubiquitous reference point in mid-nineteenth-century culture, but they also affected it, fragmenting and diversifying the popular understanding of *Uncle Tom's Cabin*. *Tom* mania not only produced the meaning of Stowe's book in the culture of the 1850s, it ensured that it took on a variety of meanings.

The rewritings of *Uncle Tom's Cabin* form a fascinating testing ground for the questions literary critics have traditionally asked about reading: "Is reading determined by the text, by the reader's subjective responses, by social, cultural and economic factors, by conventions of reading, or by a combination of these?"[28] In different guises *Tom* mania could be used to support most of these positions. As might be assumed from its intervention in the slavery debate, Stowe's novel is designed to elicit certain responses from readers: it "spurs the reader into action" and attempts to control the reader in processes resembling those identified by Wolfgang Iser and other theorists who have characterized the way texts construct their audiences.[29] However, Iser also describes the process as bilateral, "a dynamic *interaction* between text and reader," and subsequent writers have attributed more of the business to the reader, Michel de Certeau famously arguing, for instance, that readers are far from passive consumers, that they "[invent] in texts something different from what they 'intended,'" and John Glavin contending that all reading is a kind of adaptation: "If a novel, a poem, a play is to be read at all, it's got to be retrieved, put back together, refurbished."[30] The rewriters of *Uncle Tom's Cabin* demonstrate such independence in their readings of Stowe's book, though of course they in turn press their interpretations upon their own audiences, asserting themselves over *Uncle Tom's Cabin* while hoping for compliance in other readers. Each new product in *Tom* mania represented another sortie in this struggle between readers and texts.

Thus, paying attention to *Uncle Tom* and its many offshoots helps uncover the "cultural conversation" in which they were engaged; but it also necessitates an awareness of the forms and genres conscripted for the purpose.[31] As Leah Price has pointed out, all texts, as evidence about reading, are complicated by the circumstances within which they themselves are produced: "What readers respond to (at least in forms to which more than telepathy can give us access) is never just a text: they respond to the editor's demand for a review, to the teacher's demand for an exam answer, to the interviewer's demand for a statement, to the publisher's demand for an edition."[32] New *Uncle Tom*s adapted themselves not only to the conventions of professional forms like reviews but also to minstrel sketches, melodramas, and plantation novels, not to mention the extraliterary shapes of wallpaper, spoons, and china figurines.

These mutations can also be seen as translations (and of course *Uncle Tom* was translated into dozens of languages), but these were just as often "intracultural translations," rewriting in English that could amount to mimicry, appropriation, manipulation, and transformation.[33] Adaptations were often willful "misreadings," deliberately partial, and of course especially loaded in their attitudes to slavery. *Uncle Tom*'s movement from the United States to Britain also necessitated a significant reinterpretation, as did its migration from Northern antislavery texts to proslavery and Southern ones and from white to black readings. As with all translations, Stowe's text was reconfigured by the forms and the circumstances into which it was relocated.

Some *Uncle Tom*s were targeted at specifically British or American audiences, a few at both; they were variously designed for public or private, masculine or feminine, working-class or bourgeois consumption, the most obvious division being whether they were destined for the parlor or the stage. *Tom* mania highlights some of these distinctions, partly because the extraordinary interest in *Uncle Tom*s caused spectators to stray (and to commentate) outside of their usual spheres, so that in New York middle-class reviewers shared a theater with woolen-shirted Bowery boys, and in London critics made rare trips to the less respectable theaters. In these observers' distasteful references to popular melodrama and to "theatres which stand below the level of dramatic criticism" are revealed the workings of class and privilege through culture, testimony to the "institutions of social reproduction" that John Guillory has argued are at stake in notions of cultural value.[34] *Uncle Tom's Cabin* traversed audience and genre boundaries that were usually strictly observed, but for us the commentary that tracked its progress helps lay bare some of those distinctions.

And Stowe's novel not only generated intertexts, it was itself intertextual. *Uncle Tom's Cabin*, which rapidly became one of the most influential representations of African Americans in its time, was indebted to another—blackface minstrelsy. One of my arguments is that the minstrel elements of Stowe's book may have facilitated its rereading and rewriting by drawing on the inherent instabilities and ambivalences in the racial politics of blackface.

Extraordinarily popular both as a specific type of show and as a related set of conventions in dance, music, and theater, minstrelsy prefigured the success of Stowe's novel in the 1850s. The mania for *Uncle Tom's Cabin* coincided with dozens of minstrel troupes and even dedicated minstrel halls, a craze that, in Robert Toll's words, "swept the nation in the 1840s, from the White House to the California gold fields . . . and [for] over half a century . . . remained the most popular entertainment form in the country."[35] Minstrelsy not only survived into the twentieth century, but it also left traces in a myriad of successors, from vaudeville to Disney cartoons. Like *Uncle Tom's Cabin*, blackface could be translated into a seemingly endless number of different genres. As Robert Cantwell contended: "From ragtime and jazz to standup comedy and the circus ring, there are few forms of American popular entertainment that do not have a root in the minstrel show."[36]

Minstrelsy's origins are obscure, but some of its ancestry may lie in European folk rituals that involved blacking up, such as mummers' plays, callithumps, and impromptu shivarees. In these practices, blackened faces signaled that the activity was metaphorical, performative, or ritual. This resonance later translated into minstrelsy's strong associations with burlesque, where blackface was the sign that something was being travestied.[37] In America, however, blackface also took on racial connotations, so that by the 1820s it was sometimes known as "Ethiopian delineation." Variety pieces performed by blacked-up white men provided entr'actes for working-class theaters or were staged at circuses, medicine shows, and menageries. This racial aspect was confirmed by the introduction of the term "Negro minstrels," which coincided in the early 1840s with the development of a whole evening's blackface entertainment and the emergence of the minstrel show.

The minstrel show opened with the company sitting in a semicircle singing and cracking jokes, while the second act comprised a medley of musical or comical novelties. Often there was a mock sermon or political speech (the stump speech), which parodied popular speakers or burlesqued topical subjects with grandiloquent but nonsensical oratory in a "black" accent. The finale consisted of a one-act skit, until the mid-1850s usually set on a Southern plantation, though afterward it was often a travesty of a recent theatrical hit.[38] In general, the show supplied, in Eric Lott's formulation, "kneeslapping musical numbers punctuated by comic dialogues, bad puns, and petit-bourgeois ribaldry."[39] Its musical sound was largely shaped by its instruments: banjos, fiddles, bone castanets, and tambourines.

Minstrel audiences were also distinctive: they primarily consisted of young working-class men, mostly concentrated in the cities of the northeastern United States. The minstrel show's oft-repeated claims to represent black culture and to dramatize slave life in the South should thus be treated as suspect, and its depictions of carefree slave possum hunts and dances were probably colored by the fantasies of a working class comprised of large numbers of newly urbanized immigrants from Europe.[40] However, some of minstrelsy's earliest influences may indeed have lain in interracial contacts, such as the early-nineteenth-century dancing competitions described by W. T. Lhamon, in the racially mixed (and sexually unregulated) districts of the New York slums.[41] Yet although certain tunes and dances may have had origins in black communities, even these were probably complicated in their histories; for instance, the cakewalk, a "black" dance adapted by minstrels, itself originated in black parodies of white dancing.[42]

Although there was a powerful streak of racist contempt and proslavery sympathy in blackface, as illustrated in two of its most persistent types, the joyful Southern slave "Jim Crow" and the uppity Northern dandy "Zip Coon," recent criticism has also illuminated its variety. Not only did minstrelsy mutate over time and to accommodate different consumers, but it is clear that it could incorporate ambiguous and contradictory effects, using the black mask both to stand for black people and as a disguise from which to attack middle-class strictures. The blackface figure could be viewed simultaneously as a clown and as a proxy for the audience's own rebellious desires. Minstrelsy could thus direct the class anxiety of white workers at potential black rivals and at the same time suggest the possibility of allegiance.[43] Blackface's inherent political ambiguity was enhanced by the fact that performances were topical, partly improvisatory, and acutely responsive to their audiences.

Blackface consumers were thus very different from the largely female middle classes whom critics have associated with the sentimental novel and who have been presumed to have formed the backbone of Stowe's readership. In fact, it was precisely the genteel and feminine in middle-class culture that minstrels often lampooned, and antiwomen, and later antifeminist, jokes formed a significant thread in blackface humor. Some performers even created blackface drag characters to highlight the supposed silliness and hypocrisy of the sex. So blackface may seem an unlikely relative for *Uncle Tom's Cabin*, especially given Stowe's championing of female good sense in that novel, her idealization of mothers, and the feminization of her hero, Tom.[44]

Yet blackface played a significant role in *Tom* mania. As I shall demonstrate, not only did Stowe's book borrow blackface imagery and characterization, but it made radical use of some blackface elements that in turn resonated through many of the book's imitators. Further, the comic double act with which minstrel shows often opened can be seen to form part of the

secret of *Uncle Tom*'s broad popularity and apparently infinite adaptability.
Some of the novel's most famous scenes, such as the conversations between
Topsy and Miss Ophelia, can be seen to be derived from minstrelsy's end
man–interlocutor exchange.

This piece, the exchange between the blackface end man, who sat at the
end of the semicircle, and the interlocutor, who sat in the middle and who was
not blacked up, was a central minstrel tradition. Moreover, it was predicated
on a series of ambiguities that made it possible to read the sketch as a mockery of the black character, or the white character, or both. The end man was
apparently stupid, mishearing and misunderstanding the interlocutor's con-
versational sallies, but in the process he produced a series of puns and surreal juxtapositions of ideas that were staples of minstrel amusement. The
interlocutor, moreover, was often pompous and verbose, as much a representative of middle-class pretensions as of "white" culture per se, so that working audiences could identify with the end man's disruptions of the interlocutor as well as laugh at the "black" character's speech.

This book traces the way *Uncle Tom's Cabin* harnessed these contradictions. The nods to minstrelsy in the novel did more than provide comic relief;
by turning the end man–interlocutor dialogues into conduits for disguised and
ambivalent sympathy for slave characters, they may have made its antislavery
message palatable for the cautious and scarcely noticeable for the indifferent.
Moreover, Stowe complicated the dynamic of the end man–interlocutor exchange: by introducing female interlocutors and making her end man a girl,
she hinted at an antislavery conspiracy behind the verbal antagonism.

Feminizing the end man–interlocutor dialogue, which could work both to
further and to undermine racial stereotypes, also allowed Stowe to modulate
the novel's relationship with sentimental femininity. Although *Uncle Tom's
Cabin* has been read as a powerful champion of the domestic and maternal
values associated both with sentimental fiction and with what historians have
dubbed the midcentury "cult of true womanhood," Stowe's use of blackface
routines sometimes subjects those values to uncomfortable ridicule. The end
man–interlocutor scenes in *Uncle Tom's Cabin* enable fantasies of revolt
against the ordered domestic realm the novel (mostly) endorses: such scenes
comically upset bourgeois values even as they seem to promote them.

Part of the key to *Uncle Tom*'s success thus lies in its debts to blackface,
which had pioneered the ambivalent and contradictory racial politics that allowed the minstrel show—and *Uncle Tom's Cabin*—to appeal to very wide au-

diences. The blackface debt would also help explain the way the novel "develops an aesthetics . . . that proves to be as characteristic of racism as it is of abolitionism."[45] Like minstrel show audiences, *Uncle Tom*'s readers sometimes responded to subtle or subversive appeals for sympathy and sometimes ignored them, choosing only to see black characters as crude racial types. Stowe's antislavery message was couched in a form so ambiguous about race, and at times so explicitly demeaning in its representation of black people, that it both advocated emancipation and licensed a plethora of racist imitators.

Examinations of the racial politics of *Uncle Tom's Cabin* have tended to stress its alignment with other antislavery representations of black people in which, according to Christine Bolt, "the slave was idealized, and, in consequence, dehumanized."[46] Uncle Tom himself very clearly belongs to the strand of thinking George Fredrickson has identified as "romantic racialism," which characterized black people as inherently innocent, good-natured, and receptive to Christianity.[47] It is for this reason that Douglas Lorimer associates Stowe's text with the philanthropists' racial imagery in his characterization of Victorian ideas of black people as linked either with missionary Bibles or else with minstrel banjos and bones. But *Uncle Tom's Cabin* harbors both blackface and Bible references. Lorimer argues that *Tom* mania "gave new life" to the minstrel show in Great Britain; I would argue that the two were sometimes hard to distinguish.[48] In the complex and ambiguous set of black characters in *Uncle Tom's Cabin* we find not only piety but subversive mischief, designed to inspire the same combination of sympathy and derision in which the minstrel show traded. Like minstrel show audiences, readers had cause to empathize with these characters as well as laugh at them, but, like blackface personae, Stowe's images could easily be converted to the most degrading of racial types. In the ambivalence of *Uncle Tom's Cabin,* as in the ambiguity of many minstrel acts, lay the seeds of a racial characterization that has proved to be as damaging as it has long-lived.

The variety of positions on slavery taken up by each of *Uncle Tom*'s many transformations was reflected in their selective use of blackface elements. Adaptations of *Uncle Tom's Cabin* borrowed from blackface in different ways, choosing only to take on its most unsavory habits of racial characterization or else adopting its ambiguous and parodic qualities. The American melodramas incorporated the end man–interlocutor exchanges and Stephen Foster's sentimental minstrel songs; British melodramas preferred song-and-dance routines linked to a troupe known as the Ethiopian Serenaders. Proslavery novels turned blackface into crude—and cruel—caricature; the "dramatic reader" Mary Webb used minstrel comedy as a hook to draw her audiences into appreciating the pathos of Uncle Tom's demise.

Recognizing blackface traditions can thus help us read a variety of *Uncle Toms*, but *Tom* mania also directs us to the extent of blackface's influence, spilling out of the minstrel halls and into the parlors even of those who never went to minstrel shows. Moreover, Stowe's adaptation of blackface techniques explores what happens when theatrical forms are translated into fiction. Her novel prompts us to ask how much of the knowingness, irony, stylization, and sheer play of blackface could be rendered in prose, and how much of the excitement and unpredictability of performance must necessarily have been lost when minstrelsy was absorbed into a novel.

Examining *Tom* mania reveals that *Uncle Tom's Cabin* also played an important part in the history of blackface performance. The book supplied enormous amounts of minstrel material in the 1850s: *Uncle Tom* was made the butt of minstrel jokes, lampooned in comic sketches, and rendered into the subject of songs and speeches. Some of this was pure ridicule, and some was allied with a proslavery hostility, but by no means all. Critics have missed the political diversity as well as the formal variety of minstrel commentary on *Uncle Tom's Cabin*. "Uncle Toms" appeared in stage laments about the cruelty of slavery, and some troupes staged full-scale dramatizations of the original text.

Uncle Tom's minstrel connections indicate that the novel was less genteel than has been supposed, in its debt to a notoriously rowdy entertainment, but it also reminds us that some minstrel productions already had aspirations to gentility. As I shall show, blackface already had surprising links with antislavery music that prefigured the appearance of Stowe's novel, and an increasing sentimentality in the minstrel show of the 1850s chimed with the mood of *Uncle Tom's Cabin*. Adaptations of the book contributed to minstrelsy's movement toward bourgeois tastes, which in turn facilitated the demonstration of sympathy for slaves on the blackface stage. In addition, the *Tom* shows of the later nineteenth century, which staged *Uncle Tom* in tents throughout the farthest reaches of the country, extended the earlier minstrel tradition of touring, which in the 1840s had taken troupes onto the Mississippi, along the railroads of the Northwest, and as far as the California gold rush towns.[49]

For their part, minstrel show versions of *Uncle Tom's Cabin* were hugely influential upon later characterizations of the novel, converting Stowe's char-

acter into a comic or, worse, a proslavery stooge: they helped make Uncle
Tom the figure he has become in popular memory. Like the minstrel character "Jim Crow," whose name came to symbolize the violent history of racial
segregation, "Uncle Tom" became a powerfully charged racial term. Losing
the power and moral certitude of Stowe's original Christian slave, Uncle Tom
was transformed in the minstrel shows, becoming a race traitor.

In short, blackface spread alongside *Tom* mania, and *Tom* mania's minstrelsy, like *Uncle Tom's Cabin* itself, mutated to suit its audiences. And both
for blackface and for *Uncle Tom's Cabin* some of the most crucial audiences
lay in Britain. Minstrelsy was from its earliest incarnations a transatlantic
phenomenon. For a start, some of its ancestry may have been British, both
because the practice of blacking up may have originated in British folk
rituals and because an 1820s routine developed by the British actor Charles
Mathews was a crucial prototype for Ethiopian delineation. Among the list of
American "types" Mathews performed on the London stage after a trip to
New York was a black preacher, whose comical sermon foreshadowed minstrel show stump speeches. Mathews also parodied a black actor trying in vain
to play Hamlet against a chorus of audience demands that he sing "Possum
up a Gum Tree."[50] After Mathews, blackface continued to be profitably traded
across the Atlantic, with T. D. Rice's "Jim Crow" making a hit in London in
the 1830s; the Ethiopian Serenaders, the Virginia Minstrels, and the Christy's
Minstrels enjoying popularity in the 1840s; and numerous minstrel troupes
following Rice's success throughout the nineteenth century. Eventually, there
would even be British blackface stars who dared to take their version back to
America.[51]

Minstrelsy was not only as popular in Britain as in the United States, but it
developed distinctively British offshoots with the formation of local British
troupes and even a recognizably British style of blackface, identifiable by its
costumes, its music, its puns, and its terminology. In its class affiliations, in its
cultural niche, in its audiences, and in the way stage "blackness" was read,
British minstrelsy would create subtle variations on the American form. Just
as the *Tom* plays would do in the 1850s, minstrelsy adapted itself to local tastes
and predilections when it reached foreign shores.

Thus, the blackface elements in *Uncle Tom's Cabin* offered a form of racial
representation that was familiar to the whole Atlantic world, and *Tom* mania
extended these transatlantic minstrel connections. British minstrel troupes
staged versions of *Uncle Tom's Cabin* and themselves brought it back to the
United States. *Uncle Tom* was also transformed into melodrama in London

with a whole slew of minstrel references, but these were expressly designed to appeal to British tastes in blackface performance, which even in the 1850s were quite distinct from those in the United States. As I shall discuss, the more mixed class base of British minstrel show audiences and the British preference for a more restrained style of performance were reflected in the London dramatizations of *Uncle Tom's Cabin.*

Not all of *Uncle Tom's* repercussions were textual. A recurring pattern in *Tom* mania consists of its insinuation into the lives of real people—the African Americans the novel purported to represent. In Britain Charles Mathews's impersonation of a black actor was taken to represent Ira Aldridge, the African American tragedian. Aldridge toured Britain in the 1830s and, as a result of Mathews's act, was barracked with requests for "Possum up a Gum Tree."[52] Similarly, after the publication of Stowe's novel black people were persistently asked to explain themselves and their lives in terms of *Uncle Tom's Cabin.* For some writers, Stowe's characters became irresistible templates for picturing African Americans, so that travelers in the South after 1852, such as the British writer Barbara Bodichon, describe real slaves as if they were people in *Uncle Tom's Cabin.* Stowe's novel, in other words, inspired a tradition of racial—and racist—imagery, and often blackface, itself shaping the representation of black people in both visual media and the written word, was involved in this process. Yet I shall also show that black writers and performers were themselves able to turn *Uncle Tom's Cabin* to their own purposes, even borrowing the book's fame to offer a subtle critique of its imagery or its power. And the influence of such black writers and speakers left its mark in the most unlikely outposts of *Tom* mania, so that plantation novelists created blackface apologists for slavery precisely to counter the arguments of the slave narrators or to distract from the testimony of black exiles in Britain, like Samuel Ward and William and Ellen Craft.

The book is arranged roughly in the way in which *Tom* mania spread; that is, it begins in the United States, moves on to deal with adaptations in Britain, and then charts American responses to the British reception of the novel, in which *Tom* mania can be said to have become a transatlantic topic. However, I use British sources alongside American ones throughout, and their relevance to so much of the discussion in itself suggests the extent to which the two cultures were still interlocked in the 1850s. My first chapter examines the minstrel elements in Stowe's *Uncle Tom's Cabin*, while the second explores the novel's conversion into minstrelsy, demonstrating that minstrel show *Uncle Toms* ranged from proslavery to antislavery in their sympathies. The proslavery minstrel *Tom*s concentrate on fugitive slaves, which, as my third chapter suggests, were becoming a major national anxiety in the 1850s and the subject of copycat novels, which borrowed the form of *Uncle Tom's Cabin* to challenge its argument about slavery. Chapter 4 deals with *Uncle Tom's* translation into melodrama and reform drama in the United States, while chapter 5 tracks Stowe's book to Britain, where its dramatization reflected the differences in British attitudes to slavery, the stage, minstrelsy, and class. Chapter 6 considers the way the celebrity of *Uncle Tom's Cabin* itself became the focus for transatlantic debates about gender, class, and nation. The international furor over the novel was linked at the time to debates about literary nationalism: chapter 7 examines a handful of anti-*Tom* texts that fictionalized Stowe's reception in Britain rather than slavery in America. Finally, chapter 8 reads Stowe's second antislavery novel, *Dred*, as part of the *Uncle Tom* phenomenon, as both a rewriting and a response to others' readings of *Uncle Tom's Cabin.*

Of course, *Uncle Tom's* afterlife extended beyond the 1850s—new interpretations of Stowe's novel appeared throughout the nineteenth and twentieth centuries, and no doubt there will be more to come. The persisting need to fix the message of *Uncle Tom's Cabin* suggests that the text's own ambiguities, not to mention the amorphousness and adaptability that almost infinitely extended its interpretation in *Tom* mania, are merely revived by each successive incarnation. I hope to suggest in this book how a definitive meaning for the novel has remained for so long tantalizing and always elusive.

TOPSY AND THE END MAN: BLACKFACE IN "UNCLE TOM'S CABIN"

[IT HAS] SCENES OF NEGRO HUMOUR THAT WILL SEND OUR WITS DIGGING IN A NEW VEIN, AND DRIVE THE EXHIBITORS OF NIGGER MELODISTS TO DESPAIR.

"Uncle Tom's Cabin," *Nonconformist* (London), 8 September 1852

The first reviews of *Uncle Tom's Cabin* lingered not only over the weepy deathbeds of Eva and Uncle Tom but also over comic aspects of the novel. Unlike later critics, nineteenth-century observers were particularly struck by the humor in the book, which was attested to by reviewers from both the North and the South in the United States as well as in Britain. The *National Era*, a Washington antislavery paper, noted *Uncle Tom's* "drollery," while a letter to the *New York Independent* from New Orleans reported that readers had been both "moved to tears" and "convulsed with laughter."[1] An article in New York's *Putnam's Monthly* implied that the novel inevitably produced these two extremes, relating the story of a man sleeping in a strange house: "Being annoyed by hearing somebody in the adjoining chamber alternately groaning and laughing, he knocked upon the wall and said, 'Hallo, there! What's the matter? Are you sick, or reading Uncle Tom's Cabin?'"[2]

This conjunction of comedy and sentiment was not unusual in the 1850s: a year after *Uncle Tom* came out, the narrator of Herman Melville's "Bartleby the Scrivener" would boast of his knowledge of "divers histories, at which good-natured gentlemen might smile, and sentimental souls might weep."[3] And as Robert Weisbuch points out, this particular set of reactions would have been recognized by contemporary readers as a "Dickensian effect."[4] Yet Stowe's comedy was constructed out of materials new both to Dickens and to his many American imitators.

The reviews implicitly recognized as much: their appreciations of *Uncle Tom's* comedy were accompanied by special praise for the novel's black characters. In London the *Times* declared that "a little black imp, by name TOPSY . . . [is] one of the best sketches in the book" and picked out "scenes in which the negroes are represented at their domestic labors or conversing with each other." Another review declaimed, "One Topsy is worth a dozen little Evas."[5] The *New Englander* characterized "the dramatic interest which so enlivens Uncle Tom's Cabin" in a list of aspects missing from another text: "It rarely takes the form of a dialogue; it gives no specimens of negro-English dialect; it is almost wholly destitute of humor."[6] These, by implication, were the strengths of Stowe's novel.

The emphases on comedy, on black life, and on dialogue and "negro-

English" and the fascination with Topsy's "impishness" single out aspects of *Uncle Tom's Cabin* that were also the attributes audiences claimed to enjoy in blackface entertainment. More pointedly, many reviews explicitly invoked the minstrel show as a comparison. The *Literary World* remarked that "the element of the popular performances on the stage and elsewhere, the Jim Crow oddities, the Ethiopian serenaders, the Christy minstrels ... will be found also to be the essence of the humor in Uncle Tom's Cabin."[7] Even when readers argued that Stowe's work was a new departure, it was blackface that provided the contrast. In the passage from the *Nonconformist* quoted in the epigraph to this chapter, *Uncle Tom's Cabin* is declared to contain "scenes of negro humour" that will drive minstrel show promoters to "despair." The *Times* announced that Stowe avoided "the slang of 'Ethiopian Serenaders'" and remarked "how refreshing it is to be separated for a season from the conventional Sambo of the modern stage."[8] Unusually for a pronouncement by the *Times*, this was echoed by a correspondent for *Frederick Douglass' Paper*. William Wilson also described the novel as an antidote to images derived from the theater: "Shopkeepers that heretofore ... exhibited in their windows Zip Coon, or Jim Crow, with his naked toes kicking out the panes, for general amusement, profit and loyalty to the Southern God; ... are now proud to illume those very windows through the windows of my *Uncle Tom's Cabin*, while good Old Aunt Cloe [*sic*] peeps out just to see what the matter is."[9]

Wilson's description of Uncle Tom figures replacing Jim Crows in a shop window suggests how the commercialization and duplication of Stowe's images would come to rival those of the 1840s blackface clown. Tom and Topsy would become images as ubiquitous as Jim Crow or Zip Coon and possibly even more long-lived. *Uncle Tom*'s characters would occupy some of the same structural positions in American and European culture as those of the minstrel stage: Uncle Tom and Chloe would take over not only literal shop windows but also figurative ones.

Far from signaling a break with blackface representation, the interchangeability of Stowe's characters with stage ones is an indication of their kinship. Wilson's efforts to disassociate Stowe's imagery from that of the minstrel show testify to the power of blackface, ironically indicating the necessity of measuring Stowe's characters against blackface ones like Jim Crow or Zip Coon, just as the *Times* forged the connection it sought to repudiate between the novel and the minstrel troupe the Ethiopian Serenaders. They illustrate the inescapable cultural authority blackface held in the 1850s and that it was the benchmark against which portraits of African Americans had to be tested.

Even though *Uncle Tom's Cabin* would break blackface's monopoly, these quotations suggest how much Stowe's depictions both were and would remain entwined with earlier ones.

Stowe herself almost certainly never saw a minstrel show. She famously disapproved of the theater and cautioned against even the sympathetic dramatization of *Uncle Tom's Cabin*, as it might give the form an unwarranted imprimatur of gentility.[10] It would seem all the more unlikely that she would countenance minstrelsy's rowdier style of performance. Lott admits to "equivocation" in his connection of the two cultural forms, "*Uncle Tom's Cabin* as a break from but also a continuation of blackface minstrelsy," locating these contradictions in the "unavoidable . . . ambiguity of the revolutionary 1850s."[11] Yet the conjunction of blackface and the sentimental antislavery text seems less surprising when we acknowledge the cultural power of minstrelsy in the 1850s.

By the time Stowe began her book blackface had permeated U.S. culture, and both its icons and versions of its acts could be found everywhere. As Wilson's article for *Frederick Douglass' Paper* suggests, shopkeepers used images of blackface characters for advertising in their shopwindows, and in Nathaniel Hawthorne's *The House of the Seven Gables* (published in the year *Uncle Tom* was serialized) they featured as confectionery—Hepzibah Pyncheon sells gingerbread Jim Crows.[12] Moreover, minstrel show songs were available as sheet music, its jokes and sketches were published in books, and devotees admiringly repeated its material on the streets. Many years later, Stowe's Hartford neighbor Mark Twain would try out blackface turns for guests in the parlor; it is likely that the audiences of the 1840s and 1850s also carried their enthusiasms out of the shows and into their homes.[13] Minstrelsy was as pervasive in popular culture and as readily adapted to nontheatrical purposes as *Uncle Tom* would come to be. In fact, *Uncle Tom's Cabin* was a symptom of the extent to which blackface imagery and humor were available to Americans outside the minstrel hall, and it would demonstrate how the ambiguities and ironies minstrelsy applied to racial politics could be equally useful off the stage. And in its turn, of course, *Uncle Tom* mania would extend blackface's reach into a wider culture.

It has been assumed that it was the experience of living in Cincinnati between 1832 and 1851 that eventually made slavery such a compelling topic for Stowe. The often intense racial tensions in the city during this period resulted in riots and a bitter controversy at Lane Seminary, where Stowe's father, Lyman Beecher, was president and her soon-to-be husband, Calvin, taught.[14]

In addition, Cincinnati's location just north of a slave state made it both a hub of trade with the South and a prominent stop on the Underground Railroad. It was also a place where planters took black mistresses and educated their illegitimate children.[15]

But it should also be noted that the city played an important part in the history of minstrelsy. Many blackface troupes visited Cincinnati in the 1840s: Christy's Minstrels in 1846 and 1847; the Sable Harmonists three times in 1847, once in 1848, and again in 1849; and also the Sable Troubadours, Kneass's Great Original Sable Harmonists, T. D. Rice, and Campbell's Minstrels.[16] Not only that, but one version of the legend of T. D. Rice's invention of Jim Crow, the routine that earned him his reputation as the "father of blackface," stipulated that Rice had borrowed his song from a black stage driver of that city.[17] As I discuss in chapter 2, Cincinnati was also home to minstrelsy's most famous composer, Stephen Foster, between 1846 and 1850. Commentators on both Stowe and Foster have surmised that Cincinnati could have provided experience both of black people and of racial issues that later contributed to their writing; it also offered a chance to hear minstrel songs.[18]

Blackface is usually identified with a very different audience from that of the sentimental novel: male not female, working class not bourgeois, rowdy not genteel.[19] The blackface elements in *Uncle Tom* suggest the novel's links with a very different aspect of 1850s culture and imply that the book may have had a much broader class and gender appeal even than those of its fellow sentimental novels. The moments when Stowe's book evokes the minstrel show could indicate some ambivalence about the middle-class femininity it at other times celebrates. Blackface aspects of *Uncle Tom* could also work to cushion the impact of its politics by dissolving them in irony and contradictions.

Uncle Tom's ties to minstrelsy are more comprehensible when we acknowledge the shifts in performance style in the 1850s that were bringing blackface more into line with sentimental aesthetics. By the 1850s there was plenty in blackface that would have chimed with Stowe's sensibilities. *Uncle Tom's Cabin* was only one of many antislavery productions to capitalize on the popularity of blackface, and Stowe's book also coincided with a change in the content and the projected audience of minstrel entertainments, which were coming to be pitched at more respectable bourgeois patrons and to be larded with sentimental ideals of home and family very like her own.

What Robert Winans calls the "earthy[,] . . . comic and antisentimental"

tone of early minstrel show music began to change in the mid-1840s. From
the start, many minstrel songs were republished for the home market with
more genteel lyrics and without the dialect of stage versions.[20] But whatever
real gap existed between blackface and parlor music began to narrow with the
mid-1840s development of the plantation song, which had musical and lyri-
cal ties to the sentimental ballad.[21] This form was often used for songs that
affected to have some sympathy for the slave, such as Sam Sanford's 1844
song "Lucy Neal," which describes her tragic separation from her lover, but
even in this there was room for equivocation, as there were several versions
of the lyrics whose implications for slavery varied, and the tune itself suggested a humorous tone.[22]

As minstrel tunes became more like parlor songs, the middle classes began
to come more to minstrel shows, and they in turn increasingly took on the
shape of concerts.[23] Gentlemen and even sometimes ladies were appearing in
minstrel hall audiences, especially the larger, more respectable ones in the
cities, by the 1850s, and some showmen arranged promotions especially directed at women and children.[24] Eventually, minstrelsy would become so respectable that bourgeois men began to learn the banjo, and even the British
Prince of Wales would take lessons from one of the blackface Bohee Brothers.[25] _Uncle Tom's Cabin_ thus emerged as the minstrel show itself was being
adopted by the very classes for whom Stowe's novel was designed.

Moreover, blackface's musical history was closely bound up with avowedly
antislavery music throughout the 1840s. The four-part harmonies of the
singing Austrian family, the Rainers, inspired troupes like the Virginia Minstrels and Christy's Minstrels as well as the antislavery Hutchinson Family
Singers, who campaigned as they performed but whose use of humor and
rhythm signaled their musical proximity to minstrelsy.[26] The English singer
Henry Russell, who also toured extensively in the United States, sang both
antislavery songs and "negro melodies," though he did not wear blackface;
many minstrels in turn sang Russell's songs.[27] Moreover, throughout the 1840s
and 1850s abolitionists themselves frequently put antislavery lyrics to minstrel show tunes. "Lucy Neal," "Old Dan Tucker," "Dandy Jim," "Dixie's
Land," and "Lucy Long" were all adapted in this way, and antislavery collections appeared with what Sam Dennison calls "parodies, copies, and flagrant
borrowings from the minstrel repertoire."[28]

Such attempts to package earnest arguments in an entertaining format
failed entirely to draw on the provocativeness and irony that were partly

responsible for blackface's mass appeal. The fast fiddle-dance tune of "Old
Dan Tucker," for instance, must have sat oddly with the elevated sentiment
of the lyrics sung to it at an antislavery picnic in 1845:

> Our fathers fought on Bunker's Hill
> For liberty and independence,
> And freedom fires are glowing still,
> Deep in the souls of their descendants.
> Rouse up the flame—rouse up the flame—
> Rouse up the flame, throughout the nation,
> Death to slavery and oppression![29]

Stowe's achievement in *Uncle Tom's Cabin* was to harness the tone as well
as the trappings of blackface, but she necessarily also borrowed the racial
portraiture along with them. Whereas antislavery songs dealt with abstract
principles, Stowe would try to infuse the slaves' plight with dramatic interest,
which is why *Uncle Tom's Cabin* imported all minstrelsy's ambivalent attitudes to African Americans along with its theatrical power.

The minstrel stage, meanwhile, adeptly turned the abolitionists' weapons
back at them. The Hutchinson Family Singers, who were famous for Jesse
Hutchinson's 1844 emancipation song "Get off the Track" (itself set to "Old
Dan Tucker"), were often parodied there.[30] "Get off the Track" also shared
blackface's fascination with the railroad: while in the Hutchinsons' lyrics the
"Car Emancipation / [Rode] majestic thro' our nation," blackface troupes
played the "Railroad Overture," an instrumental imitation of the "slocomo-
tive bullgine, dat at de fust ob de beginning is very moderate, den as de steam
rises, de power of de circumvolution exaggerates itself into a can'tstopmiza-
tion, and runs clar ob de track."[31]

As W. T. Lhamon has pointed out, the blackface trick of imitating a locomotive's whistle is duplicated by both Harry and Topsy in *Uncle Tom's Cabin*,
but the most famous juxtaposition of abolitionism with this midcentury fascination with locomotive technology lies, of course, in the idea of the Underground Railroad.[32] The term inspired both George Allen's antislavery parlor
song "The Underground Rail Car, or Song of the Fugitive" and Dan Rice's
blackface jokes about "De Railroad dat's *underground*."[33]

In exploiting each other's success abolitionists and blackface artistes increasingly blurred their respective positioning in class and cultural niches.
While the showmen mocked the Hutchinsons as a sign of the genteel taste to
which the family troupe appealed (along with many other such signs), and

while abolitionist songwriters in the 1840s had attempted to take over the cultural territory of blackface by adapting its songs, by the 1850s the two kinds of performance and of racial representation had an increasing tendency to merge.

If minstrelsy's co-option by abolitionist forces in the 1840s may have suggested Stowe's adoption of blackface in *Uncle Tom's Cabin*, it was also already offering a fictional version of the plantation that was readily adapted for the novel. The fantasy plantations of the minstrel show purported to offer audiences an ethnographic glimpse of real slave life. Parts of the show in 1840s programs were explicitly labeled "as Southern Darkies" or "as Plantation Darkies," while the Virginia Minstrels advertised themselves as an insight into slave life in America, promising "sports and pastimes of the Virginia Colored Race, through the medium of Songs, Refrains, and Ditties as sung by the Southern slaves."[34]

That Stowe's idea of plantation life closely resembled such representations is suggested by a facetious article about minstrelsy in an 1845 *Knickerbocker Magazine* that sketched out a plot mingling blackface with domestic sentiment. This could also have described, almost exactly, that of *Uncle Tom's Cabin*. James Kennard's article "Who Are Our National Poets?" was self-consciously ludicrous, but it would take only a small shift in tone to render it into a crude outline of Stowe's novel.

Kennard's tongue-in-cheek argument was that our national poets were blackface ones and that minstrel songs were the first American poetry. He built a little scene of slave life around two current tunes of the minstrel stage whose plot and characterization bear striking similarities to the book Stowe later wrote. Kennard imagines a character, "poor Sambo," hoeing while he sings about a master and mistress who promised him his freedom but died, leaving him still "hillin'-up corn!" Kennard sympathizes: "Poor fellow! it seems a hard case. His 'massa and misse' are freed from *their* bonds, but Sambo still wears his." But Kennard's creation is uncomplaining and grateful for small mercies: "He might here very properly stop and water the corn with his tears. But no; Sambo is too much of a philosopher for *that*. Having uttered his plaint, he instantly consoles himself with the thought that he has many blessings yet to be thankful for." Kennard's Sambo thus prefigures Uncle Tom not only in his disappointment at not being manumitted (in Tom's case St. Clare promises him his freedom but then dies before he can effect it) but in his possession of the kind of "grateful joyous" heart that makes him bear his trials stoically.[35]

Both Sambo and Tom live in happy domestic comfort and in log cabins overgrown with flowers: Tom's is "covered by a large scarlet bignonia and a native multiflora rose" and has "flourishing" flower and vegetable beds, and Sambo's "is embowered in Catalpa and Pride-of-India trees."[36] They also have capable wives: Aunt Chloe cooks "corn-cake, in all its varieties of hoe-cake, dodgers, muffins, and other species too numerous to mention," and scolds the children, while Sambo's Jenny "gives the hommony another stir, looks at the hoe-cake, and [gives] the young ones a tight cuff or two on the side of the head, to make them 'hush.' "[37] Even the fate Stowe envisages for her hero is foreshadowed in Kennard's imaginary scene setting for his minstrel songs, for, like Tom, Sambo is subject to the financial situation of his master, who squanders his fortune on the horses, "and poor Sambo and his family may be sold, separated, and sent just where their new masters please; possibly to labor on a sugar plantation—the hell of the blacks."[38] In *Uncle Tom's Cabin* Tom's master, Shelby, makes similar "speculations" that of course result in Tom being sold away from his family, and he too ends up doing back-breaking work in a plantation "hell" (*UTC*, 16–17).

What was different was the tone. Kennard's is a fake sympathy in the parodic tradition of early minstrelsy's mockery of genteel and sentimental culture. His apparent praise for black creativity is a staple of blackface humor, drawing attention to the travesty by pretending to take it for reality.[39] Sambo's predicament afflicts real people, but Kennard derives amusement from imagining blackface as also subject to it, confusing slaves with blackface characters. Although he calls on his audience to sympathize with his slave in the same way as Stowe does for Tom, Sambo is actually a mechanism to celebrate the artifice of blackface.

Despite Kennard's use of it, however, blackface sometimes allied itself more sincerely with sympathy for the slave. Some early minstrel songs, for instance, dealt with the cruelty of white people to black ones, including among the charges sexual exploitation, the separation of families, underfeeding, over-working, and brutality. However, shows were inconsistent, and such songs would be freely mingled with cheerful or comic ones. As Robert Toll asserts, "contradictory feelings about slavery" could be fostered by the structure of the minstrel show, in which the same evening's entertainment could feature both complacency and disquiet.[40]

In this way, watching a minstrel show worked very differently from reading a sentimental novel: rather than directing emotion inward, the show generated contradictory feeling and then diffused it, dispelling by laughter not internalization. The minstrel show could offer complex devices for winning over the public, mechanisms in which slave characters were endeared to audiences even as they were apparently demeaned. *Uncle Tom*'s neutralizing effect on the disturbing question of slavery may well be the reason mid-nineteenth-century readers found it so compelling, but that effect could be due not only to sentimental tears but to blackface comedy.

The mystery of *Uncle Tom's Cabin*'s extraordinary success at a time when publishers believed that books about slavery did not sell has been explained by the antirevolutionary reassurance that the novel's sentimentality offered readers. Eric Sundquist argues that "sentiment, not antislavery made the book popular" and that the popular appropriation of *Uncle Tom* "gave conventional expression to subversion and thereby contained and controlled it."[41] Sundquist's analysis builds on a succession of critics' emphasis on the "sentimental power" of the novel—its direct appeal to readers' emotions, its idealization of motherhood and domesticity. These qualities have been assumed to explain its sales figures, aligning it with the other sentimental novels produced in the 1850s, many of which were also written by women, featured female heroines, and were commercially successful. These novels also helped produce what Ann Douglas called the "feminization of American culture" in the mid-nineteenth century.[42] Clearly, part of the answer does lie here in the way Stowe privileges passive martyrdom and feminine "influence" over more direct or aggressive approaches to political change. But perhaps *Uncle Tom's* popularity bears more than a coincidental relationship to the equally remarkable craze for minstrelsy in the 1850s.

Certainly, if one is conscious of the contemporary prevalence of blackface performance, it is immediately apparent that a number of characters in Stowe's novel are minstrel show types.[43] Both little Harry and Topsy are explicitly called "Jim Crow" and perform for white audiences: Harry dances and does imitations, while Topsy combines her dance with acrobatics and her startling whistle. It has even been ingeniously suggested that George Harris's disguise during his escape is a kind of blacking-up.[44] Tom is the novel's only black character without close blackface cousins, though, as I have suggested, he may have an ancestor in Kennard's Sambo, and on the stage he was later conflated with the old "uncle" figures of sentimental songs like Foster's (see chapters 2 and 4).

However, *Uncle Tom's Cabin* draws not only on minstrel conventions of characterization but also on comic routines from the blackface tradition. Patterns of dialogue, the structure of the double act—these are transported from the stage and converted into some of the novel's most distinctive moments. Stowe's borrowing was creative not derivative, and her transformations of theatrical material contributed to the realignment of the traditional gender and class positions of much early blackface performance.[45] But *Uncle Tom*'s version of blackface also complicated the sentimental identifications with domestic femininity that are often assumed to be the crux of the novel. Blackface moments in the book sometimes encapsulate sentimental values and sometimes convey ambivalence about them, and at one point the two are explicitly contrasted. Recent criticism has emphasized the way the text celebrates bourgeois femininity, but the novel also cracks jokes at its expense. The feminized heroism of Uncle Tom is shadowed, sometimes supportively, sometimes subversively, by Stowe's recasting of Jim Crow.

Minstrel show set pieces, which themselves contained a number of possible ways of relating to the characters on the stage, were converted in Stowe's novel into powerful devices for reallocating sympathy. One tradition Stowe reworked with particular subtlety, the dialogues between the end man and the interlocutor, worked in the minstrel show both to dramatize class tension and to supplant conflict with the ludicrous and nonsensical. Class is crucial in Stowe's writing—her sentimental vision of matriarchal power is implicitly middle class. However, the end man–interlocutor scenes in the minstrel show are highly ambivalent about precisely the social world *Uncle Tom* valorizes, approaching it with a fine balance of mockery and aspiration. By incorporating such scenes into her novel, even in an adapted form, Stowe complicated its class appeal, positing an ironic distance from bourgeois values as well as an identification with them. Like the members of minstrel show audiences, *Uncle Tom*'s readers inhabit several positions at once.

In the minstrel show the debates between the end man and the interlocutor took place in the first act, between performers sitting in a semicircle on the stage. The end men, who wore rags and spoke with "black" accents, bantered with the immaculately suited interlocutor, whose diction was not only middle class but prone to exaggeratedly complex and Latinate phrasing. As they traded remarks, the end men frequently misunderstood and vulgarized the interlocutor's point, while the interlocutor struggled vainly to assert the respectable, or standard English, interpretation of his utterance. Often he took on specific roles, imitating reformers, preachers, or academics, all those "who from the vantage point of superior class, education, or morality, presumed to lecture the mob."[46] As with most blackface, the weight of the comedy varied in different performances, but often the jibes were not only directed at "black"

misuse of language but also worked to undercut the genteel airs of the interlocutor. What appeared to be and sometimes was also a racist attack on black
speakers was also a dig at the standardizing and ornate language of the upper
echelons.

These exchanges are echoed a number of times in *Uncle Tom's Cabin*, and
Stowe not only reproduced the double-edged quality of the stage satire but
also extended and complicated its possibilities. In an early scene that dramatizes the way positions can be simultaneously censored and celebrated in the
novel, Mrs. Shelby is instructing Sam to help the slave catcher go after Eliza
and her child. She is also signaling, less overtly, that she would rather be help-
ing them get away. In the midst of her doublespeak, Mrs. Shelby herself is distracted by Sam's propensity for taking his Maker's name in vain. What ensues
could be an end man–interlocutor exchange, during which Mrs. Shelby takes
on the interlocutor role, ordering, teaching, and reforming, and Sam becomes the end man, disrupting, mocking, and blaspheming:

> "Why have you been loitering so, Sam? I sent Andy to tell you to hurry."
>
> "Lord bless you, Missis!" said Sam, "horses won't be cotched all in a mimit;
> they'd done clared out way down to the south pasture, and the Lord knows
> whar!"
>
> "Sam, how often must I tell you not to say 'Lord bless you, and the Lord
> knows,' and such things? It's wicked."
>
> "O, Lord bless my soul! I done forgot, Missis! I won't say nothing of the sort
> no more."
>
> "Why, Sam, you just *have* said it again."
>
> "Did I? O, Lord! I mean—I didn't go fur to say it."
>
> "You must be *careful* Sam."
>
> "Just let me get my breath, Missis, and I'll start fair. I'll be berry careful."
>
> "Well, Sam, you are to go with Mr. Haley, to show him the road, and help
> him. Be careful of the horses, Sam; you know Jerry was a little lame last week;
> *don't ride them too fast.*" (*UTC*, 39–40)[47]

Mrs. Shelby, as interlocutor, instructs Sam in correct linguistic practice and
demands reverent comportment. Persistently transgressing, Sam achieves the
end man's dance between ignorance and mockery in his counterproductive
attempts to stop blaspheming. He conceals a hint of cheek in a hopeless attempt to conform. Yet in the larger context of the slave-catching chapters, this
scene's class configurations are more subtle and more surprising than the
minstrel duality would suggest.

Sam has been tipped off that Mrs. Shelby privately hopes that the fugitives will get away. His blasphemies, which necessitate Mrs. Shelby's reprimands and instruction, cause delay, which buys time for Eliza and Harry. Although Sam's language appears to challenge Mrs. Shelby and to set up confrontation, its time-consuming provocation also works in her interest, increasing the chances that the runaways will escape. Thus, the interval produced by this end man–interlocutor role play represents both class conflict and also a cross-class alliance. The end man and the interlocutor's combat is also a conspiracy. To mix matters up still further, Haley, the white slave catcher, has been established in the opening scenes of the novel as deeply uncouth, in speech as in all else. While Sam's slips and errors work in alignment with Mrs. Shelby's prim disapproval, their opponent is "coarse," "low," and "over-dressed." White gentility is in league with black vulgarity against white "coarseness": Sam's exclamations, however sacrilegious themselves, are arraigned against the "profane" slave trader (*UTC*, 1).

This alliance is still in operation when Sam induces Haley's horse to unseat his owner, "accidently" waves his palm leaf in its eyes, and unleashes "a miscellaneous scene of confusion" while horses bolt, dogs bark, and Mike, Mose, Mandy, and Fanny "raced, clapped hands, whooped, and shouted, with outrageous officiousness and untiring zeal" (*UTC*, 41). This could be minstrel show slapstick; as on the stage, it could also represent a disruption of the industrial work ethic, enabling first-generation urban audiences to laugh with as much as at black characters who would rather dance and go hunting than put in long hours of labor.[48] Yet if this scene similarly enshrines both an apparent critique of black shiftlessness and a delight in it, it differs from the minstrel show in suggesting the genteel sanction of Mrs. Shelby. Stowe includes her middle-class forces of discipline and order in the novel; unlike those of the stage interlocutors, they are often explicitly feminine, and here they are also in league with blackface chaos.

Uncle Tom's Cabin thus adapts the minstrel show's capacity, in Dale Cockrell's words, "to ridicule both up and down the social ladder simultaneously," reapplying it with significant adjustments to class and gender.[49] It is not just ridicule that moves in this scene but also sympathy, and it is not a straightforward journey. Whether the reader identifies most with Sam's linguistic license or with Mrs. Shelby's corrective impulse, procrastination brings the two into collusion. Social position here cannot be marked out simply as rungs on a ladder, and sympathy must chart a path complicated enough to encompass both mistress and slave without visiting the lower-class white.

The oscillating satire and sympathy of the end man–interlocutor dialogues demonstrate the way in which comically uneducated, self-serving, or cowardly characters can also serve to make digs at white slave-owning society. If the novel is inspected for blackface dualities, some of its most demeaning portraits can be found at points where sentiment has the greatest force. The sentimental also amplifies the comedy, adding another layer of meaning to blackface wordplay that is often an antislavery point. On the stage, parodies of sermons, lectures, and stump speeches evinced the same pattern of overt mockery of (and discreet pleasure in) linguistic anarchy as the end man dialogues, and the novel also adapted this blackface convention.

After his triumph over the slave catcher Sam shows off his "speechifying" (*UTC*, 64). Like blackface oratory, this is a self-aggrandizing affair that evinces errors of logic, narcissism, and overinflated and inaccurate use of language. He asserts that his afternoon's work is an example of his determination to "stand up fer [his people's] rights," explaining that his wavering intentions were a sign of his "*conscience*," one of a series of terms he glosses in contradiction to conventional usage: "[W]hen I thought of gwine arter Lizy, I railly spected Mas'r was sot dat way. When I found Missis was sot the contrar, dat ar was conscience *more yet*,–cause fellers allers gets more by stickin' to Missis's side,–so yer see I's persistent either way, and sticks up to conscience, and holds on to principles" (*UTC*, 66).

Sam's "black" accent and his novel definitions–of "persistence," "conscience," and "principles"–were all staples of the blackface form. He also produces other common aspects of such performances–muddled terms of address ("ladies of de other sex"), self-serving and circular arguments (it is a matter of conscience both to go after Eliza and not to go after her; he is principled because he acts in the belief that "fellers allers gets more by stickin' to Missis's side"), and malapropisms and neologisms ("they's perquisite to dese yer times, and ter *all* times") (*UTC*, 66).[50]

This speech could appear to work merely as unpleasant ridicule, painting Sam as ignorant and conceited and his listeners as gullible. When Andy questions Sam's account, he receives a reply in the same nonsensical vein: "[B]oys like you, Andy, means well, but they can't be spected to collusitate the great principles of action." Nevertheless, the protest is quelled, "rebuked, particularly by the hard word collusitate, which most of the youngerly members of the company seemed to consider as a settler in the case" (*UTC*, 66). If all the mockery in this scene were directed at Sam and his listeners, the reader would function here like those minstrel show spectators who may have felt superior

and witty in contrast to the speaker. But the stump speech did not always or
not only work to mark off the punters' abilities from those of the characters
on the stage. Parts of the speech could poke fun at the audience, parts at black
speakers, parts at the middle-class aficionados of its many "highbrow" targets: Shakespeare, opera, phrenology, politics, religion, and science. Lhamon
argues that the language of the stump speech actually identified the speaker
as a trickster, highlighting and partly endorsing his assaults on taboo. Adroit-
ness with language in the form of puns was part of the pleasure of such pieces,
especially when embedded in examples of apparent clumsiness.[51] Holmberg
and Schneider suggest further subtleties. Stump speakers, particularly in sermons, addressed the audience as if it were a black one, making it participate
in their disarranging of language and logic. The audience could thus participate in the joke or else was mocked itself in quips masked by the momentary
confusion over who was being addressed.[52]

Not all of these ambiguities are possible in the novel, where the narration
mediates between Sam and the reader, partly cutting off the possibility of our
identification with his listeners. The page cannot encompass all the shades of
identification of minstrel performances, but even here the stump speech offers
some complications. Sam's perorations, like the ones in minstrel shows, are
also sometimes double-edged. Sam accompanies Shelby to political meetings,

> where, roosted on some rail fence, or perched aloft in some tree, he would sit
> watching the orators, with the greatest apparent gusto, and then, descending
> among the various brethren of his own color, assembled on the same errand,
> he would edify and delight them with the most ludicrous burlesques and imi-
> tations, all delivered with the most imperturbable earnestness and solemnity;
> and though the auditors immediately about him were generally of his own
> color, it not unfrequently happened that they were fringed pretty deeply with
> those of a fairer complexion, who listened, laughing and winking, to Sam's
> great self-congratulation. (UTC, 64)

Like those aspects of blackface that may have been derived from black
parodies of white dancing, speech, or style, Sam's oratory is sometimes a lampoon of white performances at political events. He is as liable to expose the
weaknesses and self-aggrandizements of white speakers as to demonstrate
the fallibilities of black ones. His audiences are complicit with him in this (not
the butts of the joke but themselves enjoying it), and his white spectators occupy the fringes, not the prime seats. It is claimed that black dancing for
mixed audiences may have contributed to the origins of blackface; this scene

stages a white enjoyment of black performative skills alongside a black commentary on white ones.[53] Sam's discussion of the slave-catching exhibits a number of the racially derogatory characteristics of minstrel show speeches—the non sequiturs, mispronunciations, and digressions. However, his antics at political meetings offer the "clever sallies at local personalities and public affairs" that undercut the effects of his minstrel speech traits, again finding targets across the social spectrum.[54]

One of the most typical elements of the set-piece speech in the minstrel show, the malapropism, itself demonstrates some of the complexities of Sam's language. Linguists have described the way the malapropism can itself be in fact a sophisticated play on words, both in minstrel show versions and in the black linguistic practices to which they allude.[55] Sam thoroughly misleads Haley about the road they should take, achieving the paradox of convincing him that Eliza has taken the dirt track while truthfully explaining that it would be impossible. In the course of this elaborate deception he uses a malapropism with a sting. Haley believes that Sam is trying to trick him to take the turnpike, but it is in fact a sophisticated double bluff. Sam wants Haley to use the other road, so when he says, "Now, when I study 'pon it, I think de straight road do best, *deridedly*," it is not so much a mistake as it appears (*UTC*, 50). While the straight road would "decidedly" be the best one, his word coinage reveals another truth: he is in fact deriding the slave trader.

The reader's sympathy in this instance helps convert the apparent malapropism into something entirely apropos, and it makes both Sam's hidden meaning and the joke itself accessible. Sympathy is not just linked with the comedy in this case, it is an integral part of it, and together they conspire to transform Sam's language from a sign of ignorance into a hint of his power.

Chloe's idiosyncratic pronunciation in the novel also embeds multiple significances in blackface malapropism, but where the comedy of Sam's vocabulary conceals sentiment, Chloe's openly directs the reader to empathize with her. As with Sam's speech, Chloe's can be read against conventional usage, but the effect is more poignant than comic. Chloe, we are told, "had a particular fancy for calling poultry poetry," and she also persists in calling the confectioner (to whom she hires herself out in an attempt to buy back her husband) a "perfectioner." These transpositions take place in a scene where Mr. Shelby has callously suggested that she forget Tom and "marry" someone else. Chloe is at this point pitiable but also heroic, because when Mrs. Shelby offers to raise the money to redeem Tom, Chloe volunteers to earn it herself. Chloe is not a risible figure at this point, and, given her enthusiasm for cooking fowl, calling poultry "poetry" is not in her case inappropriate. Considering the urgent reason for her stint at the confectioner's, even "perfectioner's" may not be incorrect. Here the blackface convention is conscripted to assist the sentiment in the novel, where the laughter and the tears demanded by the genre were evoked almost in the same moment and by the same device.

But the novel allocates sympathies in more complex ways than these. In some blackface performance comedy was only apparently disparaging, often cloaking a guilty fascination. Outrageous inclinations, at least for its genteel readers, were also at work in *Uncle Tom's Cabin*, despite the exemplary role models it also provided in the forms of Eva and Tom. As well as offering official aspirations to follow these paragons, the book takes a secret pleasure in behavior that provides a systematic contrast. Its unofficial celebrations of a blackface style form one of the most remembered aspects of the novel, and they also provide one of its most concentrated antislavery hits. These moments in the text derive from blackface at its most subtle and paradoxical, and they are extraordinarily effective.

The scenes in which Miss Ophelia is pitted against Topsy could be interpreted as symbolic of a clash of values, in which immaculate New England housekeeping wars with domestic chaos. As several critics have shown, Stowe uses good housekeeping as a marker of decent society. Gillian Brown has argued that the disarray of Dinah's kitchen, with its onions and hair grease and damask tablecloths jumbled together in drawers, can serve as an explanation of the novel's critique of slavery.[56]

In her relation to Dinah's kitchen, though, as in her relation to Topsy, Miss Ophelia is a difficult figure to identify with. There is an element in the text that secretly condones Dinah's style, and she is, after all, "a native and essential cook, as much as Aunt Chloe" (*UTC*, 179). In Dinah's case, as in Topsy's, the novel pulls in two different directions, overtly lamenting chaos and quietly allowing, even encouraging, readers to enjoy it. Both Dinah and Topsy simultaneously reinforce and suggest an escape from the middle-class domestic ideal. This tension between identification and denial clearly echoes a central feature of blackface performance, during which audiences were able both to enjoy the attributes and antics of the men on stage and to use the burnt cork mask to distance themselves from it.

Topsy's encounters with Miss Ophelia replicate this tension, in contrast to the unalloyed sentimental instruction of her scenes with Eva. Topsy's appearance suggests the exaggerated makeup and impoverished attire of Jim

Crow, but a feminized one. Jim Crow was, in fact, played by the seven-year-old Miss Wray in 1835, though women performers were otherwise rare.[57] There were female characters in blackface, usually played in drag (in the 1830s there was a stage "Mrs. Crow," and the minstrel show later developed a female "wench" figure), but they were adult roles and often highly sexualized. For these transvestite "wenches," the incongruity of white men dressed as black women was often the focus of the joke.[58] In what were often vicious blackface songs, such as the extremely popular "Lucy Long," the singers lusted after women described not only as unattractive but specifically as unattractive because of racial characteristics. Their skin was dark and their mouths were wide, as their blackface makeup confirmed, and their feet or heels were long, as their oversized floppy shoes implied. Though the wench danced, it was probably another ("male") performer who sang about her.[59] Topsy, on the other hand, does her own singing, as well as dancing, somersaults, and whistling. Unlike Lucy Long, Topsy is a child, her hair still "braided in sundry little tails, which stuck out in every direction," and never in the novel is she associated with sexual innuendo (*UTC*, 206). Whereas songs like "Lucy Long" presume that the signs of blackness are physically repulsive, Topsy's function is to demonstrate the irrationality and inhumanity of such a feeling: her need for love teaches Miss Ophelia to overcome her fear of black bodies.

Topsy's most memorable lines in the novel occur in duets with Ophelia, mimicking the classic minstrel double act. Like Mrs. Shelby, Miss Ophelia is a feminine interlocutor, representing the forces of decency and respectability, which Topsy, like a good end man, disrupts.[60] As with the earlier invocations of end man and interlocutor in the novel, the exchanges between Topsy and Miss Ophelia work on a number of levels, enabling virtually contradictory interpretations. Topsy's perversion of the catechism is a good example. The scene echoes Pearl's failure to repeat hers in Hawthorne's *The Scarlet Letter*, scandalizing the Puritan elders, but Pearl's behavior is purely mischievous—she is withholding what she knows.[61] Topsy's error is a product of the ignorance engendered by slavery. In the course of her enforced call-and-response, Topsy is expected to respond, "Our first parents, being left to the freedom of their own will, fell from the state wherein they were created." She interrupts the recitation with a question, "Was dat ar state Kintuck?" (*UTC*, 218). Topsy's willful misparroting of the formula personalizes and even domesticates it, echoing the end man's reinterpretation of educated or sentimental culture in prosaic and ludicrous terms.

An undated minstrel show sketch called "Blackberrying" illustrates this process, showing how much Stowe's famous scene resembles the structure of such blackface humor. In "Blackberrying" the interlocutor is called "Tambo":

BONES: Den she axed me if I would go to the 'pothecary shop for some medicine. I said yes; so I went down to Dr. Night Bell—

TAMBO: No, not to Dr. Night Bell; that's the name of the bell on the door, the night bell.

BONES: Well, I called him Dr. Night Bell, anyhow.

TAMBO: I presume he was a pretty good physician?

BONES: No, he wasn't fishin', he was home.

TAMBO: Oh no, I mean he was a doctor of some note.

BONES: Yes, he was counting out his notes when I went in.

TAMBO: No, Bones, you do not understand. I mean he was a doctor of some standing.

BONES: No, he wasn't standin', he was sittin' on a three-legged stool.[62]

Bones's interpretation of the sign on the doctor's door works both to illustrate his capacity to misunderstand and to undermine the conventions of polite speakers like Tambo and the doctor himself. Bones's misapprehensions and mishearings interrupt the flow of Tambo's questions, so that every line of inquiry is arrested by the necessity to rephrase or reexplain. Topsy's interjections serve the same purpose, distracting Miss Ophelia from the solemn progression of the catechism. With his anarchic imagery, Bones simultaneously reveals and undermines Tambo's value system, as Tambo's status-conscious inquiries about the doctor's professional standing serve paradoxically to evoke the ludicrous and venal picture of the physician counting his money on a three-legged stool. Topsy's transformation of the phrase from the catechism into the irreverent image of Adam and Eve "falling" out of Kentucky works the same way, perfecting an alteration from the sublime to the ridiculous.

Topsy's jokes involve the same kind of seditious literalism or faux naïveté that the end man used to undermine his opponent. Her false confessions of theft also echo this kind of play: "'Why, Missis said I must 'fess; and I couldn't think of nothin' else to 'fess'" (*UTC*, 213). Like Bones's, Topsy's interpretation is ostensibly wrong, but it allows her to best Miss Ophelia, just as Bones's error in the sketch reduces the doctor to the sign of his nighttime summons. Topsy's apparent illogic and ignorance take on Miss Ophelia's (and the reader's) worldview and refute it. The end man in the minstrel show could license the audience's identification with the forces of disorder; in the same way Topsy's function here is to provide enjoyable pokes at authority. One of Topsy's roles in the novel is to demonstrate the destructiveness of slavery and the redeeming power of its antithesis, Little Eva. Topsy lies and steals and knows no better because slavery has deprived her both of family and a moral order. One drift of the narrative confirms this, as Eva teaches her to love and Ophelia makes a missionary of her. But the novel also pulls in another direction, fostering the secret desire to revel in Topsy's upsets and oddities, to challenge the constraint and self-discipline represented by Miss Ophelia.

Some of Topsy's most profound challenges to convention are also attacks on the domestic and the feminine. In these episodes too the text provokes conflicting responses. The scene in which she disperses a bed instead of making it, scattering sheets and spreads and feathers, dressing "the bolster up in Miss Ophelia's night-clothes, and enact[ing] various scenic performances with that," brings her style of theatrical disorder to housekeeping, and she mounts a similar assault on the delicate pursuit of needlework: "[S]he broke her needles, threw them slyly out of windows, or down in chinks of the walls; she tangled, broke, and dirtied her thread, or, with a sly movement, would throw away a spool altogether. . . . [T]hough Miss Ophelia could not help feeling that so many accidents could not possibly happen in succession, yet she could not, without a watchfulness which would leave her no time for anything else, detect her" (*UTC*, 216, 215).

These vignettes are reminiscent of minstrelsy's fantasies of revolt against the middle-class work ethic, but Topsy's recalcitrance is directed at *domestic* work, at the insistence that she sew fine stitches and help keep a spotless house. Topsy's rebellion is against the feminine version of the factory ideal, the well-ordered home. Richard Beale Davis calls Topsy "a bundle of perversities reflecting the guilty consciences of her owners."[63] Her mischief is obviously a reflection as well as a product of the moral disarray Stowe believes is occasioned by slavery, but it would also appeal to anyone who has secretly chafed at the domestic yoke: it is blackface subversion for girls.

Topsy's catchphrase, "I'se so wicked," was later turned into two songs, singling out her defiance of conventional piety as her most marketable characteristic.[64] In this as in her exchanges with Ophelia Topsy's resistance is enjoyable: comic, punishable, ultimately to be corrected, but also potentially delicious. Given what we know of Stowe's own scatty and impatient approach to housework and her extended flight from domestic responsibility to the Brattleboro Water Cure, the writer herself may have taken some pleasure in Topsy's assault on the home.[65]

Yet just as Stowe invoked blackface comedy to solicit forbidden sympathy for Topsy the imp, so she also used it to press home the plight of Topsy the slave. In this, the sketch "Blackberrying" again elucidates Stowe's method:

> BONES: Ah! Tambo, she's gone dead.
>
> TAMBO: Is she dead, Bones?
>
> BONES: Yes, Tambo. She sent for me three days after she died.
>
> TAMBO: No, Bones, you mean three days previous to her decease.
>
> BONES: No; she had no niece; she was an orphan.[66]

Topsy's assertion, upon well-meaning interrogation, that she "never was born" exactly parallels Bones's assertion that his girl sent for him "three days after she died": it is an affront both to reason and to the interrogator. Topsy's illogical outburst, "I 'spect I grow'd," is closely related to Bones's, and both work by challenging our common assumptions about life, death, and family structures. Like Bones's denial of the finality of death, Topsy's rejection of the necessity of birth is, at one level, a comic display of ignorance and, at another level, oddly disturbing.[67] Topsy's statement upsets Ophelia's attempts to establish origins and order, and it is amusing as much because it nonplusses the interlocutor as because it makes no sense. Yet despite the reader's strong temptation to enjoy them, Topsy's rejections of order and logic also unsettle the reader, and the text's invocation of such contradictory feelings is especially powerful here. In Topsy's case the comedy is intensified by pathos: she has been "raised by a speculator," and so her ignorance of her birth reflects the slave owner's indifference to her humanity. Stowe is both playing with a comic convention in Topsy's line and giving it a moral resonance. Topsy's "never was born" can be compared not only with the blackface sketch but with the opening of slave narratives, in which the absence of the usual biographical details makes the same point.[68]

Topsy's famous comment used a minstrel device to extraordinary political effect. However, although blackface assisted in the novel's complex marshaling of readerly emotion, and although some of the most potentially derogatory scenes in the novel also encourage readerly identification with slaves, it should not be forgotten that Stowe's antislavery weapon here is a minstrel figure. Blackface, so politically elusive, always so close to mockery, would ever be a mischievous servant. Despite the power Stowe invested in the ambiguities of Topsy's characterization, it was not difficult for later readers to convert Stowe's character into a sign of irrepressible black childishness, especially for proslavery propaganda. Like many blackface figures, Topsy was a fantasy projection for those afflicted by bourgeois repressions, but although this role complicated her relation to race, it did not negate it.

Worse, just as the minstrel show itself could harbor violently degrading images alongside invitations to imagine oneself with the characters on the stage, so does *Uncle Tom's Cabin*. Some of the most highly charged scenes of black-white encounter in the novel seem to owe more to the fear or disgust expressed in some minstrel performance than to those acts that encoded fascination or a sense of shared conspiracy. These episodes lack the fine balance of empathy and amusement that make earlier scenes both powerful and open to multiple readings, and they demonstrate the dangers of conscripting blackface to do antislavery work. Where Stowe's racial portraiture is least equivocal, there is most indication of how it might also be damaging.

A certain unease is manifested first in the characterization of St. Clare's household. The valet, Adolph, is very like the blackface dandy, typified by Zip Coon, in his dress, manner, and speech (*UTC*, 142–43). However, Adolph, unlike Chloe, is not a sentimentalized version of a blackface tradition, nor does his role, unlike Sam's, involve a complex antislavery play across its conventions. Adolph's activities in the novel are unsavory: he pilfers from his master, flirts with Jane and Rosa, and despises Ophelia for working: "[S]he was no lady" (*UTC*, 206). Jane and Rosa, who are similarly overdressed and inclined to "airs," scoff at Dinah, who is too dark to go to the "light-colored" ball, and at Topsy too. Unlike the scenes with Sam or Topsy, these instances of dandyism are not complicated by any reversals of sentiment in the novel, and there are no secret devices to endear these characters to the reader. In fact, they are partly punished in the narrative, for when St. Clare dies his wife takes the opportunity to have Rosa whipped and Adolph sold.

In the minstrel show figures like Adolph could satirize both working-class dandies and the upper-class style they aspired to, as well as expressing anxiety about wealthy free blacks, but in the novel, which so frequently makes a white middle-class lifestyle normative, the satire is not so broadly shared.[69] Whereas Topsy's sallies against bourgeois femininity may offer the reader the pleasures of vicarious rebellion, it is Adolph, Jane, and Rosa who are ridiculed, not "airs" per se. Black dandies in the novel indicate a narrower set of transgressions than those on the stage, as Stowe's characters get above their station, rather than lampooning their self-styled betters. In these moments Stowe's characterization is far less generous to her fictional slaves even than her blackface model; it presages more the vicious slurs typical of later proslavery novels (see chapter 3).

Those novels would have even more use for Sambo and Quimbo.[70] Legree's black adjuncts are, like Topsy, illustrative of the effects of cruel and irresponsible enslavement, but they have none of her redeeming hilarity. Stowe paints a grotesque and frightening portrait of these two, who are positively menacing in appearance: "coarse, dark, heavy features; their great eyes, rolling enviously on each other." Their language reinforces this impression: "barbarous, guttural, half-brute intonation" (*UTC*, 299–300). As with Topsy, the contrast between Sambo's and Quimbo's dark features and their eyes imitates blackface makeup, and "their dilapidated garments fluttering in the wind" mimic minstrel costume, but the "barbarous" accents are a far cry from Sam's acute malapropisms (*UTC*, 300). As we see Quimbo "viciously [driving] two or three tired women" from the corn mill, or Sambo kicking Lucy to fainting point, there is none of the oscillation of sympathy that Stowe motivates for Sam or for Topsy (*UTC*, 301, 305–6). Like those characters, however, they are immeasurably more powerful when hell raising than when heaven-bent, as when Cassy hears "the sound of wild shrieking, whooping, halloing, and singing . . . mingled with the barking of dogs, and other symptoms of general uproar" (*UTC*, 325). This passage is reminiscent of the "rough noise" that Cockrell identifies as one of the folk practices behind early blackface or the raising Cain that Lhamon argues remained one of its primary impulses. It is also not far off from the uproar produced when the Shelby slaves delay the slave hunt or from the commotion Topsy tends to engender. But in Legree's house rowdiness is sinister; it is not a festival of misrule. Legree and his overseers are "in a state of furious intoxication," and their "making all manner of ludicrous and horrid grimaces at each other" is not rebellious role play but a possible precursor of real violence (*UTC*, 325).

Blackface in the final section of the novel is thus the source of sinister images, not, as earlier, of comic pleasures or a dose of antislavery sentiment. There is no longer the sense, as in many of the scenes set on the Shelby and St. Clare plantations, that blackface is designed to snare readerly sympathy for the forces of riot; rather, gentility and order are endorsed more completely. The signal for this comes when Legree demands a song from the "dispirited" slaves he is carrying home. When Tom strikes up a "Methodist hymn" Legree silences him and demands a song that could easily belong to the blackface repertoire: "Mas'r See'd Me Cotch a Coon."[71] Stowe calls the song "one of those unmeaning songs, common among the slaves," a judgment she almost immediately contradicts, observing that "there was a prayer in it, which Simon could not hear" (*UTC*, 297).[72]

This snatch of blackface signals a deep rift between white and black signi-
fication, in stark contrast to the earlier alliances between Mrs. Shelby and
Sam or Topsy and the reader. The secreting of a "prayer" in a song, which
partly parallels Stowe's blackface envelopes for antislavery messages, is also
a desperate measure. Tom's fellows are not exploiting the distance between
genteel and blackface culture in the way that the novel itself does in earlier
episodes. At this point the reader is not encouraged to enjoy the "rowdy" entertainment, even unofficially. The song is pitted against piety, but, where the
text winked at Topsy's and Sam's irreverence, here sanctity prevails. Legree
believes that when his slaves sing they are neither expressing despondent
feelings nor experiencing them, which is easier on his conscience and useful
in his efforts to subdue his workforce. The song's rowdiness links it with
Legree's degenerative rejection of middle-class values and makes it incompatible with Uncle Tom's godly tunes.

In her later defense of the novel, *The Key to Uncle Tom's Cabin*, Stowe's
collection of documents to "prove" the central tenets of *Uncle Tom's Cabin*
reveals what she believes to be crucial to the novel's argument. Tom's piety
and domesticity are emphasized. A whole chapter is devoted to historical examples of black people with Tom's qualities, as is one to those of George Harris. Stowe does not accord her borrowings from blackface the same importance. It is striking that the *Key* does not produce authenticating examples of
blackface behavior. There are no sources cited for Sam and Andy, and although there is a chapter devoted to the issues raised by Topsy, this is restricted to the possibility of educating slaves: "[T]he appeal to the more generous part of the negro character is seldom made in vain."[73] Although Stowe
used minstrel characterization and set pieces in her novel, she did not spell
out any ideological implications for them in the way she did for Uncle Tom's
piety or the state of Chloe's cabin. Yet the association of minstrel songs with
Legree in the novel does suggest some unease about blackface.

Whereas Topsy's Jim Crow act could coexist with a susceptibility to Eva's
instruction, Tom is only ever a moral beacon. In Tom Stowe signaled most
clearly where readers' sympathies should be directed: his personification of
Christian strength works without the ambiguities of other figures in the text.
Tom's religion protects him from the dismissive readings Topsy's blackface act
leaves open, and whenever Uncle Tom is the novel's focus of sympathy, blackface is once more the antithesis of feminine sentimental culture: impious and
uncouth. All through the novel multiple, conflicting, and even contrary identifications are opened up for the reader, and its quiet encouragement to cheer

for Topsy's chaos or Sam's insurrections could also call out other more oblique readings. Minstrel show devices could help *Uncle Tom's Cabin* inspire antislavery feeling in stealthy, unconfrontational ways, but they could not guarantee it. *Uncle Tom*'s readers, like blackface audiences, could take from the novel what they wished, and that included less benign interpretations.

The blackface in *Uncle Tom* suggests that many of the ambiguities and unpredictabilities of performance could be incorporated into fiction. Lott has suggested that audience responses at the minstrel show blended apparent contradictions: "mordant irony and suspension of disbelief" and "disavowal or ridicule of the Other and interracial identification with it." Lott compares this with theories of the contemporary cinema, at which spectators "successively identify, across gender lines, with logical screen representatives of ourselves (heroes, victims), then with seeming adversaries (villains, killers)."[74] In the same way the viewer of blackface could serially imagine solidarity with or his own superiority to the racialized figure on the stage. Yet many of the same paradoxes of audience identification are apparent in the process of reading fiction. Even with a novel readers can interpolate themselves into narratives in peculiar ways.

Some of the possibilities are suggested by Frances Hodgson Burnett's recollection of the impact of *Uncle Tom's Cabin* on her as a child in England in the 1850s. Burnett's imaginative appropriation of Stowe's novel suggests that its readers could harbor sympathies as multiple and perverse as those of any blackface audience. She describes acting out the novel in solitary play, recasting *Uncle Tom* with herself, at different times, in almost every role. In the following passage, in which Burnett coyly refers to her younger self as the "Small Person," she suggests how the plot was advanced with the characters shared among the child and a couple of dolls:

> [A] cheerful black doll was procured immediately and called Topsy; her "best doll," which fortunately had brown hair in its wig, was Eva, and was kept actively employed slowly fading away and dying, while she talked about the New Jerusalem, with a hectic flush on her cheeks. She converted Topsy, and totally changed her gutta-percha nature, though it was impossible to alter her gutta-percha grin. She conversed with Uncle Tom (then the Small Person was Uncle Tom), she cut off "her long golden-brown curls" . . . and presented them to the weeping slaves. (Then the Small Person was all the weeping slaves at once.)[75]

The confusion of pronouns in this passage (who exactly converts Topsy?) suggests the rapid shifting of identities under way, and the writer seems to be as absorbed in Eva's conversion as in Topsy's resistance. But the most surprising identification the girl makes is manifested in a scene her mother accidentally stumbles upon, starring the doll who had hitherto played Topsy. The child is discovered, "apparently furious with insensate rage, muttering to herself as she brutally lashed with one of her brother's toy whips, a cheerfully hideous black gutta-percha doll who was tied to the candelabra stand and appeared to be enjoying the situation."[76]

Here the Small Person, formerly Uncle Tom and "all the weeping slaves at once," has been transformed into Legree, while the doll, formerly Topsy, has become Uncle Tom. The doll, because of the fixed grin on its inanimate face, seems in its unchanged expression to retain the irrepressible good humor of its earlier role, and this impression helps to convert Burnett's version of Stowe's antislavery image into something more like masochistic fantasy. The young girl and Stowe's villain have been fused together into a "little fury with the flying hair," while Uncle Tom and Topsy have together coalesced into a rubber doll who is taking Tom's fatal punishment with every sign of enjoyment.[77]

This scenario, which the child's mother finds "alarming" and "distressing," surely denotes an unexpected allocation of empathy in Stowe's young reader. Critical readings of slave narratives have revealed the pornographic function of the accounts of whippings such texts produced as evidence of the victimization of women slaves. Deborah Mcdowell's analysis of such scenes highlights the aptness of Frederick Douglass's comment that he was not only a "witness" of such events but thereby also a "participant."[78] Burnett's anecdote illustrates the way identification with the injured can also be disturbingly inflected by a fascination with the violence of the scene. Jenny Franchot suggests that Douglass's description of his Aunt Esther's whipping disrupts the narrative path of his autobiographies, its "aesthetic power" arresting their trajectory of self-liberation.[79] Franchot's argument offers the possibility that Douglass's whipping scene resonates beyond its antislavery function and that it spills out from its illustrative role in the narrative. Burnett's story indicates that the whipping of Uncle Tom could similarly escape its primary role in Stowe's novel. Legree is an intense object of interest even for a reader who sympathizes with "all the weeping slaves." Not simply evoking "feeling" or "sympathy," Legree's physical assault on Tom could itself attract a guilty identification, even from a child who at other moments was imagining herself as the abused martyr. As well as the sentimental heroine and the comic, tragic, and incidental slave characters, Burnett's "feeling" could also take in the villain.

Burnett manages in the course of her games to identify across gulfs of age, class, gender, and race. Not only does her play illustrate the "movement of sympathy in all its anxious appeals" across such grounds of difference, which Shirley Samuels describes as the work of sentimental literature, it turns the crossing of those lines into a multidirectional roller-coaster ride. Samuels argues that "the sentimental complex . . . situates the reader or viewer: that is, the act of emotional response the work evokes also produces the sentimental subject who consumes the work."[80] Stowe bears this out in the declaration in her preface that her "object" has been "to awaken sympathy and feeling for the African race, as they exist among us," and her plea in the conclusion that readers "see to it that *they feel right*" (*UTC*, xiii, 385). The parting of Tom from his family, Eliza's flight across the ice, the deaths of Tom and Little Eva are all clearly designed to inspire empathy of this kind. Yet Burnett's example indicates that this process may be only partially successful: her acting out of the novel does make her the kind of sentimental subject who "feels right," but it also involves a much more experimental kind of readerly subjectivity.

Burnett's staging of *Uncle Tom's Cabin* in the nursery points to the intricacies of the play of sympathy in the novel, echoing a complexity that was not confined to the imagination of her childhood reenactments. Even at the most apparent structural levels of the text, it is not only the virtuous who monopolize the reader's emotions or who inspire a sense of kinship. There are scenes in the novel that demand sympathy without pity or pathos or that even play with readerly sympathy, shuttling it between antagonistic characters and surreptitiously attracting it to unlikely recipients. Sympathy takes circuitous, evanescent, and sometimes multiple simultaneous routes through the text, creating a slipperiness and paradoxicality that is more typical of the minstrel show. Burnett's rapid imaginative movements across identity boundaries are anticipated in the book when Stowe complicates even the crossings and blurrings characteristic of blackface, sometimes radically redistributing minstrelsy's most typical class and gender loyalties.

Most commentators overlooked what Burnett unconsciously recognizes, the way Stowe's book borrowed some of the performative ambiguities of minstrelsy. Blackness in the shows was theatrical, and its staginess licensed readers to make silent identifications with characters' prankish assaults on gentility. Minstrel audiences could at once laugh at "black" characters on the stage and simultaneously delight in their affronts to decent society and respectable manners. Richard Butsch asserts that minstrelsy offered "a dual message of racism and anti-intellectualism"; it could also be described as hiding class conflict in apparent (and often offensive) racial parody.[81] *Uncle Tom's Cabin* captured for the novel some of the multiple meanings blackface embedded in performance, offering readers a comedy of secret sympathy in which black characters could be at once ludicrous, seductively subversive, and aligned with moral rectitude. Blackface structures in the novel opened conduits for cross-class and cross-racial empathy, both overt and antislavery in purpose and also more covert and rebellious in their effects.

But if, like a blackface show, *Uncle Tom's Cabin* could be read with multiple and even competing sympathies, it could also be read as straightforward racial portraiture. The reviews of Stowe's novel also cast light on a longstanding controversy amongst commentators on blackface—was it really taken to represent black people? By assuming that the portrayal of African Americans was blackface's preserve, *Uncle Tom's* readers suggest it was. Most recently, critics have been fascinated by the complexities and ambiguities of blackface performance, Cockrell and Lhamon arguing that in its earliest forms it mingled interracial cultural exchange and social subversiveness.[82] In these accounts blackface was neither entirely white in culture nor only inspired by racism. Yet nineteenth-century celebrations of minstrelsy often claimed it was derived from specific black musicians and dancers.[83] Constance Rourke was arguing as late as 1931 that many of the rhythms in minstrel music, its dances, and the content of many of its songs showed unmistakable "negro" origins.[84] Such assertions distracted from the facts that historians have since emphasized: that many early minstrels and their music had white and Northern origins, that minstrelsy was "shaped by white expectations and desires and not by black realities," and that white working-class rivalry lay behind blackface, making stage blacks the objects both of envy and of contempt.[85] The insistence on blackface's verisimilitude, while it may not have been entirely specious, obscured the racist purposes minstrelsy could serve. The naturalization of blackface imagery in *Uncle Tom's Cabin* may have reinforced this effect: most commentators ignored white culture's investment in Stowe's images, just as they did with blackface. Like the minstrel show spectators who turned Jim Crow into a "representative of the negro," some contemporaries took Stowe's characters to be the definitive *literary* representations.

As *Uncle Tom's Cabin* increasingly supplied the reference points for transatlantic discussions of slavery in the United States, many of these reviewers, like Burnett, were British. The *Times* review of the novel declared, "We know of no book in which the negro character finds such successful interpretation, and appears so life-like and so fresh. The scenes in which the negroes are rep-

resented at their domestic labours or conversing with each other reveal a familiar acquaintance with negro life, and a capacity for displaying it that cannot be mistaken."[86]

George Eliot shared this confidence in the fidelity of Stowe's representation of the "negro character" and "negro life," asserting in an 1856 review of
Stowe's second novel, *Dred*, that "Mrs Stowe has *invented* the Negro novel."[87]
Uncle Tom's Cabin's many imitators—the pro- and antislavery novels, the
slave narratives, the parodies, dramatizations, and rewritings—are testimony
enough to its hold on representations of slavery in the 1850s and beyond. As
Richard Yarborough has asserted, Stowe "helped to establish a range of character types that served to bind and restrict black authors for decades."[88] For
the rest of the century and beyond, *Uncle Tom* tended to determine and de-
limit the scope for putting African Americans in fiction, just as minstrelsy
dominated their portrayal on the stage.

Moreover, *Uncle Tom's* hegemony extended farther than fiction. After reading the novel, Stowe's former colleague, the teacher Mary Dutton, remembered a trip they had taken in 1833 to visit the family of a pupil on their farm
in Kentucky: "Harriet did not seem to notice anything that happened, but sat
much of the time abstracted in thought. When the negroes did funny things
and cut up capers, she did not seem to pay the slightest attention to them. Af-
terwards however, in reading 'Uncle Tom,' I recognised scene after scene of
that visit portrayed with the most minute fidelity."[89] What is striking about this
passage is Dutton's conflation of "the negroes," Stowe's novel, and minstrel-
type theatricality. It seems merely a matter of course that they should do
"funny things and cut up capers" and for Dutton to describe her memories
with the dramatic term "scenes." Blackface plays through Dutton's recollec-
tions, and it is used to align them with her impressions of *Uncle Tom's Cabin*.

Uncle Tom and blackface between them helped structure Dutton's memories of slaves after the event, but they also exerted an influence over interpretations of Southern encounters as they were experienced. In 1857 a newly
married British couple took a wedding trip through North America. The
wife—feminist, reformer, and painter Barbara Bodichon—had strong antislavery sympathies.[90] While they traveled in Louisiana, Bodichon's views were in
part fueled by *Uncle Tom*, to which she referred several times in letters.[91]

Stowe's novel becomes in Bodichon's writings a touchstone on the slavery
question. She reads its absence from Southern homes as a sign of pervasive
misinformation: "The lies I have read! here in newspapers and *Cabins* (answers to *Uncle Tom* which deluge the South, where the original is not to be

found on any table)," and when Bodichon meets a Southern woman claim-ing to hate Mrs. Beecher, she observes that "every trace of humanity disap-peared, under the influence of this feeling."[92] By the time of Bodichon's jour-ney Stowe had become an obvious guide for a British traveler attempting to interpret the South. Bodichon was also filtering her impressions through her reading of Stowe, ironically so, since the novelist had herself only ever made the one trip South, and that no deeper than Kentucky. Yet the traveler's en-counters were shaped by her reading, and Bodichon was seeing as well as writing after *Uncle Tom's Cabin*. Encountering a group of black children in Carrolton, Bodichon turns the event into a weak comic dialogue about her unusual sketching dress—blue-tinted spectacles, large hat, and Balmoral boots: "Six negro children who were playing stopped, stared and then began to run away, frightened by my appearance. 'I do not eat niggers,' I said—so they came up to me and one said, 'why it's a woman!' 'Why do you wear boots?' 'Because it is wet!' 'Why do you wear spectacles?' 'Because I can't see without.' 'Why do you wear a hat?' 'Because I can't carry a parasol!' So we be-came good friends."[93]

This exchange falls far short of the end man–interlocutor acts it faintly re-sembles, though, interestingly it is the black children who take up the inter-locutor position in this case, questioning Bodichon's deviation from conven-tional dress for a woman of her race and class. Sadly, Bodichon's assertions of the practicality of her getup don't make for much of a joke, and it is not as obvious as she implies why the children make friends, especially given the epithet she applies to them. But Bodichon does more than borrow the comic device Stowe had adapted from the minstrel show. Stowe's novel provides the model for Bodichon's understanding of these "jolly children, half naked," and a real child is transformed in the Englishwoman's account into a fictional character: "One was a real little Topsy who sang and danced, and then seized the youngest and screamed to me, 'I'll sell you this child for two dollars.' The poor little thing howled and cried and I gave Topsy a scolding for such a wicked joke."[94]

A naughty little girl becomes, for Bodichon, Stowe's creation, and the im-age in the novel absorbs the identity of the young slave. Disturbingly, of course, Bodichon's "Topsy" is herself mimicking slave society, satirizing the commodification of human life. Bodichon could have seen her as a Louisiana trickster with a vital point to make about slavery. Instead she reads her—and writes her—as *Uncle Tom*'s blackface slave girl. The fluidity of identification that Frances Hodgson Burnett had discovered in her Manchester nursery has gone. Whereas the English girl could slip in and out of a range of imaginative roles derived from Stowe's novel, the black child's role is determined by it.

Uncle Tom's Cabin harnessed the minstrel show's potential for ambiguity and developed it to an extraordinary extent. Minstrelsy relied on performative conventions to sidestep the contentious, and it used theatrical unreality to allay anxieties about race and slavery. *Uncle Tom* reorganized stage material precisely to mine those anxieties, exploring even under an innocuous and irreverent surface the desperate human circumstances that occasioned them. But the flexibility, the paradoxicality, and the multiplication of sympathies in the text, which partly lent it its power, also laid it open to endless reappropriation and helped impress its images on the likes of Bodichon's "Topsy." Blackface was valued for its ability to make whiteness merge into blackness. Bodichon's story suggests how Stowe's novel could, for some readers, allow blackness to disappear into blackface.

MINSTREL VARIATIONS: "UNCLE TOMS" IN THE MINSTREL SHOW

IT WOULD SEEM ALMOST
ABSURD TO SAY IT,
CONSIDERING THE USE
THAT HAS BEEN MADE OF
THEM, [BUT] WE HAVE
ALLIES IN THE ETHIOPIAN
SONGS; THOSE SONGS
THAT CONSTITUTE OUR
NATIONAL MUSIC, AND
WITHOUT WHICH WE HAVE
NO NATIONAL MUSIC.

Frederick Douglass,
"The Anti-Slavery Movement"

It has been argued that the increasing gentility of minstrelsy in the mid-1850s helped to dilute the music's antislavery content, because without the bourgeoisie for a target, minstrel songs staged racial difference rather than class.[1] Nevertheless, minstrelsy was neither a homogeneous form nor a static one. *Uncle Tom's Cabin* itself was deeply implicated in the shift in minstrel performance in the 1850s, and there was more variety in minstrel versions of the book than critics have recognized: the minstrel show *Uncle Tom*s sometimes even promoted antislavery arguments. Just as Stowe's novel harbored contradictory impulses, incorporating minstrelsy's opportunities to identify with black characters and also its tendency to demean them, so minstrelsy's responses to her text could be sympathetic both to slaves and to the institution of slavery. The ambivalence in Stowe's novel was amplified and exploited by minstrel troupes; blackface *Uncle Tom*s demonstrate that, like earlier forms, the minstrelsy of the 1850s could equivocate about slavery.

Minstrelsy's ideological flexibility on the slavery question is clear not only from the range of its *Uncle Tom*s but from the multiple uses it found for the music of the most successful composer of the period, Stephen Foster. Foster's songs were employed so consistently in *Uncle Tom*s that they could be called a central pillar of *Tom* mania, and in the end Stowe herself created a version of *Uncle Tom* in which Tom sang a Foster tune. Like *Uncle Tom's Cabin* itself, Foster's music was equally used for abolitionist and proslavery purposes.

Born in 1826, Stephen Foster composed nearly two hundred songs before his death in 1864; he became the first American to earn his living by writing music and accumulated a string of hits, many of which remain famous. His compositions include "Oh! Susanna," "Camptown Races," "Old Folks at Home," "Come Where My Love Lies Dreaming," and "Jeanie with the Light Brown Hair."[2] Raised in and near Pittsburgh in a well-connected but usually impoverished family, Foster began to earn pocket money at the age of nine by performing blackface music with other boys in an impromptu theater (*Doo-Dah!* 55). By the late 1840s he was producing comic songs, including "Oh! Susanna" (1847) and "Camptown Races" (1850), for minstrel troupes. His first blackface numbers included conventionally comic characters who sang in heavy "dialect" and were sometimes crass racial caricatures.[3] But in

1848 there were signs of a new sensibility at work in his "Old Uncle Ned," which expressed some fondness for the deceased slave: "He's dead long ago long ago."[4] However, it also borrowed from the grotesque tradition of black-face comedy in enumerating Ned's physical peculiarities:

> He had no wool on de top ob de head
> De place where de wool ought to grow.
>
> . . . .
>
> His fingers were long like de cane in de brake
> He had no eyes for to see
> He had no teeffe to eat de oae cake
> So he had to luf dat oae cake be.

Although the lyrics remark compassionately that there will be "no more hard work for poor old Ned," their description of his person is still closer to Kennard's mockery than to Stowe's antislavery "uncle": sentiment in this song does not entirely translate into sympathy.

However, Foster's later songs minimized these contradictions. In his most famous plantation melody, "Old Folks at Home" (copyrighted in October 1851), the compassion is directed toward the presumed speaker. The listener is asked to identify with the blackface singer:

> Way down upon the Swanee ribber,
>   Far, far away,
> Dere's wha my heart is turning ebber,
> Dere's wha de old folks stay.
> All up and down de whole creation,
>   Sadly I roam,
> Still longing for de old plantation
> And for de old folks at home.[5]

"Old Folks" generates fellow feeling for slaves by dwelling on ideas central to the middle-class culture of sentiment: domesticity and the family. Yet although his lyrics attempted to reconcile bourgeois ideals with the blackface version of the plantation, Foster's own relationship with minstrelsy was initially ambivalent. When he first began composing, Foster copyrighted his parlor music but not his minstrel songs, and though he had a long promotional arrangement with E. P. Christy, putting Christy's name on his blackface material, Foster never saw the Christy troupe perform (*Doo-Dah!* 177). When the dynamics of their relationship began to change and Foster's songs were becoming famous, he attempted to prize back the right to be acknowledged as their composer. His letter to Christy of 25 May 1852 signaled that the public perception of blackface was changing: "I had the intention of omitting my name on my Ethiopian songs, owing to the prejudice against them by some, which might injure my reputation as a writer of another style of music." But by this time Foster felt that it was no longer incompatible to be the author both of parlor ballads and of minstrel songs: "I have concluded to reinstate my name on my songs and to pursue the Ethiopian business without fear or shame." Not only was Foster conscious of a new respectability in the "Ethiopian business," he took the credit for it: "I find that by my efforts I have done a great deal to build up a taste for the Ethiopian songs among refined people by making the words suitable to their taste, instead of the trashy and really offensive words which belong to some songs of that order" (*Doo-Dah!* 183).

His biographers have concurred. Emerson argues that Foster's music "subsume[d] and synthesize[d]" both the parlor and blackface strains (*Doo-Dah!* 102).[6] In a peculiar endorsement of this argument L. V. H. Crosby's indisputably parlor ballad, "The Slave Mother," quotes from one of Foster's earlier blackface songs:

> She learns her little child to talk,
> She teaches it to pray;
> And sing "Susanna don't you cry,"
> And on the banjo play.[7]

Crosby's allusion to Foster indicates the way in which even his rowdier tunes could be assimilated by a genteel sensibility and also demonstrates the phenomenon we have seen earlier in the uses made of *Uncle Tom's Cabin* as well as of minstrelsy. In Mary Dutton's retrospective reading of slave behavior on the Kentucky plantation, in Barbara Bodichon's observations in Louisiana, and in James Kennard's joke about minstrelsy in the *Knickerbocker* blackface imagery could be used to overlay the reality of slavery. Just as *Uncle Tom's Cabin* helped Dutton to rewrite her holiday memories as blackface frolics and enabled Bodichon to turn slave children into Topsies, here the parlor ballad imagines slaves singing Foster's tunes. More than ever, the gentrification of blackface allowed its audiences to take its representations of slave life for the genuine article.

Foster's part in bringing blackface to the middle classes suggests one way in which his work echoed Stowe's in *Uncle Tom's Cabin*, as does the precise coincidence of the date of his letter to Christy with the early months of the novel's success. There were other connections too. Foster spent 1846 to 1850 in Cincinnati, where Stowe also lived between 1832 and 1851.[8] Commentators on both Stowe and Foster have surmised that Cincinnati could have provided experience both of black people and of racial issues that later contributed to their writing; as I have suggested, it also offered a chance for them to hear minstrel songs.

Foster, like Stowe, was conspicuously successful. "Old Folks at Home" earned him fifteen thousand dollars in sales, and his publishers advertised in September 1852 that it had sold nearly forty thousand copies.[9] The scale of this triumph echoes that of Stowe's novel and happened at almost exactly the same moment. These bestsellers would be joined by *Uncle Tom's Cabin* on the stage, which in George Aiken's version achieved long runs in the 1850s and then became the backbone of American touring theater for over fifty years. In many places these markets overlapped, as when the Aiken production played Foster's songs and as in the career of E. P. Christy, who claimed the authorship of Foster's work and also turned *Uncle Tom* into a minstrel sketch in 1854. Clearly, this was the age of the runaway hit, but Stowe's work, Foster's songs, and the *Tom* shows were locked together in a mutually sustaining explosion of celebrity.

Like *Uncle Tom's Cabin*, Foster's music also harbored ambiguities about slavery that enabled its users to make it mean a variety of things. While those who rewrote *Uncle Tom* were consciously re-creating it in their desired image, Foster's songs were necessarily open to interpretation with every performance. Abolitionists set new lyrics to Foster's tunes as they did to other minstrel music, though his were especially popular for such purposes. Both his earlier and later works were open to such treatment: there were versions of "Oh! Susannah," "Camptown Races," "Uncle Ned," "Old Folks at Home," "Massa's in the Cold, Cold Ground," and "My Old Kentucky Home" (*Doo-Dah!* 10).[10] His music was also incorporated wholesale into antislavery campaigns: the Hutchinson Family Singers adopted his "Nelly Bly" to show support for Lincoln. In the 1850s "Old Folks" was part of the repertoire of the black singer Elizabeth Greenfield (see chapter 6), while the Fisk Jubilee singers sang it after the Civil War (*Doo-Dah!* 59, 15).

Performance contexts helped determine how Foster's work was read so that his songs were glossed by their positioning in concerts, plays, and minstrel sketches. To some extent, of course, this process of adaptation was an inevitable part of the way stage music was transmitted in midcentury popular culture: since minstrels and abolitionists were already trading tunes, it was inevitable that Foster's would be caught up in their exchanges. But Foster's music also enabled this process.

The crucial quality in Foster's oeuvre was also the key to his reconciliation of blackface with middle-class audiences—his harnessing of what Charles Hamm calls "the most popular emotion of the day," nostalgia.[11] Nostalgia played a central part in the Foster family's own mythology, since his parents and older siblings hankered for years after their beloved "White Cottage," lost to them when the Bank of the United States foreclosed on the improvident William Foster in 1827 (*Doo-Dah!* 29). This personal loss meshed with a wider cultural concern perhaps fueled by the nineteenth-century American experiences of migration, urbanization, and industrialization. Foster could draw on the parlor tradition of "home" songs initiated by Thomas Moore, the most famous example of which, John Howard Payne's "Home Sweet Home," was performed in the United States in 1823.[12] When the implied singer of "Old Folks at Home" found himself "Still longing for de old plantation, / And for de old folks at home," Foster had transported the genre of the home song to an imaginary plantation, and he attributed that most contemporary of musical feelings to a slave.

But "Old Folks" is crucially ambiguous about what precisely this shared nostalgia is for. Is it (politically neutrally) for a place, time, and people; is it (an antislavery) longing for the family and home from which the singer has been cruelly parted; or is it a yearning for a return to the social relations of slavery itself? "Old Folks" was incorporated into *Tom* shows in such a way as to suggest all three. In different productions listeners were called upon to sympathize with a "black" character who variously missed home, mourned an involuntary removal, or made an idyll of slave life. The nostalgia of "Old Folks" readily became a political tool, but the song's politics were indeterminate in the song itself and mutable in its application. The feelings evoked by "Old Folks at Home" and especially by the device of the slave yearning for a lost world were made central to a host of versions of *Uncle Tom*, whose political differences determined the meaning of the song on any specific occasion. Foster's songs were taken up by the whole spectrum of the novel's revisionists, and they bolstered arguments ranging from the abolitionist to passionate apologias for slavery. According to proslavery texts, the most powerful emotion in midcentury America was evinced by ex-slaves missing the plantation, while in abolitionist ones it came from slaves yearning for the families slavery took from them. Emerson remarks on the frequency with which Foster uses the phrase "no more" and that it can signify both regret and exhortation, working equally to mark mourning and to express the hope that slavery will end (*Doo-Dah!* 198). It was on precisely this knife edge of nuance that the multiple uses of Foster's songs turned.

It is intriguing, given the persistent association of Foster's music with *Uncle Tom's Cabin* and that scores of *Uncle Tom*–related tunes were being published in the 1850s, that Foster abandoned his only attempt to write a song that referred to the book. He may have been unusual in picking Tom as his protagonist, though: according to *Dwight's Journal*, "all the minor composers were . . . busy on this theme," for "every music publisher . . . [must] have his 'Little Eva' song."[13]

As if to emphasize the utility of his nostalgic slave songs when thinking about Stowe's novel, Foster himself attempted to reproduce the spirit of "Old Folks" when he tried to write about *Uncle Tom*. The song that eventually became "My Old Kentucky Home" develops the situation implied in "Old Folks" and ties it to Stowe's fictional site for the first part of her novel. The song was begun while *Uncle Tom's Cabin* was still being serialized, and in Foster's early drafts the lyrics featured the chorus:

> Oh good night, good night, good night
> Poor Uncle Tom
> Grieve not for your old Kentucky home
> You'r bound for a better land
> Old Uncle Tom.[14]

The song would thus express Tom's longing for his family after he has been sold South and also hint at his religious martyrdom—in the novel the dying Tom comforts George Shelby, who is too late to save him: "The Lord's bought me, and is going to take me home,—and I long to go. Heaven is better than Kintuck!" (*UTC*, 362). It was replaced with

> Weep no more, my lady,
> Oh! weep no more today!
> We will sing one song
> For the old Kentucky Home,
> For the old Kentucky Home, far away. (*Doo-Dah!* 195)

Stowe's point combined both religiosity and an antislavery message; Foster's original lines hinted at the same mixture in their reference to a "better land," but the second version transfers the emotion to a "lady." Because the song uses standard English, not blackface dialect, in its final form, we may presume she is white. Foster had removed all traces of religion and the slavery question from his song along with *Uncle Tom's Cabin*, but despite all his best efforts, "My Old Kentucky Home," like his other songs, was soon associated with the book. The Philadelphia minstrel Sam Sanford incorporated it into his troupe's famous blackface sketch, "Uncle Tom's Cabin! or Life in Old Kentuck."[15]

Given their usual quickness to interpret, parody, or otherwise exploit the modish or popular elements of contemporary culture, it was entirely characteristic of minstrel troupes to take up *Uncle Tom's Cabin*. Minstrelsy quickly cannibalized Stowe's novel, and intertextual borrowing executed a full circle as the novel's references to blackface traditions led to reworkings of *Uncle Tom* by the minstrels themselves. Some of the book's characterization had been borrowed from blackface, blackface in turn incurred debts to *Uncle Tom*, and minstrelsy not only played into *Uncle Tom's Cabin* but out of it too. Minstrel shows staged their own *Uncle Toms*—of varying fidelity to the original but often self-consciously offering to answer it.

For some performers the book supplied a staple object of burlesque throughout the 1850s, and, in the end, minstrels adapted and parodied *Uncle Tom's Cabin* so often that it became a minstrel fixture, making appearances in manuals for the amateur minstrel. Thus, even people who did not go to minstrel shows might have created their own blackface *Uncle Tom* in home entertainments. In *G. W. Moore's Ethiopian Anecdotes and Goakes* the novel was cited as a model for "a representation of the sayings and doings of the negro" at which the blackface performer should aim: "[T]hose of my readers who have perused the far-famed *Uncle Tom*, will understand that the dialect of the negro must be retained."[16] Another handbook for the home entertainer produced in 1899 included *Uncle Tom's Cabin* in a list of suggested sketches for the amateur blackface company to perform.[17] This sketch makes literal the end man role I have suggested Topsy takes in the novel: she is duplicated in the image, seated at both ends of the semicircle, playing the tambourine on one side and the bones on the other, being both Tambo and Bones.

Not only does Stowe's story form a characteristic set piece, but the handbook also seems to suggest that her central character had himself become indispensable to the blackface stage. The detailed instructions on "HOW TO BLACK UP" show two possible variations: a young black figure in burnt cork or an old character with bald head and snowy beard. For the latter the instructor describes how to blacken the face, add a "bald" wig, and put on a pair of brass spectacles, and voilà: "[Y]ou've got an old 'Uncle Tom.'"[18] Not only

had Uncle Tom become a minstrel type, but the jokes themselves linked
Stowe's character, stage history, and the minstrel show. Referring to a dance
largely made popular by minstrelsy in the 1890s, the exchange went:

> END: . . . Do you remember when cake-walks were done for the first time on
> the stage?
>
> MIDDLE: No, I do not. Do you know?
>
> END: Yes; cake-walks were done for the first time on the stage in "Uncle
> Tom's Cabin," when Eliza crossed the river on the *ice—cakes of ice.*[19]

Minstrels put Stowe's novel to an astonishing range of uses. References ranged
from lame puns on the title and allusions to it in stump speeches to *Uncle Tom*
songs, sketches, burlesques, tableaux vivants, and full-scale musical adaptations. In some cases Stowe's novel merits just a fleeting mention. For instance,
in a book of stump speeches it is among the middle-class cultural texts that
the blackface speaker muddles up: "De text for dis evening's discourse am
taken from de ninety-fust volume of Shakespeare's comic song-book called
Uncle Tom's Cabin." The reference to Shakespeare and multivolume tomes
signals the class and cultural niche *Uncle Tom* was being assigned, as does the
question "Has any ob you ladies or gemmon got de book wid you?"[20]

Yet while some shows joked about genteel culture, others courted it—a special price for children was offered at Sanford's Opera House to see Frank
Brower dance his "Happy Uncle Tom" and also at Christy and Wood's Hall,
where "Front Seats [were] invariably reserved for ladies."[21] In songs like
"Poor Uncle Tom," which Wood's Minstrels sang at Minstrel Hall in New York,
blackface *Uncle Tom*s encompassed the sentimental style appropriate to such
performances.[22]

In politics, too, there was enormous diversity. Discussion of the minstrel
*Uncle Tom*s has usually described an absence of politics or has assumed a
proslavery stance, but they varied widely on this point.[23] Some references eschew the slavery question, some achieve a perfectly judged ambivalence, some
seem sympathetic to slaves, and others preach specific positions, from colonization to the proslavery argument. During the Civil War Harry Pell attacked
secession in his *Uncle Tom* "discourse," instructing "Jeff Davis . . . you should
never let / yourself on treason sup" and exhorting General Grant to catch "ole
King Cotton by de slack part ob his trouserloons, an' shakes de debil out ob
him!"[24] In their *Uncle Tom* references, minstrel troupes demonstrated both
blackface's capacity to avoid politics and its occasional willingness to embrace

it, and where they took a position on slavery it was neither uniform nor predictable.

The minstrel show *Uncle Toms* have been dismissed as "emasculating the story."[25] A number of acts indicated some relation with Stowe's work in their titles (Harry Birdoff recorded "Uncle Dad's Cabin," "Old Dad's Cabin," "Aunt Dinah's Cabin," and "My Aunt's Cabin"), yet many recalled *Uncle Tom's Cabin* in little more than name.[26] No connection with Stowe is apparent in "Uncle Tom: An Ethiopian Interlude in One Scene," in which Uncle Tom wears a gray wig and patched clothes and gulls his brightly dressed companion Pete into buying a turtle. The (somewhat crude) comedy consists of Tom's malapropisms ("snackin' Turple") and the turtle's biting Pete on the behind.[27] Even Frank Brower's "Happy Uncle Tom: A Celebrated Plantation Scene," although it was sometimes incorporated into more political and pointedly anti-Stowe productions such as Sanford's, was, in itself, neither. In it Tom played the end man to a banjo player called Jeff. Jeff was circumlocutory, and Tom was slow to understand:

> JEFF: Nothin' but steel and brass.
> TOM: You steel'd de brass?[28]

C. H. White's twenty-five-minute sketch, "Old Dad's Cabin," featured a cast of characters with no equivalents in the novel (Mrs. Arabella Brown, Old Dad Brown, Lucy Brown, and a peddler), and its business consisted of the peddler's repeated attempts to sneak into the kitchen and court Lucy.[29] One version of "Aunt Dinah's Cabin" similarly involved Uncle Breve, Rattle, Cliff, Aunty Dinah, and Leader of Orchestra, none of whom suggest affinities with *Uncle Tom*.[30]

These sketches, which reneged on their titles' promise to comment on Stowe's novel, nevertheless helped associate it with minstrel subjects, making the cabins of old uncles and aunts familiar blackface paraphernalia. Tom himself, never a comic character in the novel, was incorporated into the end man–interlocutor duet, which stripped him of the dignity and pathos with which Stowe had endowed him. By making Tom an end man, the sketches made him dull-witted, self-interested, and perhaps a little criminal, almost the opposite of Stowe's model Christian. These characters could never be martyrs to the cruelty of slavery; rather, their joking and banjo playing suggested that nothing was amiss. By not commenting on slavery in such "celebrated plantation scene[s]" they implied that it was unremarkable.

Thus, of course, even those sketches that ignored the slavery question were political. Stowe's novel was associated with a contentious stance on slavery, and it is telling that some shows tried to exploit the novel's audience without detonating the novel's political charge. Leaving out the controversy could be an important (and, of course, itself politically motivated) way of rewriting *Uncle Tom's Cabin*.

The minstrel show *Tom*s to which critics have paid most attention are the proslavery versions. Many were used for the third part of the minstrel show, which traditionally purported to represent a faithful picture of slave life in the South but increasingly consisted of a burlesque of something currently playing in the theater or the opera.[31] *Uncle Tom*, of course, could be fitted into both categories. These shows demonstrate the same indignant opposition to the antislavery elements of Stowe's book as the novels I discuss in chapter 4; as I show, they shared an interest in fugitive slaves. Indeed, in the indiscriminately voracious manner of all minstrelsy, some sketches may have been constructed with reference to proslavery novels as well as to Stowe's original.

The proslavery *Tom*s created counterplots that reversed all Stowe's politically significant events and conscripted music and spectacle to demonstrate that slavery was a blessing. Similarities between sketches suggest that minstrel managers looked to each other as well as to Stowe's novel itself for ideas, and both scripts and performers moved readily between minstrel shows. Sam Sanford, who sometimes played Uncle Tom with his own troupe, also played him, in his own adaptation, with Sam Sharpley's Opera House in Philadelphia.[32]

Nelson Kneass's "operatic burletta" for the Christy and Wood's Hall formed the "Southern" part of a show whose first part professed to represent "The Dandy Negroes of the North." As with most shows, the second part consisted of variety acts, while his "Uncle Tom's Cabin: or, Hearts and Homes" concluded the evening. Toll argues that it "differed from the standard plantation closing act only in name," and certainly its three "tableaux" featured numerous song-and-dance numbers and very little plot.[33] However, a conscious response to the novel may be discerned in Kneass's insistence that slaves are happy and in the burletta's pointed reversal of the threats and tragedies Stowe's characters undergo, which add up to a detailed refutation of *Uncle Tom*'s portrait of slavery. The outline may look inconsequential, a mere vehicle for a medley of songs, dances, and imitations, but the paucity of events is itself part of the message.

In the first tableau Tom returns from a camp meeting and tells Chloe of the free blacks he has met there "and his preference for Old Kentuck." Thus, the opening constitutes a clear endorsement of slavery. Then follows a string of musical interludes: Topsy sings and dances, Tom and Chloe perform a duet, and there is a chorus. The second tableau is apparently even more direction-less: George serenades Liza, they sing a duet with bird imitations, a chorus is sung to Eva, Topsy is involved in a duet, and Tom and Chloe are "amazed and overcome by the power of music." In the third there are six songs, celebra-tions for the Fourth of July and a wedding, and a "characteristic dance." Cru-cially, however, if this sequence is read against Stowe's novel, the apparently disconnected pieces invert many of the events in the book. Tom is not sold at the opening but returned to his wife; George and Eliza are not parted but mar-ried; and both Tom and Eva live. Every one of Stowe's tragedies is averted, and, most reassuringly, at the end "hearts and homes are as should be found everywhere."[34]

This New York *Uncle Tom* shared several characteristics with Sam San-ford's Philadelphia show, *Happy Uncle Tom; or, Life among the Happy*, which Sanford himself had written and in which he took the lead part. It played first in 1853, but there were also revivals in 1855 and 1859, and the script was fran-chised by other troupes.[35] However, Sanford's was a more aggressive rewrit-ing of Stowe: slavery was benevolent, and free Northern black people were miserable. Moreover, it specifically attacked abolitionists, and its closing song reversed Stowe's attack on the Fugitive Slave Acts. As with the New York adaptation, *Life among the Happy* was also designed to be entertaining, in-corporating comic turns, songs, dances, and camp-meeting chants, but most of them were directly tied to its defense of slavery.[36]

In the opening scene Sanford's Aunt Chloe tells "A Tale about the Aboli-tionists" and declares that she disliked her glimpse of free Cincinnati: "I'd radder by on de Old Plantation," echoing Tom's contempt for free black life in Christy and Wood's sketch, "Uncle Tom's Cabin: or, Hearts and Homes." As in that piece, Tom's first appearance is also a return from a "Camp Meet-ing"—in this case it is accompanied by "happy time and plenty money." In the second scene George Harris, who in the novel has an extraordinarily selfish master, here defends slave owners in the song "White Folks dat don't own Nig-gers very good to talk." The other slaves reinforce this complacency: "Massa is no stingy man." The closing song spells out the drama's differences from the novel—"Oh! White Folks, we'll have you know / Dis am not de version of Mrs Stowe"—but disingenuously implies that the difference is a matter of fortune rather than politics: "Wid her de Darks am all unlucky, / But we am de boys of Old Kentucky." However, the final lines lay bare the connection between representing slave life as comfortable, even fun, and reinforcing the status quo when they return to the anxieties expressed in the opening—that "Abolitionists" are trying to tempt slaves to flee with exaggerated promises of the benefits of freedom:

> Den hand de Banjo down to play,
> We'll make it ring both night and day;
> And we care not what de white folks say,
> Dey can't get us to run away.[37]

There are several more similarities with Christy and Wood's play: they share a character not derived from Stowe (Lame Jake, who in Christy and Wood's synopsis courts Topsy), and in both George and Eliza are married by jumping over a broomstick.[38]

Sanford's publicity material links the production's proslavery stance to his troupe's patronage by Southerners, announcing a revival of "Uncle Tom's Cabin . . . [a]t the many requests of our Southern friends." Sanford claimed that "the students of the University [presumably of Pennsylvania] presented him with a valuable service of silver for thus defending their institutions and showing the slaves in their proper light, and not the abuses written by Mrs. Beecher Stowe."[39]

Sanford's claims about his play's ability to promote sectional harmony must have been tested when he presented *Happy Uncle Tom* at the New Orleans Academy of Music in November 1863, during the city's occupation by Federal troops.[40] Joseph Roppolo disregards the Philadelphia troupe's production in his accounts of New Orleans *Uncle Tom*s because of the circumstances, yet in a sense this fraught context represented precisely the political challenge for which Sanford had tailored it. *Happy Uncle Tom* was not only as sensitive to Southern prejudices as a New Orleans audience could have hoped but was specifically designed to please audiences that were already divided, tense, and defensive at its first performance in 1853. Sanford's shows also offered special pleasures for those Northern audiences for whom Southern sounds were a curiosity, as his self-promotion indicates: "Sanford is recognized as the Greatest Dialect Performer in the Negro business, his representation of the various Slave States and their peculiarities has been without a parallel."[41]

The antifugitive theme hinted at in Sanford's "Dey can't get us to run away" was the most widely used defense of slavery in the minstrel *Uncle Tom*s.

The trope of the disappointed fugitive was given the most elaborate treatment in the Bowery Theatre's 1860 production, the plot of which differed significantly from Sanford's and from Christy and Wood's, but like them it linked abolitionists and fugitive slaves in its "Southern Drama of the Old Plantation." The Bowery's boasted fewer songs than the other two adaptations but an abundance of incident. First, a fugitive who has gone North "to pick up gold in the street" returns, "satisfied that he has been deceived by an Abolitionist." He "resolves to stay at home." Just to confirm the sectional implications raised so far, "Scorem, a foreigner to the South, and a cruel slaveholder, [is] reprimanded for his inhumanity, by a real Southerner." Then a "Splendid view of a plantation," with singing and dancing, is disrupted by an alarm: "'Whar's Daisy? Whar's Daisy?' Stolen, carried off by an Abolitionist."[42]

This event is, of course, a good excuse to contrast the lot of free blacks in the North with life on the plantation. Uncle Tom, dispatched to rescue Daisy, is "disgusted with the climate." He encounters those blackface political bogeys, a black dandy and a (black) "female . . . bloomer," intended to signify an abhorrent Northern liberalism in matters of race and gender that has allowed both women and black men to become uppity. The Bowery's Uncle Tom, evidently a natural conservative, "thinks the menagerie is broke loose." The plot then produces a sequence of sensations: Daisy is eventually found; the abolitionist "shows the cloven foot"; Uncle Tom rescues Daisy; Daisy's clothes are stolen by the female bloomer (presumably signaling that feminine clothing is hard to resist, even for a feminist); Uncle Tom sees black people freezing to death in unsanitary conditions; Daisy is saved again. In the final act they return home, and there is a "Happy reunion." The social, political, and climatic inferiority of the free states is underlined by the demonstration of "Uncle Tom's delight in getting back to de Bressed Old Souf."[43]

All this idealization of the South was not confined to Northern minstrel troupes: George Kunkel's Baltimore company, the Nightingale Serenaders, also attempted one. According to Birdoff, Kunkel read Stowe's novel while on tour in Wilmington, North Carolina, and created a forty-five-minute play, which he first played in Charleston at the end of his regular show. This astonished his audience, which was expecting the conventionally much shorter and more musical burletta in that slot.[44] But Kunkel's production is unlikely to have offended Southern patriots. His "Aunt Harriet Becha Stowe," one of the most famous minstrel anti-*Tom* songs, reproduced the connections made in the Sanford and Bowery plays between abolitionists, misinformed fugitives, and free blacks suffering in the North:

> Dey treated dis here child, as doe I was a Turk,
>
> Den tole me for to leave dem and go away to work;
>
> And den I wish dis Fugitive was back to ole Virginny.

Just to spell out the implications of this, the song advocates submitting willingly to bondage:

> Oh! when I was a picanin, Old Uncle Tom would say,
>
> Be true unto your Massa, and neber run away,
>
> He tole me dis at home, he tole me dis at partin'
>
> Ned, don't you trust de white folks,
>
> For dey am quite unsartin.[45]

Here Tom, as in the Bowery and Christy and Wood's dramatizations, is made the mouthpiece of the slavery side. Unlikely as it may seem, the minstrel reading of *Uncle Tom's Cabin* is thus a precursor of twentieth-century critics of the novel who have argued that Tom is compliant, even collusive, with the slave-owning regime, that he is, in the slang term that epitomizes the idea, an "Uncle Tom."[46]

In the novel Tom does not counsel against flight but calls it Eliza's "right," and he only chooses to submit to his own painful fate in order to save the other slaves on the plantation: "'No, no—I an't going. Let Eliza go—it's her right! I wouldn't be the one to say no—'tan't in *natur* for her to stay; but you heard what she said! If I must be sold, or all the people on the place, and everything go to rack, why, let me be sold. I s'pose I can b'ar it as well as any on 'em'" (*UTC*, 34). Stowe makes the extent of his sacrifice clear: as he speaks, "something like a sob and sigh shook his broad, rough chest convulsively" (*UTC*, 34). Tom's refusal to flee, in other words, is one of his most heroic moments, a denial of his own interests for the sake of his fellow slaves. The proslavery minstrel shows willfully misinterpret this, making Tom the avatar of slave loyalty, the advocate of bondage, and the disparager of freedom. But as Kunkel's song shows, if Stowe's character was a traitor to his race, it was blackface minstrelsy that made him one.

Kunkel's was one of many proslavery musical numbers. The New Orleans Serenaders sang an "Uncle Tom's Cabin Song" that alternately preached against slaves running away and warbled nostalgia for the slave quarters, where "[w]e played the banjo, sung and tripp'd it lightly": "Oh! how I love my own dear cabin Home."[47] The protagonist of Dan Rice's "Uncle Tom's Cabin" sang about "strange adventures among the Nordern States," where he is impoverished—"cold and starvin' from de elbow to de knee"—and deceived by abolitionists—"Dey tried to make me b'lieb 'em, and said dey lub'd me well"—who promise equality but actually exploit him: "Dey called me brudder Thomas, an' said you're quite secure, / An' locked me up to prove it, till I broke down de door."[48] Several songs attacked not the novel but its author. One attributed to Dan Emmett and called, among other names, "Jordan Is a Hard Road to Trabel" and "The Other Side of Jordan" was played repeatedly in minstrel shows. The many versions of this song concern themselves with America's international relations, referring disparagingly to Irishmen, Cubans, Lajos Kossuth, and Louis Napoleon and bragging that "the Americans will show them what they will do, / on this and the other side of Jordan."[49] Stowe's role in the assertion of the "Yankee" patriotism promoted by the songs was that of traitor, since she was held to have told tales on her country about the mistreatment of slaves. One lyric suggested she should turn her attention to the British poor instead:

> Poor Mrs. Beacher Stow, she thinks herself so brave,
> So she left her own country accordin',
> She went on to England for to see dere White Slaves,
> For to write about on t'odder side o' Jordan.[50]

Similar allegations were made in blackface lyrics to the English dance tune "Pop Goes the Weasel."[51]

Not all minstrel versions of *Uncle Tom* were as militantly proslavery and pro-Southern as Kunkel's and the Bowery's. For a start, the antislavery lobby itself produced and circulated some *Uncle Tom*–related blackface material. Two songs could have come straight out of the minstrel tradition. "The Ghost of Uncle Tom," composed by Martha Hill and sung by the Hutchinson Family Singers, featured blackface dialect and (perhaps unintentionally) ludicrous lyrics:

> Knock! Knock! Knock! When de hour ob midnight come—
> Oh who is dat a knocking?
> Tis the Ghost of "Uncle Tom."

The song borrowed the railroad-emancipation connection of Jesse Hutchinson's "Get off the Track," but it infantilized the supposed black singer and freely used the term "nigger" in the manner of comic blackface songs. In the fourth verse, for instance, the character sings:

> Oh! dere is a railroad "un-der-ground,"
> On which de nigger slopes,
> And when he's got his ticket,
> Den his bosom's full of hope.[52]

Not only did the Hutchinsons sing this stuff, they produced their own. Asa Hutchinson composed (and dedicated to his mother) "Little Topsy's Song," whose words, by Eliza Cook, also employed dialect, offensive racial epithets, and an astonishingly patronizing premise. In it, Topsy progresses from wicked child to Eva's convert, as the choruses indicate, moving from the ironic:

> This is Topsy's savage song
> Topsy's cute and clever,
> Hurrah then for the white man's right
> Sla-ver-y for-ever!

to the celebratory:

> This is Topsy's human song
> Under Love's endeavor,
> Hurrah then for the white child's work
> Hu-man-i-ty for-ever![53]

In its attribution of Topsy's redemption solely to "the white child's work," the song does not seem to demonstrate much progress beyond the white supremacy it lampoons. Both songs illustrate how the racial attitudes we associate with blackface translated as easily into other political contexts as its form did to other performance traditions.

More unexpectedly, minstrel troupes themselves created antislavery *Uncle Tom's Cabins*. Ordway's Aeolians, who offered "Varieties" at their hall in Boston, produced an *Uncle Tom* in ten tableaux "in strict Accordance with the Book."[54] Ordway's attractions were more genteel than other versions: its playbill stressed "beautiful scenery and new music," including Chromatrope views, which involved two brightly colored magic-lantern projections that could be slid over each other for dramatic effect.[55] The tableaux played on Wednesday and Saturday afternoons, which would also appeal to ladies and family audiences. The production's political allegiances were clearly signaled at the top of the playbill with a pointed quotation from Stowe's novel: "Men do not know what Slavery is and from this arose my desire to exhibit it in a living Dramatic reality."[56] This line not only neatly justified making Stowe's tale into a literal drama but also hinted at a controversial argument—a far cry from the sketches that divested the name "Uncle Tom" of any political significance.

The production must have been fairly long (it covered most of the central details of the novel's plot), and the scenes it selected highlighted the suffering of the sold and mistreated slaves. In so doing it necessarily staked out a position critical of slavery. It began with Tom's writing lesson in his cabin, into which Eliza duly burst and informed him that he had been sold, along with her child. The second scene featured Sam and Andy describing her escape to the other slaves; the third George Harris's appearance at the inn during *his* escape; the fourth St. Clare purchasing Tom; the fifth St. Clare's household, with much detail about individual slaves; the sixth introduced Topsy; the seventh contained the sale of all the slaves; the eighth described the arrival at Legree's plantation; the ninth Tom's punishment for refusing to flog other slaves and his death; the tenth George Shelby's account of all this back at the Kentucky plantation. Not only was this "in strict accordance with the book," but it made a host of enslaved black characters the objects of sympathy.

In fact, it laid out a very precise political program, arguably a clearer one even than Stowe's, although it contained one significant difference. In the novel George Harris takes his family to Africa, which could be taken as an endorsement of the American Colonization Society's scheme to send freed slaves to Liberia (*UTC*, 376). However, in a passage that is often overlooked, Stowe refutes this interpretation in her concluding remarks, stating that "to fill up Liberia with an ignorant, inexperienced, half-barbarized race, just escaped from the chains of slavery, would be only to prolong, for ages, the period of struggle and conflict which attends the inception of new enterprises." She urges the church of the North to "receive these poor sufferers in the spirit of Christ" (*UTC*, 386). She offers another option in the shape of George Shelby, who frees his surviving slaves, though one declares, "We don't want to be no freer than we are." They will remain on his farm but be paid wages (*UTC*, 379).

The Ordway *Uncle Tom* moved away from Stowe on this issue and joined forces with the Colonizationists. In Ordway's version, when George Shelby liberates his slaves, he "tells them of 'Liberia,' a free Republic on the shores of Africa." To the sound of a "Hymn to Freedom," the scene closes "with a picture of Liberia, a free African tribe visiting the city, which dissolves into a Chromotrope, view of FREEDOM TO AFRICA."[57] Thus, the finale, with spectacular special effects, linked emancipation with a "return" of the black population to a (literally) hazy projection of an African city. The clear implication was that Ordway's Aeolians' solution to the miseries of slavery was to send America's black population away and to fulfill the Colonizationists' dream of Liberia.

Ordway's Aeolians were not the only minstrels to put on an antislavery *Uncle Tom*, although their Colonizationist position seems to have been unusual. The Moore and Burgess Minstrels, originally a British troupe, transformed Stowe's tale into musical tableaux vivants that were straightforwardly abolitionist and probably produced after the Civil War. The dust jacket of *G. W. Moore's Ethiopian Anecdotes and Goakes* shows Moore positioned between a Stars and Stripes and a Union Jack; the final tableau in the Moore and Burgess production attempted a similar minstrel linking of the two nations in its allegorical "Thanksgiving Hymn of the Freed Slaves to Britannia and Columbia."[58]

As in the Ordway version, the Moore and Burgess Legree kills Tom, and Eliza flees across the frozen river; but there were also similarities to the proslavery versions: there is a camp meeting, "which Tom has often attended," and in the opening scene "the happy darkies sing," although here this is not a sign of slavery's beneficence, because they are "unconscious of the cruel fate which awaits them." More was also made of scenes that did not have a direct bearing on the slavery question: there was a tableau devoted to Tom and Eva, one to Topsy's mischief, and one to Eva's death, which involved an "invisible chorus of angels."[59]

Even troupes that performed proslavery sketches of *Uncle Tom's Cabin* may at times also have used material of a different character. Sam Sanford's troupe played Foster's "My Old Kentucky Home," while the Bowery production ended its second act with "Old Folks at Home."[60] In their hands, of course, slaves were longing for plantation life; they were not reduced to misery because of it. Yet both Christy's Minstrels and Wood's Minstrels separately published sheet music for sentimental Uncle Tom songs that acknowledged his tragic end. Whereas the Tom in the sketches thrived, the one in the songs expired. One of Christy's songs included a version of Kunkel's attack on "Aunt Harriet Becha Stow."[61] Another songbook incorporated these lyrics:

> Uncle Tom's gone to rest, let us pray for his soul,
> He will answer no more to the call of the roll.
>
> .   .   .   .
>
> His children are weeping, Aunt Chloe's heart's sore,
> Can but pray that he's gone where his troubles are o'er.[62]

Similarly, in the sorrowful three verses and chorus published by Wood's Minstrels, Tom is sold, rescues Eva, and dies, while "those who knew him best, / Mourn for the slave."[63]

The contradictory politics of minstrel show *Uncle Tom's Cabin*s may have elicited surprising responses from their audiences. Frederick Douglass attacked minstrelsy in 1848, calling its practitioners "the filthy scum of white society, who have stolen from us a complexion denied to them by nature, in which to make money, and pander to the corrupt taste of their white fellow citizens," but in 1849 he hoped that a black troupe might "yet be instrumental in removing the prejudice against our race," and he later argued in a lecture to the Rochester Ladies' Anti-slavery Society that "we have allies in the Ethiopian songs."[64] Naming three slave laments, two of them Foster's, he pointed out that "Lucy Neale," "Old Kentucky Home," and "Uncle Ned" "can make the heart sad as well as merry, and can call forth a tear as well as a smile. They awaken the sympathies for the slave, in which Anti-Slavery principles take root, grow up, and flourish." Interestingly, he made a similar argument on that occasion about Stowe's novel, which "could light a million camp fires in front of the imbattled hosts of Slavery."[65]

Douglass's cautious approval of the sentimental strain of minstrelsy casts light on a curious phenomenon. There is some evidence that there were black spectators at minstrel *Uncle Tom*s. The Bowery Theatre advertised seats in its "Colored Person's gallery" on playbills for its minstrel *Tom* show. This sign that it hoped to attract black audiences—to segregated seating—uses language considerably more polite than that of its plot synopses, which refer to "nigger" characters.[66] Nevertheless, the Bowery may have had black patrons at the show. In Charleston black attendance at the Nightingale Serenaders' dramatization was even significant enough to cause a controversy. The city council forbade blacks from entering the hall; the council's policy was publicly condemned by Parson William Gannaway Brownlow, the proslavery minister and newspaper editor who later sided with the Union and in 1865 became governor of Tennessee.[67] Meanwhile, black spectators were smuggled in for exorbitant sums between five and ten dollars. (The Bowery's "Colored Person's gallery," by contrast, cost twelve cents.)[68]

One can only speculate about why black audiences in Charleston were so eager to see a proslavery *Uncle Tom's Cabin*. Perhaps, like the thousands who read the novel and attended the play elsewhere, they were just curious to see this popular phenomenon. Yet it is suggestive that the city council placed it out of bounds to them. Could the *idea* of Stowe's creation have retained its emancipatory connotations, both for the city council and for the black audience, despite Kunkel's best efforts to spin it another way? Could these observers have identified with blackface subversion or even with the unfortunate runaways by reading the plays against their plots? Just as we must acknowledge the determination with which proslavery minstrel troupes rewrote Stowe's work to suit their purposes, so we should perhaps imagine their audiences reading the shows, equally deliberately, to suit theirs. While Sanford's and Kunkel's characters sang the praises of the "Old Plantation," some observers may have been able to conjure entirely another sort of dream out of this travesty of Stowe's tale. Perhaps Kunkel's *Uncle Tom*, despite itself, fostered some hopes of freedom.

COPYCAT CRITICS: THE ANTI-"TOM" NOVEL AND THE FUGITIVE SLAVE

"YOU HAVE A VERY
ATTENTIVE BOY, SIR,
BUT YOU HAD BETTER
WATCH HIM LIKE A
HAWK WHEN YOU GET
ON TO THE NORTH."

William and Ellen Craft, *Running
a Thousand Miles for Freedom*

While the politics of minstrel adaptations of *Uncle Tom's Cabin* were unpredictable, another genre unambiguously rewrote Stowe's book as propaganda. Proslavery novels attacked *Uncle Tom's Cabin* but borrowed its form and some of its techniques: they were anti-*Tom* books and also paradoxically themselves an aspect of *Tom* mania.

In 1852 both Northern and Southern periodicals called for writers to answer Stowe in novel form: George Frederick Holmes argued in the *Southern Literary Messenger* for "a native and domestic literature" to provide the most telling response to *Uncle Tom*, while the *Pennsylvanian* asked "friends of the Union" to "array fiction against fiction."[1] These calls were answered by a rash of novels loudly championing slavery and self-consciously produced in the wake of *Uncle Tom's Cabin*. Between them Francis Pendleton Gaines, Jane Gardiner, and Thomas Gossett list thirty-four texts that made some claim to be replies to *Uncle Tom's Cabin*.[2] Not all the authors were from the South— Gossett attributes eight novels to Northerners and several more to writers with Northern origins.[3] Caroline Lee Hentz even belonged to the same literary society in Cincinnati, the Semi-Colon Club, as Stowe in the 1830s.[4] And the books' politics were far from identical. The *Dover Morning Star* jokingly asked of *Aunt Phillis's Cabin*, "Was it written by a friend or foe of slavery?"; individually, the anti-*Tom* novels covered many shades in between.[5] *Mr. Frank: The Underground Mail-Agent* offered an ostentatiously moderate viewpoint that was not proslavery, not Colonizationist, nor yet in favor of immediate emancipation.[6] *The Master's House* painted the slave owners as benevolent but also depicted cruelty to slaves, which it put down to overseers and poor whites.[7] Two novels by "Northerners" (Sarah Josepha Hale's *Liberia* and the Reverend Bayard R. Hall's *Frank Freeman's Barber's Shop*, which positioned itself between Northern and Southern "hotheads") expressed some unease about slavery but promoted colonization rather than outright abolition.[8]

Intentionally or otherwise, these anti-*Tom* novels were commercially parasitic on Stowe's book, much in the fashion of the minstrel sketches that capitalized on its fame. But many of the novels also mount a fierce and focused ideological challenge to Stowe. Antislavery politics is their explicit target, and like minstrel shows they are much exercised by the question of fugitive slaves. Stowe's attack on the 1850 Fugitive Slave Act in *Uncle Tom's Cabin* was a central but not the sole impetus for this concern, for the books demonstrate how significant the question of fugitives had become to the national debate about slavery. In dramatizing their plight Stowe had politicized the Southern plantation novel, but by running away the fugitives were themselves supplying evidence of the insupportability of the slave condition. They created texts too: certain exceptional individuals published autobiographies—slave narratives— that eloquently demolished arguments about the naturalness of slavery and the happiness of slaves.[9] The anti-*Tom* novels return obsessively to the subject of runaways, and in the frequency of their references they point to the impact fugitive slaves were themselves making upon the argument. The novels attempt to blame white agitators for black discontent, or they turn to blackface for images of carefree and contented slaves. They attempt to drown real fugitives' voices in the blackface "dialect" of minstrelized slave characters. Ironically, the anti-*Tom* novels adopted a Northern mythology about the South, minstrelsy, despite their constant claims that Northerners misrepresented the slave states.

Mrs. G. M. Flanders's *The Ebony Idol* neatly illustrates the function of blackface in the anti-*Tom* novels. Children in Flanders's novel take to blackface to satirize reformers like the "sentimental demi-intellectual" spinster who holds a reception for a fugitive slave: "Little boys forming all sorts of processions, paraded up and down the street, singing negro melodies, and shouting forth defiant and abusive phrases. . . . [W]ith blackened faces they trudged through the streets, bearing a banner with the rebellious motto, 'Niggers is riz!' "[10] Flanders's scene closely resembles the rituals of "rough noise" or "raising Cain" that fed into early examples of blackface performance. It mirrors historical examples of blackface in racial politics, as in 1834, when antiabolitionist rioters in Philadelphia blacked their faces and donned tatty Jim Crow coats and a New York mob attempted minstrel-style mock oratory in the Chatham Street Chapel.[11] In the same way, blackface parodies in these novels are made to be the antithesis of sympathy with black people: they assert and are supposed to illustrate the ridiculousness of liberatory politics. Displacing black speakers and subjects, they substitute instead the "negro melodies" and "blackened faces" that stand for them. Speaking for or instead of ex-slaves in abolition meetings, they proclaim absurd the idea that black people could "rise."

Many texts signaled a relationship with *Uncle Tom's Cabin* in their titles. The most obvious include the nod in *The Lofty and the Lowly* to Stowe's subtitle *Life among the Lowly* and the cabins in *Aunt Phillis's Cabin* and *Uncle*

Robin's Cabin in Virginia and Tom Without One in Boston. Others attacked *Uncle Tom* in a preface or commented explicitly on it within the text.[12] Two characters in *Buckingham Hall*, for instance, discuss the book for several pages, while the narrator in *Aunt Phillis's Cabin* devotes a lengthy set of "Concluding Remarks" to the subject.[13] Other books like *Ellen, Louise Elton*, and *Mr. Frank* do not directly invoke Stowe, but they make slavery a central issue, and since the natural comparison for such fiction in the 1850s was with *Uncle Tom's Cabin*, it is not extravagant to read them among the novels conceived as "replies" to it.[14] That by 1857 such adversarial positioning against other texts was commonplace in fiction about slavery is suggested by James M. Smythe's joke that his book was "intended as an answer to . . . noone in particular."[15]

However, we should be careful about reading all these as a single coherent genre, not least because the extent to which they actually engaged with Stowe's text varied dramatically, and for some authors, associating themselves with Stowe's book was merely a cynical appeal to the market. For instance, the subtitle of Calvin Henderson Wiley's *Life at the South: A Companion to Uncle Tom's Cabin* represented a calculated deception, since it contained no reference to Stowe and very little to slavery. In fact, the book had first appeared—as *The Adventures of Old Dan Tucker*—two years before Stowe's.[16]

Even when novels were seriously concerned with *Uncle Tom's Cabin*, commercial considerations sometimes worked to obscure the nature of their relationship with that text. Publishers trumpeted connections with *Uncle Tom* and kept to a mutter the information that they were critical works. W. L. G. Smith's book *Uncle Tom's Cabin As It Is* was promoted as "Another *Uncle Tom's Cabin!*" in large letters, while its oppositional political stance was buried in much smaller print.[17] Certain firms in the 1850s made good business out of the rush to answer *Uncle Tom*: although dwarfed by the unassailable achievements of Stowe's book, some replies sold very well. It was claimed that *Aunt Phillis's Cabin* achieved sales of 18,000, while *Uncle Tom's Cabin As It Is* was supposed to have shifted 15,000 copies in fifteen days. Others, like T. B. Thorpe's *The Master's House*, ran to several editions.[18] Some presses profited from the productions of both sides of the slavery argument. In London, Clarke, Beeton published *The Key to Uncle Tom's Cabin*, but it also brought out Charles Jacobs Peterson's *Cabin and Parlour* (with the English spelling) to put the contrary point of view.[19] J. B. Lippincott, who during the Civil War would help found Philadelphia's Union Club to counteract the city's Southern sympathies, played a significant role in the production of anti-*Tom* novels in the 1850s. His firm capitalized on the interest in *Uncle Tom* by publishing seven of the "answers": *Aunt Phillis's Cabin, Antifanaticism, Mr. Frank, Louise Elton, The Olive Branch, The Black Gauntlet,* and *The Slaveholder Abroad.*[20] T. B. Peterson of Philadelphia published not only Wiley but a whole collection of spin-offs, including the anti-*Tom* novel *Cabin and Parlor,* which was written under a pseudonym by the publisher's brother. *Cabin and Parlor* was advertised not even as a reply to Stowe's novel but as "fully equal in points of interest to *Uncle Tom's Cabin.*"[21] T. B. Peterson's catalog bracketed the three texts together and emphasized the connection with Stowe's novel, printing a review that proclaims of Peterson's character, " 'Uncle Peter' is more than a match for 'Uncle Tom.' "[22] In the light of this commercial puffery Charles Peterson looks less than candid when his preface denies any intention of riding on the back of Stowe's success: "The author disclaims, in advance[,] the idea of having written this work for mercenary considerations; as has been said of another, 'to steal a part of the profits of a *lady's* hard earned reputation.' " Peterson calls such accusations "disingenuous attempts to silence reply to 'Uncle Tom's Cabin,' " but his publisher, at least, was as interested in "mercenary considerations" as in quashing Stowe's arguments.[23]

Although Peterson affected distaste for the market that Stowe's novel had created, he was, along with most of the anti-*Tom* novelists, attempting to create a commercial space for his own stance on slavery. In this context the *Southern Literary Messenger*'s review of *Cabin and Parlor* missed the point in its "regret that by similarity of title and the time of its publication, it should be associated, in any way, with Mrs. Beecher Stowe's volumes."[24] The *Messenger* failed to grasp that Peterson's novel had several inevitable relationships with *Uncle Tom's Cabin.* It had a discursive one, in that it constituted a reply to that text, and a commercial one, in that its potential market had been partly created and certainly enormously expanded by the interest engendered by Stowe's book. As I shall shortly explain, it also had a generic one, in their common debt to the plantation novel. Whether financially calculating or not, these novelists were inescapably a part of *Uncle Tom* mania.

Disingenuousness about the motives for publishing these books was matched by that about their racial politics. Just as the specter of Stowe's novel hovered inevitably around "replies" to it, so the testimony of the slave narrators and the implicit argument of every runaway haunted the novels, whose arguments against slavery turned repeatedly (and ultimately ineffectively) to the question of the fugitives.

Those replies to *Uncle Tom's Cabin* that set out to be political retorts and that were careful to differentiate themselves from commercial spin-offs characterized the novel as a provocation rather than a source of profitable imitation. Ironically, of course, they also contributed to the *Uncle Tom* phenomenon even as they protested against it. They themselves invoked Stowe's novel in their attempts at refutation, and they were read and reviewed alongside it too.

Charles Holbrook, a New York visitor to a North Carolina plantation in October 1852, brought as presents copies both of *Uncle Tom* and of *Aunt Phillis's Cabin*.[25] Proslavery commentators would have been gratified to see Stowe "balanced" by Eastman in this gift, but the pairing of the novels also demonstrated that the replies to *Uncle Tom's Cabin* necessarily presupposed the existence of the original.

Reviews reinforced the anti-*Tom* books' dependence on their opponent by reading them alongside *Uncle Tom's Cabin*.[26] The *North British Review* assessed Stowe's novel at the same time as *Aunt Phillis's Cabin*; *Graham's Magazine* reviewed it with *Cabin and Parlor*; the *New Englander* examined *Uncle Tom* along with three "answers" and another antislavery novel, *The White Slave*.[27] The *Liberator*, which reproduced articles about Stowe's book as evidence of its widespread instigation of discussion about slavery, included in its evidence notices of the anti-*Tom* novels.[28]

Unsurprisingly, critics of the *Uncle Tom* phenomenon lumped them together: *Graham's Magazine* complained about the "Cabin Literature" produced by both Stowe and her opponents, under which, it said, "the shelves of booksellers groan."[29] The *Boston Post* went so far as to hold Stowe responsible for her enemies: "Mrs. Stowe will have much to answer for, if good paper and ink are to be wasted, and the public pocket picked, by any more of these 'replies' to her 'Uncle Tom.'"[30] By classifying the "answers" with the original, the *Boston Post* demonstrated the inescapability of their connection: even when the books were not directly read together, *Aunt Phillis's Cabin* would have conjured up the ghost of *Uncle Tom*.

For the majority, "answering Stowe" meant standing up for the South. Martha Haines Butt excused herself for bursting into print "but two years out of school" by referring to "her duty, as a warm-hearted Virginian, to defend the South."[31] The *New Orleans Weekly Picayune* charged *Uncle Tom's Cabin* with depicting "the whole body of the people of the south as living in a state of profligacy, cruelty, and crime—tyrants, who fear not God, and cruelly oppress their fellow-creatures."[32] The "people of the South" here were all presumed white, and Louisa S. McCord's review similarly subjected Stowe's

white characters to detailed scrutiny but glossed over her black ones.[33] Some
of Stowe's most heinous crimes were to show Southern ladies and gentlemen
using vulgar New England expressions and admitting lower-class rogues into
their homes: "Mrs. Stowe evidently does not know what 'a gentleman' is," and
"she is ignorant alike of our manners, feelings and even habits of language."[34]
Butt likewise argued in the preface to her novel that because "wealthy Southerners" generally harbor "refined and delicate feelings," they could not treat
slaves in the way Stowe describes.[35]

In combative novels like *Ellen* the retaliation took the form of attacks on
the North: it was also a cradle of villains in *North and South, Cabin and Parlor, Uncle Robin's Cabin,* and *Uncle Tom's Cabin As It Is.*[36] However, *The
Planter's Northern Bride* blamed the economic system rather than the people
of the North, implying that free labor made misery inevitable for the poor.

Despite the North-South antagonisms created and supposedly enacted in
their plots, these novels' generic kinship with Stowe's book nevertheless
illustrates how much they were drawing on shared traditions in representing the South. *Uncle Tom's Cabin* bears many resemblances to the plantation
fiction of Robert Pendleton Kennedy, William Gilmore Simms, and George
Tucker.[37] In her sympathetic portraits of the Shelby and St. Clare plantations
and in her dwelling on the languorous, elegant, and hospitable lifestyle of
wealthy Southerners, Stowe echoed such writers' earlier idealization of this
section of Southern society. And although her novel denounced slavery, it
also conveyed the seductiveness of the slave owners' way of life. As a child in
Britain during the Civil War, Frances Hodgson Burnett's knowledge of the
South was largely formed by Stowe: "To her the South was the land of 'Uncle
Tom's Cabin.'" Yet she found herself sympathizing with the Confederates,
and not just because of the suffering produced in Manchester by the shortage
of cotton for the mills: "She did not in the least know what the war was about,
but she could not help sympathising with the South because magnolias grew
there, and people dressed in white sat on verandas covered with vines. Also
there were so many roses. How could one help loving a place where there
were so many roses?"[38] As the *New Englander* claimed, Stowe's idealization
of the plantation was "incomparably the fairest and most attractive," even
compared with texts designed to "show the bright side of the negro's life in
slavery."[39]

In some senses the proslavery novelists were copycat critics, sharing some
of Stowe's structure, setting, and characters even while they denounced her.
Yet their paths had been smoothed by Stowe's own borrowings from the ear-

lier incarnations of the plantation novel. Stowe had entwined the slavery debate with domestic imagery, and they accepted the connection, as their titles
suggest: *The Master's House, "Uncle Tom's Cabin" Contrasted with Buckingham Hall, Aunt Phillis's Cabin, Uncle Robin's Cabin in Virginia and Tom Without One in Boston.* In addition, their portraits of the South were not dissimilar from Stowe's, even when local color, and especially the Southern
landscape, became part of the argument. Stowe contrasted Tom and Chloe's
cabin, covered with bright flowers, with Legree's estate, where "mildewed jes-
samine or honeysuckle hung raggedly" and the garden was "grown over with
weeds" (*UTC*, 17, 298). Flowers were important in the ideology of the well-
run house in midcentury domestic literature; in Stowe's version, the decorative gardening around the slave cabin signified a healthy household, while
Legree's blighted plantation mirrored slavery's corruption of the South.[40]

The "answers" to *Uncle Tom* used the same symbols but reversed the message: in them the South's abundant plant life signaled the felicities of slave
life. Peterson's Uncle Peter lives in a "neatly whitewashed" cabin that boasts
a "vegetable plot," a "flower garden," and a "rude arbor," covered in honeysuckle, over the door.[41] Aunt Phillis lives in a "neatly white-washed cottage"
adorned with roses.[42] Whereas Tom's flowery cabin in Stowe's novel reflects
his domestic sensibilities and confirms him as a sentimental hero, in the answers to her book the picturesque slave cabin is a credit to the master rather
than to the slave. In *Buckingham Hall* the comfort of the slave quarters helps
to evangelize an English visitor, who is converted to slavery by observation
of "the neatness of the out-buildings and the rural appearance of the white-
washed cabins, in which resided most of the slaves. They were surrounded by
flowers and creeping plants, and in a little garden attached to each were
plenty of chickens and other poultry running about."[43]

Such visions of order and plenty were frequently made to demonstrate the
virtues of the slave system in anti-*Tom* novels. *The Planter's Northern Bride*
is most explicit about the purpose of scenes like these; they are there to combat the tropes of antislavery literature: "I had heard many a tale of the woes
and sufferings of this enslaved race; but I looked in vain for scars and stripes
and chains. I saw comfortable cabins erected for their accommodation, comfortable raiment and food provided for them."[44] Whereas the spotlessness of
Uncle Tom's cabin pleads for him by demonstrating that he prizes the same
lifestyle as Stowe's bourgeois readers, Hentz's cabins demonstrate the generosity and efficiency of the slave system.

One aspect of *Uncle Tom's Cabin* that the "answers" to the novel rejected was *Uncle Tom*'s abjuration of a love interest. The *North British Review* was especially struck by this: "[T]he omission is what hardly any writer of fiction, bad or good, has ever ventured on since Shakspeare."[45] Instead, of course, Stowe shows slavery separating black families—Tom from Chloe, George from Eliza. The majority of replies, however, incorporated a marriage plot among the white characters; in many cases they used a North-South alliance to show off the South to Northern readers. *The Planter's Northern Bride* used the motif to argue for national harmony: its heroine was an "angel of conciliation" who made the hero want to "bind the North as well as the South in one common embrace."[46]

Nevertheless, the replies did take up *Uncle Tom*'s other significant deviation from the traditional plantation novel. As Richard Beale Davis argues, the novel "enlarge[d] the dimensions of the form" in its creation of a host of black characters and in making them the central focus of its plot.[47] It was to this innovation, of course, that George Eliot paid tribute in the claim that Stowe had "invented the negro novel" (see chapter 1). Although McCord's review largely ignored this aspect of *Uncle Tom's Cabin*, it was by concentrating on slavery and by making all its critics "provide the argument in regard" to it that Stowe helped politicize the plantation tradition.

The shift from the plantation novels' incidental treatment of slavery to its centrality in the anti-*Tom* texts is apparent in the differences between William Gilmore Simms's *The Sword and the Distaff* and its successors. Although it has often been included among the anti-*Tom* books, *The Sword and the Distaff* was published so close in time to *Uncle Tom's Cabin* in 1852 that it is unlikely to have been composed in response, especially as it does not mention Stowe and does not labor to defend slavery or the South.[48] Simms complained in a letter to a friend about the dearth of reviews of his book, "though it is probably as good an answer to Mrs. Stowe as has been published," yet compared with novels written specifically to "answer" Stowe, *The Sword and the Distaff* seems remarkably free of anxiety about the condition of slaves.[49] The episode in *Cabin and Parlor*, for instance, where a planter family loses its money is designed to show Southerners agonizing about selling their slaves, and the neighbors in the novel buy up whole families in order to prevent them from being uprooted or separated.[50] *The Sword and the Distaff* exhibits none of this self-consciousness. In it the slaves are relatively minor figures. Simms's debt-ridden Captain Porgy mortgages and sells his slaves without a qualm: the plot hinges on slaves as property, not as people. Porgy

reflects that if the sheriff attempts to seize his slave Tom, he will shoot his possession rather than let him "fall into the hands of a scamp."[51]

As slavery became a central concern of the post–*Uncle Tom* plantation
novel, black characters became more significant. As the reader for *Graham's
Magazine* spelled out, the slaves in *Cabin and Parlor* are modeled on those
in Stowe: "[T]here are Uncle Peter and Aunt Violet–corresponding to Uncle
Tom and Aunt Chloe, and Charles and Cora–corresponding to George and
Eliza."[52] *Aunt Phillis, Uncle Robin's Cabin,* and *Uncle Tom's Cabin As It Is* followed Stowe enough to name the text after a slave. More commonly, Uncle
Tom himself was reinvented in a succession of sentimental black "aunts" and
"uncles" who matched him for warmth and humility, but they testified rather
to the benevolence of slavery than to its brutality.

In the opening chapters of Stowe's documentary defense of her novel, *The
Key to Uncle Tom's Cabin,* she defends its realism by offering nonfictional
counterparts for some of her dramatis personae. Tom's prototypes are included to show that "the negro race is confessedly more simple, docile, child-
like, and affectionate, than other races; and hence the divine graces of love
and faith, when in-breathed by the Holy Spirit, find in their natural temperament a more congenial atmosphere."[53] This is the point of *Uncle Tom* as
attested by Stowe, that black people are more naturally religious, and it is on
this basis that she declares enslaving them wrong. Yet plenty of anti-*Tom*
novels were prepared to reiterate the first point while vehemently refuting
the second. Aunt Phillis's master describes her in terms that mirror Uncle
Tom for virtue: "Her industry, her honesty, her attachment to our family ex-
ceeds everything. . . . [H]er whole life has been a recommendation of the religion of the Bible." The difference is that this feminine version of Stowe's
martyr is a model for the benefits of her condition: "I wish Abolitionists would
imitate one of her virtues–humility."[54] Like Stowe's Uncle Tom, too, Page's
Uncle Robin keeps a Sunday school, and McIntosh's Daddy Cato wants to
learn to read the Bible.[55] Peterson's Uncle Peter is also sold to pay off debts
and echoes Tom in his declaration that he will "[t]rust in de Lord." His wife,
like Stowe's Chloe, is a proud cook, and she is "unrivalled" in the prepara-
tion of "corn-cake." When their former owners are in need, Uncle Peter and
Aunt Vi'let match the magnanimity of their originals by leaving secret gifts of
chicken and turkey in the white folks' larder.[56]

But if the anti-*Tom* novels found the model of the domestic black character useful, they would revel in the possibilities offered by the blackface one.

Blackface in the answers to *Uncle Tom* was unabashedly polemical. Despite their allegations about Northern misconceptions of Southern life, the myths about slavery enshrined in (Northern) minstrelsy proved extremely useful to the anti-*Tom* novelists. While Stowe had exploited minstrelsy's ambiguities, the answers flattened them, stressing the form's claims to racial "delineation," rather than its connection with travesty, and making the "racial characteristics" of minstrelsy vindicate the practice of slavery. Blackface characterization and behavior is in fact one of the most recurring features of these novels, and it is designed to suggest that slavery is beneficial, even fun. There is very little of the ambiguity and double-edged mockery apparent in end man-interlocutor scenes on the stage or in the exchanges that Stowe molded from them. Instead, the replies to her text referred primarily to blackface songs and described bouts of energetic and implausible dancing, which they contended were constant features of plantation life. The novels used blackface to make black characters lazy, ignorant, and feckless rather than subversive and telling. Black speech in these novels is usually the compendium of grammatical oddities and stereotyped accents it was on the minstrel stage: "I is so glad I gwine from dis place... Masser."[57] Slaves employ malapropisms and customize words: "[T]hat's about as close as Robin ever comes to correct pronunciation."[58] Unlike their use on the stage, however, linguistic slips and oddities are not used here to poke fun at aspects of white culture, only to make black characters ludicrous. Worse, in *Antifanaticism* Uncle Dick is comically unaware of his own absurdity: "[W]hen Charles would laugh at the droll pronunciation of his words, Uncle Dick would think he had said something very witty, and join heartily in the laugh."[59]

Songs from the blackface tradition constantly crop up in these novels. A slave sings Stephen Foster's "Old Uncle Ned" in *The Olive Branch*; one in *Frank Freeman's Barber's Shop* sings "Take Me Back to Ole Virginee" and "Possum up a Gum Tree"; in *Antifanaticism* "Dinah Crow" is sung; "Zip Coon" and "Old Dan Tucker" are played at the ball in *Cabin and Parlor*; and in *Uncle Tom's Cabin As It Is* slave characters adapt Foster's "Camptown Races" and sing "Lubly Rosa," "Virginia Reel," and "Lucy Bell."[60] Unusually, it is the English character in *Buckingham Hall* who performs Foster's "Oh! Susanna."[61]

These minstrel songs usually denote happiness in the novels. In the final paragraphs of *Buckingham Hall* the slaves celebrate the master's marriage with impromptu verses that make it clear that this blackface-style entertainment is tied to an explicit defense of slavery:

> Darkies dey don't wan' be free,
> Cause dey happy as dey be:
> Massa gibs 'em plenty meat.[62]

Whereas blackface on stage was often politically ambiguous and even contradictory, its use in these novels is baldly connected to their argument. In *Mr.
Frank* the slaves ask not to be freed because, as their master says, "all that
they ask is to be let alone . . . to enjoy themselves in hoeing corn, picking tobacco, . . . singing Lucy Neal to their heart's content" (on "Lucy Neal" see
chapters 2 and 5).[63]

It was especially cheeky to use blackface voices to praise slavery, of course,
in view of the wealth of contradictory black testimony abroad in the 1850s.
Some of these texts come close to recognizing it, even pinpointing the quality in slave music that W. E. B. Du Bois would later enshrine in the term "sorrow songs." However, where black writers like Du Bois and Frederick Douglass emphasized the pain behind such music, the anti-*Tom* novelists carefully
denied that there was any such thing.[64] In Douglass's famous formulation,
"[S]laves sing most when they are most unhappy. The songs of the slave represent the sorrows of his heart."[65] The slaves' thoughts, by contrast, in *The
Planter* are of "how happy they are": "This is indicated both in their sacred,
and in their secular songs."[66]

Peterson, too, asserts that the music is only sad to the white listener: the
slaves' "mirth finds its food as well as its expression, in music that to more advanced races is always mournful." He illustrates this with a story of travelers
on the Nile hearing "the music of the Ethiopians," which, "though often
drawing tears to the listener's eyes, appears to afford only mirthful enjoyment
to the African himself."[67] Similarly, Hall concedes that the musicians' conflicting emotions may lie behind the music's special qualities, but he too cannot imagine that the slaves are anything but content with their lot: "The negroes seem to sing as caged birds, willing to be free and yet loath to fly away
even when the door is left purposely open. And that renders the boat-song so
resistlessly powerful to move the soul with melancholy and compassion, and
yet with emotions akin to those of fun and frolic."[68]

Dances, which accompany many of these songs, are similarly used in these
novels to justify slavery. The characters' propensity for dancing is made a sign
both of racial characteristics and of the benevolence of their masters. "Negroes let alone would keep an eternal saturnalia," according to *Uncle Robin's
Cabin*.[69] In *The Planter's Northern Bride* the slave "gives care and trouble to

the winds," while the "Northern labourer has anxious thoughts for the mor-
row, fears that the daily bread for which he is toiling may be withheld." He is
not threatened by the adverse circumstances that could impoverish a free
laborer, and it is impossible to suppress his appetite for pleasure: "No matter
how hard he has been at work, if it be a moonlight night, he steals off on a
'possum hunt, or a fishing frolic, or if he hears a violin, he is up and dancing
the Virginian breakdown, or the Georgia rattlesnake."[70]

The assumption here, that dancing is a central feature of slave life, is common to many of the novels. *Cabin and Parlor* opens with a ball for the planter's
daughter, and it closes with the entire slave community going off to dance.[71]
Buckingham Hall features no fewer than five episodes of slave singing and
dancing, and two of these scenes were picked out for illustrations, suggesting
that such tableaux were especially significant or interesting moments.[72]
Readers were often placed in the position of white observers in the novels, re-
garding such frolics with detached amusement, especially when they degenerated into slapstick. An extended sequence in *Aunt Phillis's Cabin* combines
most of the elements of blackface entertainment: gymnastics, physical comedy, and musicality. The dancer "cut[s] the pigeonwing," rolls an old man off
a barrel, and switches rapidly between "dancing with every limb," "making
the most curious contortions of his face," stretching out snoring on the grass,
leaping into song, and then making a leapfrog getaway.[73] Similarly, the children in *Uncle Robin's Cabin* progress from tumbling to imitations to gymnastics and end with banjo dances.[74] For white characters such displays are in-
tensely amusing. The "ridiculous antics" of the slaves in *Buckingham Hall*
cause the whites to laugh "till they could laugh no longer from sheer ex-
haustion."[75] As well as making the black characters ludicrous, these episodes,
like the singing, confirm the fact that they are happy. Kennard's jokey article
on minstrelsy for New York's *Knickerbocker Magazine* spelled out this connection in 1845: "This thing is well understood at the South. A laughing,
singing, fiddling negro is almost invariably a faithful servant. Possibly he may be lazy and idle, but 'treasons, stratagems and spoils' form not
the subject of *his* meditations."[76] Kennard promoted a mythology of blackface as Southern life, in which minstrel-type performance reassured owners
of the slaves' compliance. In *Uncle Robin's Cabin* a Northerner makes the
mistake of asking if all this dancing is designed to relieve "the sorrows of the
heart." His Southern companion rejects this thesis as bluntly as other novels
deny it in relation to song: "[T]hey are . . . imagined sorrows."[77] *Cabin and
Parlor* juxtaposes a scene of Northern wretchedness with a chapter featuring

a joyful slave wedding, itself a deliberate refutation of the abolitionist claim that slave owners encouraged immorality and broke up marriages. In this "the happy faces, the very *abandon* of merriment" are described as if they would come as a surprise to Northern readers: "Ye who never having crossed the Potomac, regard the slave as a haggard, emaciated, broken-hearted victim! go to a negro wedding . . . and learn how grievously you have been disappointed."[78]

It was disingenuous, of course, to claim that such pictures of the South were unfamiliar in the North, for exaggeratedly "happy faces" and merry "abandon" were customary on the minstrel stage. Just as the anti-*Tom* novels derived their cozy slave cabins from Stowe and yet explicitly opposed them to abolitionism, so the proslavery plantation dances were already familiar to supposedly hostile Northern readers. In *Mr. Frank* the protagonist is surprised, because "his mind had hitherto been so completely filled up with ideas of 'chains, fetters, stripes, scars, and negro groans,' as to entirely preclude his realizing such a thing as a negro frolic."[79] Mr. Frank clearly did not go to minstrel shows.[80]

Yet it was only part of blackface's appeal that was transferred to the anti-*Tom* novels. Their creation of a fictional white audience, amused by physical comedy, ludicrous behavior, and songs marked as specifically "black" music, exemplifies the fascination with the transcultural encounter that lay behind all minstrelsy's myths of songs and dances lifted from specific black performers. The stories of Rice's appropriations for his act and the tale of the song stolen from the original "Watermelon Man" both invoke blackness staged for a white audience.[81] Reproduced here too is the assumption that this version of blackness is grotesque and that the correct response is hilarity. But what is missing from the novels is the knowingness in the Jim Crow stories, the joking about the very fact that the blackness on the stage is theatrical. The biggest joke, that it wasn't real blackness, was airbrushed out of these novels.

The answers to *Uncle Tom* had little use for minstrelsy's ability to undermine the white-over-black hierarchies it seemed to promote. Only a couple of novels attempted to borrow the forms of the stump speech or the dialogues between the end man and interlocutor, no doubt because it was in these forms that the blackface speaker so often undercut white pomposity and cultural norms on the stage. In the closest approximation to the ironies such scenes could generate, a black coachman in *Mr. Frank* takes to a stump—"Feller citizens"—in imitation of antislavery oratory. He parodies white, albeit Northern white, political agitation. His speech attacks "de mas'rs ob de Norf" who are oppressing "prentices, factory-boys, sewin'-girls, and oder poor persons."[82] Elsewhere the status quo is inverted so that, as in George Aiken's version of the end man and interlocutor, the white character gets the punch line. Echoing the grandiloquence of the stage interlocutor, the white Quaker in *The Olive Branch* inflates the song "Old Uncle Ned" to "Aged Uncle Edward."[83] *Aunt Phillis's Cabin* avoids the complications of such interchanges altogether: it pilfers Stowe's famous duet between Topsy and Ophelia but makes it a sentimental moment rather than a comic one. In this novel the religious spinster tells the slave that Jesus died on the cross, which causes her to examine the sky anxiously, wondering if God, too, is mortal.[84] The problem with Eastman's scene is that it lacks Topsy's mischief, trying to retain the sentimental scene of instruction without allowing the slave character her moment of comic triumph.

Black characters in these texts are not allowed to subvert their masters; instead, they must, in the most extreme versions, parrot the proslavery views of their authors. In *Antifanaticism* it is the slave Rufus who reassures a solicitous Northerner, "'Yes sar, dis nigger never leab his master to go wid nobody; 'caze he know dat nobody ain't gwine to treat him good no how like massa does.'"[85] These moments of ventriloquism, where the writers place their arguments in the mouths of black characters, reflect the driving purpose behind these novels, for one of the most crucial tenets of these defenses of slavery was that slaves were comfortable and happy in their servitude and that they would never think to seek anything else.

It was for this reason that the major theme in these novels—it occurs in fifteen—is that of fugitive slaves.[86] In many the plot revolves around them. This frequency suggests the freight of anxiety in these texts about the implications of slave escapes—the possibility that slaves resented their condition or might long for freedom. Paradoxically, these texts were obsessed with fugitives, while their primary argument was that slaves did not want to run away.

Almost unanimously, the anti-*Tom* books pronounced that the blame for slave escapes lay with abolitionists. They reflected in fiction the Southern fears Kenneth Stampp describes during the "insurrection panics" of 1856 and 1860, in which "unscrupulous" white men were presumed to be conspiring with slaves.[87] In the South of these books, abolitionists had "emissaries constantly passing through this country" with the object of "enticing" slaves "for ever from servitude."[88] Mr. Frank's work consists of "running away a few hundreds of negroes, annually, from their masters."[89] Such agents would stop at nothing: one mother has even "had a young child stolen from her."[90] Smith's

Uncle Tom is persuaded to leave by a monster who then seduces a slave girl and encourages her to leave her husband for freedom.[91] In *Ellen* a runaway slave is trained to be a burglar.[92]

The novels represented such activity as even more widespread in the North, where antislavery fanatics were kept busy by the surprising number of holidaying masters who exposed their slaves to temptation. Many fictional slave owners were warned not to take their slaves away for that very reason.[93] Still, they persisted. In *The Planter's Northern Bride* the faithful Albert cleaves to his master in Massachusetts despite antislavery blandishments, but the flighty Crissy deserts her mistress in Cincinnati.[94] The credulous Frank and Carrie in *Frank Freeman's Barber's Shop* are led by Bostonian trick preaching to think that Providence intends them to run off.[95] Over the river in Cambridge, Massachusetts, the abolitionists in *The Lofty and the Lowly* degenerate into a mob, baying outside the Southerners' home and demanding to "liberate" a terrified Daddy Cato, who begs, "[P]lease, my dear Misses, no to gib me up."[96] Even in New York City Uncle Peter in *Ellen* has been scarred by his experience of abolitionists, who persuaded him to leave his master: "[W]hen out of humour with any of his fellow servants, his most vindictive wish was, that his master would send the offenders North and set them free."[97]

It is inconvenient for the slave owner when his property absconds on holiday. In *The Planter's Northern Bride* Ildegerte is in a strange city when she loses her husband to consumption and her slave to abolitionists all in one night.[98] Nevertheless, flight is usually worse for the fugitives. The novels make escape their loss rather than the planters'. In *Uncle Robin's Cabin* they start off "just as comfortably situated as they could possibly wish," "having on the plantation, parents, brothers, and sisters," and they voluntarily deprive themselves, "determining to leave them, and be separated from them for ever."[99] Deposited in the North penniless and naive, the slaves are either cruelly exploited or abandoned with the unfamiliar task of finding their own way in the world. In cities those who cannot find work starve in slums and are rebuffed by philanthropists who will send aid only to slaves. They are tricked out of their money, charged for lodging with "friends," and exploited for their labor.[100] Where once they were well fed and comfortable, they find themselves poor and overworked.[101] If they have the misfortune to be ill, their saviors confiscate their savings to compensate for lost work time.[102] Worst of all, the philanthropists turn out to be racists, calling the slaves names and barring them from the philanthropists' tables and pews and from public transport.[103] In the North the slaves find themselves surrounded by "caricatured representations of the negro . . . and . . . placarded bills, in which very black faces, very thick and red lips and very staring white eyes figured continuously."[104]

These episodes blame abolitionism for the fugitive slave problem. A few of these fictional abolitionists go so far as to foment rebellion, distributing incendiary documents and organizing insurrections.[105] A number of books contend that abolitionism is self-defeating, actually promoting slavery and the abuses against which it protests: "If those Northern abolitionists were to stop their meddling in our concerns, the condition of the slaves would be much improved. . . . If they were to let us alone, there is no doubt that, in the course of years, not a slave state would be in existence."[106] It is the bad behavior they inspire in slaves that forces owners to sell the slaves off or that keeps the unscrupulous slave dealers occupied: "[T]he abolitionists . . . entice them off, and we grab them flying."[107] Northern meddling also results in the separation of families.[108] It is because abolitionists pressed for the Wilmot Proviso, banning slavery in the territories acquired from Texas, that masters moving west have to sell their slaves, fueling the slave trade.[109] They have "ruined" domestics in Washington, D.C., rendering them dishonest, so that families employ the Irish instead.[110] Misunderstood masters, in sheer frustration, have become "more tyrannical," and abolition has forestalled reform in the South.[111]

Although all these accusations against abolitionists of ill will and evildoing serve an obvious purpose in these novels, they also have another function. It is telling that the responses to Stowe's novel are peopled with "ultra" abolitionists: Stowe, of course, did not belong to an antislavery society, nor did her novel appeal for immediate emancipation. The anti-*Tom* novels attacked her book as if it were more dangerous than it was, in some cases perhaps because they had not read it, in others with the view of discrediting it by association. Yet the textual abolitionists had another crucial job, which was to provide the source of all disharmony in the South. Blaming antislavery men for causing any and all dissatisfaction on the plantation absolved the slaves from reflecting on their condition, and it reinforced the contention that they had no reason for unhappiness. The constant reiteration in these texts that it was Northern meddlers who created runaways worked alongside the denial that slaves ever dreamed of freedom unprompted. In several novels when they are offered their liberty, they turn it down.[112]

Arguably, the recurrence of runaways was a sign of imperfectly suppressed anxiety. One might ask why, in all these fictional cases of idyllic plantations, there always is a fugitive. The *New York Observer* printed a rumor in 1852 that a slave in Kentucky "who had obtained a copy of 'Uncle Tom's Cabin,' read it to his fellow slaves, and in consequence, 25 of them escaped to Ohio, and were passed on the 'underground railroad' to Canada."[113] The anti-*Tom* novels never fretted that Stowe's book might have that effect in other cases. They were too intent on proving the rarity of runaways. And yet in every text that set out to disprove his reality, the specter of the fugitive was invoked and reinforced. Not only that, but this insistence that slaves never left their masters flew in the face of the facts.

Outside proslavery fiction slaves made off with themselves in large numbers during the antebellum period. In life escapees were not the few isolated malcontents they were in the novels: slave owners placed thousands of advertisements for the return of runaways every year, and it is likely that many more escaped than were recorded in this way. One estimate is that sixty thousand slaves escaped between 1830 and 1860.[114] The black antislavery activist Henry Highland Garnet believed he had given shelter to 150 runaways passing through New York City in one year alone, while the Quaker Levi Coffin claimed he had helped 2,000 in the course of his long career.[115] So rather than being the uncommon occurrences these novels made them out to be, fugitive slaves were numerous enough to be noticeable both as absences in the South and as arrivals in Northern cities.

Neither were all these real disappearances the work of white abolitionists, as the novels claimed. Although there is evidence that there was antislavery activity in the South, the majority of slave fugitives made it on their own.[116] Abolitionists did, of course, play a part in the Underground Railroad, which hid and supported fugitives on their way through the Northern states and also helped them start new lives as free persons. In the books such activities figure as pecuniary exploitation, and the promotion of ex-slave lecturers appears as a selfish way of garnering attention. But all such fictional aid to black characters comes from whites. There is no whisper in these texts of the "vigilance committees" black communities formed in the North to assist ex-slaves or of black participants in the Underground Railroad. White abolitionist James G. Birney recognized that "such matters are almost uniformly managed by the colored people"; in the novels it was exactly the reverse.[117]

The problem of fugitive slaves constituted one of the most serious fault lines of North-South politics in the 1850s, and the anti-*Tom* novels were thus tapping into a major national controversy. The runaways in Stowe's novel were themselves a response to a political manifestation of anxiety about the issue: the second Fugitive Slave Act, which was incorporated into the Compromise of 1850. The law revived and strengthened the Fugitive Slave Act of

1793, making it easier for Southerners to retrieve escaped slaves from Northern states. In itself the law represented a response to perceptions within the slave-owning states that Northerners had been facilitating the disappearance of their "property." Dispensing with the need for warrants, the legislation allowed an owner who had seized his former slave merely to prove his possession to a specially appointed federal commissioner, a more convenient proposition than previous arrangements. Precisely reflecting the suspicion enshrined in the succession of fictional abolitionists who enticed away slaves in the anti-*Tom* novels, the law also made it an offense to assist runaways.[118] So major was the political and cultural significance this legislation took on that Stowe described it as a central piece of American literature in an article of 1856. In response to a friend's request for "a specimen of a purely and peculiarly American production to send to France," Stowe dryly suggested "a copy of the American Fugitive Slave Law."[119]

In their indifference to the facts about the numbers and the volition of fugitive slaves, the anti-*Tom* novels wrote initiative and ingenuity out of their slave populations. Above all, the insistence that abolitionists lay behind attempts to escape expunged the possibility that slaves themselves might independently object to their condition. The *North British Review* recognized that fugitives challenged "the Anti-Abolitionist" line that "the slaves are the happiest people in the world," asking, if that was the case, what was "the meaning of the countless advertisements, offering rewards for the apprehension of runaway slaves, to be recognized by marks sufficient to prove the 'happy' state they left?"[120] The flights that later historians saw as "an important form of protest against bondage" either were made to disappear in the novels or were turned into the byproducts of external malice.[121] In the same way as proslavery scientists theorized away fugitives by transforming their motives into a disease (in 1851 Samuel Cartwright pathologized the desire for freedom by labeling the need to escape "drapetomania," from the ancient Greek verb *drapetein*, "to run away"), the anti-*Tom* novelists explained them with reference to abolitionists.[122] A similar process dictated the constant description in these texts of blacks in the North as "degraded." They longed to return to slavery themselves rather than help anyone out of it; in fiction, freedom profited no one. Benjamin Quarles argues that Southerners ignored black participation in the Underground Railroad because to acknowledge it "would have been to undercut the Southerners' own position that the docile and apathetic sons of Africa were well-adapted, loyal slaves."[123] It was for exactly the same reason that the anti-*Tom* novels denied the possibility of the Railroad's existence and attacked Stowe's novel instead. This process was perfectly, and cruelly, reproduced in the documented case of Samuel Green, a black preacher in Maryland who was thought to be assisting fugitives. Green was imprisoned for ten years in the 1850s, not for abetting fellow blacks in their flight from servitude but for possessing a copy of *Uncle Tom's Cabin*.[124]

The prominence of the fugitive issue in these novels may also have been influenced by the ubiquity of escaped slaves in antislavery propaganda. Marcus Wood has argued that the fugitive is a central figure in "the literature and art generated by slavery" from the mid–eighteenth century to this period. A common strategy in antislavery propaganda was to use Southern advertisements for runaways to illustrate the callousness of slave owners and the sufferings of their property. The most famous example, Theodore Weld and the Grimké sisters' 1839 book *American Slavery As It Is*, had fed Stowe's imagination while she was writing her novel.[125] The anti-*Tom* novels respond partly to this tradition and partly to its manifestation in *Uncle Tom's Cabin* in the stories of Eliza's dash across the ice floes and George's journey north in disguise. In 1853 Stowe had reinforced the power of the fugitive question when she borrowed the technique from *American Slavery As It Is* for *The Key to Uncle Tom's Cabin*, printing nearly twenty pages of advertisements culled from newspapers from the latter half of 1852. Stowe drew readers' attention to the telling details unselfconsciously revealed in such texts by slave owners. The frequency of references to scars implied cruel treatment; descriptions of light coloring and complexion bore witness to violent or immoral sexual relations between owners and slaves; mention of the intelligence of the fugitive suggested the waste of talent and life in slavery; the notices that unclaimed captives would be sold to pay jail fees demonstrated that even free black people could be enslaved on suspicion. One interpretation of *Key* distilled the whole text into a famous fugitive case. *Key* devoted a chapter to the story of the Edmondson family, part of a group of seventy-seven slaves who in 1848 attempted to escape from slavery in Washington, D.C., by stowing away on the schooner *Pearl*. After they were recaptured the *Pearl* fugitives were mostly sold South, while the whites who had helped them were imprisoned.[126] When Aiken followed the success of his *Uncle Tom* by transforming the unwieldy *Key* into a play, he did it by dramatizing the story of the Edmondson family.[127] In other words, just as the anti-*Tom* novels boiled the *Uncle Tom* issue down to the question of fugitives, so Aiken reduced *Key*—Stowe's justification of *Uncle Tom's Cabin*—to the story of one escape attempt.

The antislavery use of runaway advertisements addressed the proslavery arguments about the *condition* of slaves, tackling the assertions both that they were kindly treated and that they were not mentally fit for any other state of life. The fugitives themselves made an even more fundamental challenge to the ideology of slavery, since by running away, even from "good" homes, they demonstrated that an intractable principle was at stake. They wanted to be *free*, even if freedom entailed poverty and discomfort. It was this aspect of the fugitive slave issue that rendered it so insistently subversive.

Slave narratives contained the most powerful articulation of the feeling that the anti-*Tom* novels labored to suppress. Most obviously, the majority of the antebellum autobiographies of fugitive slaves would never have been written if their authors had not escaped. Not only were their narratives crucial to abolitionist propaganda, but these authors founded an African American literary tradition and launched political and journalistic careers like that of Frederick Douglass.[128] Running away allowed narrators to produce accounts not only of conditions under slavery but also, crucially, of slaves' irrepressible longing for freedom.

It was in this context that the anti-*Tom* novels tried to assert the contradictory positions that there were no fugitives, that running away was never a slave's own idea, and that it made slave lives worse. *The Master's House* even tried to make the case that slave narratives profited the hunters of men. In it a slave dealer hunts runaways from a "Free Sile Album" like the antislavery annuals in which many slave narratives were published: "There at a glance could be seen, every published account of runaway negroes, who had escaped to the North or Canada, for the last fifteen years." "By the means of this book" the slave dealer works out the whereabouts of fugitives, and "with the assistance of spies" he catches them and gets "great bargains at little cost."[129]

Obviously, fugitives who put their new identities into print did run a great risk of reenslavement, but the idea of using the slave narrative for that purpose also represents a vindictive fantasy. Thorpe's fiction here reflected the fact that for at least a decade the narratives of fugitive slaves had been demonstrating the arguments adopted in proslavery novels to be palpably false: without the ministrations of abolitionist bogey figures, escaping slaves could still strike out for freedom and oppose slave-owning society's most central beliefs. The incessant redrafting of the figure of the runaway in the anti-*Tom* novels reflects the power of the slave narratives they either ignore or dismiss with Thorpe's "Free Sile Album." Implicitly, they argue against the autobiographies of ex-slaves and against the physical protests of the thousands of runaways whose existence they so repetitiously deny. Yet like their refutations of Stowe, these efforts at negation keep the specter of their opponent alongside the text. The blackface ventriloquism so many of these books attempt, using "black" characters to affirm their ideology, is marked just as surely by the black voices they pass over as by *Uncle Tom's Cabin.*

Ironically, while the answers to Uncle Tom obsessively fretted about Northerners running slaves off, the news in the 1850s was full of examples of the reverse: black people fleeing for themselves and being returned South by Northerners complying with the Fugitive Slave Act. The constable of the Northern city in *Uncle Robin's Cabin* who will not let Mammy return to Virginia in case she is reenslaved inverts the cases of scores of real slaves whose return to their owners was enforced by the law.[130] Instances of slave recapture made a huge political impact in both the North and the South. Forcible seizures brought crowds to the streets of Boston and other cities, and extensive public sympathy was expressed for black people taken back south against their will. Emotions were equally aroused in the South at reports of dramatic rescue attempts and at a number of states' counterlegislation to limit the jurisdiction of the Fugitive Slave Act.[131] In Boston in February 1851 a fifty-strong black mob carried off a man called Shadrack from a courtroom before he could be sent south, but in April 1851 the Georgia runaway Thomas Sims was seized and escorted to a ship by one hundred policemen. In Pennsylvania in September 1851 four people were killed in a battle between slaveholders and fugitives and their friends at the home of William Parker, a black Underground Railroad agent. In November 1851 black and white abolitionists rescued a former slave known as Jerry from a police station in Syracuse, New York, and sent him to Canada. In May 1854, when another Boston rescue mob failed to abstract Anthony Burns from the courthouse, buildings were draped in black, and fifty thousand spectators lined the street as state and federal troops marched him through the town to a waiting ship.[132]

These were recent or contemporary incidents for the writers of the anti-*Tom* novels. There was a terrible irony in their claims that "abolitionists" were stealing male slaves from the plantation, seducing slave women from their mistresses, and kidnapping slave children from their mothers. It was highlighted by the notice posted by the Boston Vigilance Committee after Thomas Sims was returned to slavery, warning the "Colored People of Boston" not to talk to watchmen and police officers and to "keep a sharp look out for kidnappers."[133] Both sides accused the other of trafficking in stolen lives, but the anti-*Tom* novelists had the least justification. Ex-slaves in this period fled *from* the Northern United States, as many as twenty thousand to Canada between 1850 and 1860, and a number of well-known writers and lecturers elected to stay in Britain during the 1850s rather than risk reenslavement under the Fugitive Slave Act.[134]

There was another poignancy in the repetition in these novels of the claim that slaves who accompanied their owners on trips to the Free States were decoyed off to penury by unscrupulous abolitionists. As these books were being written, Dred Scott was attempting to claim his freedom through the courts on the grounds that his master had taken him to live for long periods in the Wisconsin Territory, where slavery was illegal.[135] While the anti-*Tom* novelists penned stories of slaves who were duped into leaving and bitterly regretted it, Dred Scott was publicly demonstrating his seriousness about obtaining his liberty for himself. For Dred Scott it was difficult, time consuming, expensive, and in the end impossible to do something that in the books happened almost at the drop of a hat. Granted, during the early stages of Scott's travails his efforts were not widely known. By the time *Uncle Tom* was published he had lost his first case in the St. Louis Circuit Court in 1847, the jury in that court had found for him in 1850, and the Missouri Supreme Court had overturned that decision in 1852. But by 1854, when the majority of the anti-*Tom* novels had been published, Scott's case was before the United States Circuit Court, and at the end of that year Scott had appealed to the Supreme Court. By the time the Court reached its decision in 1857, the Dred Scott case was controversial enough to spark accusations of a political conspiracy, and in 1860 it became an election issue.[136] The verdict—that Dred Scott not only would remain a slave but as a black person was not entitled to resort to the law—provoked understandable outrage in the antislavery camp, but it is notable that Scott's case contradicted another of the anti-*Tom* books' contentions, that it was always Northerners who helped slaves out of bondage. Dred Scott's financial backing came not only from the South but from a slave-owning family: the sons of his former master, Peter Blow.[137] Unlike those in the anti-*Tom* fiction, some real slaveholders were acutely aware of Dred Scott's determination to be free.

The insistence that slaves were comfortable in slavery depended on the assumption, propagated in all the "answers" to *Uncle Tom's Cabin*, that black people were fundamentally different from white ones. This aspect of proslavery propaganda was most stridently represented in the obsession with racial purity. The presumption that amalgamation was dangerous was, of course, something that many antislavery thinkers shared: in *The Key to Uncle Tom's*

Cabin Stowe drew attention to the light coloring mentioned in runaway advertisements:

> In reading the following little sketches of "slaves as they are," let the reader notice:
>
> 1. The colour and complexion of the majority of them.

Stowe's sarcastic comments, interspersed between her documentation, implied that this was scandalous evidence not only of extramarital sexual relations but of interracial ones. After reprinting the notice of a reward for a runaway whose "hair curls without showing black blood," she notes, "Another 'very intelligent,' straight-haired man. Who was his father?"[138]

But whereas *Uncle Tom's Cabin* had made the prevalence of interracial sex one of its charges against slavery, in the anti-*Tom* novels it is abolitionists, not slave owners, who embody this possibility. The "she Abolitionist" in *Aunt Phillis's Cabin* not only "considers Southerners heathens" and "wants Frederick Douglass to be the next President," she argues for amalgamation. *Aunt Phillis's Cabin* treats the idea with good-humored ridicule: the Southern girl mocks that "Uncle Bacchus would just suit her, with his airs and graces; but I do not think she is stylish enough for him."[139] However, in other texts the prospect is more threatening. For *The Planter's Northern Bride* the idea is so unnatural that although the "most ultra Northern philanthropist . . . may advocate amalgamation with his lips . . . in his heart, he recoils from it with horror."[140] Not so for the abolitionists in *Mr. Frank*. The antislavery society meeting is scandalously mixed, as "Vidi" slyly insinuates: "[A] white person was nearly always found between two blacks, and a black one between two whites." The effect of this commingling of the races seems to be that the delegates turn lecherous: "Everybody seemed to be well pleased with this arrangement; especially several rakish-looking old Quakers, who were situated between buxom-looking negro-wenches; and some huge, amorous-looking negro-gallants, whom Fate, or their own sense of the beautiful, had thrown amongst exceedingly pretty country-girls."[141] If there are sexual predators, in other words, they are Northern Quakers or free black men, whereas implicitly for the proslavery anti-*Tom* novelist, the prospect and possibility of such encounters is appalling.

But anxieties about amalgamation were not all about sex. One of Stowe's warnings about the runaway slave advertisements was that they revealed that the differences between black and white, and, necessarily, between the en-

slaved and the free, were not always self-evident. It is a short step from wondering if a runaway had a white parent to worrying that he may never have
been black: "[W]hite children have sometimes been kidnapped and sold into
slavery." She quotes the Reverend George Bourne's account of a seven-year-
old white boy stolen from his parents, "immersed in a tan-vat to change his
complexion, tattooed and sold." Once again, Stowe asserts that it is slave owners not abolitionists who steal people from their families—"the tanning process is not necessary now, as a fair skin is no presumption against slavery."
The slave laws have become a charter for abduction: "That kidnappers may
steal and sell white children at the South now, is evident from these advertisements. . . . When the mind once becomes familiarized with the process of
slavery, . . . and when blue eyes and golden hair are advertised as properties
of *negroes*—what protection will there be for poor white people, especially
as under the present fugitive law they can be carried away without a jury
trial?"[142] Stowe's sensational revelation of the instability of racial boundaries,
which she is both blaming on slavery and using to undercut its ideological basis, attacks proslavery certitude about the inevitability of slavery or freedom.
Her question plays on her readers' prejudice, implying as it does that the
possibility of enslaved white people is more shocking than the known fate of
thousands of black ones. But it also cuts at those justifications of slavery that
relied on theories of racial difference. "White"-looking "black" people undermine the possibilities for such categorization. No doubt for the same reason there are relatively few characters in the anti-*Tom* novels who are identified as "mulatto" or otherwise of mixed racial origin. It would be otherwise
harder to produce racial explanations for the suitability of the slave system,
such as the argument in *Frank Freeman's Barber's Shop* that slaves do not
suffer when separated from their families because they are not like their
masters, and "man [*sic*] differs from black creatures radically."[143]

As with the claims that slaves did not run away, anti-*Tom* novels touched
upon a significant contemporary anxiety in their assertion that racial difference was a vast and unbridgeable gulf and that it was obvious who was a slave
and who was not. It could easily be argued that the popularity of blackface
minstrelsy itself was in some part a manifestation of a concern with the nature and distinctiveness of race. On the one hand, white performers could
take on a kind of "blackness" for theatrical purposes, rendering racial lines
permeable. On the other hand, the assumption of the burnt cork mask reinforced the immutability of the actor's whiteness beneath: blackface would
always wash off.

An anecdote incorporated into the publicity material of Sam Sanford's Philadelphia troupe perfectly captures the contiguity of the basic minstrel joke with the issues at stake in the 1850s arguments about slavery and the Fugitive Slave Act. Advertising for the 1860–61 theatrical season, Sanford printed in his program an implausible tale he presented as fact. "The Wrong Negro" described his troupe's recent tour to Richmond, where the show was attended by local man Charles Loxley, who had recently lost a slave. During the performance Loxley was struck by Sanford's apparent resemblance to his runaway. When Loxley seized him from the stage, the showman played along and accompanied the Virginian to the alderman's office, still in full blackface and costume. Loxley made his solemn oath that Sanford was his slave and returned with his prize to his hotel, followed by an amused crowd. Sanford asked to wash and change, and in front of Loxley's eyes Sanford's "color, voice, gait and demeanor were all changed in a twinkle, and from an old greasy negro, he came out a finished gentleman, as everybody knows him to be." Loxley was reduced to a laughingstock, while news of these events drew flocks to Sanford's shows, and he returned to Philadelphia "satisfied with his experience in Virginia, and the peculiar institution of the sunny South."[144]

Sanford's story advertises both his show's authenticity and the delights of its falsity; ostensibly, it establishes the verisimilitude of his performance, but it simultaneously revels in its trickery and travesty. The ambiguity and the studied amorality of "The Wrong Negro," as well as the deft way in which it manages its contradictions, were all symptomatic of midcentury minstrel performance. Minstrelsy was precisely designed to raise the contentious and the difficult while muffling it in conspiratorial illusion. Loxley's response to Sanford's show was most ludicrous because he took it straight. What is extraordinary about "The Wrong Negro" is its apparent indifference to its implications for the institution of slavery: it treats this story of a failed recapture as though it has no special moral or political charge. "The Wrong Negro" offers no sympathy for the real escaped slave, but the structure of the narrative insists that we condemn Loxley's detention of another human being, since the suspense is created by the arrest of the "wrong" man. Meanwhile, it subjects the slave owner to humiliating mockery. But there is not the slightest hint that the injustice committed here might reflect one in Loxley's claim over the real fugitive, Josh. Sanford's escapade may illustrate the arbitrary horror of enslavement, may even suggest some deeply buried fear that a white skin provides no protection. It is certainly anxious to assert Sanford's true identity: "a finished gentleman, as everyone knows him to be." But it pointedly draws no

conclusions about slavery itself: the plight of the authentic slave is not allowed to enter into it. Instead, Sanford makes a profit ("those iron handcuffs
were to him bracelets of gold"), and he discovers pecuniary "reasons" to be
pleased both with Virginia and with the "peculiar institution" itself. Cheerfully denying the current political climate in 1860, Sanford's tale of slavery
demonstrates a wonderful North-South rapport, even though the slave owner
is discomfited and the Philadelphia showman makes a mint.

Most unexpectedly, too, Sanford's jokey narrative could also serve to reinforce the racial anxieties enshrined in Stowe's question about the fugitive
slave law: "[W]hen blue eyes and golden hair are advertised as properties of
negroes—what protection will there be for poor white people?"

A decade before Sanford published "The Wrong Negro," a documented
case of slave flight and recapture turned precisely on the possibility of misidentification it toyed with: what happens when a system of servitude determined by racial categorization finds itself unable to pin race down? In 1850 a
woman arrived in New Albany, Indiana, from Kentucky and settled there with
her daughter and grandson. All three appeared, and were assumed to be,
white. A few months later a man called Dennis Framell arrived in the town,
also from Kentucky, and obtained a warrant for their arrest as fugitive slaves.
The next day they were impounded and brought to court, where they claimed
that they had never been slaves, but under the terms of the Fugitive Slave
Act their testimony was not acceptable as evidence. The tribunal found for
Framell, and a federal marshal handed them over to him in Kentucky. The
capture and return of Framell's claimed slaves aroused significant public feeling in New Albany, perhaps in part because they had always been taken to be
white. This episode might thus have served to reinforce the antislavery point
that slaves were indistinguishable from Northern whites in their domestic aspirations, using their visual identity with the white residents of New Albany
to affirm a moral one too. However, subsequent events bore out Stowe's concern in *Key* that where race eludes certain classification, the threat of slavery
potentially reaches out to everyone.

The citizens of Caseyville, Kentucky, also believed that the family were
white: they formed a mob to rescue them from Framell, and a local court declared the family white and free. It was a Southern mob and a Southern judge,
in other words, that obstructed the prosecution of the Fugitive Slave Act. In
doing so, of course, they called it into question: if the Kentucky judge was
right and the disputed family was always free, then their case was a perfect
demonstration of the law's vulnerability to fraud. If this group of people could

have been saved by the right to testify, might not others be at risk? Doubts seem to have been raised because this family seemed white, but they were also surely applicable to other arrestees. Yet the incident did more than expose a sympathetic bias toward the paler victims of the Fugitive Slave Act. The confusion illustrated how unsatisfactory race could be in deciding who should have legal rights and who should not.

In New Albany unease persisted, even after the Caseyville judge's pronouncement, about whether the family really was black or white. Just to be sure, their supporters clubbed together $600 to "buy" them from Framell and make their liberty unquestionable, even if his legal claim to them was correct.[145]

Sanford's story was thus an eerie distortion of the plight of the New Albany family. In "The Wrong Negro" Sanford proves that he is not black in order to demonstrate that he cannot be a slave. There is no "proof" in New Albany nor even in Caseyville that the family is not black. There are merely society's consensus and the concurrence of the judge. But just as in Sanford's story, whether they are slaves is dependent on whether they are black. The outrage of the slaveholders of Caseyville over the perceived misidentification of Framell's captives works to uphold the Southerners' conception of racial lines, reiterating the connection between whiteness and freedom, but it is motivated by the urgency of Stowe's charge in *A Key to Uncle Tom's Cabin*. If there is no identifiable difference between slaves and freemen, the assurances of the anti-*Tom* novels that slaves are fortuitously adapted to their condition ring hollow. And the dispute itself threw into question the very distinction that the Caseyville court attempted to establish. Whiteness, which Sanford asserted would always announce itself in the end, was not always ineluctable: race might be impossible to call with certainty. The family at the center of this case demonstrated the uncomfortable truth that Sanford's Virginia anecdote both explores and attempts to suppress. It is also the thing the anti-*Tom* novels are so desperate to deny, so desperate that they conscript blackface voices to obliterate the testimony of thousands of acts of flight and hundreds of slave narratives. What the anti-*Tom* novels cannot face, and what Sanford sheers away from acknowledging, is that enslaved people are morally indistinguishable from the free.

MINSTRELSY, MELODRAMA, AND REFORM DRAMA: "UNCLE TOM" PLAYS IN NEW YORK

WEEP AT THE DEATH
OF EVA, SYMPATHIZE
WITH POOR UNCLE TOM,
LAUGH AT THE
VAGARIES OF TOPSY . . .

"Uncle Tom's Cabin,"
Playbill,
People's Hall,
Montpelier (1880s)

The inadequacy of copyright regulations came together with the theater's insatiable greed for plots in the mid-nineteenth century, so that plays were blithely lifted from novels, translated from the French, and traded across the Atlantic. Not surprisingly, *Uncle Tom's Cabin* was also quickly absorbed into the repertoire. At least nine versions of *Uncle Tom's Cabin* were produced in the American theater in the 1850s, in Baltimore, Boston, Troy, Philadelphia, New York, New Orleans, Chicago, and Detroit.[1] Thousands of people, many of whom had not read the book, would have attended a performance of *Uncle Tom's Cabin* in the 1850s. Even for those who had encountered the novel, the dramatizations functioned in part as mediating or exegetic texts, conditioning the way such audiences "read" the original, whether they did so afterward, remembered it in retrospect, or never did so at all. The wider assimilation of a sense of Stowe's novel was thus closely dependent on the process of dramatic adaptation, and the plays expanded and altered the meanings of the *Tom* phenomenon. Making *Uncle Tom* theatrical inevitably affected its politics and modified its position on slavery.

As we have seen, the more sentimental and straightforward minstrel adaptations of *Uncle Tom's Cabin* did not always differ significantly from those found in the conventional theater. In fact, for individual performers the line between the two frequently blurred as actors moved between minstrel halls and theaters and back again. Thus, T. D. Rice, the legendary creator of the blackface act "Jim Crow," played Uncle Tom at the Bowery Theatre in January 1854. Frank Brower of the Virginia Minstrels burlesqued *Uncle Tom* for Wood's Minstrels with his "Uncle Tom Jig" in the fall of 1853, but in May 1854 he took over T. D. Rice's role at the Bowery, while his fellow minstrel John Mulligan played Topsy. In September 1859 Brower was back in a minstrel version, appearing with Sam Sanford's troupe in a "Happy Uncle Tom Dance."[2] Eventually, the two *Uncle Tom* traditions coalesced: when in 1899 Frank Dumont suggested that the amateur minstrel close his show with an Uncle Tom, his "Illustrated Guide to create an 'Uncle Toms Cabin' scene" included Deacon Perry, a character from George Aiken's dramatization. Dumont's illustration also made twins of several characters, in imitation of the giant "double mammoth" touring theater productions of the late nineteenth century.[3]

For their part, minstrel elements invaded the theaters. The *Tom* plays turned the slave auction into a kind of minstrel olio, or variety act, as each "slave" was required to show off his musical and comic talents to buyers. One playbill explicitly called this part the "Grand Minstrel Scene."[4] Minstrel songs were also readily incorporated into the theatrical *Uncle Toms*. A Pittsburgh production in 1853 featured "Old Folks at Home" sung by Tom, "My Old Kentucky Home" by Topsy, and "Massa's in de Cold Ground" by a chorus.[5] George Aiken's homesick Tom sang "Old Folks at Home" on Legree's plantation, and "My Old Kentucky Home" was later added to this production; in G. W. Jamison's proslavery production the song was applied to fugitive slaves who found themselves cold and unloved in the North.[6] Stowe herself had Tom sing a slightly altered version in her 1856 dramatization, *The Christian Slave*.[7] Civil War *Uncle Toms* included "Old Black Joe," and "Dolcy Jones," "Nelly Bly," and "Ring de Banjo" also appeared on occasion.[8]

Blackface influenced dramatizations of *Uncle Tom's Cabin*, but the plays did not precisely reproduce either Stowe's adaptation of minstrelsy or the minstrel's reinvention of *Uncle Tom*. Minstrelsy was mixed with melodrama and "moral," or reform, drama in the theatrical *Uncle Toms*: these three generic traditions structured the reimagining of Stowe's novel for the stage. Their interplay is apparent in the two most documented plays (the ones for which we have scripts), written by George Aiken and H. J. Conway. Conway's was first played in November 1852 at the Boston Museum, Aiken's in the same month in Troy, New York.[9] They were later imported to New York City on the strength of long runs. Conway's ran for two months at Barnum's Museum at the end of 1853 and for a fortnight in an 1855 revival.[10] Aiken's triumph was even greater at A. H. Purdy's National Theatre, then known for its insalubrious location and sensational fare. His *Uncle Tom* drew record crowds for most of the period between July 1853 and May 1854.[11] Aiken's play resurfaced in the 1870s and was toured all over the United States by dozens of tent parties, for whom it was a staple until at least the end of the century. Conway's, too, was revived in the 1870s and was also performed as far afield as Australia, New Zealand, and South America in the 1850s.[12]

More important, in the two months when these two versions played simultaneously in New York they were advertised and reviewed as competitors and as taking diametrically opposed positions on slavery. P. T. Barnum's advertisement for the Conway play boasts of its racism—"it represents the Southern negro embracing all its abhorrent deformities, its cruelties, and barbarities"—and implicitly damns any sympathetic slave portraits in its competitors: "[I]t does not foolishly and unjustly elevate the negro above the white man in intellect or morals. . . . It exhibits a true picture of Negro life in the South, instead of absurdly representing the ignorant slave as possessed of all the polish of the drawing room, and the refinement of the educated whites."[13] The National Theatre also attacked its rival in advertisements and in new lines that referred to Barnum. It was in turn accused of immorality by the *Observer* newspaper and defended by the *Atlas*; the *Liberator* charged Barnum with omitting "all the strikes at the slave system, and . . . so [shaping] his drama as to make it quite an agreeable thing to be a slave."[14] Despite this apparent ideological contrast, William Lloyd Garrison preferred Conway's play, which he had seen in Boston, to Aiken's, and in comparison to some minstrel adaptations the differences were less pronounced than the dispute suggested.[15]

Contemporary commentators saw the *Tom* plays as extremely significant. They were fascinated by the dramas' popularity, seizing upon them as a chance to observe a mass public response to a text that not only was a notorious tearjerker but also had serious ideological implications. The theatrical production offered the possibility of participating, with a very large gathering, in a simultaneous encounter with *Uncle Tom's Cabin*. The auditorium in the 1850s was so lit that Uncle Tom's audience could watch each other as well as him, and spectators were able to observe and interact with their fellows as well as with the representation on the stage.[16] Stowe's appeal to private emotion and her construction of a domestic empathy could thus be transformed on the stage both into a public exhibition and into a spectacle of the play's effect upon hundreds of onlookers. This shared experience of *Uncle Tom's Cabin* fascinated reviewers. The *New York Herald* writer explained that "the effect of the piece on the audience was what most interested us, and we took a seat in a stage-box so as to witness the play of countenance of the crowd in pit and boxes."[17]

In a discussion of English melodrama in this period Elaine Hadley contrasts "sentimental literature's unitary readership of the literate middle class" with melodrama, which she argues "confronts an audience . . . that is disunited and suspicious."[18] Yet in the case of the *Uncle Tom* play, a piece of sentimental literature converted into melodrama, reports stressed that a spectrum of social groups shared both the experience and their emotions. In the novel's dialogues between Sam and Mrs. Shelby, Stowe had subversively linked characters from different social worlds. The spectators of the *Tom* plays also experienced a temporary sense of community, and reviewers were struck by the plays' power to elicit sympathy across social divides.

The *Troy Daily Times* recorded that the audiences for George Aiken's production in that town were "respectable" and comprised of "the best people."[19] The abolitionist Parker Pillsbury noted with delight that a Boston production drew wealthy patrons, "one of the largest and best looking audiences I ever saw in any theater. And five hundred people bought tickets . . . for *secured seats, at double price*."[20] An article in the *New York Daily Times,* "Uncle Tom among the Bowery Boys," focused on "a very attentive audience of ragged, dirty lads" at the other end of the social scale, "children often who have no home, who know nothing of the Church and the School," who watched Aiken's play at the National Theatre; the *New York Atlas,* too, drew attention to the occupants of the gallery and to their workingmen's attire—"a heroic class of people, many of them in red woollen shirts."[21] For the antislavery party this type of audience was especially interesting because, as the *Liberator* put it, "those ragged, coatless men and boys in the pit" are "the very *material* of which mobs are made."[22] Abolitionists themselves had been the targets of mob violence many times, but "[n]o mob would have dared to disturb the Abolition part[y] at the National Theatre," explained the *New York Tribune,* for it was itself "composed largely of the stuff which demagogues acting under oligarchs have used for the purpose of burning down halls."[23]

It was for this reason that the newspaper correspondents were interested in their responses. The *Herald*'s reporter noted that "tears were freely shed by the audience," including men, women, and children, and interpreted this sign of emotion, this "touch of nature [as] a true Abolitionist," assuming that the drama, "its scenes palpitating with verisimilitude," represented "the strongest form of Abolition-teaching."[24] The *New York Daily Times* recorded the reactions of the Bowery Boys almost to each scene and speech, approving of the moments at which their interest perked up, which demonstrated them to be friends to the slave—they were "wrought up to the highest pitch" when Eliza was in danger of recapture and produced "a grand cheer" when she escaped. Political radicals while they watched, the Bowery Boys applauded George's declaration of his right to freedom in an antislavery impulse that would previously have been anathema: "The caps wave, and the 'Hey' sounds with almost every sentence, at words which would be hissed down in most public meetings, and be coldly received in the churches—but which, somehow, seem to strike some strange chord in the dirty, ragged audience."[25] The *New York Tribune* declared that the Bowery's "B'hoys were on the side of the fugitives."[26]

These records of theatrical encounters may have been couched in terms of the slavery question and how *Uncle Tom*'s take on it was being received, but they were also symptoms of a wider phenomenon in the theater. In some ways it was actually less remarkable that the Bowery Boys were in the theater than that there were so many middle-class observers there with them. American melodrama was undergoing a shift in tone, and its audiences were changing accordingly.

In its original French and English forms, melodrama merely meant musical drama: it was defined by frequent songs and a musical accompaniment.[27] By the mid–nineteenth century it also encompassed spectacular scenic effects and far-off settings, excitingly complex plots, and stark moral contrasts in characterization. Unfathomably wicked villains plotted to dishonor virtuous young heroes and heroines. Earthquakes and avalanches, pirates and bandits contributed to the thrills. Exotic animals appeared; ships floated in huge tanks; cascades streamed on stage. Diorama backcloths made the scenery move; gaslight and gauze were combined for atmospheric effects. And in the final scenes wickedness was always thwarted, the villain was foiled, and goodness received its reward. In America Louisa Hamblin's *Nick of the Woods* (1838) typified the genre. As with countless of these plays, the plot was borrowed from elsewhere.[28] Set on the western frontier, the play featured bloodthirsty Indian raiders, blustering backwoodsmen, and a variety of kidnaps and ambushes for the heroic immigrants. In its most exciting scene a disguised "Indian-killer" made a rescue bid for the captured heroine "precipitated down the cataract in a canoe of fire."[29]

Melodrama in Europe in this period held a special appeal for working-class audiences. While the middle classes in London patronized a variety of theatrical entertainments, among the East End poor the only competition for melodrama was the pantomime at Christmas; in Michael Booth's words, "[M]elodrama . . . *was* the working-class theater."[30] For Frank Rahill it constituted "a kind of composite self-portrait" of "the uprooted and disinherited poor of the nineteenth-century city."[31] Despite this, melodrama was rarely a revolutionary form. Jeffrey Mason argues that melodrama's "substructure" was conservative, since it tended to individualize issues and reduce them to matters of private choice. Where suffering or a social problem could be blamed on the villainy of a single character, there was little room to denounce an oppressive class or institution.[32]

This individualism chimed with American melodrama's gentrifying drift toward sentimentality in the 1840s. Melodramatic theater increasingly adapted its tone to attract middle-class audiences in those years, almost exactly mirroring contemporary developments in minstrel song. At a moment when the middle classes themselves were expanding, middle-class behavior and taste were being codified, and increasing value was being placed on sentimental and domestic themes, museum lecture halls began to attract middle-class audiences to what was effectively theater.[33] They promised edification rather than titillation, family-oriented entertainment, and the matinee. Where the theater was rowdy and disreputable, serving alcohol and accommodating prostitution, the museum would be improving. The "moral drama," which critic Bruce McConachie calls a "minor revolution in theater," complemented this shift in audience culture, using the stage to advocate moral reform. The melodramatic patterns of virtue and villainy were used to dramatize the issues championed by benevolent movements, and spectatorial pleasure was tempered with moral evangelism, enabling a pious and decorous enjoyment of the dramatic. In earlier melodrama stark morality and sensational effects had been designed to elicit specific and clearly defined audience responses. In this respect melodrama resembled the sentimental novel and contrasted with minstrelsy, which licensed a variety of audience interpretations and identifications. The new developments in this period capitalized on melodrama's tight control over audience reactions and, like the sentimental novel, used it didactically. This technique would prove especially useful in the staging of *Uncle Tom's Cabin*.

Moral drama also made a special appeal to women. Like sentimental literature, it was very closely aligned with the midcentury obsessions (the family, domesticity), which reflected most pointedly on women's roles and duties, but women's parts were more modest in these plays than in the novels. William Henry Smith's 1844 temperance play *The Drunkard* has a domestic setting, and its whole moral is designed to reinforce the sentimental cult of the family. The musical accompaniment to the final tableau is "Home, Sweet Home."[34] Nevertheless, the suffering wife, Mary Middleton, is relatively minor: she quietly endures, while her eponymous husband is rescued by a male philanthropist.

All this would suggest an identity, or at least a similarity, between the readers of *Uncle Tom's Cabin* and the enthusiasts of moral drama. As *Uncle Tom's Cabin* couched the slavery question in this theater's preferred terms (moral absolutes, idealized homes, and an appeal to the "feeling" of individual readers), it was perfectly adapted for this moment in theatrical history, so much so that it is sometimes seen to have provoked it. At least one critic has read the enthusiastic adoption of Stowe's story for this new cultural niche as causal.[35] As late as the 1880s another claimed that *Uncle Tom's Cabin* was the only play he was allowed to watch as a boy: "'The School for Scandal,' no.

'Romeo and Juliet,' no. A minstrel show, oh, horrors! But 'Uncle Tom's Cabin' was something altogether different. That was a moral lesson."[36]

Yet although Stowe herself distrusted the theater at the time when stage managers were rushing to dramatize her novel, as McConachie observes, her attitude was already old-fashioned.[37] And all of the stage versions of the novel were written for audiences significantly more diverse than Stowe's original market, the subscribers who first read her novel as a serial in the *National Era*. Even the scripts produced for museum theaters would have presumed audiences more male, working class, and antiabolition than Stowe's likely readers.[38] This was how middle-class commentators found themselves sharing theatrical experiences with Bowery Boys.

The adaptations of *Uncle Tom's Cabin* struggled to rework Stowe's story in the terms of three competing and partly overlapping theatrical forms. Melodramatic conventions demanded an emphasis on scenery and spectacle, while stage traditions shaped characterization, language, and gesture. Moral drama was created by transfiguring the novel's sentimental femininity into a theatrical picture of saintliness, with celestial imagery, blinding white lighting, and a soundtrack of heavenly choirs. And the pleasures of minstrelsy were invoked in song-and-dance scenes and comic interludes, sometimes in straightforward imitation of the minstrel stage, sometimes borrowing from the novel's blackface variations, and occasionally finding yet more uses for its ambiguities. The diversity these productions achieved suggest that even if there was an inherent class politics in melodrama, it did not translate into a single or predetermined position on slavery.

Aiken's and Conway's plays have both been judged to have fallen short of Stowe's political radicalism. McConachie notes that both water down the novel's attacks on capitalism and avoid Stowe's endorsement of a feminine ethos.[39] Conway's has been characterized as Compromise dramatized, a desperate attempt to appeal to the majority on both sides.[40]

Yet both scripts retained something of Stowe's antislavery tone. Aiken's Eva tells her father that she would rather be in heaven because "I feel sad for our poor people. . . . I wish, papa, they were all *free!*" (Aiken, *UTC*, 3.2). An exchange between Tom and St. Clare counters the argument put forward in the proslavery minstrel shows, that slaves were materially better off than freemen:

> ST. CLARE: Why, Tom, you couldn't possibly have earned, by your work, such clothes and such living as I have given you.

TOM: I know all that, Mas'r St. Clare—mas'r's been too good; but I'd rather have poor clothes, poor house, poor everything, and have 'em *mine*, than have the best, if they belonged to someone else. (Aiken, *UTC*, 4.2)

Aiken also refers to the racial inequalities enshrined in slave law: Cassy tells Tom on Legree's plantation that there is "not a white person here who could testify, if you were burned alive. There's no law here that can do you, or any of us, the least good" (Aiken, *UTC*, 6.1). Conway's George Harris matches such moments with a speech that not only declares his own rights—"why am I not a man, as much as anybody?"—but also indicts the slave system for cruelty: "I had a father, one of your gentlemen—who didn't think enough of me to keep me from being sold with his dogs and horses. I saw my mother put up at Sheriff's Sale, with her seven children. They were sold before her eyes, one by one, all to different masters, and I was the youngest. She came and kneeled down before my master and begged him to buy her with me—he kicked her away with his heavy boot" (Conway, *UTC*, 1.5).

However, such moments of genuine protest were mitigated in the plays by the demands of melodrama. At the end of the novel, Legree is unrepentant and unpunishable (again because there have been no white witnesses), and George Shelby cannot help his remaining slaves, who "[look] dejected, and [walk] off in silence" (*UTC*, 365). But melodramatic villains were customarily punished, and poetic justice kills off the Legrees of both Aiken and Conway, which, as critics have suggested, potentially dulls the antislavery outrage of the plays. If the problem is solved with Legree's death, then there is no larger social question to worry about. Worse, in Conway Legree is made responsible for everything—he kidnaps Eliza from Canada, obtains Tom by fraud, and is driven to ill-treat him by a personal feud with St. Clare. His is what David Grimstead calls "mere personal villainy" and not, as in Stowe, the inevitable symptom of a vicious institution.[41]

Though this evidence from the scripts is suggestive, we must, of course, also allow for possible differences in the way the plays were performed at different theaters: the 1876 Conway script, for instance, has extensive revisions in a second hand that suggest that in at least one performance a number of speeches and even scenes were cut. Many of these episodes have a direct bearing on the slavery question, such as the persecution of the slaves in the warehouse, Legree's declaration of his intention to be cruel to Tom, an exchange between two buyers on the undesirability of St. Clare's former slaves ("independent as the devil"), and a discussion of slave law (Conway, *UTC*, 5.1, 5.3, 6.1).

It is also possible that the moral emphases of the scripts helped distract audiences from their politics. In making *Uncle Tom* into moral drama, Aiken and Conway were linking it with other plays that espoused causes dear to the reform movements of the 1830s and 1840s, such as the crusades against alcohol and seduction. In their hands Stowe's tale became what Rosemarie Bank calls a "regulating text."[42] Both writers paid lip service to the temperance tradition: a number of the Aiken *Uncle Tom's Cabin* cast had featured in the first production of *The Drunkard*, and his Tom gives St. Clare a lecture on alcohol (Aiken, *UTC*, 3.1). The program description of the death of Conway's St. Clare suggests stock elements of the "drunkard drama": "Grief and desolation. Agony of the wife and child. . . . Apotheosies of his mother."[43] Pointedly linking this theme with slavery, Conway's slave buyers frequent the bar during the auction scene (Conway, *UTC*, 5.3).

The plays also used religious exhortation to maintain the tone of moral uplift. In Aiken's first scene George Harris's misery, induced by a cruel master, is also a spiritual crisis. Eliza counsels that "heaven . . . will deliver you"; he retorts that "I can't trust in heaven," and she adjures that "we must all have faith" (Aiken, *UTC*, 1.1). This almost becomes a refrain—Tom advises his fellows to "trust in the Lord—He is our best friend,—our only comforter!" For his own part, Tom believes that "Him that saved Daniel in the den of lions . . . He's alive yet! and I've faith to believe He can deliver me!" (Aiken, *UTC*, 1.3). Later he almost converts St. Clare, urging him to "look up—up where our dear Miss Eva is." St. Clare responds, "That faithful fellow's words have excited a train of thoughts that almost bear me, on the strong tide of faith and feeling, to the gates of that heaven I so vividly conceive" (Aiken, *UTC*, 4.2). Several of the plays' tableaux have religious implications: Conway's Legree drops dead at the sight of a spiritual allegory (Cassy and Eliza's staging of Legree's mother's ghost pointing to heaven [Conway, *UTC*, 6.3]), and in the "picture" at the end of Aiken's act 2 George and Eliza "kneel in an attitude of thanksgiving" (Aiken, *UTC*, 2.6). Attending these plays must have come close to a religious experience in itself: McConachie points out that the succession of emotional responses they solicited—weeping, applauding, terror—would have replicated the experience of a revival meeting.[44] These elements helped ensure that Aiken's play brought in new bourgeois, "respectable" audiences to the National Theatre. The manager, Purdy, encouraged this new clientele with the introduction of matinees, the banishment of "females of an improper character," and the announcement of "the manager's intention to make this a strictly moral theatre."[45]

In Aiken, one of the main beneficiaries of this spiritual emphasis was Little
Eva. Distilling the novel's many virtuous characters (Mrs. Shelby, Mrs. Bird,
Rachel Halliday, and others in the Quaker settlement), the script intensifies
Tom's and Eva's roles and charges the slave and the sick child with a super-
human religiosity. In the process the play creates a new element in moral
drama. While Legree's persecution of Tom translates easily into the tradition
of the stage villain, it is difficult to fit Eva's death with that pattern, since it
involves no human agency. Eva's expiry made for a theatrical sensation and
would become one of the most distinctive contributions to the popular conception of *Uncle Tom*.

It was thus in rendering sanctity into spectacle that the plays partly staked
their claim to the "moral." They belonged to this branch of the drama not
because they boldly denounced a specific vice or even because they showed
virtue tempted but because they represented goodness transcendent. The
plays' object became the staging of Tom's and Eva's luminous piety, and it was
virtue itself that they made spectacular.

Aiken's famous closing scene encapsulated the effect for which this drama
strove: "*Gorgeous clouds, tinted with sunlight. Eva, robed in white, is discovered on the back of a milk-white dove, with expanded wings, as if just soaring
upward. Her hands are extended in benediction over St. Clare and Uncle Tom,
who are kneeling and gazing up to her. Impressive music.—Slow curtain*"
(Aiken, *UTC*, 6.6). This "picture" effectively duplicated all three deaths in the
text. Eva had already expired in act 3 with a "feeble smile" and the exclamation "Oh! love! joy! peace!" (Aiken, *UTC*, 3.4); St. Clare at the end of act 4
died energetically, exclaiming, "At last! at last! Eva, I come!" (Aiken, *UTC*,
4.5); and act 6, scene 5 closed with special effects in honor of Tom's demise:
"*Solemn music.—George covers Uncle Tom with his cloak, and kneels over him.
Clouds work on and conceal them, and then work off*" (Aiken, *UTC*, 6.5). Although in the 1853 performances Eva did not die, the 1876 version of Conway imported that scene from Aiken, and a note on the script calls for "white
fire" to light a similarly pious "tableau of Eva in Heaven" (Conway, *UTC*, 4.5).
That play also featured a vision of St. Clare's deceased mother in his deathbed
"picture."[46]

Eva's death, which Stowe both idealized and charged with tearful power,
is a perfect example of what Ann Douglas calls the "consolation literature" of
the mid–nineteenth century. Douglas sees an alliance of clerical and feminine
forces behind the period's "domestication of death," the same constituency
with which she and many critics associate Stowe.[47] Conway and Aiken were

writing in the first instance for similar audiences, and their stagings of Eva in heavenly glory were another manifestation of the fascination in novels and tracts of the period with the celestial.

H. E. Stevens's production for the Bowery in January 1854 shows how the taste for moral theater was proliferating in the early 1850s and how the bourgeois appeal of the moral drama was also beginning to transfer to the regular stage. This production collected crowds around its themed ticket office, which was decorated to look like a slave cabin.[48] Whereas the National's *Uncle Tom* showed that museums' moral pieces could be profitably transported to the theater, the Bowery proved that theaters could devise their own reform dramas. Although more accustomed to providing the thrills of spectacular melodrama, the Bowery followed the museum plays in enacting solemnity. The Bowery's usual audiences were very unlike the bourgeois families and clerical flocks who would have recognized Eva's apotheosis from the imagery of consolation literature, but Stevens's adaptation for the theater aspired to the same tone. In its "Grand Fourth Act Finale" Eva's deathbed is "beheld with Deep Sympathy[,] and Breathless Silence Reigns, as the sacred vocal choir is accompanied by the Deep Organ's Peal."[49] Picked out in its advertising as the Bowery's great achievement in this production, the reverent atmosphere was the quality Stevens was attempting to absorb from the museum *Uncle Toms*. The dramatic capital Aiken and Conway made of Eva's death epitomized the churchy transformation of melodrama: what Stevens had borrowed and was selling to the habitués of the Bowery was funereal theater.

The *Daily Times*'s review of Aiken's play directly speculated on its value as missionary work, commenting on its effect on the "ragged" boys in the audience who had had the benefit of neither church nor school. Boys who "could not be got to listen to a sermon. They would not be moved by it if they did" have heard, in *Uncle Tom's Cabin*, "grand religious sentiments and the truest feelings of humanity."[50] The moment of shared feeling is transmuted into evidence of *Uncle Tom's* miraculous powers of spiritual enlightenment.

Despite their "moral" emphasis, Aiken and Conway were not averse to incorporating some of the excitements that characterized spectacular melodrama. Charles Western Taylor's production for Purdy's National Theatre, which lasted for only around a dozen performances in August and September 1852, suggests the similarities.[51] Taylor's was a typical sensational melodrama, an afterpiece meant to fill a space in a program rather than to cause controversy. It played on different nights alongside a nautical drama, a tightrope walker, and a blackface burlesque of Verdi's opera *Otello*. Only loosely derived from Stowe's text, Taylor's piece renamed characters and used Tom in just two scenes, remaining true to the melodramatic formula. The slave dealers sound like classic stage villains, agents of an implacable and reasonless malice. A playbill's summary of act 1 suggests their activities: "Slave Dealers on Hand; . . . the Mother's Appeal; Capture of Morna; . . . Midnight Escape." As well as the virtuous heroine, her stout protector, and the encroaching villains, Taylor's *Uncle Tom* provided the spectacle and suspense to which the audiences of the National were accustomed. The second act offered "Excitement . . . Dark Threatenings . . . Snow Storm; Flight . . . Pursuit . . . Desperate Resolve and Escape . . . Mountain Torrent and Ravine . . . Maniac's Protection; Desperate Encounter . . . Fall . . . Meeting . . . Escape."[52]

In the novel most of the basis for this action is found in two chapters, "The Mother's Struggle" and "The Freeman's Defence," but Taylor works it up into fifteen scenes involving at least five pieces of impressive scenery: the frozen Ohio river with floating ice, the "mountain torrent and ravine," the cave, the bridge, and the "mountain rocks." For good measure he creates a character, Crazy Mag, who presumably offered scope for interesting behavior. The fight scenes were energetic too, for Wilmot (Taylor's version of George Harris) "shoots down [their] pursuers in real Christian style, as fast as they come."[53] Slavery was rendered as stylized suffering, with exaggerated violence and extreme imagery. According to the *Herald*, "The negro traders, with their long whips, cut and slash their poor slaves about the stage for mere pastime, and a gang of poor wretches, handcuffed to a chain . . . are thrashed like cattle to quicken their pace. Uncle Tom is scourged by the trader."[54]

The props in this description are an aestheticized paraphernalia of cruelty (long whips, cuffs, and chains), and the play intensifies the horrific aspects of the original, with the frequency of assaults upon Uncle Tom very much exceeding that in the book. This was a year before Aiken's transfer to the National, when sensation was still the theater's stock-in-trade, and its *Uncle Tom* offered a typical dose. As the advertisement for the play indicated, the scenery was more prominent than its depiction of slavery. Nevertheless, as with the reviews of Aiken and Conway, the *New York Herald* leaped to political conclusions, expressing outrage in a fiercely antiabolition review even at the decision to stage the book. The *Herald*'s insistence on reading Taylor's production, so clearly designed without pretensions to political gravity, as an intervention in the slavery question suggests once again that *Uncle Tom's Cabin* escaped the intentions of its adaptors. Just as they sought to deploy

Stowe's text for their own purposes, so their own work was in turn read in unexpected ways.

As critics have observed, the escapes of Eliza, George, and Harry fitted very easily into the patterns of sensational melodrama.[55] Not surprisingly, then, Taylor made a feature of his "Floating Ice," the Bowery production had a similar scene, and Eliza's flight across the frozen Ohio was regarded as a highlight of Aiken's play, especially when later productions incorporated bloodhounds (Aiken, *UTC*, 1.6).[56] Conway's had a cataract instead, like that in *Nick of the Woods* (Conway, *UTC*, 1.7).[57] His playbill even made special mention of the scene painter. Lighting effects were similarly intense. Legree's terrified conscience is suggested by his being "suddenly . . . illuminated with white fire" (Conway, *UTC*, 6.3).[58]

Aiken, Conway, and Stevens also theatricalized other aspects of Stowe's text. Cassy's appearance in the novel, her wild outbursts and elliptical references to sexual exploitation, could easily translate into a traditional stage confrontation between feminine innocence and masculine villainy. Conway's melodramatic idiom paints this relationship starkly: "the monster who now owns you, and who will sacrifice you to his brutal lust." His sensational vocabulary is both overdetermined and economical, as very short speeches set up the moral contrast between Legree and his victims (Conway, *UTC*, 5.2). This typically melodramatic combination of high emotion and brief dialogue echoed extremes on the stage of sadistic power and absolute vulnerability. When Cassy falls on her knees to beg for Tom's life Legree "turns[,] looks at her—folds his arms and laughs" (Conway, *UTC*, 6.3).

Staginess was not confined to moments of heightened terror in these plays. Comic roles in melodrama, or even the parts of the heroes' decent allies, were often marked by linguistic peculiarities. In *The Drunkard* the spinster is prone to malapropism, and other characters in that play speak theatrical "Yankee." In *Nick of the Woods* the "ring-tailed squealer" Ralph Stackpole communicates in an extravagant mixture of earthy neologism and frontier boast: "Arn't I the crittur to shake old Salt by the forepaw? Arn't I the leaping trout of the waters? . . . If I can't, may I be tee-to-taciously explunctified!"[59] In Aiken's script Phineas Fletcher's trademark "teetotally" echoes one of Stackpole's coinages in this speech (Aiken, *UTC*, 1.4). Such verbal tics or tags are allocated to a number of characters in both Aiken and Conway. Aiken's Aunt Ophelia and Conway's Aunty Vermont share a disapproving "shiftless!" Conway's Sam makes "Lor knows!" his constant refrain, and Drover John utters an involuntary "ha!" whenever he finds slavery "sticks in his throat." Aiken's Topsy not only habitually proclaims her own wickedness but makes it the subject of her theme song.[60]

The emphasis on dramatic scenery, the melodramatic vocabulary and gestures, even the taglines were not entirely untrue to the novel. Legree's physical exultation over Cassy on the stage, for instance, is an effective shorthand for the relationships sketched out at more length by Stowe, while Ophelia's "shiftless" and Sam's "Lor knows" also appear in the book. Comic and melodramatic effects derive easily from Stowe's narrative, which at times is itself not far removed from the relevant stage genres.

These playwrights also seem to have felt a structural necessity for another character type, the "cute" Yankee abroad in the South. All invented a version of the Yankee, and Conway used him as a vehicle for a mixture of sectional pride and racial prejudice similar to that which Stowe awards to Aunt Ophelia. The Bowery's Everlasting Perseverance Peabody, Conway's Penetrate Partyside, and Aiken's Gumption Cute were also paired with Miss Ophelia, embroiling her in absurd courtships. Cute is an unsympathetic fraud who ridicules Topsy and woos Ophelia for her money, while Penetrate is a focus both for his play's rigid delineation of gender roles and for anxieties about its stance on slavery.

The plays made alterations not only to *Uncle Tom*'s take on slavery but also to its position on women. They retained few traces of the book's loudest counterpoint to the slavery theme, the promotion and also secret mockery of a sentimental ideal of femininity. The novel linked its critique of slavery both to glorified pictures of womanhood (in Mrs. Shelby, Bird, and Halliday) and to a sly rebellion against it (in Topsy's interactions with Ophelia). The plays offered some examples of female characters exerting moral influence. In the Conway script Mrs. Shelby is mentioned in act 3 working with Chloe to free Tom in a demonstration of solidarity and active concern quite in keeping with their originals in the novel. Perhaps surprisingly, Chloe, a relatively minor character in the novel, was not cut from any of these plays, even starring in a deathbed tableau in the Bowery version. However, for the most part, as McConachie has observed, the aspect of *Uncle Tom's Cabin* that has appealed most to twentieth-century feminists is missing from Aiken and Conway.[61] Women's roles in many reform dramas were confined to the supporting variety: in the process of dramatizing *Uncle Tom's Cabin* many of the more powerful female characters were watered down or even dropped. There are no scenes in Aiken, Conway, or Stevens where Eliza warns Tom or where Mrs.

Shelby and Mrs. Bird remonstrate with misguided husbands. In minstrelsy, of course, female roles were even more limited, and it was traditional for women to be played by men. Moral dramas may have put up a better show in this respect than the minstrels' rival *Toms*, but both forms diminished the impact of the women Stowe wrote.

In keeping with the downgrading of women characters in the stage plays, Miss Ophelia became more ridiculous, especially in Aiken and Conway. Stowe's flawed but golden-hearted character was reduced on the stage to a comic figure, recognizable as the stock spinster of melodrama. Conway's Aunty Vermont, for instance, marries his invention, Penetrate Partyside, and provokes a series of jokes about gender confusion that work to register women as laughable. In one scene Penetrate blunders into Vermont's steamboat cabin by accident and inadvertently arrays himself in her cap and nightgown before being discovered sprawled over the spinster's bonnet case (Conway, *UTC*, 2.3). This ridicule of the feminine contradicts the spirit of Stowe's novel, and Conway is even further from it in the slave auction episode, which is torn between unease about slavery's reduction of humanity to livestock and misogynist alarm. Aunt Vermont accompanies Penetrate to the market, hoping to save Tom. The other participants stare, and Penetrate's explanation demonstrates the transgressive nature of her presence: "I guess you're suthin' of a show here; women don't come here without they come to be sold ginerally, but . . . you come to do a woman's duty" (Conway, *UTC*, 5.3).

Penetrate's observation that women only come to the slave marts to be sold has a shock value equivalent to Stowe's portrait of a young girl being marketed as a concubine. But Conway turns this episode into a running joke. Haley threatens to add "and lady!" every time he calls on the assembled "gentlemen"; Penetrate protests. This burlesque of "a woman's duty" to save slaves is absolutely antithetical to Stowe's mission, implicitly directing women away from the slavery debate. It also lessens the impact of Conway's scene.

The comic business at the slave market is the accompaniment to Legree's conspiracy to acquire Tom by fixing the auction and his promise to exact a fearsome revenge for earlier frustrations (Conway, *UTC*, 5.3). One of Aiken's reviews had specially picked out the power of the slave market on the stage ("To see an apparently real slave mart . . . is equally a dramatic and historic novelty in this city"),[62] but in Conway the device's potential for indicting the whole slave system is undermined by these jokes and by attributing its worst aspects to Legree's melodramatic scheming.

The ambivalence about attacking slavery manifested in this scene is a symptom of the much larger struggle Conway's play conducts with its own radical implications. Conway's script is not only reluctant to sympathize too much with women but is also very conflicted about slaves. Just as these productions to some degree played down the antislavery implications of their source by making Eva's apotheosis stand in for the "moral" of the drama, so they counterweighted their politics with comedy in the slave scenes and unflattering racial characterization. This may explain the reviews of Conway's production that interpreted it as an outright apology for slavery.

In fact, Conway's play seems more muddled in its politics than calculating. Penetrate is constantly the butt of jokes, yet he is also the conduit of the play's antislavery sympathy. The book he is writing on the South is the excuse for a number of satiric observations on slavery, but their bite is undercut by his blundering. His notebook jottings on a slave coffle reflect like a good Garrisonian on the ironies of American ideology: they are chained in "the home of the free and the land of the brave" (Conway, *UTC*, 2.2). When he overhears two slave dealers discussing their merchandise, his long-drawn-out failure to guess their subject, thinking that they must be talking of cotton, then machines, then cattle, then pigs, reflects the inhumanity of their conversation. He also turns the traders' talk of "hogs" and animals back on them when he writes, "Nigger babby ten months old, hefting thirty five pounds—sold on the waters of the wide and free Mississippi for fortyfive dollars—by one cussed hog and bought by another darned brute" (Conway, *UTC*, 2.2). Yet despite the strong terms of this condemnation, it is embedded in a comic scene. The scandal of the baby being itemized for sale is counterpointed with the comedy of Penetrate's interjections, as he assumes the discussion of the baby's weight is about that of a pig:

> HALEY: How much? Why may be 35 pounds or more.
> PENETRATE: Thirty five pounds! Why didn't I hear you say he was ten months old?
> HALEY: So he is!
> PENETRATE: Oh! hogs lard and sassages! Ten months old and weighs only thirty five pounds, the runt of the litter, and you refuse ten dollars for him? (Conway, *UTC*, 2.2)

That this is intended to be funny makes the episode's tone uncertain; Penetrate's misapprehension blunts the impact of his strike against slavery. Comparing it with Stowe's use of comic scenes for serious purposes is instructive. Her novel offered the possibility of readerly alliance with put-upon slave characters like Sam and Topsy, whereas in Conway protest and the ludicrous are juxtaposed without irony and with a suddenness that jars. Stowe successfully disguised her appeal to sympathy; Conway's mechanism detracts from his.

Stowe herself strove not to antagonize Southerners, moderating any apparent critique by making Legree a Northerner, in showing Ophelia's racial prejudice, and in carefully evenhanded remarks like "[s]outh as well as north, there are women who have an extraordinary talent for command, and tact in educating" (*UTC*, 178). Conway labored even more obviously to paint the South, slavery aside, in a good light. Initially, Penetrate is shocked that St. Clare is willing to buy a slave, even if it is to ensure that Tom will have a decent life. St. Clare's defense of his behavior "throws new light on the matter," and Penetrate grows to admire his hosts: "You Southerners are warm hearted and generous, and would fight to your knees in blood for your own liberty" (Conway, *UTC*, 3.2). As in the novel, St. Clare compares slavery with conditions for the poor in Europe and the North, and Penetrate's studies of slave law lead him to a grudging respect for slave-owning paternalism (Conway, *UTC*, 2.3, 6.1). By the end of the play Penetrate is participating in the slave system himself by attempting to pay for Tom's freedom. Like many proslavery critiques of Stowe's novel, Conway was emphatically rejecting the abolitionist purism manifested in the Garrisonian motto "no union with slaveholders."

Conway also avoids Stowe's outright condemnation of the slave-owning classes. His Shelby goes out of his way to say good-bye to Tom, who is comforted by it: "I have seen him—and I begin to feel reconciled to the Lord's will now" (Conway, *UTC*, 1.3); whereas Stowe's Shelby shirks the leave-taking out of guilt and embarrassment: "[T]hat he might not witness the unpleasant scenes . . . he had gone on a short business tour up the country, hoping that all would be over before he returned" (*UTC*, 85). Instead, Conway is harsher on his black characters. True, Topsy's history is explicitly related to the miserable treatment of children under the yoke when she is described as a "specimen of neglected uneducated black humanity" (Conway, *UTC*, dramatis personae). But there is a whole series of hints that dishonesty and disloyalty are endemic among the black characters. Sam betrays Eliza by bringing her handkerchief to Haley and his bloodhounds, in a reversal of the mischievous support he shows her in the novel (Conway, *UTC*, 1.5). Topsy in the play is not light-fingered because of her abused childhood but because she has learned such tricks from St. Clare's pampered valet (Conway, *UTC*, 3.1). And Adolph's freedom with his master's belongings in the novel has escalated in the play into a full-scale philosophy of theft. St. Clare explains: "Adolph being my property, considers himself part and parcel of myself: and uses my other property as his own occasionally" (Conway, *UTC*, 3.1). Penetrate's response to this speech, although in the vein of his other comparisons of North and South, recasts Adolph's behavior as criminal: "Guess if a white man was to do it North, he'd be fitted with a full suit at the state[']s expense, and provided with lodgings besides in the stone jug" (Conway, *UTC*, 3.1). The implication here that Adolph ought to be locked up could be a disparagement of Southern justice, or it could be an aspersion on Adolph's race. It is also symptomatic of a strong reluctance in Conway's play to cast slave characters as the blameless victims of an inhuman system. Topsy's inability to relate the salient details of her history is transformed from the political indictment it represents in Stowe into a disturbing echo of the racist argument for slavery, as Penetrate presumes she is stupid: "Wall since I've been here, I've seen two distinct specimens of the nigger creation generally—one altered externally into a full blown puppy—and the other ain't equal intellectually to a half grown squash!" (Conway, *UTC*, 3.1).

The racial politics of such scenes was derived from blackface. In commissioning the script, Moses Kimball had asked Conway to blend "the grave and the gay."[63] Some of the "gay" material was supplied by minstrelsy, which was incorporated into all the *Tom* plays, confirming the 1850s cultural equation that put blackface into any Southern setting with a number of black characters. Yet the legends that accumulated around Aiken's play explicitly distinguished it from minstrelsy. G. C. Germon refused to take the role of Tom at first because he was a "straight actor," and a "Jim Crow darkey" was beneath him. One review similarly suggested that audiences prepared to laugh when they saw Uncle Tom because his accent "in the theater, is associated always with the comic." Yet his opening words were "so earnest that the first laugh . . . died away into deep stillness."[64]

Such audience expectations were not always disappointed, however. Taylor's production made the conjunction of *Uncle Tom* and minstrelsy seem automatic, since it opened with a blackface spectacle, a "Negro celebration," that included a chorus of "Nigga in de Cornfield" and a "Kentucky Breakdown Dance." There were other song-and-dance acts between dramatic cliffhangers: "Come Then to the Feast" and "We Darkies Hoe de Corn."[65] Taylor was drawing on the stage's endowment of black music and dance with a theatrical value that could be marshaled in his production both as an attraction in itself and as a shorthand for the South.

Aiken's play hints at some ambivalence about minstrelsy. After Topsy is

converted she stops dancing breakdowns, suggesting that such activity is in-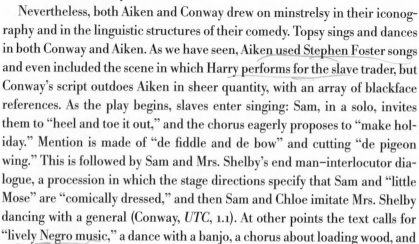
compatible with the godliness promoted by the text (Aiken, *UTC*, 5.4). Sambo
and Quimbo sing and dance to keep Legree's conscience at bay, which associates entertainment not only with his sin but also with his cruelty as a slaveholder (Aiken, *UTC*, 6.3). Conway's letter to Kimball suggests a different
problem—that Stowe's adaptation of blackface elements are too unconven-
tional to transfer easily back to the stage: "We must depend for our comic parts
on Topsy (hard thing to do as a female negro)."[66] As Lott points out, Conway's
Topsy "was a departure from the minstrel show's typical female types," whose
attributes were usually sexual.[67]

Nevertheless, both Aiken and Conway drew on minstrelsy in their iconography and in the linguistic structures of their comedy. Topsy sings and dances
in both Conway and Aiken. As we have seen, Aiken used Stephen Foster songs
and even included the scene in which Harry performs for the slave trader, but
Conway's script outdoes Aiken in sheer quantity, with an array of blackface
references. As the play begins, slaves enter singing: Sam, in a solo, invites
them to "heel and toe it out," and the chorus eagerly proposes to "make holiday." Mention is made of "de fiddle and de bow" and cutting "de pigeon
wing." This is followed by Sam and Mrs. Shelby's end man—interlocutor dialogue, a procession in which the stage directions specify that Sam and "little
Mose" are "comically dressed," and then Sam and Chloe imitate Mrs. Shelby
dancing with a general (Conway, *UTC*, 1.1). At other points the text calls for
"lively Negro music," a dance with a banjo, a chorus about loading wood, and
dancing in the slave warehouse (Conway, *UTC*, 1.1, 2.3, 5.1).

Much of the dancing and joking in these scenes represented the rowdier
end of the minstrel spectrum. Conway's Penetrate sums up the entertainment
provided by these derivations of blackface, a spectacle of black Southernness
designed to amaze the Northerner, when a look off stage causes him to ex-
claim to St. Clare: "Squire, the niggers outside act ridiculous! [T]hey cut up
all manner of shines—laughing—hollering, and dancing" (Conway, *UTC*, 3.1).
Penetrate's rendering of the play's black characters as ludicrous mirrors minstrelsy's equation of blackness with noisiness, physicality, and music. In the
intensity of his response, however, he also reflects the unspoken identifications with such qualities that caused minstrel audiences to be so drawn to
"shines" on the stage. The stage directions instruct him to be "very loud and
excited, imitating dancers." This makes him both the ideal minstrel audience
and a reproduction of blackface itself: an excited, imitative, but also demeaning response to black culture. Like much blackface performance, Pen-

etrate espouses the ridiculous as he attempts to denounce it, and it was the same process that these plays borrowed from the minstrel show, reducing blackface to its simplest possible function: producing a theatricalized version of black bodies and black culture.

Such effects seem crude in comparison to Stowe's exploitation of black-face. At points Aiken and Conway even unravel the webs of sympathy created in the book's end man–interlocutor scenes. Conway, for instance, excises all the irony and reversibility from Sam's dialogue with Mrs. Shelby. His version occurs shortly after the opening, before there is a whisper of a threat to any of the slaves. So Sam's cheek is not, as in the novel, delaying the slave trader, and Mrs. Shelby's reprimands are real and not a fig leaf for her delight that he has aided Eliza's escape (Conway, *UTC*, 1.4, 1.1). There is no conspiracy in Conway, as there is in Stowe, between the mistress and the slave, and the theater audience is not secretly invited to side with Sam, as the novel's readers are. Stowe's sophisticated play with blackface sympathy is reduced in Conway's version to a representation of black incompetence. While Stowe's narrative encourages the reader to identify with Sam's incorrigible profanity and against genteel manners, Conway's repositioning of the scene renders such spectatorial empathy unlikely.

Aiken rearranges the original even more drastically to give white characters the jokes. Sam's definition of sticking to principles in the novel sounds more like sacrificing them. He thinks of chasing Eliza because "I railly spected Mas'r was sot dat way." However, when he finds out his mistress is against the hunt he obstructs it, and "dat ar was conscience *more yet*,–cause fellers allers gets more by stickin' to Missis' side,–so yer see I's persistent either way, and sticks up to conscience, and holds on to principles. . . . [W]hat's principles good for, if we isn't persistent, I wanter know?" (*UTC*, 66). In the novel Sam's errors and puns echo both the most obvious intimation of a blackface stump speech—that black speakers are linguistically substandard—and its secret enjoyment of the disruption and corruption of educated English. Stowe encourages this private pleasure, so a snobbish dismissal of Sam would rebound on the reader, who would have missed the joke and failed to rejoice in his part in the slave dealer's downfall.

When Aiken reproduces Sam's quip, he almost exactly reverses the power relations in the novel. His text lifts Sam's verbal distortions and gives them to the Yankee, Gumption Cute, who is in conversation with the equally unscrupulous lawyer, Marks. Not only are both speakers white, but Marks is trying to recruit his companion for the business of catching runaway slaves.

MARKS: You're afraid, then?

CUTE: No, I ain't; it's against my principles.

MARKS: Your principles—how so?

CUTE: Because my principles are to keep a sharp lookout for No. 1. (Aiken, *UTC*, 4.1)

Cute's perversion of the idea of "principles" is a fair reflection of his character. However, the positioning of this wordplay in Aiken allies it with the forces of slavery, not with those of resistance. At one level, this move would seem to bypass the racial implications that haunt all blackface, removing the possibility that the comedy could be read as a characterization of blackness. But by taking the slave's funniest lines and giving them to slave catchers, Aiken partly redeems his villains. Stowe's evil characters work to damn their trade, but Aiken transferred to them some of Sam's comic glamour: taking a scene in which a slave triumphed over his would-be masters, Aiken transformed it into one that offered to make those very masters endearing.

The potential confusion of sympathy deriving from the blackface conventions underlying this dialogue was rendered all the more likely because of the discussion that immediately precedes it in the play. Not only does Aiken pinch Sam's punning for his Marks and Cute double act, he also incorporates an end man–interlocutor scene. Again, Cute takes the blackface role, here the end man, while Marks supplies the interlocutor's straight-man feeds:

MARKS: I suppose you gave up the spirits [spiritual rappings], after that?

CUTE: Well, I reckon I did; it had such an effect on my spirits.

MARKS: It's a wonder they didn't tar and feather you.

CUTE: There was some mention made of that, but when they said *feathers*, I felt as if I had wings, and flew away.

MARKS: You cut and run?

CUTE: Yes; I didn't like their company, and I cut it. (Aiken, *UTC*, 4.1)

There is precisely the same pattern of persistent double entendre in the question-and-answer rhythm here as in Tambo and Bones sketches like "Blackberrying." Similarly, the surreal imagery created by the literal interpretation of the figure of speech, "I felt as if I had wings, and flew away," mirrors the defiance of logic in Topsy's "never was born." Unlike Topsy's declaration in the novel, however, the humor in this sketch is not linked to a polemical point, and Cute's absurdity undermines the horror of Mark's slave driving. The end man's frustration of the interlocutor on the stage is usually

designed to elicit audience sympathy, for he is upsetting the meanings enshrined in polite and educated language. Placing Marks and Cute in the positions of Tambo and Bones was thus more likely to endear them to an audience than to stamp them as villains.

Elsewhere in his script Aiken has Cute play the interlocutor in a conversation with Topsy. Cute's ornate expression and knowing references to
Topsy's blackness, calling her "charcoal" and by the names of a number of
blacking products, mark out his whiteface role. Topsy, by contrast, leaves the
wordplay, such as it is, entirely to Cute:

> CUTE: Look here, Charcoal!
>
> TOPSY: My name isn't Charcoal—it's Topsy.
>
> CUTE: Oh! Your name is Topsy, is it, you juvenile specimen of Day & Martin?
>
> TOPSY: Tell you I don't know nothin' 'bout Day & Martin. I's Topsy and I be-
> long to Miss Feely St. Clare.
>
> CUTE: I'm much obleeged to you, you small extract of Japan, for your infor-
> mation. (Aiken, *UTC*, 5.2)

Cute's references to blacking (the firm of Day and Martin produced a black
polish, and "extract of Japan" was a varnish) are oddly placed here.[68] In the
minstrel show such moments reinforce the tacit understanding between audience and performers that this is a travesty, that stage blackness is makeup,
and that the stylized differences between end man and interlocutor are performative. In the 1850s productions of Aiken's play Topsy wore burnt cork,
making hers literally as well as generically a blackface role. But though her
comic turns were derived from the minstrel stage, both in Stowe and in Aiken
Topsy's part was also a sentimental one, and her conversion from heathen to
missionary could only be effected by divesting the character of the irony and
knowingness that usually accompanied stage blackface. To solicit tears as well
as laughter, the actress playing Topsy had to make the audience suspend its
awareness that she was blacked up. Perhaps it is for this reason that Aiken has
Topsy assert and reassert her blackness in the face of Cute's innuendo:

> CUTE: Walk your chalks!
>
> TOPSY: By golly! dere ain't no chalk 'bout me. . . .
>
> CUTE: Chowder, how green you are!
>
> TOPSY: [*Indignantly*] Sar, I hab you to know, I's not green; I's brack. (Aiken,
> *UTC*, 5.2)

Topsy stands in this scene for authenticity and integrity, rejecting Cute's offer to exhibit her in the dig at P. T. Barnum incorporated in later productions (Aiken, *UTC*, 5.2).

Yet these quips about Topsy's color were designed to amuse the audience as well as to establish Cute's bumptiousness. And the playwright did not reserve these jests for Cute, whose moral dubiousness might help to discredit them. Aiken's most controversial jibe was apportioned to Deacon Perry, Miss Ophelia's beau. After adopting Topsy, Ophelia introduces her to Perry:

> OPHELIA: She is my daughter.
>
> DEACON: [*Aside*] Her daughter! Then she must have married a coloured man off South. I was not aware that you had been married, Miss Ophelia?
>
> OPHELIA: Married! Sakes alive! what made you think I had been married?
>
> DEACON: Good gracious! I'm getting confused. Didn't I understand you to say that this—somewhat tanned—young lady was your daughter? (Aiken, *UTC*, 5.2)

Given the fear with which the idea of "amalgamation," or interracial sex, was invested in the period, the deacon's mistake here is risky indeed. Deacon Perry has for a moment conjured up a proslavery fantasy, that the antislavery Northerner—Ophelia—has exercised in the South her secret inclination for interracial sex. Women's involvement in antislavery activities had long attracted the accusation of immoral sexual inclinations, culminating in the presumption that abolitionists were advocating amalgamation.[69] New York's race riots of the 1830s had been inflamed by James Watson Webb's claims in the *Courier and Enquirer* that "abolitionists and amalgamators" were identical.[70] Philip Lapsansky has unearthed "lacerating graphics" that similarly promoted "antiabolitionist rhetoric joining antislavery and amalgamation," as in the 1839 lithograph *Practical Amalgamation*, which showed a white woman sitting on a black man's knee and a white man kneeling adoringly before a black woman.[71] Abolitionists denied the charges, the American Anti-Slavery Society issuing disclaimers after the 1834 riots on handbills and in a letter to the mayor, disclaiming "any desire to promote or encourage intermarriages between white and colored persons."[72] Not only that, but they too made use of the horror provoked by the idea in their exploitation of very white skinned slaves like Ellen Craft, whose appearance at an 1848 antislavery meeting in Salem, Ohio, "produced a thrill of interest and feeling that can hardly be conceived, and certainly not described."[73] Stowe, of course, had made a similar point in the "quadroon" characters Eliza, Emmeline, and Cassy and in the

lascivious interest they attract from unsavory slave owners like Haley and
Legree. Conway emphasized this with his Eliza: he justified cutting the part of
Harry on the grounds that it would make his female relatives less attractive
("to make *Cassy* a *Grandmother* would destroy her not only with the audience
but with the personator"), so in his version Haley buys Eliza, and her flight
from him is driven by a fear of coerced sex rather than outraged maternity.[74]

All these characters have "white" fathers and "black" mothers, which, as
Jennifer DeVere Brody suggests, was the most common nineteenth-century
representation of the children of "intermarriage."[75] So the deacon's suspi-
cions about Ophelia not only would have been scandalous in themselves but
would have jarred with "the image of miscegenation promoted by a range of
discourses" in the period that "was that of the black woman and the white
man."[76] Aiken thus risks reviving all the popular representations of abolitionists as immoral and so detracting from the emotional power of Ophelia's
conversion of Topsy. The impact of such a suggestion is underlined by the
deacon's next misapprehension, that Ophelia has given birth without even
the sanctification of marriage.

Shocking as Aiken's miscegenation joke may have been, Conway was willing not only to match but even to outdo it. When Eva determines to buy Tom
in that play, Haley remarks, "Well, the young lady seems to be sot on him, and
nut'rally enough." Penetrate reads his expression as sexual and registers
astonishment: "A young lady sot on a nigger and naturally enough, must put
that down under the head of no accounting for tastes" (Conway, *UTC*, 2.2).
Linking Eva and Tom in this way is even more extraordinary than imputing
irregular behavior to Ophelia. Ophelia is a comic figure, and suggesting unlikely partners for her falls within the tradition of such spinsters in melodrama, but Eva is a heroine and a child. Conway undermines at a stroke both
her purity and Tom's devoted passivity, the very crux of Stowe's imaginative
attack on slavery. It is the piety of Eva's link with Tom that in the novel endorses their gentle brand of opposition to slavery. Conway's script by contrast
here exhibits a conspicuous lack of control. His play seems to lay itself open
to all the fears fed by the proslavery camp just where it seeks to distance itself from fanatical abolitionism. For moral drama it was making distinctly
salacious suggestions, and, rather than playing safe politically, it was encroaching on taboo.

The plays illustrate the ways in which generic conventions helped determine the political significance of *Uncle Tom's Cabin*. Their differences help
us identify the plays as interpretations, as each a reading of the original text.

Their similarities—the recurrence of these influences in an ostensibly diverse set of plays—reveal that such readings were not entirely willful but were also conditioned by contemporary expectations of the form into which *Uncle Tom* was being converted. All these productions were commercial before they were political, and their conscription of minstrelsy was directed by the popularity of its generic conventions, as was their use of sensational and moral melodrama. Dramatists were more obviously motivated by the exigencies of commercial production than by fierce conviction on the slavery question, and so the stage *Uncle Toms* were formed by a combination of generic expectation, theatrical business sense, and the dramatic characteristics of Stowe's novel itself. As a result, their adaptations of blackface erred disturbingly on the side of racial denigration, and they opted to ditch Stowe's domestic brand of defiance. There is a vast difference between Topsy snapping her needles in the novel and Conway's jokes about women speaking up in public. However, just as Stowe's novel was susceptible to multiple readings and rewritings, so the interpretation of these plays lay partly in the eyes of their beholders. Abolitionists persisted in seeing the power of Aiken's drama to convert, while some proslavery writers saw every dramatization of Stowe as an attack.

— 1ᵉ BAS BLEU. — Profitons de l'occasion.. L'ONCLE TOM est à la mode.. hâtons-nous d'écrire
un roman intitulé LA TANTE TOM.
— 2ᵐᵉ BAS BLEU — Ça me botte !..

In this French cartoon, Paris Bluestockings decide to write an "Aunt Tom's Cabin."
Honoré Daumier, "Actualités," *Le Charivari* (Paris), 18 November 1852, 3.
Courtesy of the British Library.

supports to the upper part.

What were the emotions of the Small Person's Mamma, who was the gentlest and kindest of her sex, on coming upon her offspring one day, on descending the staircase, to find her apparently furious with insensate rage, muttering to herself as she brutally lashed with one of her brother's toy whips, a cheer-

SHE WAS LASHING THAT POOR BLACK DOLL AND TALKING TO HERSELF LIKE A LITTLE FURY.

Left: A girl playing Simon Legree. R. B. Birch, illustration for Frances Hodgson Burnett's autobiography, *The One I Knew the Best of All* (London: Frederick Warne, 1893). Reproduced by permission of the Syndics of Cambridge University Library.

Below: Instructions for a home minstrel-show production of *Uncle Tom's Cabin*. From Frank Dumont, *The Witmark Amateur Minstrel Guide and Burnt Cork Encylopaedia* (Chicago: M. Witmark, 1899), 85. Reproduced by permission of the Syndics of Cambridge University Library.

"UNCLE TOM'S CABIN." (FIRST PART.)

S. S. SANFORD,
AS HAPPY UNCLE TOM.

Above: S. S. Sanford playing Uncle Tom in a
proslavery minstrel show version. *Our Day*
(pamphlet, n.d.). Harvard Theatre Collection.
Courtesy of the Houghton Library, Harvard
University.

Right: Playbill for the Howard family playing
Aiken's *Uncle Tom's Cabin.* Harvard Theatre
Collection. Reprinted by permission of the
Houghton Library, Harvard University.

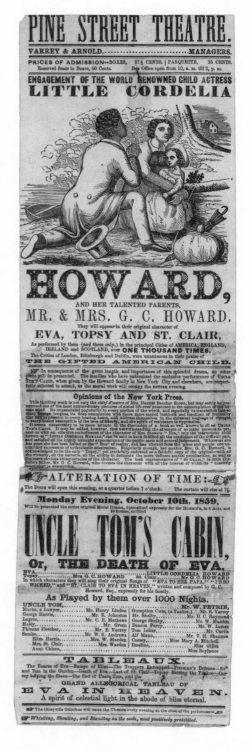

CHORUS—SING, DARKEYS, SING.

THE HOLIDAY DANCE.

Happy slaves dancing, two of many such scenes in proslavery novels. *Above:* from Robert Criswell, *"Uncle Tom's Cabin" Contrasted with Buckingham Hall, the Planter's Home; or, A Fair View of the Slavery Question* (New York: Fanshaw, 1852); *left:* from Charles Jacobs Peterson (pseud. J. Thornton Randolph), *The Cabin and Parlor; or, Slaves and Masters* (Philadelphia: T. B. Peterson, 1852). Courtesy of the Library Company of Philadelphia.

THE POLITICAL TOPSY.
"I 'SPECTS NOBODY CAN'T DO NOTHIN' WITH ME!"—*Vide* "*Uncle Tom's Cabin.*"

October 23, 1852.

Left: Uncle Tom's Topsy used in a London satire on Prime Minister Disraeli. From *Punch: or, the London Charivari* (1852), 198. Reproduced by permission of the Syndics of Cambridge University Library.

Right: British anti-American satire that condemns the United States for slavery. Richard Doyle, *Punch: or, the London Charivari* (1847), 209. Reproduced by permission of the Syndics of Cambridge University Library.

THE LAND OF LIBERTY.
RECOMMENDED TO THE CONSIDERATION OF "BROTHER JONATHAN."

Above: Title page of a song book for the Ethiopian Serenaders, the most popular American minstrel troupe in Britain. Harvard Theatre Collection. Reprinted by permission of the Houghton Library, Harvard University.

Facing page: Playbill for the Female American Serenaders, a British imitation of the Ethiopian Serenaders. Courtesy of the British Library.

St. James's Assembly Rooms,
(Late Crockford's.)

GREATEST NOVELTY IN THE METROPOLIS.

First Appearance in London!
OF THE
FEMALE AMERICAN
SERENADERS!

The **FEMALE AMERICAN SERENADERS**, Mesdames CORA, WOMBA, YARICO, WOSKI, JUMBA, MIAMI, and ROSA, having been received with the most enthusiastic applause in Liverpool and Manchester, will have the distinguished honor of making their first appearance in London

ON WEDNESDAY, APRIL 21st, 1847.
Their Performance will consist of a Grand
AMERICAN CONCERT,
OF VOCAL AND INSTRUMENTAL MUSIC,
Including the principal Songs and Airs with which the Public have been familiarised by the celebrated Ethiopian Serenaders, and also several Native Melodies, and other compositions entirely new to European associations.

PROGRAMME OF THE ENTERTAINMENT:
NEW CHARACTERISTIC OVERTURE, in which is introduced several

	Native Melodies	.	FULL BAND
CHORUS	" The American Serenaders"	.	By the COMPANY
BALLAD	" Flora May"	.	CORA
SONG	" I'm going ober de Mountain"	.	JUMBA
SOLOS and CHORUS	" De Programme for de Concert"		By the COMPANY

(Ten Minutes allowed between each Part.)

PART II.
OVERTURE, consisting of Selections of Airs from " Masaniello"	.	FULL BAND
DUET and CHORUS	" The Indian Gleaners"	CORA, WOSKI, and COMPANY
ROMANCE	" De Phantom Canoe"	.	YARICO
SONG	" Who's dat knocking at de door ?"	.	JUMBA
SONG	" Mary Blanc"	.	CORA
SOLOS and CHORUS	" De Invitation to de Ball"	.	By the COMPANY

PART III.
MEDLEY OVERTURE		.	FULL BAND
CHORUS	" The Raccoon Hunters"	.	By the COMPANY
BARCAROLE	" De Jolly Skiffsman"	.	WOSKI
SONG	" The American Jack Sheppard."		
CHORUS	" Buffalo Girls"	.	By the COMPANY
FINALE, the celebrated " Railroad Overture," with all its astounding effects,		FULL BAND

The Public is respectfully informed that all the NEW MUSIC sung by the Female American Serenaders is Published by D'ALMAINE AND Co., Soho-square, London, that Firm having purchased the Copyright: and all parties are cautioned against publishing the same.

Morning Performance at half-past 2 o'clock ; Evening, half-past 8 o'clock. Doors open at 2 and 8 o'clock.

Family Tickets, to admit Six, Half-a-Guinea, to be had of D'Almaine and Co., Soho-square, and at the St. James's Assembly Rooms. Single Admission HALF-A-CROWN.

Left: In this Parisian cartoon, rival theater managers fight over *Uncle Tom.* "Revue de La Semaine," *Le Charivari* (23 January 1853), 3. Courtesy of the British Library.

Below: Characters designed for a children's theater version of an *Uncle Tom* pantomime. Barry Clarke Collection, London.

One of many Tom-themed household goods produced in the 1850s. *Uncle Tom's Cabin* banner on cloth, ca. 1852. The Gilder Lehrman Collection, GLC 6894, courtesy of the Gilder Lehrman Institute of American History.

Ceramic Uncle Tom and Eva, probably produced in the 1850s. Courtesy of the
Harriet Beecher Stowe Center Library, Hartford, Connecticut.

"UNCLE TOM" IN LONDON: BRITISH DRAMATIZATIONS

[T]HEIR EXHIBITION IS . . . CALCULATED FROM ITS FORCE, TRUTHFULNESS, AND MIXTURE OF THE LUDICROUS WITH SENTIMENT, TO RAISE FEELINGS WHICH MAY AT NO DISTANT PERIOD PRODUCE RESULTS THAT EVERY FRIEND OF NEGRO EMANCIPATION WOULD HAIL WITH SATISFACTION.

"Ethiopian Serenaders—St James's Theatre," *Daily News* (London), 18 March 1846

London's theater managers seized upon *Uncle Tom's Cabin* even more voraciously than had their counterparts in New York, and Stowe's novel was translated into British melodrama as well as American moral reform plays. British hack writers set to work on *Uncle Tom*, attempting to harness its commercial success in the same manner as the American plays and minstrel sketches were doing, and, like them, the London dramatists necessarily negotiated its politics. Although slavery was not their primary interest in tackling Stowe's text, revising the book involved taking a stance on the issue. When *Uncle Tom's Cabin* transferred to the London stage, it became a vehicle for popular British attitudes to slavery as well as to the United States. Where the American dramatizations had been cautious about the racial and regional politics they negotiated, British *Tom* plays dared to imagine the overthrow of America's "peculiar institution." And cultural as well as political differences are apparent in the British *Tom* plays. The proliferation of versions in London drew comment, in contrast to the handful of New York productions, which were distinguished by the huge numbers that saw them. The diversity and class fragmentation of British theater was thus reflected in the London *Uncle Toms*, as it was in British theatrical conventions. These plays, like other British melodramas, avoided religious references, promoted patriotic themes, and at the same time thrilled to "foreign" spectacles of "Americanness." They did share their American counterparts' willingness to borrow from minstrelsy, but the blackface they referred to was itself already a variant on American forms, as *Uncle Tom* in London played its part in the development of a distinctively British blackface tradition.

A letter to the *Times* of London in 1852 took issue with Stowe's book on the grounds that it pandered to "profane" tastes such as those that inclined to sensational melodrama. The writer feared that the novel "will be immortalized at the Victoria and the Bower Saloon, and no doubt 'The Secret Chamber in Legree's House,' and the 'Death of Tom at the Whipping Post,' will be faithfully recorded: or 'Legree the Man of Crime and the Murderer of Uncle Tom,' will attract the unwashed inhabitants of the Transpontine districts."[1]

Some of the writer's anxieties would prove prophetic. Not only was *Uncle Tom* eagerly adopted by the London theaters, including the Victoria and working-class establishments, but the plays did pick out the most violent and

Gothic scenes in order to thrill their audiences. Reviewers would come to lament both the poor taste of the *Tom* plays and the enthusiasm for them of London's "unwashed." The *Spectator* described "the mob that has read a popular book . . . rushing to see the leading personages placed in a visible shape before its eyes" and called the resulting theatrical activity "Tom-mania."[2]

The letter to the *Times* also accused Stowe of undue leniency to slaveholders. Pointing out the preponderance of good masters in the novel, it argued that the slaves in it led "such happy lives" that the book was unlikely to win many converts to abolitionism. But the theatrical productions the writer so scathingly predicted were not necessarily ineffectual as critiques of slavery. The London plays tended to be uncompromising in their politics: like the New York stagings, the London dramas sometimes equivocated about slavery, but many also condemned it outright and suggested remedies that in the United States would have seemed terrifyingly inflammatory. In England Stowe's "Christian slave" threatened to become a revolutionary.

Two months after it appeared in Boston a pirated edition of *Uncle Tom's Cabin* had been published by Clarke in London, priced at two shillings and sixpence. Between August and December fifteen more British publishers had produced their own versions. These illicit editions proved even more profitable, though not for Stowe, than the American ones: by the end of the year the *Eclectic Review* estimated that the number of copies in circulation exceeded a million.[3] Thus, *Uncle Tom* was even more of a hit across the Atlantic than it had been at home, which is why the managers of the London theaters, for whom adaptations of novels were a relatively cheap and popular source of new plays, quickly began to exploit it. The playwright Edward Fitzball wrote of the 1850s that "all the managers [were] mad to produce [*Uncle Tom*] on the stage. Every theatre[,] nearly[,] produced its version."[4] Between 1852 and 1855 there were at least twenty different *Uncle Tom's Cabin* productions in London, as well as performances of "Scenes and Sketches" or "Scenes and Songs" from the novel, *Uncle Tom* "Living Marionettes," amateur or one-off performances, *Uncle Tom* pantomimes and burlesques, and a horseback production. The Christmas pantomime at the Sadler's Wells Theatre boasted not one but a multitude of *Uncle Tom*s. There were also, of course, productions at most provincial theaters.[5] The toy theater industry, which customarily extended theatrical culture by producing condensed melodramas for children, also participated in *Tom* mania. Five sets of abridged scripts and plates of characters and scenery were printed to enable children to stage *Tom* shows at home. Another company brought out *Uncle Tom* as an eight-page "Pictorial

Play" for children.[6] So ubiquitous were the dramatizations of Stowe's novel that when *Punch* satirized Disraeli's political opportunism by casting him as Topsy ("Who made you politically? . . . Nobody as I knows on"), the magazine referred not to Stowe's book but to the plays, imagining *Uncle Tom's Cabin* played at "Westminster Theatre."[7]

Fitzball, who "was engaged by three managers to write three distinct pieces," claimed that the process of adaptation "did not require any remarkable ability, as it was only to select scenes and join them together."[8] It was common practice to create scripts just by transcribing Stowe's dialogue, as the *Theatrical Journal* suggested by reserving special praise for adaptors who had "not been content with merely dividing the novel into acts and scenes, leaving the descriptive portions to the painter and machinist, and turning the other portions into dialogue for the actors."[9]

Like American audiences, Londoners were used to spectacle, and their *Uncle Tom*s provided it. Fitzball claimed that Mr. James of the Queen's Theatre, "a first-rate artist, assisted by his equally talented son[,] . . . contributed immensely to the run of [his] piece" with "some beautiful scenery . . . , especially the Sea of Ice."[10] The *Theatrical Journal* commended "the effective scenery, by Mr. Shalders" at the Olympic, where another Fitzball version was playing and where the *Critic* noted that "a great point is made of the quadroon Eliza crossing the Ohio upon the floating ice."[11] Of the Adelphi's *Slave Life*, the *Critic* said that "the *mise en scène* does credit to the audience" and that "the various tableaux and pieces of sentiment with which the entire piece is filled appeared to afford unmitigated satisfaction."[12] At the "little Cabinet Theatre" Stowe's story was condensed into visual and musical vignettes "in a series of well executed cabinet scenes of Mrs. Stowe's great work, each scene being accompanied by a song or ballad founded upon some pathetic passage in the novel."[13] Not surprisingly, Astley's Amphitheatre, which specialized in circus-type shows, including horseback acrobatics and performing animals, excelled at converting *Uncle Tom's Cabin* into thrilling spectacles. As the *Theatrical Journal* noted, Astley's demonstrated that "there are in the story abundant situations in which equine performers may be introduced with advantage." As the review explained, in this performance Sam and Andy placed the nut under Haley's saddle on stage, and he was "repeatedly thrown to the ground in his attempts to mount the plunging steed." Then the scenes showing the flights of George and Eliza Harris were used to introduce a variety of vehicles onto the stage: "[W]e have the arrival of Eliza's pursuers on horseback at the inn on the Ohio, where George soon after arrives in a handsome phaeton and pair, and Mr. Wilson his old master makes his appearance in a diminutive pony chaise. The escape of George, his wife and child, in the wagon, is next shown." The reviewer was also impressed by "Haley being pushed into the chasm," the "effective and picturesque" slave market, and the slave hunt on Legree's plantation, "in which whites, blacks, dogs and horses join in wild clamour."[14]

The *Tom* plays' conformity with the melodramatic tradition was comically illustrated by one of the burlesques in the Sensation Series published by Thomas Hailes Lacy. Lacy's 1864 *The Tyrant! The Slave!! The Victim!!! & The Tar!!!!* provides an amusing parody of the British *Uncle Toms* and also offers some clues about their staging. The hyperbolic proliferation of exclamation marks in the title reveals the mocking tone of this little ten-page pamphlet, borne out by the echo of theatrical advertisements in its subtitle, *An Entirely and Supernaturally Original Nautico-Domestic Transatlantic Sensation Drama*, and by its proposed setting, which melded melodrama's fondness for the exotic and its carelessness with plausibility in a surreal panoply of animals and locations: a "Boa Constrictor . . . a group of Walrus and Buffaloes . . . [and] infant Alligators . . . disporting on the frozen surface of the boundless Savannah."[15] Moreover, the text follows many of the 1850s dramatizations in taking liberties with the book: a note in *The Tyrant!* warns that "the plot and interest of Mrs Beecher Stowe's popular work have not been closely adhered to." In the "Programme of Incidents" the novel is reduced to the substance of its final chapters. As "The Southern Tyrant Legree" persecutes "the lovely and distressed Octoroon Eliza," Uncle Tom tries to save her, but a remedy is only effected by the arrival of a British tar and a bathetic "GRAND COMBAT OF SIX."[16] The Jack Tar hero links *Uncle Tom* with the patriotism of nautical melodrama and signals the ways that Stowe's text had been reworked for local purposes.

The British melodramas and the American "moral" *Uncle Toms* should be regarded as completely distinct varieties of adaptation. For a start, theater historians have not treated the London *Tom* plays as particularly significant, whereas great claims have been made for George Aiken's dramatization—that it was the first six-act play, performed without afterpieces, that it was the first to create dignified "black" roles, and that it attracted a new kind of audience to the theater. Hence, it is held to have earned its recognized place in a national tradition.[17] The British plays, on the other hand, like C. W. Taylor's sensational New York production, merely attempted to meet the expectations of the audience, and they made few claims to a grander moral purpose, happily coinciding on programs with comedies, burlettas, farces, singers, tableaux, "Poses Plastiques," and "Living Marionettes."[18] And as with all those who adapted Stowe's novel for their own purposes, British playwrights and theater managers made it their own. *Uncle Tom* was dramatized in a way that suited the special customs and conditions of the British stage, and it came to represent international relationships in a way it could not in the United States.

The plots of these productions were almost as diverse as they were plentiful. Several revoked the martyr's death Stowe had reserved for Tom: in the Pictorial Plays Tom heals Legree's wounds and his master frees him, declaring, "African, thy virtues have subdued me," and Tom makes his way to Canada. At the Standard Legree's claim over Tom was disproved, and he returned to "the bosom of my family." At the Royal Surrey he and his family were freed by Shelby. At the Olympic he was freed and his homecoming frozen in a tableau with his children. The Victoria Theatre had it both ways, killing Tom off in its production of September 1852 but then reviving him so that St. Clare could free him and send him home the following February.[19] Similarly, the episode that had become the iconic symbol of Aiken's production—Eliza and the ice—was omitted entirely from both Victoria Theatre productions and the Pictorial Play version, while at Astley's Amphitheatre it happened off stage and was merely reported by one of the characters. This was perhaps a surprising missed opportunity, given that Astley had worked so hard to provide vehicular and equestrian thrills for his audiences.[20] At the Olympic Fitzball introduced a variation: George poled his wife and child across the stage on an ice floe.[21]

In other departures from the original, the Surrey Theatre had Legree arrested as a pirate, and the Victoria's February play, *The Slave Hunt! or, St. Clare and the Happy Days of Uncle Tom*, featured entirely new characters, opened at a gambling house in Louisville, and saw St. Clare lose Cassy on a bet to one of the new villains, who was later "torn apart by his own dogs" off stage. This did not, however, prevent him from coming back on to complete a remorseful death.[22] Mark Lemon and Tom Taylor's exciting version opened with Shelby's return and a discussion of Topsy's dress and behavior, Eliza took Eva's lines in the book offering love to the reprobate, the slaves sang and exclaimed about the kindness of their masters, and Harry did a "grotesque dance." The play returned to the plot of the novel with the advent of a slave trader—here Legree rather than Haley—who provoked maternal outrage by threatening to buy Harry. Uncle Tom did not appear until act 2. Meanwhile, Topsy had advised on and assisted in Eliza's escape, and she subsequently dressed as a boy to confirm George Harris's disguise as he tried to join his wife. Legree recaptured all of them, made eyes at Eliza, and stabbed Tom with a Bowie knife; but the other slaves all escaped safely, and Cassy finally shot Legree as he pursued them through a rocky pass. The piece ended with a tableau of the grateful slaves on the rocks.[23]

Very few London plays transferred to New York or vice versa. However, in 1856 the Howard family came to London under the management of P. T. Barnum, with a compressed version of Aiken's script. At Marylebone they reduced Aiken's work to three acts, ending with Eva's death and omitting the scenes with Cassy and Legree. They also performed at the Strand and at Sadler's Wells, sometimes offering *The Death of Eva* on its own, and occasionally they were joined by Barnum's other protégé, Tom Thumb. They stayed only a few months, but Tom Thumb extended his visit into a successful European tour.[24] Conversely, the script of Lemon and Taylor's *Slave Life* was sold in Boston, and it was performed in Philadelphia in May 1864.[25]

It may have been difficult to bring American plays to London because of the peculiarities of the British theatrical climate. Aiken had made the spectacle of Christian martyrdom a central feature of his play not only in Tom's religious devotion but in Eva's death and heavenly ascension. In the United States this aspect of the Aiken script attracted its "moral" audiences and helped palliate its potentially contentious political implications. In Britain, however, Eva was frequently omitted from the dramatis personae altogether, perhaps because she is so closely associated with the book's Christianity. She does not appear in Lemon and Taylor's script for the Adelphi, Fitzball's Olympic production, the Royal Surrey's *Uncle Tom*, the Victoria's September 1852 version, the Standard's version, the Pictorial Play, or Webb's Juvenile Drama. Not surprisingly, *The Tyrant!* saw no need to incorporate Eva into its *Uncle Tom* burlesque either. Tom's faith, too, was much less conspicuous. Only in one play, Fitzball's *Uncle Tom's Cabin*, did Tom fall to his knees and pray, and even then he conspicuously did not address any deity directly, calling on "One, whose eye seed eberyting!"[26] This evasion of a central feature of Stowe's characterization or, at the very least, circumspection about staging it was due to British licensing laws. It was commonly regarded as blasphemous to include references to religious matters in the theater in London. Putting a show of religion upon the stage as Aiken had done would have been provocative in the extreme, even where it was possible. The examiner of plays at the Lord Chamberlain's Office refused to license scripts that mentioned religion, politics, or public figures or that seemed to offend taste or morality. In the

1820s Examiner George Colman had become infamous for striking out references to heaven, God, Lord, and angels, and although the 1850s deputy examiner, William Bodham Donne, tried to be more flexible on this matter, the clergy and the press complained bitterly if norms were breached. It was even forbidden to mention the Bible or use it as a property on the stage, so Tom could never have pursued his scriptural studies in the British theater.[27]

The *Spectator* made these cultural differences explicit in its attack on the profusion of *Tom* plays. Offering to cite "intrinsic evidence that [the novel] was not designed by its author for stage-adaptation," it pointed to the book's "tone . . . of a positive religion. . . . The piety of the book is no mere accident . . . but it is the moral basis on which the whole superstructure is raised." And it was this aspect of the novel, the reviewer concluded, that made it unfit for theatrical representation: "[I]t need not be explained to the merest smatterer in knowledge of the English character, that anything like an allusion to sacred personages on the London stage, is not only objectionable, but morally impossible. A Methodistical play and an Atheistical play would be equally rejected."[28] As the *Athenaeum* put it, Uncle Tom was not a character fitted for the English stage: as his "religious elements . . . are, as it were, the flesh and blood of the character, when deprived of them a skeleton alone remains."[29] Thus, what made Aiken's play "moral" for audiences in New York would probably have made it immoral in London.

Similarly, the politics of many British plays might have been unpalatable in the United States. Although Uncle Tom himself usually remained the pacifist Stowe had designed, firmly reiterating the lines about accepting his imminent sale ("Let Eliza go, it's her right" [*UTC*, 293]), the London plays were violent. Legree frequently uttered the boast about his fist being calloused from knocking down slaves, but in the City of London Theatre an antislavery character showed him his own calluses—from knocking down men such as Legree.[30] In Webb's Juvenile Drama the slave catchers are physically attacked by the slave's supporters, while Sam and Andy laugh.[31] Other plays went further. Even in Aiken and Conway slaves had been seen to defend themselves, but London theaters introduced the frightening possibility that they might do more. At the City of London Theatre Cassy threatened the outcome that slave owners dreaded, suggesting that Legree's slaves "one day at the voice of a bold leader will each uplift a weapon . . . to strike at [him]."[32] Some productions staged slave revolts outright. In one Tom refuses to kill Legree, but his fellow slaves are less scrupulous, and Cassy sets fire to the slave prison, while the stage directions indicate "Plantation in a state of insurrection."[33] The Royal Surrey Theatre was bolder even than this. In its production slave rebellion becomes a crucial moral focus: first the majority of Legree's slaves "mutiny, setting buildings on fire and attacking their master with the words 'Down with the oppressor.'"[34] Legree unjustly holds Tom responsible for this "mutineering." For his part, Tom is initially a moderate, offering to tell his fellows that it is "bad to disobey the massa and rise agin 'em," but the violence worsens on the plantation, with a fight between Legree and his slaves, burning buildings, and a riot. Finally, Legree's brutality is too much even for Tom, and when the slave owner threatens to plunge a child into the flames, Tom mounts a rescue: "[I]f him never did mutiny, he will now!" The moral seems to be that some crimes are too heinous to endure peacefully, a conclusion almost totally opposed to Stowe's vision of the slave's redemptive suffering. New York reviewers had been appalled that George defended himself in Charles W. Taylor's production; Barnum had sold Conway's play on the grounds that it would be inoffensive to slaveholders and their sympathizers. Yet where American productions were constrained by the fear of provoking sectional conflict, British dramatists wished it onto the stage. And while in the United States few abolitionists were advocating revolt in the early 1850s, not least because it would alienate public opinion, that very prospect spiced up London melodramas a treat.

It was far less uncomfortable for Britons, of course, to imagine slave revolts on the other side of the ocean, but the *Tom* plays may also have encouraged British workers to identify with their stage slaves. When the actors cried, "Down with the oppressor!" spectators might also have thought of their own masters as they cheered, much as they were sometimes encouraged to equate villainy in other melodramas with their own downtrodden position and as they may have identified with George in Aiken and Conway. The letter to the *Times* that decried the likely influence of Stowe's novel itself suggested that the political temper of theater audiences suited antislavery sentiments when it sneered that the "philanthropical remarks" in the book "would soon bring down the gallery of the Victoria."[35]

Some contemporary observers were disturbed by the international political implications of the London *Uncle Toms*. The *British Army Despatch*, which disapproved of the novel, of abolitionism, and of meddling in American affairs, suggested that the plays were upsetting American expatriates: "Every American in London is disgusted with the Uncle Tom mania here. If he go to a theatre, he is insulted and shocked. The English people, on the other hand, are deluded into the falsest notions of America. When the slave in the drama escapes into British India, there is a cheer. That cheer may cost us some day our best alliance."[36]

Although New York audiences were uncomfortably aware that a major national question was being examined and enacted in the *Tom* plays, Aiken's and Conway's dramatizations did not project an overarching idea of America in the way that some British versions explicitly set out to do. The exaggerated virtues of the British tar who saved Uncle Tom in *The Tyrant!* were not too far removed from the way some plays laid out the relative moral positions of the two nations. *Uncle Tom's Cabin* made a useful cause for British self-congratulation, based on a peculiar image of America that was refracted and distorted by the conventions of melodrama. And, as with all judgments on somewhere else, the plays reveal something of the judges. The London plays incorporated some peculiarly British responses to slavery, to minstrelsy, and to *Uncle Tom's Cabin*.

In the nautical dramas that *The Tyrant!* burlesqued, the Jack Tar character has two functions. One is to provide a kind of maritime exoticism, which is evinced by the hornpipes and "nautical slang" that accompany his every appearance, and the second is to provide a focus for patriotic sentiments. His role is identical in *The Tyrant!* The piece ends with Jack calling for a "national" dance, "and then hey for old England, and Britons never shall be slaves."[37] This yoking of nationalism with a distaste for slavery was not uncommon in the mid–nineteenth century, and both were frequently invoked in British comments on America. As Michel Rezé has pointed out, a number of recent causes of Anglo-American tension—the annexation of Oregon, the fisheries dispute, and the more general distrust embodied in the travelogues of Trollope, Dickens, and Martineau—helped shape the British response to *Uncle Tom's Cabin*.[38] A *Punch* cartoon of 1847 showed the Yankee "Brother Jonathan" dreaming of "slavery," "Repudiation," and "Mexico," with the papers for Texas and Oregon lying beside him.[39]

Raising a cheer for England was a traditional practice in the melodramas, especially the nautical ones, and many of the *Tom* plays used the slavery issue to do it. At the Pavilion Theatre George asked audiences to pray not only for him but "for England and the Emancipation of the slave," and an *Uncle Tom* burlesque made reference to the intractability of "the Fishery Question between England and America."[40] More commonly, the plays exploited George and Eliza's escape to Canada in the novel, as the majority of versions spelled out that it was the British laws pertaining there that ensured the fugitives' freedom. Rousing speeches in defense of human liberty thus became in many plays self-congratulation for British foresight, which had produced emancipation in the colonies nearly twenty years before. In the Royal Surrey Theatre George headed for "Canada, where Britain's star of liberty lights all"; at the City of London Theatre he fled "[t]o the British land, . . . to the shore that with one touch can break thro' the bond of slavery as a thread, and shake defiance with her flag to all nations that encouraged it!" At Astley's Amphitheatre he left for "Canada, where freedom's flag is raised triumphant and the poor slave is cherished"; in the operatic version he apostrophized that country again: "[A]ll are free there—where British justice regulated the law." Finally, in the Pictorial Plays the governor of Canada declares the runaways free under a Union Jack to the music of "Rule Britannia."[41]

The recurrence of the imagery of flags underlines the obvious way these plays paraded their national symbolism (the U.S. flag is also at the center of the *Punch* cartoon), and a couple went so far as to cast aspersions on America's "star-spangled banner." At the Standard Theatre a character declared that it "would look all the brighter for having the stain of slavery washed from its folds," while at the Surrey Britain championed liberty, "though her banners be not shotted with its emblem," and a slave echoed Frederick Douglass in noting the irony of the Fourth of July speeches on liberty.[42] Webb's Juvenile Drama extends this imagery of Britain still further in its cutout characters for the toy stage, as the soldiers who come to arrest Legree are depicted as English redcoats.[43] Though this may have been an oversight on the part of the illustrator, the eruption of English soldiers onto the Louisiana scene demonstrates the processes by which transporting *Uncle Tom* across the Atlantic and onto the British stage also became a kind of translation, and Stowe's tale was read with an English imagination as well as from an ostentatiously British (and even antagonistic) perspective.

Despite the anti-American patriotism of many British productions, "Americanness" also became a part of their dramatic interest. Character types, accents, scenery, and lifestyle were flagged on the stage as being especially American, and they amounted in some plays to a vicarious or theatrical tourism. The *Theatrical Journal* proclaimed that "great credit" was due to the manager of the Adelphi, Madame Celeste, who had "visited the localities in which the action of the drama is supposed to take place" during a recent tour through the United States.[44] A *Spectator* review of a French *Uncle Tom* speculated that the introduction of a rifle duel and the change of a character's name had been effected to make the drama seem more American, and a number of London plays made similar efforts.[45] A stage direction in the

Adelphi production calls for Eliza to "name some American songs," and, as in other dramatizations, characters in that one drink "juleps."[46] The *Theatrical Journal* praised the portrayal of a character in one play, calling attention to the "peculiar twang, odd phraseology, loose swinging gait and singular costume . . . copied to the life by the actor [who] has had the advantage of personal observation of the character during his sojourn in the States."[47]

In the same vein the "Yankee pedlar" in London is not a focus for sectional tension, as are Gumption Cute and Penetrate Partyside in Aiken and Conway, but functions more as a comic "type." Fitzball's Jonathan Slingsby manifests the traits of the stage Yankee in his speech, in his references, and in his unscrupulous pursuit of profit as he tries to get Tom to buy Chloe a gown "sich as one worn by the President's Lady at Tammany Hall." More sympathetic than Aiken's character and more partisan than Conway's, the London Yankee comforts Tom when he is sold and actively helps the runaways.[48] The New Englander's unabashed support for the escapees and his undermining of slave laws pose a clear contrast with Conway's production, in which the "Yankee" sought so ostentatiously for amity between the play's Northern and Southern characters.

Although some of these innovations, like the staging of the slave revolts, reflected the differing political sensitivities for British and American dramatists, others reflected a less-than-perfect acquaintance with the geography of the United States. Eliza crossed the Ohio River and found herself in Canada, or she headed north from Kentucky and ended up in Louisiana, while the Indiana Quaker settlement was mysteriously located on the lower Mississippi.[49] Others introduced their slave characters to British cuisine: at the Olympic Chloe prepared "chicken pudding and giblets," and elsewhere she was famous for "black pudding."[50] American tourists complained that the British played Uncle Tom and Eva with Cockney accents, while George Harris spoke "Oxford."[51]

Some plays made this Anglicization conscious, introducing not only a British but specifically a Cockney character, who offered Londoners a mouthpiece for what might be their own responses to all this staged foreignness. Like the Yankee characters in American productions, the Cockneys could be read as the audience's representatives in the plays, but they were also a focus for conflict with the slave-owning South they depicted. At the same time, like Cute and Partyside, these characters were comic, which may have helped diffuse the tensions they set up. In a production at the Victoria, Timothy Tickler emulated Partyside's compromise with slave owning by buying a slave with benevolent intent: "[I]f he serves me faithfully—he shall be free." In a remark intended by the playwright to comment both on the relative humanity of British and American customs and on the current popularity of Stowe's creation, the slave trader retorts, "I see these Britishers know how to make Tom fools of themselves."[52] As the pun suggests, these versions were to some extent conscious of or even knowing about the fact that they were producing a British take on Stowe's novel. Well informed or not about American specificities, they were repackaging *Uncle Tom's Cabin* for audiences an ocean away from the United States and its slaves.

British reviewers, however, did partly resemble American ones in their fascination with poor and working-class audiences. The best-selling versions of the novel in Britain were the one-shilling railway editions, and *Uncle Tom* also found most favor as a play at the cheaper end of the market. Working-class audiences could see *Uncle Tom's Cabin* on the stage all over London: south of the river there were two productions at the Victoria; in the East End *Uncle Tom* was playing at the Pavilion, the Standard, and the City of London; and in the west Stowe's hero appeared at the Royal Surrey in Marylebone. There were even more versions of the play dispersed in "Penny Gaff" establishments, described with horror by Henry Mayhew as "shops which have been turned into a kind of temporary theatre (admission one penny), where dancing and singing take place every night." Mayhew claims that these theaters, which were much frequented by costermongers, flagrantly promoted immoral attitudes, being "a platform to teach the cruelest debauchery. . . . [They were] infamous places."[53] According to the *Times*, one such "penny" *Uncle Tom* was staged a hundred yards away from its more professional competition at the Pavilion.[54]

Perhaps surprisingly, these productions refrained from drawing too many analogies between poorly paid workers and slaves. Very few referred to the episode in the book where St. Clare compares slavery in America with poverty in Britain (Stowe, *UTC*, 199–200). But at the Surrey, Ophelia, whose antislavery opinions were allied with British ones by making her Canadian, declared, "How in the world can the two things be compared. The English labourer is not sold, parted from his family and whipped," and St. Clare concurred: "[O]ur[s] is the most bold and palpable infringement of human rights."[55]

Yet despite their common interest in working-class onlookers, London reviewers' reactions to them contrasted starkly with those in New York. The American observers saw the attendance of "mechanics" at Aiken's play as a blessing likely to result both in antislavery conversions and in a more general

moral uplift. Critics in London, by contrast, were interested in neither the
morality of audiences nor their politics: their judgments were based instead
on a mixture of class and cultural snobbery. Audrey Fisch has helpfully described such responses to *Tom* mania in terms of the midcentury "cultural crisis" that pitted "High Culture" against the mob.[56] They also highlight the gulf
between the two nations' sensitivities over the slavery debate, as well as the
contrast between contemporary American anxieties about the morality of the
theater and the corresponding British ones about aesthetics.

The ubiquity of the *Tom* phenomenon necessitated some comment in the
theatrical press, but reviewers signaled that they were compromising their
dignity in this. The *Spectator* noted how many proprietors were "exhibiting
Uncle Tom in some shape or other" but dismissed these venues as "those theatres which stand below the level of dramatic criticism." The *Critic* welcomed
a satire on "the present mania for our coloured brethren," and it yielded a
lukewarm commendation of the Adelphi Theatre for offering "the least con-
temptible version" of *Uncle Tom's Cabin*. The *Athenaeum* admitted that "the
enthusiasm of the [Olympic] audience at the different crises of the interest
was unbounded." But, the reviewer sniffed, "this kind of stage adaptation of
political or even ethical novels has no claim on the score of Art." Lemon and
Taylor's play at the Adelphi was the only one to attract much praise at all, and
even then the *Spectator* called it "a perfectly inoffensive drama," though the
Theatrical Journal called it "truly the most clever version of the novel." The
Critic declared the dialogue in one of Fitzball's dramatizations, at the
Olympic, "the *ne plus ultra* of inane flatness," and it called another of his versions "dull, tame, and destitute of all the melodramatic qualities which are
necessary to make a story of that sort agreeable to a London audience." The
snobbish proviso to this statement is telling: "—at least at this end of town."
Fitzball had been invited by his former manager at the Marylebone Theatre,
in then unfashionable west London, to do a second script for his new establishment at Drury Lane, and the *Critic* was implying that a different sort of
product altogether was required at this more upmarket theater. The reviewer
recommended that Smith exile "both Mr. Fitzball and his piece to the purlieus of Paddington."[57]

Uncle Tom thus traversed a spectrum of London stages, from working-class
saloons in Stepney and Shoreditch to the West End grandeur of Drury Lane.
But while Aiken and Conway were praised for creating drama of which genteel Americans approved and at which rowdy ones cheered, in London *Uncle
Toms* were divided and distinguished by the social positions of the theaters in

which they appeared. As in America the critics registered the cross-class appeal of Stowe's creation, but they were disturbed, not excited, by it. However, this class division helps explain the multiplication and fragmentation of British *Uncle Tom* plays for different audiences and its dispersal and consumption at separate venues.

If anything, the London plays were more interested in women than in workers. *The Tyrant!* drew attention to the decorative or titillating function of incidents that placed feminine virtue under threat—"her muslin robes and macassar curled locks evince the heroine devoted to unheard of perils"—and expressed cynicism about the exaggerated morality of staged terrors: "[T]he monster demands (morality insists that the frightful proposition should be darkly hinted at in hieroglyphics only) a [k]iss."[58] The heroine's subsequent "Splendid Explosion of Indignant Virtue" in the burlesque points to the fact that such scenes did provide energetic roles for actresses in perversely dynamic exhibitions of female passivity. Stowe's Eliza would on the British stage revel precisely in her "indignant virtue."

Kerry Powell has claimed that in the adaptations of Stowe, as of other women novelists, "the centrality of women was denied," citing the many omissions of Eliza crossing the ice and the Royal Olympic's transferal of the scene's heroism to her husband by having George push the floe across with his staff.[59] Yet there are also moments in these plays that echo Stowe's own championship of a female morality, such as at the Olympic: "*Mrs S*[:] You men of business, as you call yourselves[,] affect, I know, to despise the opinions of *women*, but what have women to expect of men, who despise humanity."[60] Also, some of Stowe's minor "good mother" characters who do not appear in Aiken and Conway were retained by British dramatists. Mrs. Bird appeared at the Surrey and at the Standard, where she remonstrated with her husband against the new slave law: "Are not the Coloured Race men and women like ourselves[?]"[61] At the City of London and in the first Victoria production, Rachael Halliday united Eliza and George, and at the end of the latter she restored their son to them.[62] In addition, the Surrey created the magnificent Mrs. Budd, landlady of the Ferry-house who helps Eliza on her way and "brains" Haley with her frying pan in the fugitive's defense.[63] And Lemon and Taylor's script for the Adelphi contains a profusion of excellent parts for women. In it Cassy tries to protect Eliza from Legree and makes a stirring speech, explaining that he fears her not only because "I've got the devil in me!" but "[b]ecause you had a mother—a woman, such as I am. You remember the lessons that you learned beside her knees, before your evil courses broke her gentle heart. In the dead of night, in the hour of sickness, her teachings are remembered." Not only does Cassy here reiterate Stowe's own ideas about the benefits of maternal influence, but she and the other women in the play repeatedly come to each other's aid. Topsy warns Eliza about her imminent sale; her mistress is overheard pleading for the mother and child; and when Eliza makes her escape she "exits from window watched by Cassy in moonlight." The ferryman's wife helps delay the pursuers; Topsy advises Eliza how to get away and risks her life to help George rescue Eliza and Harry; while Cassy encourages the other slaves to flee Legree and finally shoots him dead.[64]

The efforts of individual actresses could also help to ameliorate the blandness of their parts, as the *Theatrical Journal* suggested of Mrs. Walter Lacy, playing Eliza at the Olympic: "[She] exerted herself to give a dramatic colouring to the part which it can hardly be said to possess either in the novel or in the drama . . . if we except her perilous crossing of the Ohio on the broken ice."[65] In good parts, on the other hand, women could excel, as the reports suggest Mrs. Keeley did playing Lemon and Taylor's Topsy: the *Spectator* called her Topsy "one of those bold though highly-finished pictures of character which, however small, stand out from the general mass"; the *Critic* called her "the great feature in the piece" and drew attention to the "disadvantage" for other actresses who took the role "of following so great an artist." The *Era* was presumably thinking of Mrs. Keeley when it compared British Topsies with Mrs. Howard's, declaring the English version "the droll, half idiot, wholly ignorant," while the American one was "shrewd, cunning, naturally wicked, almost impish."[66]

However, the British plays not only celebrated women but also, as with Aiken's and Conway's plays, sometimes cracked jokes at their expense. One script opens on feminine frivolity, as Mrs. Shelby makes a fuss over a new bonnet in which she is to go out.[67] Although the Standard Theatre went so far as to include Mrs. Bird, it also subverted her scenes, which in the novel champion womanly "feeling" over manmade politics by giving her the comic lines: "I'm a woman and I never listen to men. . . . [W]omen are generally right. . . . Mr B don't argue, you'll get the worst of it."[68] At the Victoria Theatre a slave raised a laugh with "Missus is always Massa in de end."[69] The City of London's Ophelia was more ludicrous even than Aiken's or Conway's: like them she is a comic spinster, fancying that Legree is in love with her when he lusts after her land. When Topsy apprises her of his real motives, she exclaims, "It's very hard a virgin can't entertain an idea of connubial bliss, but must have her hopes blighted by such a little devil." Female sentimentality is also a source of skepticism at the City of London, as the play reveals in Ophelia's ridiculous response to Topsy's "spose I grow'd": "[W]hat a dear ignorant stupid little darling it is.... [S]uch a shrewd little ignoramus[;] it's quite a treat to talk to her."[70]

These plays also shared their American counterparts' interest in interracial sex. Sometimes it was used to condemn slavery, as in Lemon and Taylor's script, where the stage directions indicate that Legree "smacks his lips" as he describes Eliza as "a real picture, no more color in your own sister."[71] Elsewhere, as in Aiken and Conway, British writers joked about the idea of amalgamation. At both the Pavilion and the Victoria it was the Cockney characters who made or contemplated interracial unions, directly placing British characters in such scenes. Were the Cockneys in the audience invited to identify with "Billy Bombast" the London costermonger, whose "wife was a black . . . taken away by the Chicktaws"?[72] The tone of these plays suggests not, for both Bombast and his counterpart at the Victoria, Timothy Tickler, were comic characters, and their would-be paramours sported jokey names that drew further attention to their race ("Snowball" at the Pavilion, "Milkwhite" at the Victoria). Tickler himself is ambiguous about his flirtation too, expressing anxiety about Milkwhite's attentions that seems only partly due to the fact that he has a wife back in London: "I'm afraid she's getting too agreeable. Oh Mrs Tickler, I wish your arms were long enough to reach me."[73] In an entirely different spirit, the Pictorial Plays' Kentuckian abolitionist, Van Tromp, proudly declares himself to be the son of a mixed marriage, again involving a British man: "Yes my father was an Englishman, who being above vulgar prejudice, admired a black beauty. I was born in this country, and the sun gave a gentle tinge to my complexion to mark me as a favourite."[74] Thus, the suggestion of amalgamation, which the New York plays introduced only fleetingly, was rendered obvious in the London ones, the anxieties and the secret attractions it contained openly staged.

As Timothy Tickler's purchase of a slave at the Victoria suggests, the plays did not necessarily take an orthodox abolitionist line on the slave question, and often they were neither coherent nor consistent in their attitudes either to slavery or to slaves themselves. The script produced for the Standard Theatre incorporated an explicit attack on racial prejudice that was entirely the invention of the dramatist, with no equivalent in the novel:

TOM: It isn't everyone would give his hand to a man of colour. Many have an antipathy to black.

VAN TROMP: If a man was Blue and I liked him I'd shake hands with him. It isn't in the colour of the face[,] its the case to the heart I look at and every honest man be he Brown Pink Green or Yallow I should be proud to grasp hands with.[75]

Despite Van Tromp's comparison of blackness to an unnatural spectrum of colors, the moral of this exchange is clearly that respect for a person's inner qualities both precludes racism and is a virtue in itself. For all its advocation of equality, however, the script is reluctant to condemn slavery outright. Tom declares that George would never have left his master "had he been treated like a man," and he goes on to endorse a benevolent version of slavery even more when he bewails his removal from the Shelby plantation, wishing he could have "died amidst the bright eyes and familiar faces. That made sweet the bondage and light the labour of the contented and happy negro."[76] Slavery, for this playwright, is not only bearable but "sweet" and "light," as long as the slave has his family about him. The Lemon and Taylor version suggests something similar when its slaves conclude that they have "cause to be thankful" because their "good" master and mistress only allow the whip "now and den," and Topsy sighs, " 'Twas lucky day for me when Mass'r Shelby swapped me for that old brown mare."[77] Such remarks suggest some unease about representing unmitigated white cruelty to slaves: the dying St. Clare in *The Slave Hunt!* went so far as to exhort the freed Tom to "tell your country people that all white men are not cruel—that there are those that give their hearts' blood in the cause of Africa's captive sons."[78]

Such confused messages about race and slavery were enforced, as in Aiken and Conway, by the London *Tom* shows' indebtedness to blackface. Blackface entertainment had preceded *Uncle Tom* across the Atlantic at least fifteen years before, and the history of its success in Britain and its adaptation there both predicts and helps explain many of the characteristics of the London *Tom* plays.

One of the possible sources of blackface caricature was himself British.[79] The comedian Charles Mathews used a trip to the United States in the 1820s to create a number of American comic types for the London stage; promising a friend that he would be "rich in black fun," he claimed that he had been observing black Americans specifically for the purpose of impersonating them: "I have studied their broken English carefully."[80] The celebrated sketch that followed popularized the song "Possum up a Gum Tree" in Britain. Thus, Mathews may be seen to have been a pioneer for blackface in Britain or at least to have helped prepare British audiences for it. Certainly, American blackface acts that toured in Britain after the 1820s were received with rapture. T. D. Rice brought "Jim Crow" to London in the 1830s, and it provoked a "mania" reminiscent of the later one for *Uncle Tom*.[81] Other artistes followed, including the Ethiopian Serenaders, the Virginia Minstrels, and Christy's Minstrels, and blackface became in Britain, as it did in the States, one of the most popular forms of entertainment for the rest of the century.[82] Many minstrels also stopped off in Ireland: Douglas Riach calculates that fifteen blackface troupes visited Dublin before the Civil War.[83] British audiences loved local imitations just as much: John Dunn and J. A. Cave did "Jim Crow" after Rice; Cave also copied the banjo playing of Joseph Sweeney and imitated "Yankee" Smith and "Piccaniny" Coleman; the Ethiopian Serenaders inspired the British Columbian Minstrels (later the Lantum Serenaders), the Female American Serenaders, and bands of "male and female 'Ethiopians'" at the Hanover-Square Rooms.[84] Even Karl Marx is reported to have sung minstrel songs on family outings.[85] There were also transatlantic minstrel careers. The English Buckley family, who immigrated to America in 1839, formed a blackface quartet in 1843 and toured successfully in both countries, while the American impresario "Colonel Jack" Haverly set up huge minstrel spectaculars in Britain in the 1880s.[86] Similar connections help explain the combined British and American symbolism employed by the Moore and Burgess Minstrels mentioned in chapter 2: the dust jacket linking the Union Jack and the Stars and Stripes, and the hymns to Britannia and Columbia in their *Tom* play.[87]

Just as in the United States, British blackface evolved over the century, developing from "Ethiopian delineation" by individual performers to the tripartite structure and ensemble playing of the minstrel show, and finally turning into the lavish productions and huge troupes that arrived in the 1870s.[88] Blackface entertained Britons at the theater, at the music hall, and, in the form of itinerant troupes of buskers, on the streets and at fairs, races, markets, and the seaside. A Jim Crow puppet even appeared in some Punch and Judy shows.[89]

Yet although British audiences greeted this American innovation with delight, there were quickly differences in the reception and the performance of British minstrelsy. Musicality, harmony, and sentiment characterized British blackface styles more than American ones, largely because they were the hallmarks of the Ethiopian Serenaders, whose hugely successful tour of

London and the provinces in 1846 and 1847 made them greater favorites in Britain than at home.[90] Playing over four hundred performances in eighteen months, the Serenaders drew fashionable audiences, good reviews, and parodies in *Punch*. When *Uncle Tom* arrived in London there were indigenous "Ethiopian" troupes in the streets and on the concert platforms, and their name had been adopted as the generic British term for minstrels.[91] This "British" style of minstrelsy would condition the blackface elements of London *Tom* plays.

Just as the *Tom* plays were customized for British patrons, blackface had already been tuned to London tastes. Minstrel routines adapted to local conditions as quickly as they did in the United States: the song "Jump Jim Crow" was rewritten with British references, and subsequent blackface acts tailored topical allusions and satires to their audiences, while minstrel jokes shifted to accommodate the British comic preference for puns over malapropisms.[92] The British even rechristened the end men "cornermen."[93]

There is also evidence that minstrelsy came to occupy a different cultural niche from the one it had established in the United States. In Britain a much larger proportion of blackface took place on the street, and busking minstrels were as significant as established troupes.[94] More startlingly, perhaps, in the theaters blackface was perceived as a cross-class, even a family, entertainment. Troupes like the Serenaders attracted the fashionable upper echelons, and blackface seems to have been patronized by the respectable types, including clergymen, who avoided other forms of theater.[95]

This exceptional class dimension to British minstrelsy may cast light on the politics of the *Tom* plays, although the disdainful middle-class reviewers seem to have bracketed them more with the melodramas the middle classes spurned than with the minstrels they enjoyed. However, the identifications between class and racial oppression we have seen in some *Tom* plays may have had a precedent in blackface, especially when the numbers of black people in London were relatively low.[96] Michael Pickering has speculated that "[m]instrelsy was just as much about English social relations as it was about a scantily known Afro-American population" and that "[r]ace relations abroad were perceived in the light of class relations at home."[97] This may help to explain the significance of Cockney characters like Billy Bombast and Timothy Tickler in the *Tom* plays, although, as we have seen, they were not simply equated with blackface figures: the *Tom* plays were testing the sympathies that blackface shows had already set up between London laborers and supposed American slaves.

Nevertheless, although the numbers of black people in London had declined since the eighteenth century, they had not disappeared altogether, and, as I shall shortly suggest, it is interesting to consider how much audiences figured them into their responses to blackface. A review of the Ethiopian Serenaders suggested that some British audiences were too unsophisticated to recognize their theatricality: "[T]he deception created is so great that wagers have been offered that they are really 'darkies,'" although perhaps this is just another version of the recurrent myth of misrecognition in American minstrelsy, of which Sam Sanford's story of being taken for a slave was a particularly elaborate example.[98]

Certainly, minstrelsy served a different purpose away from the special sensitivities about race and slavery in the United States: as J. S. Bratton has remarked, "[T]he average Englishman had no need of an art form which would help him deal with complex problems of identity and confrontation with a black population."[99] She argues that blackface primarily functioned in Britain as a sign of theatricality, which, as we have seen, was also one of its roles in the United States. George Rehin confirms this, noting that British observers of blackface buskers were rarely concerned with the "quality of impersonation."[100] Still, minstrelsy may also have resonated with reports of other racial encounters in Britain, to whose imperial concerns it was sometimes obliquely linked. Pickering has argued that blackface imparted a complacent sense of racial superiority and "was undoubtedly integrated into the Victorian culture of imperialism, not in a relation of cause and effect but as a powerful agent of reinforcement."[101] *Punch* made connections between minstrelsy and the peoples of the British Empire, though it did so in a jokey and ironic way that suggested that the link was not automatic.[102] A sketch in *Punch* remarked on the way blackface played fast and loose with geographic associations: "[O]ne of the oddest combinations of talent we have heard of for some time, is that represented by the New Orleans Ethiopians. Our map tells us that New Orleans and Ethiopia are a good way apart; but by a rare combination they seem to be brought together in one of the parties of Serenaders now delighting the Metropolis." *Punch* then proceeded to match this troupe's yoking of an American city and an African people with some invented collaborations between exotic peoples and localities in London: "If this sort of association is found effective, we shall be hearing next of the Brentford Bohemians, the Chelsea Cherokees, and the Mary-le-bone Mulattoes. We have already been given to understand that the Kensington Coolies will shortly be announced in conjunction with the Houndsditch Half-Castes, who will, together, furnish an Entertainment of the most attractive character."[103] If we put aside the seductively alliterating Bohemians, we can see *Punch* here moving from American racial types and terms ("Cherokees") to the imperial vocabulary of the Far East ("Coolies"), while the American derogatory term for racial mixture ("Mulattoes") gives way to the one that became common in India ("Half-Castes"). Minstrelsy certainly offered scope for imperial fantasies in Britain, even if they were only explored on the pages of *Punch*.

Blackface had also already demonstrated the potential for national preening over slavery that distinguished so many British *Tom* plays. Bratton has demonstrated that "self-congratulation" was a strong element in the sympathy British audiences extended to sentimental blackface figures, arguing that "[a]s soon as the Englishman could claim to be free of the taint of slaveholding, he turned self-righteously upon the Americans with a show of horror."[104] The evangelical and humanitarian influences that had fueled the British antislavery movement earlier in the century could also have been at work, however misguidedly, in the affection that British audiences showed for these stage slaves.[105] Still, British minstrelsy may have been pernicious enough: one *Illustrated London News* review of black dancer William Henry Lane moved seamlessly into an account of the Ethiopian Serenaders, an early example of the long line of conflations of blackface with black people.[106] And worse, in 1859 Frederick Douglass blamed the influence of minstrelsy for what he perceived as an increase in racial discrimination in Britain since his visit in 1846.[107]

Minstrelsy in the *Tom* plays reflected many of the distinguishing characteristics of British blackface. To some extent the London plays, like the American ones, merely capitalized on the blackface moments in the novel. The Olympic opened with slaves dancing, and Harry went through his song-and-dance routine in several versions.[108] In two plays not only is Harry called "Jim Crow," as in the book, but the script specifically demands that he perform an imitation of that stage act.[109]

Nevertheless, as *The Tyrant!* demonstrated, there were specifically British markers. *The Tyrant!* belabored the link between *Uncle Tom's Cabin* and minstrelsy: Tom plays the bones and makes suitably lame jokes. (Pointing to the prostrate villains, he asks, "[W]hy is dem gentlemen like eggs for breakfast? . . . Cos dey's all cracked on de top end.") However, Tom's closing "plantation dance" is not just compared to William Henry Lane but related to the writer who first brought him to British attention, Dickens, "after the manner of Boz's inimitable Juba." Dickens had described (but not named) Lane dancing in *American Notes*. In the United States Dickens was told that Lane was "the greatest dancer known," but afterward in Britain it was felt that it was "Dickens [who] had immortalised him."[110] *The Tyrant!* also makes a reference to the Ethiopian Serenaders in its prescriptions for Tom's costume. He is to be attired in full evening dress, with "black suit, . . . large stick-up collar of writing paper, . . . burnt cork face, black kid gloves."[111] The Serenaders, too, wore smart black evening dress with paper collars and cuffs, in contrast to the ragged look affected by other troupes.

The costumes in *The Tyrant!* suggest that there may have been visual reminders of the Serenaders in the *Tom* plays, and there were certainly musical ones. Among other tunes, the Serenaders sang "Old Dan Tucker," "Clar de Kitchen," "Somebody in de House," and "Nelly Bly," which included the lines:

> Darkies all great and small
> Don't ye work too long;
> For if de day was made for toil
> De night was made for song.[112]

The Serenaders also popularized "Lucy Neal," the comic-nostalgic song of separated slave lovers.

London managers incorporated the Serenaders' songs into *Tom* shows, specifically tying *Uncle Tom's Cabin* to the blackface repertoire that was most familiar to their audiences. American plays absorbed Stephen Foster's songs and associated them with Stowe's characters, but British plays used the songs of the Ethiopian Serenaders: "Old Dan Tucker" was sung in two stage *Uncle Toms*, "Lucy Neal" at the Pavilion, "Nelly Bly" and "Ole Virginny" at the Adelphi, and "Clar de Kitchen" and "Somebody in de House" at the Victoria. The songs were also turned into catchphrases or incorporated into stage business, as at the Victoria, where Dinah repeatedly yelled, "Clar de kitchen."[113] The title of one pantomime, *Uncle Tom's Cabin; or, Harlequin and Lucy Neal*, linked Stowe's hero with the Serenaders: "Lucy Neal" was both a character and a song; another minstrel song was personified as "Dandy Jem of Caroline" and in the plot "The Demon Slavery" plotted against them all.[114] That this acculturation process could go on anywhere, both for blackface and for *Uncle Tom's Cabin*, is demonstrated by a Canadian playbill for a production of Lemon and Taylor's dramatization in Toronto, which featured the Canadian Ethiopian Serenaders.[115]

The *Tom* plays transformed more than the songs. Often, where blackface moments were lifted directly from Stowe, they were deprived of the ironic context or telling juxtapositions that in the novel allowed for readings sympathetic to the slaves. The Standard Theatre's dramatization, for instance, opened with Sam's stump speech, taken almost verbatim from the book but without the authorial comment that flags his "speechifying" as a parody of white men's political meetings.[116] At the Olympic Topsy made her "never was born" statement as a free servant of Senator Bird, which deprived it of all its antislavery pathos and made her lying and stealing, which also continued in the play, both inexplicable and more reprehensible.[117] At the Victoria, too, her mischief was spiteful rather than a product of her inhuman upbringing.[118]

At other times the adaptors tried their hands at producing their own blackface, often in a way that undermined the dignity of their characters and failed to forward any antislavery conclusions. At the Olympic Uncle Tom himself became ridiculous, with his exaggerated blackface "dialect" and simpleminded jokes: "[I]f [Harry] was only a bit more blacker, den him be a beauty all ober; exact like Uncle Tom. He! he!"[119] Although they created a number of dynamic black characters who liberated themselves on their own initiative, Lemon and Taylor also conceived an execrable exchange between Adolph and Chloe that turned on the relative lightness of Adolph's skin:

> CHL: Hear the wally-de-sham- talk about nigger as do him was white hisself. Hutch! hutch! him only a quadroon.
> ADO: I know that very well, but you're a black nigger, you are.
> CHL: Dat's better dan be neither black nor white, eh niggers? Hutch! hutch![120]

These aspects of the London *Tom* plays picked up on Stowe's use of blackface, or at least on its easy incorporation into her text, but failed to see or chose to ignore the complex and barbed ways in which Stowe herself sometimes deployed it.

In some instances, however, even within the very plays that also played up the most barbaric of minstrel representations, some element of the novel's subtleties survived the transfer to the stage. Webb's Juvenile Drama asked its young impresarios to put on a compressed Topsy–Miss Ophelia exchange in which the "'spect I grow'd" line was specifically linked to the slave's upbringing by a speculator.[121] In the equestrian version at Astley's Amphitheatre Mrs. Shelby's unspoken understanding with her slaves is made obvious ("Andy, I don't want that girl caught—give her a little time"), and the confusion that attends the horse catching is revealed to be deliberate: Sam tells his companions, "You understand you are to go and look for de horses ebery whar—they are not to be found."[122] The scene is divested of the minstrel disguise (the end man—interlocutor exchange) it sports in the novel, and the antislavery alliance between mistress and slaves is more explicit. In this British performance the chaos and linguistic confusion is unambiguously a clever ploy, whereas in the novel, although Stowe signaled that it was a ruse, it could also have been read as black incompetence. The book used a potentially demeaning format to screen its subversive ironies, but the equestrian drama largely abandoned the disguise. Clownish though their language is in the Astley script, Sam and Andy's horseplay is intelligent, skillful, and exercised in a good cause. The two slaves' unhelpful assistance to the slave catcher also occurred at the City of London and the Standard Theatres, both of which included the double bluff over directions, again fully crediting the slaves with the sophistication with which Stowe had ambiguously endowed them.[123]

At the Adelphi Lemon and Taylor's script was accompanied by songs that invested black characters with sympathy, although it also contained the unflattering depictions described above. "Sambo's Lament for Uncle Tom's Cabin," a song used in the play, offered a lavishly sentimental assessment of Tom's fate alongside a more spiky comment on the American veneration of liberty:

> Far away from ole Kentucky
> Soon poor Uncle Tom must go,
> All among de big plantations
> Where de rice and cotton grow:
> We shall want him in the morning[,]
> Want him and he won't be here;
> Poor Aunt Chloe's heart is breaking
> But who minds de nigger's tear[.]
>
> Keep de wife and sell de husban'[,]
> Trade away de child'n too;
> [']Cause it is a land of freedom
> Dis is what dese freemen do![124]

The sentimentality in this production was most marked in relation to Topsy, and in her case Lemon and Taylor effected a complex shuttling between minstrel and sentimental techniques that emulated Stowe's use of blackface more nearly than other stage representations and reinforced the other strong roles Lemon and Taylor had created for women. In an episode interpolated by Lemon and Taylor themselves, Topsy helps George to escape in disguise by dressing herself as his boy slave. Her mischievousness in the scene beautifully dramatizes not only the naughtiness of Stowe's character but also her impatience with conventional femininity. She pronounces that it feels as if "I was raised for a boy, and got changed at nussin" and cannot hide her delight in her breeches: "*Top*[:] I reckon, I'se as wicked as ever again, wid dese yere tings on (*looking at her dress*). Dey a heap better than petticoats to dance in (*She begins to sing and dance to the air of 'Jim Crow'*)."[125] Topsy's easy association of the minstrel tune with cross-dressing (itself, of course, a blackface tradition, though in the minstrel show it was male performers who wore skirts) is reinforced moments later when she points to her trousers, declares she's risen in the world "[a]ll de way to de superior sex," and breaks out into another blackface song, "Sich a Gettin' up Stairs."[126]

But Topsy's cavorting at the Adelphi was not restricted to comic play; like Stowe, Lemon and Taylor leavened the hilarity with pathos and put it to good antislavery use. Topsy's catchphrase, "I'se so wicked," shifts in the text from signaling her incorrigible blackface dishonesty to marking her awareness of her shortcomings and finally to enabling an act of heroism. Struck by Eliza's offer of maternal affection (an echo of Eva's in the novel), Topsy comes to envy Eliza's child: "He not wicked—is he?" She soon reaches out herself to George Harris: "[M]ass'r George, I know I's dreffel wicked, but seems like if you died I die too." Eventually, she braves Legree's bloodhounds to save her friends: "Dogs ain't no count to Topsy; I'se so wicked, I is!"[127] The laughs raised by the recurrence of Topsy's motif are thus increasingly tinged with poignancy in the script, as the double-edged appeal for sympathy in Lemon and Taylor's comic device comes to look very like Stowe's in the novel.

As well as re-creating some of the subtleties manifested by the blackface in *Uncle Tom's Cabin*, Lemon and Taylor also put a condemnatory spin on a joke in which several other *Tom* shows happily indulged. Exaggeratedly inappropriate names for slaves that mocked their blackness appeared at several theaters. The Standard and the Pavilion had slaves called Snowball, the Olympic had one named Lilyvite, and there were also a Milkwhite and a Lillysnow.[128] Lemon and Taylor underlined the dreadfulness of this jest by putting it in the mouth of Legree, who calls the unfortunate Topsy "Snowball." Even more damningly, George Harris adopts the habit along with a "Southern drawl" when he poses as a slave owner, addressing a waiter as "my lump of snow."[129] What in other productions made an appropriate line became, in the Adelphi version, slave traders' humor. Lemon and Taylor's play demonstrated in these

incidents what it also embodied: the dangerous ambiguity of the *Tom* plays'
conjunctions of blackface and sentimentality, patriotism and antislavery
opinions. The combination of these elements in the London *Tom* plays made
for a very strange cocktail. Audiences wept for stage slaves, cheered at their
rebellions, reflected smugly on the superiority of British laws and attitudes,
and also laughed at images of dim, deceitful, and inherently comical blacks.

These damaging representations ensured that the plays kept something in
common with the extremes of proslavery material—although generally more
politically radical than American dramatizations, the British ones were also
amenable to audiences of a different persuasion. The transportation of the
Lemon and Taylor script to American cities indicates at least as much, but
even in Britain the constituents of the London *Tom* shows were easily re-
assembled into a product of a sharply different political cast. Another parody
of the London *Tom* plays, produced at the Strand Theatre in October 1852,
makes their theatrical connections with the Ethiopian Serenaders explicit
and at the same time directs a virulent attack on British antislavery activity.
In *Uncle Tom's Crib!* the eponymous character is the proprietor of a London
inn, a House of Call for Ethiopian Serenaders. His associates include "Dandy
Jim, late of Carolin[a]," and "Ginger Crow," both obviously references to
blackface songs. The play contains a variety of typically blackface entertainment: songs, dances, and burlesques of political speeches and *Romeo and
Juliet*'s balcony scene ("Look dar! What light thro' yonder winder breaks?
'tis de West and Dinah am de sun"). Blackness and blackface mingle in celebration of theatricality, as the characters describe themselves as "talented
Gentlemen ob Color which has evinced sufficient genius to please de public."[130]

The shafts at slavery come in the form of one Squashtop, who is a lecturer
at Hexminster Hall, a reference to Exeter Hall, the evangelical meeting place
whose name had become an unkind metonym for the British antislavery
movement. The play uses this character to take up the question of liberty, so
passionately defended in the other *Tom* shows but in *Uncle Tom's Crib!* the
subject of irreverent play. Tom congratulates Squashtop on his speech against
the sale of women for money, only to demand a fee for his own daughter's
hand. Tom intends to force his daughter to accept Squashtop. Tom's many
malapropisms are not an endearing trait, as Chloe's are in Stowe's novel, but
a sign in this play of the ignorance that underlies his brutality. The piece
pokes fun at the patriotic rhetoric with which the *Tom* plays dressed their
abolitionism, making Dinah reject Squashtop's advances with almost the
same phrases in which George hailed Canada in those productions: "[W]e'se

in Free England where even de poor black girl can have protection from de laws."[131] It also directs its satire at British abolitionists, as Squashtop describes gullible "old ladies" going "off into fits" at his words. He makes a cruel comment on the theatricality of such meetings ("[D]ey likes to have a real darkie among 'em") that is at the same time perhaps an apt evaluation of the degree to which black antislavery speakers were exploited in reality.[132] Eventually, Squashtop is revealed to be doubly a fraud—he is a failed crossing sweeper who has obtained his money by stealing from Dinah's true sweetheart.

Squashtop may have been more than a dramatic fancy. Crossing sweeping was among the low-paid jobs that black Londoners had taken up since the eighteenth century, and although Mayhew found very few black people among the London poor in the 1860s, he did know of a black crossing sweeper who had left five hundred pounds when he died.[133] Just as Stowe's novel helped shape the way some commentators remembered real black people in America, so the *Tom* plays provided the Strand parodist with a way of imagining London's own black crossing sweepers in terms of blackface. The play may also have been responding to the African Americans (among them Frederick Douglass, William Wells Brown, Henry "Box" Brown, William and Ellen Craft, Sarah Remond, Samuel R. Ward, and Josiah Henson) giving antislavery lectures at antislavery meetings all over Britain in the 1840s and 1850s.[134] But to come up with the antislavery speaker who also swept a crossing, the author of *Uncle Tom's Crib!* did not even need to fuse together images of black British people with *Uncle Tom* and visiting Americans. One extraordinary character seems to have combined these connections, and even gestured toward the theatricality of the *Tom* plays, in his own career.

Soon after the publication of *Uncle Tom's Cabin* the fugitive slave William Wells Brown recorded meeting an African man in London whose astonishing variety of occupations resonated tellingly with those that appeared in *Uncle Tom's Crib!* Joseph Jenkins distributed bills, played Othello at the Eagle Saloon (also the site of one of the more down-market *Tom* shows written by Fitzball), swept a crossing in Chelsea, and preached at a church in Cheapside.[135] Like the character in *Uncle Tom's Crib!* Jenkins was black, accustomed to the stage, and a crossing sweeper, and, given Wells Brown's acquaintance, he probably had antislavery connections too. He also sold psalms and tracts and served as the leader of a band. *Uncle Tom's Crib!* may have been a dig at Joseph Jenkins or someone like him (if another such polymath were possible), but even if unintended, it provides a cruel caricature of an amazingly energetic and determined individual.

Jenkins was not the only black man in Britain who found himself being ascribed a persona traceable back to Stowe's novel. At the end of the century,
the musician Samuel Coleridge-Taylor discovered that the source of the exaggerated kindness with which he was received in Hastings lay in the fact that
Uncle Tom's Cabin was playing at the theater there. Coleridge-Taylor resented the implication, for he "got out by the next train."[136]

One review of the Olympic Theatre's *Uncle Tom* praised the "perfect truthfulness" of the actor who played him, explaining that while "imitating the
voice and manner of the African, [he] suppressed the ludicrous peculiarities
that are almost identified in our minds with the negro character."[137] That "association" and those "ludicrous peculiarities" derived from blackface, but
Uncle Tom's Crib! suggests that the *Tom* plays had only adapted them not ban-
ished them altogether. To some extent these plays, which so delighted in their
country's moral superiority over the United States, were as indebted to American blackface practices as they were to an American woman's novel. None-
theless, in the manner of their borrowing, in their adaptation to local cultural
and theatrical preoccupations, they also gave a very British spin to *Uncle
Tom's Cabin*.

6

"TOM" MANIA IN BRITAIN: THE STAFFORD HOUSE ADDRESS AND "REAL UNCLE TOMS"

EVERY AMERICAN IN LONDON IS DISGUSTED WITH THE UNCLE TOM MANIA HERE.

"The Uncle Tom's Cabin Mania," *British Army Despatch*, reprinted in the *Liberator*, 21 January 1853

For some Americans, one of the most disturbing effects of the *Uncle Tom* phenomenon was its international dimension. The *Southern Literary Messenger* argued that *Uncle Tom's Cabin* was worth reviewing precisely because it was receiving so much attention abroad. "In general . . . [a]bolition attacks" were not important enough to refute, but *Uncle Tom* had "crossed the water to Great Britain, filling the minds of all who know nothing of slavery with hatred for that institution and those who uphold it."[1] *Uncle Tom* mania ensured that the complex and sensitive issue of American slavery had become a fashionable topic in the periodicals and drawing rooms of a rival country. Worse, it allowed Britain, once the colonial power and still a class-ridden monarchy, to lecture the nation whose constitution was founded on ideas of liberty and democracy. Britain had emancipated its West Indian slaves in 1833; now *Uncle Tom's Cabin* made American slavery a British cause.

However, *Tom* mania did more than travel to Britain; it was altered and expanded in the process so that some aspects of the British response to *Uncle Tom's Cabin* contributed to the meanings that accrued to the text. *Uncle Tom* inspired an antislavery petition that caused an international quarrel; Lord Shaftesbury and the Duchess of Sutherland, who sponsored the petition, thus came to be associated with the novel. In this way *Tom* mania incorporated the reputations of these two aristocrats, critiques of *Tom* mania becoming conflated with attacks on Sutherland or Shaftesbury. In the same way, *Uncle Tom's Cabin* impinged upon the receptions of the ex-slaves and antislavery lecturers who visited Britain in the 1850s. By virtue of its ubiquity in Britain, the book came to be seen as the primary available authority on American slavery, and audiences demanded that visiting Americans situate their accounts of the institution in relation to Stowe's novel. British comments on slavery, like the Duchess of Sutherland's petition, changed the shape of *Tom* mania, and in return *Tom* mania became the frame for the majority of British discussions of slavery.

This process was most striking when it affected black people. As I have indicated several times in this study, *Uncle Tom* and its offshoots sometimes powerfully altered the perception (and reception) of real people. This experience was intensified in the 1850s for the few African Americans in Britain, who were already treated as exotic novelties: antislavery lecturers, the singer Elizabeth Greenfield, and the dramatic reader Mary Webb. All found themselves interpreted in terms of *Tom* mania, effectively drawn into it, but in some cases they themselves were also able to harness the success of *Uncle Tom's Cabin*. Just as British readers could transform *Tom* mania, so could the black visitors whom it most directly affected.

Tom mania in Britain also opened up a variety of political issues aside from slavery. The response to Stowe's novel provoked questions about Anglo-American relations, the relative merits of democracy and aristocracy, and whether women should be allowed to comment on them. In Britain class and gender as well as race and region were recognized as significant for the reception of *Uncle Tom's Cabin*. As in the United States, these discussions were played out in texts: drama, as we have seen, and also travel writing, newspaper articles, petitions, poems, and songs. But, significantly, *Tom* mania in Britain also expanded to include an array of cultural events. *Uncle Tom's* celebrity meant that incidents as diverse as Stowe's 1853 visit to Britain, minstrel sketches, antislavery lectures, and the stage performances of Elizabeth Greenfield and Mary Webb were all analyzed in relation to Stowe's novel. As in the American texts, different discourses blended in this transatlantic debate, but they also battled: just as the anti-*Tom* novels had rewritten black protest as blackface frolicking, so the participants in British *Tom* mania fictionalized and caricatured their opponents, reimagining each other for their own purposes.

Americans learned of the extraordinary overseas success of *Uncle Tom's Cabin* from the London reviews, which were often reprinted in American newspapers.[2] Their effect was exacerbated by two events in 1853: Stowe's trip to Britain and an antislavery petition.

Stowe was invited to Britain by the Glasgow Ladies' New Anti-Slavery Society.[3] There were strong links between British and American antislavery societies: British groups regularly raised funds for American causes, and American abolitionists, including African Americans, toured Britain and Ireland in the 1840s.[4] American slave narratives also sold large numbers in Britain and, as Richard Blackett argues, may have "paved the way for *Uncle Tom's Cabin*" there; certainly, British abolitionists exploited the book's popularity.[5] Some organized the Uncle Tom Penny Offering campaign, which collected large sums all over the country.[6] The novel helped to stoke new interest in antislavery societies, particularly ladies' societies and those in the north of England and in Scotland, and although British abolitionists were as riven by ideological disputes as American ones, they shared out Stowe's visit eagerly, organizing the majority of the receptions and events held in her honor.[7]

Yet the trip to Britain became as much a celebrity tour as an antislavery mission. From the moment of her arrival at Liverpool docks, Stowe was followed and feted by huge crowds, large numbers were turned away from the packed halls at which she spoke, and enthusiastic mobs greeted her arrivals and departures at every railway station. The author was presented with costly gifts, collections for slaves' welfare, and publicly raised compensation for the royalties *Uncle Tom* lost in the absence of international copyright. Richard Brodhead has compared the scale and management of Stowe's reception with the enthusiasm that had greeted the American tour of the Swedish concert singer Jenny Lind in 1851–52. Stowe not only drew crowds comparable in size and excitement to Lind's and similarly made her travel plans public to accommodate those crowds, but she also "found a career, like Lind . . . as a famous object of public attention."[8] The difference was that Lind was one of a series of Europeans celebrated for bringing culture to America; Stowe, of course, was an American being lionized in Europe.

The political importance of this adulation was underlined by Queen Victoria's decision not to meet Stowe. Forrest Wilson argues that the Queen's ministers cautioned that such a gesture would upset proslavery interests in the States: the Queen was said to have remarked, "America and slavery was a question with which Great Britain had nothing to do."[9] The association of Stowe with "America and slavery" was a manifestation of a recurring concern about her reception in Britain—that *Uncle Tom's Cabin* was damaging the national interests of the United States. Stowe herself fueled these worries and contributed to the publicity given to her triumphant progress by publishing an account of her visit, *Sunny Memories of Foreign Lands*, in 1854.[10] *Sunny Memories* was partly a testimony to Stowe's welcome in Britain, with detailed attention to the events organized for her by antislavery sympathizers, and partly a gushing record of her cultural tourism, describing her ecstatic responses to historical scenes and the homes of literary giants like Scott and Shakespeare. As fascinating to Stowe in the book as the physical remnants of the past in Britain were the living celebrities she encountered, and she describes a number of introductions to famous people. As Christopher Mulvey noted, Stowe, like other nineteenth-century visitors from democratic America, was charmed by the British upper classes.[11] *Sunny Memories* not only flatters individual aristocrats but admires their lifestyles and approves of their relations with their tenants.[12] Stowe was so captivated that in 1857 she even

proposed to write a book about the British aristocracy, and she was only dis-
suaded by Calvin Stowe's concern that she would appear to be supporting
"the oppressive institutions of old."[13]

It was not farfetched for Calvin to fear that Stowe would seem to be "coun-
tenancing . . . wrong" in another country even while she denounced it in her
own. In view of the furor in 1853 Stowe's idea was astonishingly tactless. The
starstruck name-dropping in *Sunny Memories* went ill with *Uncle Tom*'s claim
to speak for "the lowly," and the British aristocracy formed a major target for
critics of *Uncle Tom* mania. This was not solely a result of *Sunny Memories*.
The crucial impetus came from a petition inspired by Stowe's book, authored
by the Earl of Shaftesbury and promoted by the Duchess of Sutherland.

As Viscount Ashley in the 1840s, Shaftesbury had campaigned for a bewil-
dering array of religious and philanthropic causes.[14] Struck by the force of
Uncle Tom's Cabin ("marvellous work!"), in November 1852 he sent a document entitled "An Affectionate and Christian Address of Many Thousands of
Women of England to Their Sisters, the Women of the United States of America" to a number of newspapers.[15] Shaftesbury gave no indication why the
petition was designed especially for his "fair fellow subjects," though when
the Duchess of Sutherland took up his suggestion that they circulate it and
collect signatures, she argued that the address should be presented by women
because "[w]e shall not be suspected of any political motives; . . . the state of
things to which we allude is one peculiarly distressing to our sex; and . . . our
interposition will be ascribed altogether to domestic, and in no respect to national, feelings."[16]

When Sutherland made this speech to a group of titled women, she highlighted precisely the issues on which critics of the Stafford House Address
would seize. Her conviction that its signatories—who included the Duchesses
of Bedford and Argyll, the Countess of Shaftesbury, the Lady Mayoress of London, and Viscountess Palmerston—would "not be suspected of political motives" was totally misplaced. Opponents divined extreme and improbable plots
behind the address and found sinister significance precisely in the distinction
of the names appended to it. But it was Sutherland's assumption that slavery's
effects were especially "distressing to our sex" that would be most firmly con-
tested, and her contrast of the "national" and "domestic" provided the terms
on which the Stafford House ladies would be challenged. Thousands of ordinary women also put their name to the Stafford House Address (by the time
it was presented to Stowe in May 1853 it had been signed by 562,448 women),
but in its wider discussion both these and Shaftesbury were ignored.[17]

The address reinforced the novel's focus on women and slavery, but it lent it an international dimension. Also, its wide discussion in British and American newspapers and in a variety of popular commentaries drew a number of other issues into association with *Uncle Tom*. Class rivalries and the old quarrels of Scotland and England became embroiled in the discussion of women's roles and responsibilities. And as with other readings of Stowe's novel, these issues transferred easily to dealings with black people. African Americans in Britain as antislavery lecturers, entertainers, and refugees from the Fugitive Slave Act found themselves part of the *Tom* mania.

The address appealed to "a common origin, a common faith, and, we sincerely believe, a common cause," asking American women to reflect on slavery's un-Christian denial to its victims of the "sanctity of marriage" and "education in the truths of the Gospel." It called on them "as sisters, as wives, and as mothers, to raise your voices to your fellow-citizens, and your prayers to God, for the removal of this affliction and disgrace from the Christian world."[18] In its stress on religious and domestic relations, in its location of a special role in protest for women, and in its stressing of influence rather than action the address neatly summed up the political emphases of Stowe's novel. Like *Uncle Tom*, the address called on women to remedy the problem of slavery by exercising their moral and spiritual influence over their "fellow-citizens"—their voting menfolk.

Also like *Uncle Tom's Cabin*, the address stopped short of advocating emancipation: "[W]e do not shut our eyes to the difficulties, nay, the dangers that might beset the immediate abolition of that long-established system." Despite this refusal to endorse "immediatist" antislavery politics, the Stafford House Address conformed with the traditions of many ladies' antislavery societies. Recent work on American women abolitionists has highlighted their diversity of opinion on women's role in the movement, ranging from those, like Lucretia Mott and Elizabeth Cady Stanton, who became woman's rights campaigners in the late 1840s to the New York ladies' societies that opposed women's participation in the main body of abolitionist activity. Differences over the exact status of women in the abolitionist movement had in fact been the catalyst for the great split between the Garrisonians and the "political" abolitionists in 1840.[19] For all antislavery societies, however, both in Britain and America, petitions were a major part of their traditional weaponry.[20] The stress in the Stafford House Address on familial relationships—basing the appeal on being "sisters, daughters, wives and mothers"—was also common among abolitionist women. In letters cited by Ruth Bogin and Jean Fagan

Yellin, for instance, Maria Weston Chapman describes the female abolition-ists' role as aiding "our husbands, brothers, and sons" and phrases an appeal as from "*wives* and *mothers . . . sisters* and *daughters*."[21] The apparently lim-ited demands of the Stafford House Address, asking women only to raise "[your] voices to your fellow-citizens and your prayers to God," may also have seemed rigorous in the context of other such petitions. For example, Angelina Grimké's motion at a New York convention in 1837 that delegates resolve that "it is the duty of woman to do all that she can by her voice and her pen and the influence of her example to overthrow the horrible system of American slavery" was highly controversial and quickly ameliorated by a resolution to urge *mothers* "to lift up their hearts to God on behalf of the captive."[22] Yet although the Stafford House Address read like many of these appeals, the British and Foreign Antislavery Society highlighted its conservatism when it set up a rival address calling for outright emancipation.[23]

The Stafford House Address was interpreted, especially in America, as sig-naling a shift in the class basis of British antislavery opinion. Although some titled individuals, like the Earl of Carlisle and the Duchess of Sutherland, had long-standing antislavery sympathies, the majority of antislavery society members were drawn from the Nonconformist middle classes.[24] There was also some working-class support, for instance, for the Uncle Tom Penny Offering.[25] As Audrey Fisch has argued, newspaper commentators expressed anxiety about this, but there was also furious scrutiny of aristocratic in-volvement.[26] *Uncle Tom*'s conscription of earls and duchesses seemed, to nineteenth-century commentators, a striking development. Shaftesbury was a prominent figure in Parliament, and the duchess was a favorite of Queen Victoria, serving periodically as her Mistress of the Robes.[27] The *National Anti-Slavery Standard* argued that it was the first time the cause had been championed by such significant people.[28] It was possible to see their mobi-lization as a sign that *Uncle Tom's Cabin* had reached the most influential members of British society: both the Queen and Prince Albert had read the novel, and so had the leaders of both main political parties.[29] However, the *Spectator* alleged that it was snobbery that drew the ladies to Stafford House, pointing out that antislavery appeals had been staged "for some years with-out recognition by the organized sisterhood: but when it is a graceful Evan-gelical Earl who asks . . . there is preferment in the work."[30] Worse, the *Spec-tator* worried that the "writ of summons" to the duchess's meeting might hereafter serve as "proof of station in the republic of fashion," and "the rank and prestige which are factitiously lent to the meeting may give it an undue importance in the eyes of Americans."[31]

This was precisely the case. In London and then in the United States letters to the press attacked the address, chiding the signatories for interfering in the politics of another country and for ignoring the abuses in their own.[32] The Duchess of Sutherland drew personal criticism. The Sutherland estates in Scotland had seen some of the most extensive and sensational incidents of cruelty during the Highland Clearances, the eviction of thousands of tenants to make way for sheep farming that resulted in suffering, starvation, and mass emigration over several decades. The worst cases involved involuntary removals, for example, that of an old woman whose home was burnt over her head. These had occurred mainly between 1811 and 1821, before the time of the 1850s duke and duchess, but some of the agents responsible remained in place, and there was still injustice and cruelty in the running of the estates at this time.[33] The duchess's championship of American slaves seemed to many, as a result, to be a bit rich. Karl Marx concluded that "the enemy of British Wage-Slavery has no right to condemn Negro-Slavery, a Duchess of Sutherland . . . never."[34] Stowe was vilified for this connection in the Edinburgh press and in Donald MacLeod's *Gloomy Memories*, a bizarre but passionate combination of social detail, Scottish nationalism, verse, and rant, containing his eyewitness descriptions of the removals on the Sutherland estates.[35] As the rest of his title suggests, he saw Stowe as colluding with English oppression: *versus Mrs. Harriet Beecher Stowe's Sunny Memories in (England) a Foreign land.* Stowe devoted a chapter of *Sunny Memories* to a vindication of the Sutherlands, but unfortunately it relied on the partisan testimony of the duke's agent and was, as a result, rather unconvincing.[36]

The Sutherland issue helped opponents to cast doubt on Stowe's concern for the "lowly." The *New York Observer* sought to redirect attention to the British poor, republishing the address with all references to slavery prefaced with "white," in an echo of William Cobbett's denunciations of "white slavery" for British laborers.[37] As Catherine Gallagher has shown, the analogy between slaves and the "free labour" of industrial capital was made for a variety of political motives, including those of West Indian planters, as well as in demands for factory legislation from the British middle classes and radical working-class agitation for suffrage.[38] The *Observer*'s example demonstrates the way these terms and arguments could also be deployed in American critiques of British society.

They even found their way into minstrel shows. The Stafford House affair suited blackface, in which ridiculing the idea of female pretensions to political influence was a comic staple. The admixture of class issues and patriotism was even more promising: the American theater was often the focus of both nationalism and class antagonism, as witnessed by the theater riots of the 1820s, 1830s, and 1840s and especially the Astor Place riot of 1849, during which working-class sections of the audience were provoked to violence by the perceived national arrogance of visiting British actors and their unpatriotic supporters in the expensive seats. *Tom* mania offered minstrelsy a compound of all these favorite elements.[39] References to Stowe's visit to Britain and the Stafford House Address appeared in blackface songs and sketches caricaturing Sutherland alongside Stowe and drawing on the imagery of "white slavery." In New York a lampoon at Burton's Theatre featured characters named the Duchess of Thunderland and Mrs. Skreecher Crow. Songs attacked Aunt Harriet Becha Stowe for hypocrisy and alleged that she was tempting slaves to run away to penury in the North.[40] At Sanford's Opera House Stowe was accused of hypocrisy for abandoning black people at home:

> Dar's Mrs. Whats-her-name,—she wrote 'bout de nigger,
> Den went across de big pond,—dar she cut a figure.
> Guess she made some money,—but gibs de nigger none.[41]

Songs also chided the English for ignoring their own paupers:

> The ladies of England, have sent a big address,
> About Slavery and all its horrors accordin',
> They had better look at home, to their own White Slaves,
> That are starving on the English side of Jordan.[42]

Even the song "Pop Goes the Weasel" incorporated references to the *Uncle Tom* affair:

> John Bull tells, in de ole cow's hum,
> How Uncle Sam used *Uncle Tom*,
> While he makes some white folks *slaves* at home.[43]

Here it was England who was the aggressor and the hypocrite, yet a number of British newspapers were using the popularity of *Uncle Tom's Cabin* to make exactly the same point. The *Times, Reynolds's Newspaper,* the *Northern Ensign,* the *Leader,* and the *Star of Freedom* all argued that "wage-slavery" or the "slavery of labour" was nearly as bad as or even worse than the plight of actual slaves in America.[44] Several British papers reprinted an American address that parodied the form and tone of the original and itemized "the immense aggregate of evils which are visited upon the poor and helpless by your husbands and brothers through the vast extent of your Sovereign's dominions."[45] The American address also employed the analogy "sisters, your land is filled with slaves—slaves to ignorance, slaves to penury, and slaves to vice." Lord Shaftesbury and the antislavery journals were forced to refute the comparison.[46]

The attacks on Stowe and her admirers were not solely concerned with their apparent neglect of the poor in Britain. Some of the commentary was devoted to the fact that the petition was circulated by women. Southern apologists made much of this point, even though some were themselves female. Recent critics have argued that women on either side of the slavery debate shared "ideological propensities" about gender as well as social constraints.[47] Some of these similarities became most apparent when proslavery women aimed to show how different their antislavery counterparts were, as hostile male reviewers condemned both sets of women in the same terms. In a strange echo of the ironies of Stowe's sister Catharine Beecher's attack on Angelina Grimké in 1837, Southern women came into print to disparage the public role being assumed by the Stafford House ladies. Beecher, who was during her career publicly associated with a number of philanthropic campaigns, including ones conducted with the aid of petitions, argued that Grimké was "without the sphere of female duty" in sending antislavery petitions to Congress.[48] The opponents of the Stafford House Address also concerned themselves with "the sphere of female duty," denouncing its signatories for stepping outside it. However, they were themselves mocked—on precisely the same grounds. The controversy over the address drew down on almost every side fierce condemnation of women's contributions to political debate; it also represented a moment of almost unprecedented female engagement, of every shade of opinion.

In Britain the most common view was expressed by the *Spectator*: the ladies had "stepped into the ducal saloon, but out of their province."[49] The *Times* published a number of letters on the subject. Lady Kay Shuttleworth, whose name had been included in the original report, wrote to distance herself from it and to promote the more appropriate cause of governesses instead.[50] "An Englishwoman" declared that the subject was one for legislation and hoped that women would not "show so entire a misconception of their own peculiar character and province" as to interfere with it. She recommended that they concern themselves with racial prejudice instead, which falls "into the domain of feeling—the domain over which women reign paramount."[51] One letter admonished the signatories for their feminine consumerism: "[Y]our own luxurious habits of dress and furniture afford the chief stimulant to the cruelties of which you complain; your own great cotton manufactories, and you, their customers, are the real supporters of American slavery."[52] These adjurations about the proper subjects for female concern and the imputation that feminine vanity was itself a cause of injustice were intensified in American responses to the address.

Southern newspapers counterattacked with letters from Southern ladies who had significant status of their own. The letter from Julia Gardiner Tyler, the wife of the former president, was reprinted by the *Times* of London, while more than fifty newspapers in the United States gave it their approbation.[53] The *Southern Literary Messenger* spelled out her significance: "[H]er social position, it must be admitted, is as high as that of the proud mistress of Stafford House, or any other titled lady of Great Britain."[54] Another letter by Louisa McCord, a frequent contributor to Southern reviews and a wealthy slaveholder, was prefaced with the information that the author was "known to fame."[55]

Such articles used the address to lecture on women's natures, roles, and duties. They questioned whether it was proper for women, especially British women, to comment on political issues in another country. Like *Uncle Tom's Cabin* itself they presumed that women's role was restricted to the domestic realm, and they did not contradict the novel's insistence that slavery was intimately lodged in this sphere. It was the slavery *question*, not the institution itself, that was outside women's sphere. Or at least it was partially outside it, for the replies also generated some ambiguity by playing on the different connotations of "domestic." They used the "national" sense of the word to assert that the issue did not concern *British* ladies, and they invoked its other meaning to imply that British women neglected their households by interesting themselves in slavery.

Sutherland's statement at the launch of the address included the hope that it would be taken as a sample of "domestic" rather than "national" feeling.[56] Instead, Tyler used "domestic" precisely to mean national, attacking "all interference with our domestic concerns." For Tyler the issue was not "domestic" for English duchesses. Another critic emphasized this point by arguing that the signatories would do better listening "to the more earnest invocations of Home."[57] The preface to McCord's letter stressed that she "prefers the discharge of domestic duties to the noisy applause of the world."[58] Tyler insisted that Southern women eschewed public activity so as not to desert the domestic post of their sex: "Do you wish to see them, you must visit their homes. . . . You will then see how utterly impossible it would be to expect the women of the United States to assemble in convention, either in person or by proxy, in order to frame an answer to your address."[59]

Slavery lay outside the domestic sphere of *British* ladies in the sense of both homes and nation, but, paradoxically, the term's peculiar connotations also justified the intervention of Southern women. For them slavery *was* a domestic issue. It not only happened in their nation, it was part of their homes.[60]

McCord also made gender the key to the question, turning on its head the address's appeal to common feminine feeling by arguing that slavery was *vindicated* by the participation of Southern women: "Woman, as a body, has never sided, never can side, with the oppressor."[61] Several Southern reviews of *Uncle Tom's Cabin* had taken the opposite tack, accusing its author of being unfeminine. In a famous letter to the *New Orleans Picayune* one woman wrote to declare that she had had some sympathy with the "supposed wrongs of women" before reading the novel, but afterward, in reaction against "the man Harriet," she had told her husband that she "would promise to 'obey' now more loudly, were we to be married all over again."[62] McCord associated Stowe with woman's rights activists Lucretia Mott and Abby Kelley, lumping her amongst "the whole corps of Reverend Misses, Lady Lecturers and M.D.s" in which she imagined abolitionists.[63] Like these assaults on Stowe, responses to the Stafford House Address implied that its signatories were unwomanly. The "Noble Ladies of England" had neglected their duties, "donning bonnet and shawl, turn[ing] remorselessly the key upon their lords, leaving them to sing in fatherly tones soft 'cradle songs,' whilst they sent loud wailings over the broad Atlantic."[64] This unflattering picture indicates the similarities of Southern ideals of femininity to their Northern and European counterparts, but there were also significant differences.

Like McCord, Tyler asserted that Southern women had been slighted by the address's call on women of the Free States, but her sense of their responsibilities is far more complex and extensive than that suggested by the abandoned English lord crooning over a cradle: "It is the province of the women of the Southern States to preside over the domestic economy of the estates and plantations of their husbands—it is emphatically their province to visit the sick, and attend to the comfort of all the laborers upon such estates; it is felt to be but a poor compliment to the women of the South, to suppose it necessary to introduce other superintendence than their own over the condition of their dependents and servants."[65]

Tyler's retort demonstrates the subtle distinctions between Southern ideals of femininity and their Northern and European counterparts. Elizabeth Fox-Genovese has argued that gender conventions for Southern white women, as for Northern women, stressed motherhood and domesticity. However, Southern women were additionally defined according to the idea of the Southern lady, which required them to embody "the privileges of their class": a "class solidarity with their husbands and fathers" would override gender affiliations.[66] Women were expected to "preside" over their husbands' estates as well as to minister to the unfortunate. Tyler's letter is, as Evelyn Pugh contends, "not only a defense of slavery, but a classic justification of the role and life-style of the idealized Southern woman."[67] Her suggestion that the address is insulting to Southern women also points to the codes of honor that buttressed Southern social hierarchies. McCord makes it clear that these are at stake when she equates the address with "a slap on the face, or a tweak of the nose . . . or . . . when some insolent puppy gives [one] the lie," listing the kind of calculated insults that in the South could provoke a duel.[68]

Tyler and McCord ranged the dignity of the Southern lady against the status of the noble ladies of England, countering the ideal of womanhood enshrined in the Stafford House Address with the South's own distinctive version, one that stressed the "corporatist" life of the plantation over the bourgeois nuclear family, and an idea of the household that contained but was not solely "women's sphere."[69] McCord spelled out the parallels and also indicated the gulf between herself and the Duchess of Sutherland, likening the master-slave relationship to that between a "Highland Chief and his kindred subjects" and mischievously suggesting that the duchess defray the cost of freeing McCord's 160 slaves, which she estimated would take "one fifteenth part of your annual income."[70]

As the analogy with the Highland chief suggests, there was a particular irony in the Southern ladies' paternalistic vision of plantation society. It could look very like the European feudalism they attacked in the British aristocracy. Stowe's own encomium to Warwick Castle in *Sunny Memories* sounds similar: "The influence of these estates on the community cannot but be in many respects beneficial."[71]

Tyler did not succeed in scotching the debate, but her accusations of unfemininity continued to resonate in it. Precisely the same sources of anxiety were invoked in reply to her letter. The *Times*, which had condemned the original address, nevertheless took up the claims that Tyler's social status was comparable to that of the duchess with a sneer at American etiquette—"Mrs. Julia Gardiner Tyler, or Mrs. ex-President Tyler, as she would be described in an American Court Circular." It also resorted to the terms of traditional misogyny, characterizing her missive as "screechy and indiscriminate ... shrill and long-winded." The *Cleveland True Democrat* suggested that it was Tyler, rather than the English ladies, who was being unfeminine: where the English aristocrats were "mild, almost timid" and spoke "with high-bred courtesy," Tyler was "as if forgetful of her sex, rude of speech, insolent in tone, and curt in manner." Her reply "is, in itself, decidedly vulgar."[72]

Yet the accusations of unwomanliness applied on both sides of the Atlantic. As the *Times* saw it, Stafford House was now confronted with "rival goddesses contending for their people and their cities in the eyes of the world."[73] Since so many commentators believed that some or all of these ladies were usurping the duties and privileges of the other sex, their husbands were also a concern. The British *Spectator* charged that the Stafford House ladies had "compromised" their spouses, tainting their names by implication. Tyler confirmed this, speculating that the ladies' names were indeed a front for their husbands, a charge that the London satirical magazine *Punch* quickly returned, asking in rhyme,

> If seriously any such notion possesses you,
> The natural question with which one addresses you
> Is, had poor MR. TYLER the irrationality
> To put into your head such a wild unreality.[74]

In New York, too, the *Tribune* called Tyler's letter "a silly, heartless, pettifogging production" that "reads a good deal more like her husband."[75]

Punch satirized Tyler with female characters in the vein of Stowe's villain (Mrs. Legree, Mrs. Jonathan Jefferson Jackson Legree, and the Misses Legree), imagining their "retort" to the English ladies and then casting doubt on its authorship: "Some have said it was not yours—no woman's work. But ... your logic was too conclusive, your statements were too exact, for mere men." The foolishness—the self-evident femininity—of their arguments explained that "[l]ogic for the Legrees" was womanly lack of it.

Punch's amusement was derived from the idea of an international incident being caused by *women*. Feminine folly was a pet topic with *Punch*—its mock almanac for 1853 featured a series of role-reversing tableaux in which women got bored shopping, drank toasts in the dining room while the gentlemen retired to the parlor, and prepared parliamentary work while their husbands fussed about domestic concerns.[76] The Stafford House controversy proved a gift for this style of comedy. Twice *Punch* imagined the exchange between the Stafford House Address and the parody address as real fisticuffs. (The minstrel song "The Duchess" had similarly envisaged a fight played to the tune of Stephen Foster's "Oh! Susanna": "Mrs. Tyler gave you what was right, / But Duchess don't you cry.")[77] *Punch* mocked the very idea of an international petition by ladies, mimicking the conciliatory feminine language of the two addresses in "The Affectionate Reproof by the Ladies Bull":

> Sisters, daughters, wives and mothers,
> Ah! our feelings how it racks,
> That your sons, sires, husbands, brothers,
>   Should so badly use their blacks!
> Oh! we speak with hearts sincerest,
>   All with love and pity rent;
> But why don't you, Sisters dearest,
>   Make your relatives repent?

Three stanzas followed of "Endearing Recrimination by the Ladies Jonathan" that similarly parodied the American address. The finale, a "Seasonable Interference by an Impartial Arbitrator," commented on the warmth of this exchange between women and pictured them gradually descending into a girlish squabble:

> Ladies, ladies, soft and fairly
>   Interchange your loving raps,
> Or you'll 'scape a quarrel barely,
>   If not come to pulling caps.[78]

In "The Ladies' Battle" *Punch* asserted that it was "advisable for females not to interfere, since . . . it is certain that a great deal more will be said than necessary, if the female tongue has anything to do with it."[79] *Punch* urged all parties to "kiss and make up," and it offered to be a proxy for all the kissing. Like commentators on both sides, *Punch* was drawing the appropriate bounds for women's opinions, which the Stafford House women and their Southern respondents had all overstepped. Although women like Tyler felt it was Sutherland who was out of place, in the resolutely masculinist view of *Punch* they should all get back in the parlor to be kissed.

Uncle Tom's Cabin was, of course, even more significant for the representation, and self-representation, of African Americans than for white women in the slavery debate. The inescapability of Stowe's novel was registered often in black writing in the United States; it was challenged, co-opted, or subtly adapted according to the needs of the writer. And the strategies that slave narrators used for conscripting *Uncle Tom's Cabin* into their own arguments were often redeployed by African Americans in Britain in the 1850s, including exiles, those on antislavery missions, and singers or other performers on tour.

In the United States *Uncle Tom's Cabin* was repeatedly reviewed and much discussed in the black abolitionist press, particularly in *Frederick Douglass' Paper*, where it was both praised and pilloried.[80] Douglass himself applauded the novel because it had opened markets for the cause: "The present will be looked to by after-coming generations, as the age of Antislavery literature—when supply on the gallop could not keep pace with demand—when a picture of a negro on the cover was a help to the sale of a book."[81] This commercial power inevitably made *Uncle Tom's Cabin* a model slave narrators had to acknowledge: in practice, they both worked with and struggled against Stowe's text. Josiah Henson's billing on his narrative as the "real Uncle Tom" seems to have stemmed originally from his editors, though he colluded in it and in the 1870s was so introduced to Queen Victoria.[82] John Brown asserted himself more boldly, not equating himself with Stowe's subject but assuming the status of a fellow antislavery writer and, as such, claiming an insight into Stowe's thinking: "Mrs Stowe has told something about Slavery. I think she must know a great deal more than she has told. I know more than I dare to tell."[83] William and Ellen Craft take up a more mediating position than Brown, appealing to readers in their narrative via the assumed common ground of *Uncle Tom's Cabin* and also offering to explain parts of it, asserting a more comprehensive knowledge of slavery than that of other readers. Their book quotes from Stowe affectionately—"as Mrs Stowe's Aunt Chloe expresses it"—but also offers glosses on *Uncle Tom's Cabin* and Stowe's later novel *Dred*: "This is the reason why Mrs. Stowe calls her characters Uncle Tom, Aunt Chloe, Uncle Tiff, &c."[84]

Solomon Northup's 1853 autobiography, *Twelve Years a Slave*, engaged even more extensively with Stowe's influence and authority. First, a whole series of intertextual references linked his book to Stowe's: *Twelve Years* was dedicated to Stowe; the *New York Times* compared it to *Uncle Tom's Cabin*; Stowe abridged a *New York Times* article on Northup for *The Key to Uncle Tom's Cabin*, and she proclaimed that Northup's account formed "a striking parallel to that history [*Uncle Tom's Cabin*]."[85] Extending the pattern of mutual allusion still further, Northup remarked in *Twelve Years* on the treatment in *Key* of the *New York Times* version of his story.[86]

Yet although Northup's text gained publicity from its association with *Uncle Tom*, he may have been obliquely criticizing the novel when he dismissed men who "write fictions portraying *lowly life as it is*, or as it is not," recalling both Stowe's subtitle, *Life among the Lowly*, and the proslavery novels that had borrowed it.[87] He was certainly taking issue with Stowe when he described being made an overseer, when he "dared not show any lenity, not having the Christian fortitude of a certain well-known Uncle Tom." Northup's strategy is made to seem superior to Uncle Tom's, to the extent that he "escaped the immediate martyrdom [Tom] suffered, and, withal, saved my companions much suffering, as it proved in the end [because he learned how to appear to whip his companions without harming them]."[88] This delicate critique bears out William Andrews's suggestion that *Uncle Tom* provoked "a campaign of literary revisionism in black autobiography of the 1850s" but offers a model of rewriting very different from Andrews's analysis of the increase in depictions of physical suffering (and the militant antiwhite tone in these texts) or from Robert Stepto's reading of Douglass's "The Heroic Slave."[89]

Douglass's 1855 narrative *My Bondage and My Freedom* did not conform either, though it too offered a gentle corrective to *Uncle Tom*.[90] In *The Key to Uncle Tom's Cabin* Stowe had discussed the part of Douglass's *Narrative* that had touched on his relationship with his mother.[91] In turn, Douglass enlarged and expanded on that very passage in *My Bondage and My Freedom*, but, where she evoked the set piece of sentimental literature, the deathbed, he explained that "[s]cenes of sacred tenderness, around the death-bed, never forgotten, and which often arrest the vicious and confirm the virtuous during life, must be looked for amongst the free."[92]

Douglass gently rejected the "scenes of sacred tenderness" that epitomized Stowe's chosen genre, and made motherhood, such a central institution in her novel, a poignant absence. Where Stowe's fictional mothers fight to retain a semblance of conventional familial relations, Douglass describes his own feeling for his mother as a troubling and unnarratable void.

Like slave narrators in the United States, black fugitives and antislavery lecturers received more public attention in Britain as a result of Stowe's book, but their new recognition also came with the risk of seeing their lives conflated with her fiction. The *Liberator* published a letter from William Wells Brown that described *Uncle Tom's Cabin* as "awakening sympathy in hearts that never before felt for the slave" and recorded Stowe's tumultuous reception at an antislavery meeting in Exeter Hall: "[T]here was a degree of excitement in the room that can better be imagined than described. The waving of hats and handkerchiefs, the clapping of hands, the stamping of feet, and the screaming and fainting of ladies went on as if it had been in the programme."[93] *Uncle Tom*'s celebrity became a focus for British interest in slave life, as speakers like Wells Brown were asked "again and again if certain portions of *Uncle Tom's Cabin* were not exaggeration."[94] Repeatedly, their lives and experiences were measured against Stowe's fiction. When an edition of Brown's *Narrative* was published in 1852, reviews in the *Critic*, the *Literary Gazette*, the *Eclectic Review*, and the *Caledonian Mercury* all made mention of *Uncle Tom's Cabin*.[95] Other black abolitionists were also marketed with reference to Stowe's book: for instance, the Leeds Anti-Slavery Society advertised an illustrated edition of the novel alongside a portrait of Ellen Craft.[96]

The inequalities of the relationship between black writers and *Uncle Tom's Cabin* were made manifest in Stowe's visit to Britain. Douglass hoped that Stowe would devote some of the proceeds from the Uncle Tom Penny Offering to setting up an industrial school for free blacks in Rochester, and while she was in England and under attack from the American press Stowe's brother, Henry Ward Beecher, publicly evoked Douglass's project to suggest that the money and attention being showered on his sister would be put to a good cause. In the end Stowe abandoned the idea, as Douglass recalled with some disappointment in his 1881 memoir.[97]

Like the slave narratives, black abolitionists in Britain responded to Stowe ambivalently. They added drama and topicality to their speeches by referring to *Uncle Tom*, but they also modified and elaborated on its account of slaveholding society. Antislavery speakers like Brown, William G. Allen, William Craft, and Sarah Remond incorporated references to Stowe's novel in their speeches, both authenticating Stowe's fiction and perhaps hoping to shed a little of its glamour on their own testimony. Allen, who protested to Douglass about Stowe's depiction of George Harris in the novel, nevertheless declared at a Leeds meeting that the book "had sprung a mine, out of which would issue prayers and sympathies for the coloured race."[98] They also corrected Stowe's vision a little, rejecting the novel's portraits of kind and cultured whites. Remond argued that poor whites in America were as ignorant as Topsy, and William Craft pointed out that, unlike Tom, he and his wife had not been taught to read by a white patron.[99]

Stowe herself met a number of the African Americans who were in Britain at the time of her trip. In *Sunny Memories* she acknowledged that their presence, like their narratives and antislavery speeches, offered another commentary on slavery. With "such witnesses as these," she declared, American readers should not assume that "our English brethren have derived their first practical knowledge of slavery from Uncle Tom's Cabin."[100] There was some modesty in this, but she floated even as she disclaimed the idea that in Britain her novel had become the primary authority on slavery. Her fiction was accorded at least equal status with their eyewitness accounts, and although Stowe may not quite have seen herself as a competitor with her fellow Americans, some observers expressed anxiety about this. Allen noted that certain British papers had accused Stowe of "seeking self-glorification." He disagreed, however, reassuring Garrison that "Mrs. Stowe . . . has too much sense and piety, and is too great-hearted, to covet honours which more properly belong to those who have led on in the forefront of this battle."[101]

The role Stowe assumes in *Sunny Memories* is that of ambassador or mediator between Britons, African Americans, and audiences at home. Several times she describes for her American readers how British people respond to their visitors. Stowe's description of the response to Congregationalist minister and American Anti-Slavery Society lecturer Samuel Ward is almost proprietorial.[102] *Sunny Memories* depicts Ward "attract[ing] attention," interacting with "lords, dukes and ambassadors," and concludes happily that "[a]ll who converse with him are satisfied that there is no native difference between the African and other men." Praising Ellen Craft's "pleasing exterior" and "sweet manners" and describing her husband as "a pleasant, intelligent young man, with handsome manners," Stowe surmises that the couple's impressive personal qualities will automatically condemn slavery to everyone who meets them: "[T]he mere knowledge that two such persons as William and Ellen Crafts [*sic*] have been rated as merchantable commodities, in any country but ours would be a sufficient comment on the system."[103]

When she introduces another woman to the Duchess of Sutherland, Stowe states herself "pleased with the kind and easy affability with which the Duchess . . . conversed with her," and she assumes the meeting to be a kind of test case of racial encounter, drawing wider conclusions from Sutherland's courtesy: "I never realised so much that there really is no natural prejudice against colour in the human mind."[104] Stowe also puts herself in an interpretative position, explaining the peculiarities of her compatriots to her new acquaintances. Stowe's account of her London tour, during which she mixed with diplomats herself, shows her occupying precisely the role James Buchanan had dreaded she would take with Queen Victoria, representing "slavery and America" to influential European society.

Commentators in the United States were aware of the impact of personal testimony in the discussion of the slavery debate in Britain. The *New York Tribune* suggested that "the slaves themselves" should be sent to make "an impression on the public sentiment of the old world." The *Tribune* was sure that such ambassadors would "convince Europe that slavery is an eminently humane, beneficent and joy-diffusing institution." This confidence that slaves themselves would make the best arguments for the proslavery camp might be perplexing, until the *Tribune* revealed what it meant by "slaves," offering a list that not only suggests blackface derivation but also specifically includes a character from a minstrel song: "[L]et Cuffee and Dinah, Sambo and Phillis, Pompey and Dandy Jim be sent out as witnesses."[105] Just as the proslavery novelists staffed their plantations with blackface slaves to spout the writers' opinions as those of black people, so the *Tribune* wished for blackface counterparts to the African Americans in Britain. Both turned to the minstrel show in their attempts to answer Stowe's own ambiguous use of blackface.

Minstrel shows themselves also took an appalled interest in just the kind of social interactions *Sunny Memories* stressed: the fascinating and, for blackface, ridiculous spectacle of the British aristocracy's patronage of black visitors. Sanford's troupe advised:

> Oh, nebber ask de pitying tear
> > From de white folks more, my brudders dear,
> But, darkeys, go to England's shore.[106]

Credulous aristocrats were shown fawning over blackface characters, seemingly oblivious to their crude speech and manners. A burlesque published in 1855 featured the letters from Europe of a blackface character, Professor Hannibal, who is asked by his English landlady, "Are you one ob thim poor hoppressed people Mrs. Butcher Store has so beautifully written on, from that barbarous savage country, North America?"[107] The question encapsulates the sensitivities that *Tom* mania was creating in the United States: Stowe threatened to confirm all the condescending misconceptions Americans feared Britons had about their country. The black man in Europe was coming, via *Uncle Tom's Cabin,* to symbolize the tarnishing of the American reputation abroad. By transforming him into a blackface man, the minstrel show could turn the imagined European accusations of backwardness on their head: in

the sketch Professor Hannibal's ludicrousness confirms the relative sophistication of the (white) American audience. The fact that the English landlady
also speaks a caricature dialect and that she is ignorant ("Mrs. Butcher Store,"
that "barbarous savage country") proclaims that the British have got America, and African Americans, all wrong. The sketch reflects a world turned
on its head and *Tom* mania bypassing the usual social order: Hannibal meets
the "Duchess of Sunderland, who calls him 'Uncle Tom's' friend," asks "all
'bout Mrs Haireyt Butcher Store and Uncle Tom," and finally invites him to
dinner.[108] In a perverted way, blackface was registering the phenomenon
Wells Brown recorded, that African Americans were automatically connected
with Stowe's creation and welcomed as an adjunct to it. The shows acknowledged the extent to which the textual representation colored the reception of
real people, and they tried in turn to reassert the primacy of stage images of
blackness.

The minstrel caricature of the black abolitionist in Britain was also employed in an anti-*Tom* novel. Ebenezer Starnes's *The Slaveholder Abroad* re-
imagined the American slave in Britain as an apologist for, not an enemy of,
slavery.[109] In place of the dignified figures cut by people like Frederick Douglass and Samuel Ward, it interpolated a blackface fool. In the novel, a Southerner takes his valet, Billy Buck, to England, and Buck amuses his master and
astonishes English people by revealing the real state—carefree and happy—of
American slaves. On one occasion he entertains some ladies with blackface
antics—mock banjo playing, "an imitation of a negro jig," and minstrel-type
songs extolling the supposed racial features of a series of girls: "Miss Sally's
fat and mighty round; / The holler o' her foot make hole in de ground"; "But
my sweetheart's got woolly har . . . / An none can with that girl compar."[110]

Buck does more than provide the light relief for Starnes's diatribe. He
works like the minstrel sketch about Professor Hannibal in Britain or the
satire on antislavery meetings in the London burlesque *Uncle Tom's Crib!* Just
as the slaves in other anti-*Tom* novels make speeches denying the implications of the fugitive crisis and of slave narratives, Buck is designed to supplant
the antislavery work of black expatriates like William Wells Brown, Samuel
Ward, and William and Ellen Craft. In a scene reminiscent of *Uncle Tom's
Crib!* Buck's blackface entertainments are transported to a meeting of the
British and Foreign Antislavery Society at Exeter Hall. This episode is dated
June 1853, when Starnes mentions that Stowe's presence is causing great "ex-
citement on the subject of slavery" in England and Scotland. *The Slaveholder
Abroad* makes a blackface mockery of the proceedings, countering the offi-

cial view in the *Observer* newspaper, which Starnes also reprints. The gathering is attended by Stowe and Samuel Ward, whom the book glosses, in startling contrast to Stowe's account of him amongst lords and dukes, as "a blackamoor from Canada."[111]

Buck is described reacting to proceedings with "waggish looks" and "comical expressions" and providing a running commentary on Ward's speech. Juxtaposing Ward's oratory with Buck's blackface English, the book undercuts the record of the black speaker with physical jokes about black people. Starnes thus frames Ward with a racist revulsion for the black body, which he places for good measure in the mouth of a "black" character. He attempts to deflect the force of the preacher's argument with the antics of his fictional slave, creating a rabidly offensive assault on the black abolitionist: "[W]hen the ... reverend gentleman complained of the separate pews and galleries reserved for colored people in the churches, 'Ki!' said Buck, 'dat gemmon talk all sem like fool now. He no know dat cost too much for buckra to set longside nigger—dem brokee deself buyin smellin-bottle.' "[112]

Starnes offers a contrast both to Ward's person and to his argument; the impression of the "reverend gentleman" is undercut by the irreverent Buck, Ward's plea for an end to religious segregation with a joke that presupposes that black churchgoers are physically revolting. Buck also contradicts Calvin Stowe, who advocates the production of free-labor cotton. Again Starnes puts a viciously racist theory in the mouth of his "black" creation, as Buck claims that only the descendants of Africans are biologically fitted to do hard labor in the sun: "Buck chuckled mightily, and exclaimed[,] '... Wa da been gwine git anybody able to work in cotton-field, in brilin hot sun, but black nigger?' "[113]

Once more Buck quotes a commonplace in proslavery argument. Louisa McCord, for instance, contended that "the white, in and near the tropics, cannot live and progress without the labour and bodily endurance of the dark race."[114] But the pseudoscience is particularly poisonous when attributed to a blackface character: Starnes countered Stowe's representation of slavery and her patronage of black people with his singing, dancing, possum-loving clown. Whereas black speakers in Britain were asked to authenticate *Uncle Tom* and were in turn endorsed by its author, Starnes's "black" character mouthed racist justifications for slavery. In his comic capers, in his language, in the topical allusions, and in his reversal of social roles (as the slave becomes the apologist for slavery), Billy Buck is derived from blackface. Unlike Stowe's slave characters, however, the minstrel caricature in Starnes is built from proslavery racial theory.

Although minstrel representations like Starnes's offered a direct challenge to black voices in Britain, some black visitors had more complicated relationships with minstrelsy, just as they did with Stowe. The singer Elizabeth Greenfield, a freed slave from Mississippi, had arrived in Britain with a contract for a tour in April 1853 but was disappointed by a faithless promoter. Her peculiar musical talent was the ability to switch effortlessly from soprano to tenor or even baritone. After she called on Stowe in London, the author introduced her to the Duchess of Sutherland, who asked her to sing at a concert at Stafford House. This in turn led to public concerts in London, Brighton, Lincoln, and Dublin.[115] Greenfield's visit to Britain, unlike the visits of antislavery lecturers such as Wells Brown, was not directly intended to proselytize but to further her singing career. However, audiences conditioned by the tours of blackface performers associated Greenfield's musicality with her race. Greenfield's nickname, the Black Swan, made a racial pun on Jenny Lind's, the Swedish Nightingale, that was itself characteristic of blackface humor. Given the way minstrel acts satirized the lions of high culture, especially fads or crazes such as those generated by famous European visitors, and given minstrelsy's readiness to convert the rarefied to the banal, it would not be surprising if it was a blackface debunking that produced the Black Swan out of the Swedish Nightingale.[116]

At home Greenfield was controversial in the black community because she had sung at white-only concerts.[117] In Britain the singer was interpreted as a representative African American, her ethnicity as part of her interest. The Prussian ambassador, Stowe reported, asked of Greenfield, " 'Are the race often as good looking?' " As with her comments on Ward's and Greenfield's success in company, Stowe's judgment in *Sunny Memories* wedded the musical experience of Greenfield's voice to conclusions about race and slavery: "[W]hat a loss to art is the enslaving of a race which might produce so much musical talent. Had she had culture equal to her voice and ear, *no* singer of any country could have surpassed her."[118] Partly illustrating Stowe's "romantic racialism" in its insistence on black musical capabilities, this is not entirely flattering to Greenfield, whose "culture" is not thought "equal to her voice and ear."[119] Greenfield's dependence on Stowe's patronage left her in a more vulnerable position than those of antislavery lecturers like the Crafts and Wells Brown, and there is no record of her offering the kind of autonomous touches with which Wells Brown and others customized their versions of *Uncle Tom's Cabin*. Part of Greenfield's repertoire, in fact, could only have reinforced the popular imagery of African Americans. Given that Stowe's patronage must inevitably have framed Greenfield for her British audiences, and in view of the established British predilection for minstrelsy, it is perhaps not surprising that Greenfield's most popular number during this trip seems to have been Foster's "The Old Folks at Home."[120] The endorsement of the author of *Uncle Tom's Cabin* meshed with the song in Greenfield's performance, confirming for her British audience the inevitability of the relationship between black Americans and these representations. As with that of other African Americans in London, Greenfield's identity was partly shaped for her listeners by both Jim Crow and Mrs. Stowe.

The significance for the antislavery argument of Greenfield's connection with Stowe is illustrated by the fact that anti-*Tom* novels condemned British treatment of the singer alongside Stowe herself. Marian Southwood's *Tit for Tat* alleged that British "philanthropists" were ignoring British social problems because "philanthropists ... were too busy, at the moment, with Mrs Stowe and the Black Swan."[121] Meanwhile, Lucien Chase dedicated his novel to "the Aristocratic ladies of Great Britain," who disregard "the horrible conditions of the substratum of English society" while they "discover fascinations in the sooty progeny of Ham." He explicitly ridiculed Sutherland's patronage of Elizabeth Greenfield, complaining that "[it is] the climax of absurdity [for] the most illustrious of England's Aristocracy, and the favorite of her Queen, [to] indulge herself in the agreeable pastime of chaperoning a negress." He also fictionalized Greenfield as "a charming negro girl from the United States, [who] sings well" and is patronized by a scheming duchess for antislavery purposes.[122]

Thus, despite Greenfield's dependence on Stowe's introductions and her adoption of a minstrel repertoire, both Southwood and Chase saw her British success, as Starnes did that of Samuel Ward, as a challenge to the images of African Americans dispensed in proslavery texts. And yet another black traveler in the 1850s succeeded in complicating Stowe's influence over the representation of African Americans in Britain. Despite profiting from Stowe's patronage and herself contributing to *Tom* mania, Mary Webb, who gave dramatic readings of a version of *Uncle Tom* in 1856, partly recovered African American performance in Britain from minstrelsy.

Webb was the daughter of a Spanish father and a slave mother who escaped before her birth in 1828. Married to black Philadelphian Frank J. Webb in the 1840s, she began giving dramatic readings after the failure of her husband's business in 1855, including performing Longfellow's *Hiawatha* in costume.[123] Despite Stowe's reservations about the theater in 1852, she was later sufficiently impressed with Webb to create a dramatic version of *Uncle Tom's Cabin*, *The Christian Slave*, especially for her. Webb performed Stowe's play solo in its debut in the winter of 1855 at Boston's Fremont Temple. She attracted an audience of 3,500 on that occasion and similar audiences in a subsequent tour of the Northern states. A year later she took the show to England.[124]

Webb's performance reconvened the personnel of the Stafford House committee, resuscitated the association of the aristocracy and *Uncle Tom*, and recalled the angry exchanges between British and American commentators. In the reviews of her show there were echoes too of the emphasis on the domestic as the proper sphere for women that underlay much of the commentary on the Stafford House Address. The interest excited by Webb's interpretation of Stowe also invoked the way other African Americans had been asked to embody the novel's characters in 1853 and 1854. However, Webb succeeded in shifting reviewers' focus from Stowe's novel to her performance, placing her own emphases on the text of *Uncle Tom* and redrawing the relationship between the white author and her black protégée.

Webb's London debut took place on 28 July 1856 at Stafford House and was attended by the Duchess of Sutherland, her daughter the Duchess of Argyll, and the Earl of Shaftesbury.[125] Webb had, of course, been recommended to Sutherland by Stowe, as had Greenfield before her. But unlike Greenfield's concert at Stafford House, Webb's reading there was not only a public event but a paying one. Webb was supporting herself and her husband during their British stay while he completed the novel *The Garies and Their Friends*, and the performance at Stafford House was designed to draw extra publicity for a tour Webb went on to make in more commercial venues. Tickets to Stafford House were advertised in the *Daily News* alongside other entertainments and sold on written application to a Mr. Mitchell at the Royal Library in Bond Street for half a guinea.[126]

The Christian Slave differed from the professional dramatizations in neglecting the conventions of melodrama and in its failure to provide spectacular thrills. It consistently opted for dialogue over incident, narrating Eliza's escape, placing Tom's whipping off stage, and excising Cassy's tearful reunion with her daughter. And rather than develop the rough speeches of the backwoods types in the novel, Stowe made her drama even more erudite, having Cassy speak French and sing in Spanish, and even giving St. Clare a song in Latin.[127] Unlike professional dramatists like Aiken and Conway, Stowe was bidding for cultural authority rather than mass appeal.

Susan Clark argues that Webb's reading was designed, by Stowe as well as by Webb herself, to counter the blackface exaggerations of melodramas like Aiken's and Conway's.[128] Nevertheless, Stowe's adaptation, like theirs, drew on the book's allusions to minstrel repertoire, revisiting those scenes with some enthusiasm. Stowe's script retained the reference to Topsy as "rather a funny specimen in the Jim Crow line." In many cases it also amplified the scenes in the novel that most owed a debt to blackface. Sam and Andy have a great deal of business, occupying scenes 4–8 and scene 11 in act 1, while Topsy "'spect[s] I grow'd," steals and lies, and muddles her catechism through three scenes in act 2. Stowe even offered performance suggestions that linked the play to contemporary blackface material. For music Stowe suggested "Old Kintuck in de Arternoon" to open the play and had Tom sing Foster's "Old Folks at Home" in dialect with a specially adapted chorus: "O, Chloe, how my heart grows weary, / Thinkin' of ye all at home!"[129] In the London edition of the script, published in 1856, Webb indicated which scenes she had omitted in her readings. The majority of Stowe's minstrel references seem to have made it to her performances.[130]

Surprisingly, Stowe's script also echoed the changes Aiken and Conway had made to the gender politics of her text. Just as their adaptations avoided the novel's empowered femininity, so Stowe herself muted her play's emphasis on women's transforming powers. Although Chloe's role is extended in *The Christian Slave* in a whole new scene in which she presides over the slaves in the kitchen, there are fewer instances of female initiative and power in *The Christian Slave* than in the novel. Stowe, too, lessens Eliza's role in her play (the character evaporates after her escape), and Mrs. Bird and the Quakers disappear from Stowe's script as well as from Aiken's and H. E. Stevens's. Mrs. Shelby's exchange with her husband is abbreviated, and her concern for the slaves is downplayed, as she "arranges her ringlets at the mirror" and worries about Haley's manners. Unlike any of the stage versions, however, *The Christian Slave* does contain a visit to Dinah's kitchen, one of the scenes in the novel that most clearly links abolitionism with good housekeeping.[131] In this regard Stowe's adaptation does not entirely forsake the domestic emphasis of the original, but in the main her script looks less like a riposte to Aiken, Conway, and their ilk than it does a companion piece. Even an adaptation of *Uncle Tom's Cabin* by its author could constitute a serious revision.

Webb's performance in Britain also threatened to revisit the earlier controversy over the Stafford House Address. This time, however, it was the British press stoking the antagonism. Just as *Punch* and the minstrel sketches had fictionalized *Uncle Tom*'s British fans, so British newspapers personified proslavery criticism, imagining Webb's performance as an extension of the occasions that had caused outrage in 1853. The *Daily News* invented a Southern figure like the opponents of the Stafford House Address, except that he was a man, and it imagined him being overcome by his own bigotry, suggesting the "pretty considerable astonishment . . . any gentleman of the Southern states of North America" would feel at Webb's recital. The projected source of his proslavery chagrin is the event's particular conjunction of race and class—the black woman and the British duchess. The imaginary Southerner "would have been confounded and disgusted at the sight of what he called a 'tarnation nigger' being listened to with the most respectful attention by no inconsiderable number of the aristocracy of England."[132]

The *Daily News* article focused attention on Webb's reading as an "event"—the Southern gentleman would be galled by the "scene," not by the reading per se or by the content of Stowe's text.[133] To some extent Webb, not *Uncle Tom*, was the point, although it was her race and her presence in the elegant surroundings of Stafford House that were the crucial parts of the equation. The quality of her performance was not the prime concern. As with the reception of Elizabeth Greenfield, Webb's made her an exotic object of sentimental feeling. Like the speeches of black abolitionists and like Greenfield's singing, Webb's performance was promoted and consumed partly on the basis that she was an African American.[134] Her race made the spectacle, was integral to the commodity audiences paid for. As they had Elizabeth Greenfield, Webb's American audiences named her after a European talent, either in homage or in parody. When Webb was called, after the British actress, the Black Siddons, it made her ethnicity as important as her talent.[135] The London reviews bore out this emphasis. The *Daily News* devoted nearly a quarter of its commentary to Webb's background—her mother, "a woman of full African blood," was an "indomitable negro-mother"—and to her appearance—"Her colour is a rich olive, and her features are remarkably delicate and expressive."[136] Like the *Daily News* and the *Illustrated London News*, the *Morning Herald* gave a detailed account of Webb's parentage and examined her skin shade and facial structure: "[S]he is a mulatto of unusually dark hue, but the contour of the face is no less handsome than the expression is amiable and pleasing."[137]

Webb's performance was also coded by her observers in terms of her gender and class. Both the *Herald* and the *Daily News* emphasized the attributes of genteel femininity, introducing her as a "mulatto lady" and by her husband's name ("Mrs Frank J. Webb"), as well as using terms like "delicate" and noting her "remarkably sweet and flexible voice, apparently without much power," and its "natural and touching feeling."[138] Like many women who made their living dramatically in the mid–nineteenth century, Webb was absorbed in a paradoxical set of conventions that demanded that she be domestic as well as commercial—that she must not be too visible despite her public position. By taking the stage Webb risked incurring denunciations similar to those that Southern reviewers had heaped on Stowe and the Duchess of Sutherland. Her dramatic reading (and it was important that it was a reading, not a full-blown drama) fitted prevailing codes of femininity: the performance in the Sutherlands' private residence was perfectly adjusted to the paradox identified by Richard Brodhead, the celebration attained by ostentatiously private, publicly domestic performing women such as Fanny Ellsler and Jenny Lind.[139] The controlled method of ticket distribution for *The Christian Slave* signaled the unusual nature of the occasion, as did its scheduling for half-past three in the afternoon, a time more suggestive of domestic teatimes than theatrical pleasures. Most of all, the price ensured exclusivity: at half a guinea, or ten shillings and sixpence, it guaranteed a wealthy audience.[140] Stowe, too, had negotiated the tightrope of feminine modesty in public life, leaving speeches to her brother or her husband throughout her tour. During the whole schedule of public appearances, soirées, teas, and meetings she sat silently while others spoke, sometimes facing crowds of more than a thousand people.[141] It was perhaps in view of this necessity that Webb's reading style remained quiet and self-contained, although the reviews hinted that it was underpowered: "[S]he was cautious on the side of restraint rather than exuberance."[142]

These markers of femininity and good taste, like Webb's married status and her connection with Stowe's text, also reflected on her class. Several writers have demonstrated how African American lecturers were appraised in terms of their social standing and the extent to which they matched the tastes and concerns of the British middle classes.[143] Henry "Box" Brown, for instance, was attacked for the sensationalism of his performances and his flashy jewelry, while Sarah Remond was praised for being "a lady every inch."[144] Webb's impact also depended upon her being recognized as a "lady," upon conforming to notions of bourgeois respectability as well as womanliness.

But, of course, it was not just the class of the performer that was at stake at the Stafford House reading. British newspapers worried about working-class audiences being carried away by the sensationalism of *Uncle Tom's Cabin* or

by the stunts and spectacular paraphernalia that accompanied the talks of
Henry "Box" Brown.[145] The audience at Webb's recital was also a factor in
the "event" newspapers analyzed, but it evoked very different emotions. The
appearance at Stafford House itself, like the endorsement and presence of
titled personages, was a crucial reason for the press attention, just as it had
been in the controversy over Shaftesbury's address. Pride, snobbery, defer-
ence, and curiosity mingled in the reports from the Sutherlands' rooms. Both
reviews comment on the number of aristocrats among the spectators. In
Sunny Memories Stowe had written ecstatically of the hall at Stafford House
during Elizabeth Greenfield's concert, describing it as "brilliant and picturesque ... picture-like and dreamy." Greenfield sang on the stairway above
a piano "perfectly banked up among hothouse flowers."[146] During Webb's
reading the *Daily News* reviewer was as conscious of the surroundings as was
Stowe on that earlier occasion. The audience was again gathered in the hall,
"one of the most magnificent in London." The *Illustrated London News*
showed Webb at a lectern at the foot of the staircase, backed by the impressive foliage of a large indoor plant.[147] *Sunny Memories*' gushing tributes to the
duchess's generosity as a patron were also echoed in the newspapers this
time: the duchess, "with characteristic kindness," had "so kindly and powerfully assisted" Webb in her career.[148]

The Duchess of Sutherland had done more than merely lend Webb her
seal of approval. She had provided an occasion and a venue for the performer's first British appearance, and she had also helped to promote Webb
by allowing her own household to become part of the spectacle. Stafford
House did not just supply the lectern, it was an object of fascination in itself,
particularly since after the reading spectators were offered a stroll around the
apartments and the picture gallery.[149] Combined with Stowe's sentimental attack on slavery and Webb's personification of the suffering of an enslaved
people, the Stafford House reading also offered the possibility of class tourism.
In a bizarre package, *The Christian Slave* performed by Webb at Stafford
House combined as spectacle a dramatization of the iniquity of American
slavery, a black embodiment of genteel femininity, and a view of upper-class
British opulence.

Stowe's relation to Webb in this matter was not a simple question of generous white patron and needy black performer. Certainly, Webb's public
readings of Stowe's work, as with the endorsements of black speakers like
William Wells Brown, could work to legitimize it. Her performances helped
counteract the criticism of black writers like William Allen and Martin De-

laney, who had rejected Stowe's portraits of slaves and slave life: Webb was a living denial of Delaney's "Mrs Stowe knows nothing about us."[150] It is likely too that for many spectators Webb's presence helped authenticate the text and that Webb herself was seen to embody the white writer's fictional African Americans. Webb risked entangling herself in the same paradox that affected African Americans who performed in minstrel shows: they were forced to add to the cultural authority of blackface representation, precisely because that authority limited theatrical possibilities for black people to minstrelsy.

Despite this, Webb's adoption of Stowe's script was complicated, and her connections with Stowe and Sutherland were contradictory. Webb was Stowe's dependent and yet at the same time stood to benefit her patron both directly and indirectly. She was the object of display, and yet in her performances Sutherland and the Stafford House circle also became part of the spectacle. Webb's professional role may have been partly compromised by these two women in her readings, but it was not wholly determined by it. Reviews of her performance also make it clear that Webb negotiated with some dignity the ironies, for a black woman, of performing Stowe's blackface set pieces.

Both in Boston and in London Webb's readings of *The Christian Slave* were promoted alongside sales of the text: in the United States Phillips, Sampson brought out the book in paper covers just as Webb began her recitals. Advertisements instructed audiences to take a copy along in order to better appreciate the effect.[151] The London edition was produced by Sampson Low, timed again to coincide with the start of Webb's efforts. *The Christian Slave* was thus a commercially symbiotic enterprise, one that benefited Stowe, Webb, and two publishing companies simultaneously. Webb was not entirely or not only dependent on Stowe as patron, and the largesse was not as clearly one-sided as had been the case with Greenfield. Where William Wells Brown's notices had exploited Stowe's text to market his own, *The Christian Slave* and Webb's recitals helped sell each other. As with any performance, too, Webb's interpretation directed the consumption of Stowe's text, her choice of scenes further refining Stowe's selection of aspects of the novel.

The *Morning Herald* was satisfied with the way she conveyed the more minstrel-related sections of the novel: "[T]o the nationalities of Sam, Aunt Chloe, and other well-known personages, she did not fail to communicate the comic tinge which the graphic dialogue of Mrs. Stowe so immediately suggests."[152] Webb seems not to have rejected the scenes of blackface badinage that Stowe's script for *The Christian Slave* retained from *Uncle Tom's Cabin*. It is certainly possible that Webb's unadorned skin and wholly different style of performance served to highlight the travesty and theatricality of those more demeaning stage representations. However, that very lack of theatrical artifice also naturalized Webb's performance and, by implication, *The Christian Slave*. Sam and Andy's antecedents in the minstrel show may have been less obvious when it was Webb who voiced their jokes and represented, at least for British audiences, one of their race.

Although Webb, like Greenfield before her, did not shy away from blackface material, it was her treatment of the tragic scenes that most struck her audiences, and reviewers implied she brought something of her own to them. The *Daily News* commended her portrait of Cassy but was especially struck by her rendition of Uncle Tom: "The hoarse negro voice, the solemn tones—those of a man living in a world which seems to be a perpetual contradiction to the laws of that God in whom he firmly believes. . . . The piety, the resignation, the humility . . . [i]t was a mixture of solemnity and pathos, quite indescribable."[153] Even if she helped to endorse Stowe's blackface moments, Webb's recitals most powerfully reiterated the dignity and humanity of *Uncle Tom's* representative slave. Webb's treatment of *The Christian Slave* confirmed Tom's martyrdom as the centerpiece of Stowe's creation. "Solemnity and pathos" was the key to Webb's *Uncle Tom's Cabin*.

In a letter of introduction written for Webb, Stowe had argued that "her success in England" would "benefit the Antislavery Cause in this country by showing of what the race is capable," echoing her earlier pleasure in *Sunny Memories* at Samuel Ward's impressive demeanor in lordly company and William and Ellen Craft's sweet manners.[154] Frank Webb's outline of the purpose of his wife's British tour was very similar to Stowe's. Although Mary Webb's recitals were part of her professional development, designed to "establish her reputation as a reader beyond cavil," they would also "serve a nobler end," proving that "the tinge on [our] brow is not the badge of inferiority . . . [that] genius [is not] . . . the exclusive attribute of one race or another."[155] Both Stowe and Frank Webb saw a political necessity in Webb's work: her readings would demonstrate the artistic capacities of her whole race; but Frank Webb carried the idea further, hoping that Mary's performances would demonstrate black genius. These ambitions, which outstretched the aims of Stowe's patronage, were reflected in Webb's commercial part in the dissemination of *Uncle Tom's Cabin*. Although, like other

African Americans in Britain, Webb was at the same time subjecting herself to commodifying scrutiny in terms of her race, class, and gender, she was also, unlike some of her fellows, turning the tables a little and embroiling her patrons in an exchange of mutual dependence and display. No less than the Duchess of Sutherland's address, Webb's performance came to characterize its own special episode in the story of *Tom* mania.

FOREIGN MANNERS AND MEMORIES: "TOM" MANIA AND TRANSATLANTIC LITERATURE

I AM INDUCED, ERE I
CONCLUDE, AGAIN TO
MENTION WHAT I CONSIDER
AS ONE OF THE MOST
REMARKABLE TRAITS
IN THE NATIONAL
CHARACTER OF THE
AMERICANS; NAMELY,
THEIR EXQUISITE
SENSITIVENESS AND
SORENESS RESPECTING
EVERY THING SAID
OR WRITTEN
CONCERNING THEM.

Frances Trollope, *Domestic Manners
of the Americans*

Although, as I have suggested in the previous chapter, cultural events helped shape British *Tom* mania as much as textual versions of *Uncle Tom's Cabin*, the transatlantic debates about society in Britain and America were closely tied to literary questions. Published at a moment of increasing insistence among reviewers and essayists that American writers should move away from the British literary tradition and create a distinctive national literature, *Uncle Tom's Cabin* was by far the most internationally successful novel the United States had yet produced. Nevertheless, the book proved a complex answer to contemporary calls for a truly American text. *Uncle Tom's* celebrity abroad both evoked and inspired what I shall call transatlantic literature: books produced in Britain and America that were written for or about the other country and that assumed and sometimes created transatlantic connections. British travel writing, like Frances Trollope's *Domestic Manners of the Americans* and Charles Dickens's *American Notes*, and American travel writing, like Stowe's *Sunny Memories of Foreign Lands*, helped form the Anglo-American relations that governed the reception of *Uncle Tom's Cabin*. Meanwhile, its readers' sense of *Uncle Tom's Cabin* as a transatlantic text—compounded by newspaper reports of its British sales, the fury over the Stafford House Address, and Stowe's account of her British triumph in *Sunny Memories*—in turn produced self-consciously transatlantic literature. This writing was yet another genre of *Tom* mania (the anti-British anti-*Tom* book), and, ironically, some of its precedents were themselves British: Dickens's "American" novel, *Martin Chuzzlewit*, and "condition of England" fiction.

Because *Uncle Tom's Cabin* provoked adverse discussion of American slavery overseas, it was less a source of national pride than of nationalist anxiety. *Tom* mania in Britain embroiled Stowe's text in long-standing arguments about the relationship of British and American literature that were themselves linked to examinations of the two countries' respective political organizations; necessarily, these referred to slavery. In the United States *Tom* mania was often read in terms of existing transatlantic discussions of American literature, culture, and politics: in their turn many of *Tom* mania's texts intervened in these debates. *Tom* mania, like *Uncle Tom's Cabin*, was the product of a literary culture that Britain and America largely shared, yet the mania acted as a painful needle to national sensitivities.

In the decades before the 1850s the political differences between Britain and America had been enshrined in famous literary quarrels: in the British periodicals' disdain for American literature and in British travelers' infamous accounts of their American visits. Texts like these yoked the literary antagonism to political questions: the United States's unique political experiment triggered a large part of the travelers' curiosity, and inevitably they commented on the disjunction between America's founding rhetoric of freedom and its continuing toleration of slavery. Yet while the literary quarrel caused British and American commentators to split on broadly national grounds, the slavery issue attracted more mixed opinion in both countries.

Robert Weisbuch has argued that "enmity [was] the keynote of Anglo-American literary relations in the mid–nineteenth century," yet *Tom* mania not only forged international alliances in literature and politics, it also constituted a series of transatlantic conversations in which national questions were disputed but by no means espoused along evenly national lines.[1] Although many in the United States read British antislavery sentiments as anti-Americanism, antislavery Americans were at least partly pleased by the expression of such opinions; opponents of slavery were cheered by the ideological support even when they were disturbed to perceive a national hostility beneath it. The proslavery camp often expressed conflicting feelings too: as with antislavery writers, their literary models were British, and they also found like minds in Britain; in their attacks on British figures, the United States' strong cultural connections with Britain were both manifest and disquieting. Even more paradoxically, they were forging transatlantic alliances with some British commentators over the principle that Britons should keep their opinions out of American slavery.

Quarrels about *Uncle Tom's Cabin* took in discussions of free and unfree labor, the condition of the poor under slavery or capitalism, and the merits of republics versus monarchies. As elsewhere, the debate struggled over texts and within texts. *Uncle Tom's Cabin* was taken (by both British and American observers of both pro- and antislavery persuasions) to emphasize the ills in American society; it inspired other texts designed to expose British problems, either in a sympathetic extension of Stowe's humanitarian effort or else in retaliatory attack. British writers invoked *Uncle Tom's Cabin* in aid of British social reforms, while some critics in the United States expressed their disgust in the anti-British anti-*Tom* book. Inspired by the furor over the Stafford

House Address, these made villains of the Stowe-supporting aristocracy, accusing it of indifference to British poverty and suffering.

Dickens had written one of the hated travelogues, and yet he was also a preeminent condition of England novelist, and the anti-*Tom* novels' contradictory invocations of Dickens illustrate precisely the ironies of their relationships with British society and British texts. Dickens was invoked for his anti-Americanism and also because his novels condemned Britain; he was lumped with Stowe among the enemies of the United States; and elsewhere he was aligned with Stowe's opponents as serious efforts were made to read his *Bleak House* as anti-*Tom* fiction. Dickens was both claimed and criticized by American audiences; the inconsistencies and anomalies of his American reception form a striking counterpoint to those of *Uncle Tom's Cabin*'s transatlantic career.

Welcoming Stowe to Dundee in April 1853, the Reverend George Gilfillan remarked, "We have long been accustomed to despise American literature—I mean as compared with our own." How strange it was, he felt, that "the most popular book of the century has appeared on the West side of the Atlantic."[2] With this speech, Gilfillan signaled *Uncle Tom's* place in a long-running—and hitherto somewhat one-sided—critical dispute over the value of American letters. His claim recalled Sydney Smith's infamous attack on American cultural achievement in an *Edinburgh Review* of 1820, in which Smith charged that the Americans "have yet done marvellously little . . . to show that their English blood has been exalted or refined by their republican training and institutions," asserting that "they have done absolutely nothing for the Sciences, for the Arts, for Literature, or even for the statesmen-like studies of Politics or Political economy." In an insult that has never been forgotten, he asked, "In the four quarters of the globe, who reads an American book?"[3] Smith's demand that the United States justify its "republican . . . institutions" with intellectual production linked American political arrangements with literature: this connection was embodied in *Uncle Tom's Cabin*.

Smith's disparagement had been echoed by a succession of British critics over the intervening decades, and their blanket dismissals were only partly mitigated by British periodical reviews of American writers like Washington Irving and James Fenimore Cooper that harped on the extent to which Americans were indebted to their British forebears.[4] When Stowe sent a copy of her novel to the British writer Charles Kingsley, his acknowledgment echoed this insistence on American originality, praising the novel for being "a really healthy indigenous growth," though, unusually, it was the influence of other

European literatures he was anxious not to see: "[It is] free from all second and third hand Germanisms and Italianisms."[5] Clarence Gohdes goes so far as to attribute to the popularity of Stowe (as well as of Hawthorne, Longfellow, and Emerson in the 1850s) a similar emphasis in British periodicals on the "autochthonous" in American literature. Now that it was fatuous to ask, "Who reads an American book?" critics began to demand that those books be uniquely American.[6]

Gilfillan's surprise at *Uncle Tom*'s success should also be read in the light of the American replies to British critics, in tones ranging from the tactful to the strident, and the now well known calls, throughout the early part of the century, for the development of a "native" American literature: the reiterated claim that American writers were not yet fully independent of what Hawthorne ironically called "Our Old Home."[7] Certainly, the British tradition was still the dominant one in the middle years of the century: among others, Edgar Allan Poe solicited Dickens's attention during that writer's first American trip, and many other American authors had literary correspondents or other connections in Britain.[8] Stowe was unquestionably a product of these transatlantic reading relationships: her favorite writers as a girl had been British; she sent presentation copies of her book on publication to British luminaries Dickens, Kingsley, Macaulay, Lord Carlisle, and the Prince Consort; like Irving and Emerson before her, she sought out living British writers when she crossed the ocean and visited the birthplaces of dead ones.[9] In *Sunny Memories* her party falls into raptures as they approach the land of Scott and Burns, wondering "how many authors it will take to enchant our country from Maine to New Orleans, as every foot of ground is enchanted here in Scotland."[10] Stowe later became an intermittent correspondent of George Eliot, and she met Elizabeth Gaskell in London, Rome, and Manchester. The connection she struck up with Lady Byron led her to risk an international scandal in 1869, when she attempted to "vindicate" the late widow by accusing Byron in print of an incestuous affair.[11]

Uncle Tom's Cabin was thus, as Gilfillan's remark indicated, necessarily implicated in this charged question of America's literary relationship with Britain, drawn into a struggle between dependence and independence, consanguinity and rupture in British-American cultural exchanges. Stowe's book was asked to represent the United States in cultural terms as well as political ones, both involved in an international rivalry and claimed in a kinship of letters. Stowe herself registered the sensitivity of this issue for Americans, reporting delightedly on finding British people acquainted with American writers and declaring it "a gratification to me that I find by every English fireside traces of one of our American poets." She also admitted deferring to British literary approbation: when the Duke of Argyll asked her about Emerson, Longfellow, and Hawthorne, she wrote that "we never value our literary men so much as when placed in a circle of intelligent foreigners."[12]

Aside from the periodical reviews, the most inflammatory texts in the construction of literary relations between the two nations were the books produced by British travelers in the United States. Unsurprisingly, America's unique origins and constitution produced curiosity all over the world, and visitors' reports on the new country were not restricted to British authors.[13] However, for many decades after American independence British travelogues were so numerous as to constitute a genre in their own right—over two hundred were published between 1815 and 1860.[14] There were varied motivations behind these reports, whose authors ranged from radicals to Tories, but certain texts were read as violently anti-American, and certainly some, such as Captain Marryat's *Diary in America* (1839), were avowedly designed "to do serious injury to the cause of democracy" by attacking the nation that had adopted it.[15] Two of the most bitterly resented in the United States were Frances Trollope's 1832 *Domestic Manners of the Americans* and Dickens's 1842 *American Notes for General Circulation*.[16] Trollope's largely unrelentingly critical stance was summed up in her infamous concluding declaration: "I do not like their principles, I do not like their manners, I do not like their opinions"; while Dickens appalled Americans by seeming to spurn the overwhelming affection and hospitality with which his readers had greeted him during his trip.[17] The American episodes in the 1844 novel *Martin Chuzzlewit*, far harsher than anything in *American Notes*, served to compound his offense.

For the majority of these commentators, slavery was an unavoidable topic, according to Christopher Mulvey, one by which British commentators "were as much fascinated as repelled."[18] Frances Trollope conceded that some slaves lived comfortably, certainly better than some servants in the Free States, but not where they were separated from their families, and she noted that slave owning seemed to dull sympathy for one's fellow creatures and to distort the compassion and morality of young Southern women.[19] Dickens was careful to acknowledge the good intentions of some slave owners, but, in the style of abolitionist tracts, he quoted Southern newspaper advertisements to show that slaves were routinely ill treated, and he argued that the institution brutalized slave-owning society, leaving it indifferent to violence. In conclu-

sion, he seemed to suggest that slavery negated all the other political and social advances the nation had achieved, which, in the light of slavery's cruelty,
were no improvement on those of the first inhabitants: "Rather, for me, re-
store the forest and the Indian village; . . . and though the death-song of a
hundred haughty warriors fill the air, it will be music to the shriek of one unhappy slave."[20]

The regularity with which British critics of America condemned slavery
made it easy to link antislavery literature with anti-Americanism, so that the
popularity of *Uncle Tom's Cabin* impugned the reputation of the United States.
Stowe's book could be invoked against the still widespread British condescension toward American literature, but its antislavery message could also
give comfort to enemies. On her first public engagement in Liverpool, the
children of a Liverpool ragged school serenaded Stowe:

> I thank the goodness and the grace
> That on my birth have smiled,
> And made me in these Christian days
> A happy English child.

Antislavery sentiments, in other words, could be indistinguishable from a
British gloating at America's expense. Describing this event in *Sunny Memories*, Stowe registered the extent to which national pride was at work in this
song: "And when one of the speakers congratulated them that they were born
in a land where no child could be bought or sold, they responded with enthusiastic cheers—cheers which made me feel rather sad; but still I could not
quarrel with English people for taking all the pride and all the comfort which
this inspiriting truth can convey."[21] Stowe recognized that her novel could be
commandeered in Britain for precisely the same purposes. On another occasion she protested against British readers who appropriated *Uncle Tom*'s antislavery message as if it appealed uniquely to them. At a Stafford House reception she tried to impress upon her listeners the fact that not all Americans were proslavery and not all British readers were friends of *Uncle Tom's
Cabin*:

> In the course of her observations, she stated that the ladies of England were not
> at all aware of the real state of feeling of the ladies of America on the subject of
> slavery. . . . The ladies of England seem not to be at all aware of the deep feel-
> ing of sympathy with which 'Uncle Tom's Cabin' was received in America long
> before it was known in England. . . . The press in America had invariably spo-

ken highly of 'Uncle Tom's Cabin'. The first word that ever appeared in print against 'Uncle Tom's Cabin' was the article in the *Times*.[22]

Two days later Calvin Stowe attacked the implicit anti-Americanism of many of their hosts while he chided England in a speech at Exeter Hall for consuming American cotton. Here, too, antislavery ties conflicted with national ones, and yet the issues were complex: the speech lost Stowe the sympathy of at least one antislavery British newspaper, and yet William Wells Brown was disappointed by the mildness of his critique of slavery.[23] The national sensitivities *Uncle Tom's Cabin* activated would prove as varied as the nuances of the midcentury slavery debate.

Stowe's treatment by her opponents echoed earlier responses to Trollope, who was also lampooned on the stage, satirized and caricatured as a harridan.[24] In turn, Stowe was herself linked to the Englishwoman in William Grayson's *The Hireling and the Slave*, which pictured her in Britain:

> There Stowe, with prostituted pen, assails
> One half her country in malignant tales;
> Careless, like Trollope, whether truth she tells,
> And anxious only how the libel sells.[25]

Yet if Frances Trollope made an obvious figure for comparison with Stowe, Dickens made a better one still. Like Trollope's, his "American" books were much resented in the United States, but the parallels with Stowe went much further than a shared denunciation of slavery.[26]

Not only was some of Stowe's writing modeled on Dickens's, but the progress of her transatlantic career in the 1850s could almost have provided a mirror image for his a decade before. More importantly, many readers saw links between *Uncle Tom's Cabin* and Dickens's 1853 novel *Bleak House*. Dickens was almost certainly not intentionally responding to Stowe, but *Tom* mania was quick to read *Uncle Tom's Cabin* into his book, even to the extent of reading *Bleak House* as an anti-*Tom* novel. Ironically, while many antislavery arguments were read as anti-Americanism, so Dickens's skepticism about the United States, itself linked in *American Notes* and *Martin Chuzzlewit* to a critique of slavery, was interpreted as hostility to *Uncle Tom's Cabin*.

Dickens suspected that he could see his own influence on *Uncle Tom's Cabin* as well as that of Mrs. Gaskell: "I seem to see a writer with whom I am very intimate (and whom nobody can possibly admire more than myself) peeping through the thinness of the paper."[27] Certainly, although it was

Walter Scott whom the young Stowe read most avidly, it was surely the children at the center of so many of Dickens's novels—Oliver, Little Nell, Paul
Dombey, and so on—who paved the way for Stowe's Eva.[28] Dickens was among
the men to whom Stowe sent a copy of the novel on first publication, and in
Sunny Memories she praised the social impact of his novels, referring to characters from several of his books in her contention that "[f]ashionable literature now arrays itself on the side of the working classes" and picturing "fine
lords and ladies hanging enchanted over the history of John the Carrier, with
his little Dot, dropping sympathetic tears into little Charlie's wash-tub, and
pursuing the fortunes of a dressmaker's apprentice, in company with poor
Smike, and honest John Brodie and his little Yorkshire wife."[29] Such characters formed the crux of a comparison of the two writers made at a Lord
Mayor's dinner in 1853 at which both authors were present. A toast was made
paying tribute to Dickens and Stowe as both "having employed fiction as a
means of awakening the attentions of the respective countries to the condition
of the oppressed and suffering classes," and Dickens returned thanks with the
observation that Stowe "would find a welcome in every English home."[30]

Like Stowe, too, Dickens had made his first trip abroad as a famous author,
and he was mobbed in America, just as she was in Britain. However, while
Stowe was greeted at Liverpool by a polite crowd, "bowing, and looking very
glad to see us," Dickens's American fans brashly pulled down the window of
his railway carriage from outside or stared through the window of the boat
cabin in which he was washing and his wife lay in bed.[31] On the other hand,
though Dickens may have had a worse time on his foreign tour than Stowe,
he was not attacked about it at home. As Stowe noted bitterly, Dickens criticized his own society too, "yet nobody cries out upon him as the slanderer of
his country."[32] However, Stowe's textual account of her trip in *Sunny Memories* was largely rose-tinted gush, while Dickens's "American" novel, *Martin
Chuzzlewit*, vigorously exercised his posttravel spleen.

One cause Dickens espoused on that U.S. trip would come to affect Stowe
too. He made himself unpopular in America by advocating a reciprocal copyright arrangement. He had lost vast sums through the piracy of American
publishers, but, as he argued, international copyright would benefit both
British and American authors.[33] Ten years later, his point was proved when
Uncle Tom's Cabin was pirated by British publishers in the same fashion as
Dickens's novels were by American ones. Unlike Dickens's, Stowe's public
was sympathetic, as *Punch* suggested in a skit called "Uncle Bull's Cribbing,"
in which *Uncle Tom* appeared as "a work admirably cribbed; beautifully

stolen; magnificently pilfered. The writer of the book is everywhere read, admired, and plundered."[34] Some publishers were even moved to make Stowe some recompense (well publicized, of course), which Stowe acknowledged in the preface to *Sunny Memories*, with the polite hope that America too would soon grant "to foreign authors those rights which her own receive from them."[35]

Martin Chuzzlewit might also be said to have preempted *Uncle Tom's Cabin* in its fierce attack on slavery, in which the British servant Mark Tapley is shocked to hear the experiences of a former slave who has been "shot in the leg; gashed in the arm, scored in his live limbs, like crimped fish; beaten out of shape; had his neck galled with an iron collar, and wore iron rings upon his wrists and ankles." Dickens dramatizes his disillusionment with American political institutions and his sense of American hypocrisy in Tapley's near hysteria as he relates the story of this ex-slave: " '[H]e's a-saving up to treat himself, afore he dies, to one small purchase; it's nothing to speak of; only his own daughter; that's all!' cried Mr Tapley, becoming excited," and he ironically deploys the American rhetoric of freedom: " 'Liberty for ever! Hurrah! Hail, Columbia!' "[36] Dickens's passionate rebuke to the slaveholders in this 1844 novel would be forgotten ten years later, when Mrs. Stowe's admirers came to read *Bleak House*.

Martin Chuzzlewit is especially cruel about American ladies, particularly political and intellectual types such as the "wiry-faced old damsel" who preaches about the rights of women or those who attend lectures on "the Philosophy of Vegetables."[37] Of course, Stowe herself came of that enquiring and energetic class of American ladies, and when Dickens similarly attacked philanthropic women in *Bleak House* in 1853, many readers assumed it was a satire on Stowe. Some readers also jumped to the conclusion that Dickens was inimical to the antislavery brand of philanthropy. *Bleak House*'s Mrs. Jellyby, whose "telescopic philanthropy" is expended on distant Africans while her household disintegrates and paupers suffer on her doorstep, presides over committees of "the Women of England, the Daughters of Britain, the Sisters of all the Cardinal Virtues separately, the Females of America."[38] It is not hard to hear echoes of the Stafford House Address in these associations, but it is unlikely that Dickens was directly parodying it: *Bleak House* was serialized almost coincidentally with *Uncle Tom's* arrival in Britain in 1852, and Mrs. Jellyby appeared in an early installment. Nevertheless, Louisa McCord explicitly likened Mrs. Jellyby to the Duchess of Sutherland, "scarcely so ridiculous, and far from being so mischievous, as these Stafford House ladies in

their misapplied efforts."[39] Caroline Rush applied Dickens's caricature to
philanthropists on both sides of the Atlantic and hinted that the description
fitted Stowe: "In England, as here, there are an abundance of Mrs. Jellybys,
mock-sympathisers . . . and occasionally authors, who pervert the genius that
might do good into plausible engines of misrepresentation."[40] Mrs. Henry R.
Schoolcraft's anti-*Tom* novel disparagingly invoked Jellyby's pet project,
Borrioboola-Gha, in her picture of an abolitionist triumph in America and
named a pair of hapless and hypocritical missionaries Mr. and Mrs. Jellabee.[41]

Stowe was also defended from this perceived attack. In Britain Lord Denman, who was a friend of Dickens as well as an abolitionist and former lord
chief justice, published six articles in the *London Standard* that attacked
Dickens for what Denman saw as his caricature of the abolition cause in the
first seven numbers of *Bleak House*. They also heaped praise on *Uncle Tom's
Cabin* and ridiculed Dickens's only criticism of *Uncle Tom* in the *Household
Words* piece, that it was "not free from the fault of overstrained conclusions
and violent extremes," by pointing out a series of implausible events in Dickens's own fiction. Again linking Mrs. Jellyby to Stowe, Denman took Stowe's
side, defending the work of "noble matrons."[42] Dickens subsequently pointed
out in a letter to Denman's daughter that Mrs. Jellyby is not supposed to be
an abolitionist: "[N]o kind of reference to slavery is made, or intended in that
connexion. It must be obvious to anyone who reads about her." He also
claimed that Stowe had told him she had been inspired to write *Uncle Tom*
"by being a reader of mine" and asked, "It is not very reasonable—do you
think it is?—to turn it as an angry weapon against me."[43]

Dickens was right to ask whether it was fair to set up the two novels as enemies, since their satire took similar forms. Jellyby's folly, like slavery in *Uncle
Tom*, is represented by chaotic domestic arrangements. In the St. Clare household lack of supervision from the languid materfamilias has allowed the slaves
to run amok, and hygiene and efficiency have been abandoned: the cook Dinah wraps raw meat in damask and stores foodstuffs together with shoes,
handkerchiefs, a hymnbook, hair grease, and more (Stowe, *UTC*, 181–82).
Much the same effect has been achieved in the home of Dickens's character,
but here the problem is the mother's misplaced zeal rather than her apathy.
Because Mrs. Jellyby devotes all her energies to her African project, her children go unnoticed (her eldest daughter "really seemed to have no article of
dress upon her, from a pin upwards, that was in its proper condition or its
right place"), and the detritus of charitable business causes her family apartments to resemble the St. Clare kitchen: "The room, which was strewn with

papers and nearly filled by a great writing-table covered with similar litter, was . . . not only very untidy, but very dirty."[44] One of the ironies of the readings of *Bleak House* as an anti-*Tom* novel—both by Stowe's supporters and her detractors—is that American slavery in Stowe and British hypocrisy in Dickens amount to much the same thing: defective housekeeping.

Uncle Tom's Cabin was thus embroiled in several ways in the complex of American sensitivities about international literary relations—by dint of its subject matter, because of its popularity abroad, and by reason of its debts to and Denman's disagreement with Charles Dickens. Inevitably, the novel's prominence was exacerbated by the subsequent furor over the Stafford House Address and Stowe's trip to Britain. And, of course, Stowe's own contribution to transatlantic travel literature heightened matters further, for *Sunny Memories* did not, unlike Irving's *Sketchbook*, offer even a gentle reproach to British accounts of American writing, nor did it achieve the distance, the slight note of disappointment with English heroes, of Emerson's *English Traits*.[45]

Worse, Stowe sometimes echoed Trollope in *Sunny Memories*, even on the very points discussed in *Domestic Manners*. Trollope had complained about the difficulty of getting servants in America, where the job was regarded as demeaning and even described by the euphemism "'help,' for it is more than petty treason to the Republic, to call a free citizen a *servant*." Egalitarian ideals, she explained, meant that young women "are taught to believe that the most abject poverty is preferable to domestic service."[46] Stowe agreed with Trollope, observing that in England "the servants seem to me quite a superior class to what are employed in that capacity with us" and enjoying the fact that "their manners are much more deferential than those of servants in our country." For the mistresses there were great benefits to this, for they kept their beauty, while American housewives "fade their cheeks lying awake nights ruminating the awful question who shall do the washing next week."[47] The British and the American housewife tended to concur on this sort of labor question, and it was only over the issues of free and unfree labor that the argument descended into what Robert Weisbuch calls the "quarrel of nation and colony, and . . . nation and nation."[48]

By the time *Uncle Tom's Cabin* was published the relative merits of labor systems (and particularly of American slavery and British capitalism) were already an established topic on both sides of the Atlantic. In addition, the comparison between the conditions of slaves and of British factory workers had become a common part of several quite different arguments. It had often been made during the debate over *British* slavery in the West Indies: the analogy was deployed by reformers working to end the suffering of both laborers and slaves and also used by those who wished to justify West Indian slavery. Meanwhile, slavery was used as a metaphor for the suffering of British workers from early in the nineteenth century. The connection had even been crystallized in the metaphorical terms "white slave" and "wage slave."[49] In the process, discussions of the respective states of free laborers and of slaves began to bleed into each other. Catherine Gallagher argues that "[i]ndustrial reformers and social critics appropriated the images, rhetoric and the tone of the antislavery movement. Simultaneously, however, they used arguments and rhetorical strategies associated with the advocates of slavery."[50] Equally, apologists for slavery in the United States borrowed from the British social reformers. By the 1850s the comparison of slaves to wage slaves was as familiar among slavery's advocates in the United States as it was in Britain. As Michael O'Brien points out, the Southern defense of slavery necessarily drew conclusions from British society because "political economy, which was often the underpinning of reasoning about slavery, was largely a British invention, with most of its evidence and logic drawn from British social experience," and because making the case for slavery was often linked to making that for the new republic itself: "[T]he proslavery argument began life as a defense of America against the old enemy [Britain]."[51] *Uncle Tom's Cabin* itself invoked the long-running debate about the relative claims on philanthropy of American slaves and British workers; it would become a mainstay of the discussion of *Uncle Tom's Cabin* as a transatlantic phenomenon and would be yoked in turn to British-American literary rivalries.

Stowe was clearly anticipating the revival of the argument that slaves were better off than factory workers: in *Uncle Tom's Cabin* she has her "own" slave owner, St. Clare, raise it. He concedes that the slave owner "is only doing, in another form, what the English aristocracy and capitalists are doing by the lower classes." Both are "*appropriating* them, body and bone, soul and spirit, to their use and convenience" (Stowe, *UTC*, 199). St. Clare acknowledges that some slaves "are better off than a large class of the population of England" but rejects his brother's contention that social difference is preordained: "So he reasons, because . . . he is born an aristocrat;—so I don't believe, because I was born a democrat" (Stowe, *UTC*, 200, 199). In other words, St. Clare holds to the ideal often flaunted as America's special preserve, the notion of equality between men. He asserts, on Stowe's behalf, that the relative comfort of his brother's slaves is not a sufficient compensation for denying them their freedom.

British readers paid special attention to this passage. The *North British Review* felt St. Clare was "putting the slaveholder's most plausible argument in the most plausible way" but refuted it utterly, arguing that "the condition of the slave is . . . infinitely worse than that of the poorest labourer in England. Indeed it must be so, as long as a position in which evil is *legally inevitable*, is worse than that in which it may be *lawfully avoided*." The crucial difference, for this reviewer, was that the English laborer could set himself to a program of bourgeois self-improvement and attain "self-dependence and self-respect," which would never be available to the slave. Unlike the slave, the British poor could improve their condition if they were "effectually taught to lay by when they have good wages, not to marry improvidently, not to bring up their children in ignorance, not to join trade unions (a horrible slavery, but self-imposed), and to guard against various other things prejudicial to their well-being and dependent upon themselves to avoid." For the laborer, as not for the slave, "no *legislative* restriction sets any limit to that improvement."[52]

Whereas the *North British Review* felt that the St. Clare passage was not sufficiently critical of slavery, the Earl of Carlisle reproached Stowe with being too hard on Britain over its treatment of its poor. In a letter thanking Stowe for her novel, he remonstrated: "Whenever you speak of England and her institutions it is in a tone which fails to do them justice. I do not know what distinct charges you think could be established against our aristocracy and capitalists, but you generally convey the impression that the same oppressions in degree, though not in kind, might be brought home to them which are now laid to the charge of Southern slave-holders." Since St. Clare's remarks are the nearest Stowe comes in the novel to speaking "of England and her institutions," it seems that it is this passage that has made Carlisle uneasy. He goes on to assert the similarities between the industrial rulers of both countries: "Our capitalists are very much the same sort of persons as your own in the Northern states."[53]

Carlisle's sensitivity about "British institutions" was mirrored by American protectiveness about those of the United States. At their most extreme, some commentators charged that British criticisms of American slavery were driven by antipathy to democratic and republican ideals and that attacks on slavery were really designed to destroy the United States—and democracy with it. *Domestic Manners* was interpreted by contemporaries as a verdict on republicanism, especially topical in Britain because its publication coincided with the reading of the 1832 Reform Bill, which argued for the extension of the franchise and changes to the parliamentary system.[54] Similarly, Julia

Gardiner Tyler surmised that the Stafford House Address was devised by the
ladies' husbands to attack American democracy. The *Times*, which endorsed
her impatience with the address, spluttered over her explanation of it: "[T]he
fair Julia is obliged to set down the cause of WILBERFORCE and CLARKSON . . .
to envy of the United States, to revenge for their successful revolt, to grief at
the loss of their market . . . to the nefarious design of sowing discord between
the Northern and Southern States."

As so often in the Stafford House affair, the *Times* retorted with a reference
to Tyler's gender: "motives intelligible to a certain class of feminine under-
standings, but utterly inconceivable to any ordinary man."[55] Nevertheless,
several men were of the same opinion. An antiabolition pamphlet published
in 1853—another attack by an American, this time on the Irish abolitionist
R. D. Webb—asserted that aristocratic philanthropy was "a backhanded way
of hitting at America" and of arguing "the inherent falsity of American democracy."[56] A similar view was debated in the New York press, the *New York Herald* publishing the theory that "the aristocrats of England and Europe . . .
fancy they are dealing a desperate blow at our institutions by their patronage
of Uncle Tom," while the *New York Independent* pronounced the idea "absurd."[57] David James McCord, husband of Louisa, put the same case with a
curious mixture of snobbery and republicanism. McCord also believed that it
was democracy not slavery that appalled the British, alleging that

> [t]hese periodic paroxysms of philanthropy, these outbreaks of pretended
> sympathy for slaves, . . . are, in fact, nothing more than significant indications
> of [British] apprehensions of the consequences ultimately to result from the
> growth of the United States, and the irresistible energies of freemen. . . .
> [Democracy], then, is no doubt the great source of offence to British philan-
> thropists. . . . Otherwise, why would that vulgar, ill-bred woman, Mrs. Stowe,
> have met with such a reception as she has received from the proud, upturned
> noses of the English aristocracy?[58]

McCord here flaunts a pride in U.S. democracy alongside a disapproval of the
British nobility's suspension of class distinctions in the case of Mrs. Stowe. In
a paradoxical attack on republicanism, the aristocracy welcomes a woman
McCord perceives, with the nicety of a South Carolina planter, to be "vulgar"
and "ill-bred."

Another line of thought, which avoided the conspiracy theory, still indicated that what was at stake in American and British attitudes to slavery was
the conflict between democracy and oligarchy. Several New York papers con-

tended that rather than bolstering the aristocracy, *Uncle Tom's Cabin* would foil it by causing British minions to rise against their oppressors and supply an ironic sequel to the upper classes' "patronage of Uncle Tom." They will "discover when it is too late that they themselves are the Legrees and the Haleys upon whom retribution must fall."[59]

Just as some British readers had used *Uncle Tom's Cabin* to emphasize American wrongs, so others, concurring with the New York papers, used it to stress shortcomings in British society. Two British novels compared suffering in Britain with the lot of the American slave. *Uncle Tom in England*, sympathetic alike to the victims of slavery, capitalism, and the remnants of feudalism, enlisted *Uncle Tom's Cabin* to advocate emancipation for all.[60] On the other hand, Charles Reade's prison-reform fiction, *It Is Never Too Late to Mend*, treated Stowe's project with some ambivalence. Reade's kindly prison chaplain gives Stowe's novel to a vicious warder in an attempt to awaken his sympathetic instincts: "This disciple of Legree is fortified against me: Mrs. Stowe may take him off his guard." But Reade is skeptical about *Uncle Tom*'s powers where British abuses are concerned, and he portrays the sentiment expended over the novel in Britain as hypocritical. While the chaplain feels for his charges as much as for Stowe's hero, both the warder and the evil governor fail to appreciate the book's application to their own case, even though they are gripped by it. Instead, like the audiences for the London dramatizations, they are moved to national self-congratulation. The complacent patriotism they express could come from the stage, but in Reade's text their remarks are horribly inappropriate. The prison governor, who tortures his charges and is supported by magistrates, creates an ironic echo of the verses the Liverpool children had sung to Stowe, telling his subordinate, "[T]hank your stars that you were born in Britain. There are no slaves here, and no buying and selling of human flesh; and one law for high and low, rich and poor, and justice for the weak as well as the strong."[61] Ironically, the "solitary" system of confinement, which Reade's entire text is designed to protest, had been pronounced by Dickens to be "cruel and wrong . . . in its effects" when he encountered it in Philadelphia.[62] As Reade was pointing out, neither nation held a monopoly on suffering.

These British texts concede the urgency of the slaves' cause while also pointing to social abuses in Britain; although Reade recognized some dangers in the universal sympathy for Uncle Tom, in both novels the different projects for social reform are compatible. However, for the American anti-*Tom* novelists, they were antithetical. The American books did what they charged the Britons with doing: highlighting only the suffering on the other side of the Atlantic. Responding to the popularity of Stowe's novel abroad and especially to the national insult for which they took the Stafford House Address, their novels were counterattacks, gunning for British society as much as for British injustice.

A peculiar collection of texts, the "answers" to *Uncle Tom's Cabin* included William Grayson's *The Hireling and the Slave*, a long poem in heroic couplets; *The Planter*, a collection of illustrative sketches and arguments; and three more conventional novels, Lucien Chase's *English Serfdom and American Slavery*, Marian Southwood's *Tit for Tat*, and Ebenezer Starnes's *The Slaveholder Abroad*.[63] These all asserted the United States' cultural parity with Britain as well as the political superiority of its institutions. Implicitly, they offered a rebuttal to British writers' accusations of American social barbarity and ideological hypocrisy as well as to *Uncle Tom's Cabin*. However, to do this they had to deny the intricate pattern of literary influence and resistance upon which their writers depended. Both generically and ideologically, the anti-*Tom* novels were inextricably bound into transatlantic debates: like *Tom* mania itself, they were rooted in political and cultural alliances as well as antagonisms.

The Planter opens like a plantation novel, but its promotion of the benefits of slavery leads to repeated digressions from its feeble pretense of a storyline. Chapter 7, for instance, comprises "Arrival—St. Augustine Harbor—Happy population—Negroes most happy—the work . . . Negroes never seem to work too hard—A free negro—THE GREAT TEACHER—Great Philosophers—PLANTATION NEGROES LUXURIATING." In an early scene, some Southern ladies are shown a clipping of the Stafford House Address. Their responses rehearse yet again the arguments of proslavery newspaper articles and minstrel show songs, this time in the guise of novelistic conversation:

> SISTER: . . . Are the negroes starving to death, like the poor people of Ireland and Scotland? and even of England and Germany?
>
> FIRST DAUGHTER: Or are they turned out of their cabins, and hunted away from their homes, as our good Peggy says the poor Irish women and children are?[64]

The Planter thus joins the many comparisons of slavery and capitalism, and its condemnation of Stowe as a "renegade traitress" suggests that it shares other commentators' belief that her influence abroad has damaged American interests. Like the attacks on the Duchess of Sutherland I discussed in the last chapter, it accused British society of hypocrisy. Ebenezer Starnes's *The Slave-holder Abroad* pretended to be a collection of letters home from a Georgia slaveholder but was in fact a disjointed mixture of statistics and fictional incidents mainly stitched together from British newspaper clippings.[65] There are letters on "Bribery and Corruption," "Betting and Horseracing," "Want of Education," and numerous varieties of "ill-treatment," "cruelty," and "brutality." No fewer than eight chapters itemize sensational examples of murders broken down into categories that include "children," "wives," and "husbands." The intention is to portray Britain as utterly benighted and so discredit any British complaints about slavery in the United States. The effect is that of a morbid scrapbook, but other texts came closer to dramatizing their allegations about British double standards.

English Serfdom neatly inverted the rhetoric about English freedoms with which the London *Tom* plays had greeted George and Eliza's escape to Canada and pointedly rewrote several scenes in the novel. A small boy is given a sentimental deathbed scene to rival the one in Stowe's book, but in *English Serfdom* Eva's message of love for the slaves is countered by little Harry's request that his father save his siblings by taking them to America, "the only asylum, for a defenceless mortal, on earth." *English Serfdom* underscored the point by having one character reverse the geography of the flight in Stowe's novel, evading the press-gang in the British colony with a dramatic flight *from Canada* into the United States: "As the boat landed at the dock at Newport, he sprang upon the shore, and pressed his lips upon the soil of freedom."[66]

Southwood and Chase explicitly addressed the transatlantic dimensions of the *Uncle Tom* debate, alluding in their prefaces not only to the book's extraordinary popularity in Britain but to the glittering society that fussed over it. Both novels make numerous references to Stafford House and Stowe's British supporters. Southwood's preface offers to address Britain's blinding by "the Uncle Tom fever," "a chronic ophthalmia" affecting "English Humanitarians, who . . . could see nothing but specks of black," lamenting dramatically, "Oh! Sutherland House! Oh! Exeter Hall!" She also makes a reference to the Clearances, calling the Sutherland estates "that field of ancient robbery."[67] As I mentioned in the last chapter, Chase's novel is dedicated to "the Aristocratic ladies of Great Britain," and Chase not only addresses Sutherland in his preface, he puts her into his novel. Among his villains are the Duke and Duchess of Sunderland, whose name, like that of their London residence, "Strafford House," is a barely disguised allusion. Exeter Hall becomes in the novel "Dexeter Hall," a center of British hypocrisy.[68]

Chase and Southwood may have had British targets, but they also had British role models, exhibiting the same mixture of admiration and antagonism that had characterized Stowe's relations with British writers. They were most indebted to what critics have called "condition of England" or "social problem" fiction, the handful of novels, written during the late 1840s and early 1850s, that addressed the social and political problems that attended rapid industrialization in Britain.[69] They included Dickens's *Hard Times*, Mrs. Gaskell's *Mary Barton* and *North and South*, Kingsley's *Alton Locke*, and Benjamin Disraeli's *Sybil*.[70]

The connection with these novels was not surprising, given that the British poor were already frequently evoked in the proslavery argument in the 1850s, and social problem fiction had been conscripted into slavery's defense before *Uncle Tom's Cabin* appeared.[71] And as F. J. Klingberg notes, *Uncle Tom's Cabin* was read alongside novels like *Mary Barton*, *Hard Times*, and *Alton Locke*. Louisa McCord, who reviewed both *Alton Locke* and *Uncle Tom's Cabin*, dismissed both with almost the same term, "wordy philanthropy."[72] Nevertheless, although McCord's essay on *Alton Locke* attacked Kingsley's sentimentality and his evident sympathy for Chartism, she quoted scenes of "wretchedness" at length from the novel in order to argue that Southern slaves were better off than British paupers, describing the "far happier, and every way more elevated, position of *our* labouring classes."[73]

Yet Southwood and Chase might also be described as "wordy philanthropy." Like Kingsley they made sentimental subjects of social problems, though unlike either Stowe or the British authors they were highlighting abuses in a foreign country. Southwood takes up the cause of British chimney sweeps and compares them with slaves, asserting that in Britain children are "bought" from their parents for this job and that their work is much harder than anything suffered in the American South.[74] Chase describes ruinous conditions for tenant farmers, degraded prisons, mercenary merchants, and the power of press-gangs, lambasting the aristocracy, Parliament, the weaving industry, the navy, and the clergy.

The novels also referred to British writers directly. In *The Planter* Dickens is once more conscripted to the anti-*Tom* cause: a character, noting that Mrs. Charles Dickens has signed the Stafford House Address, wonders if she "has read *Oliver Twist* and . . . *Bleak House?* They might point her to other work to be done, nearer home." Another puts the Dickenses on the other side, alluding to Dickens's treatment of the United States in *American Notes* and *Martin Chuzzlewit*: "[A]s her husband *insulted* our country, it is not wonderful that she should embrace such an illustrious opportunity to add an *injury* to the insult." This mixture of admiration and pique typified the attempts in these novels to conscript British fiction into their patriotic projects. In general, the characters in *The Planter* turn to British novelists for evidence of the truth of their arguments. They recommend Kingsley's *Yeast* and *Alton Locke* and also Disraeli's fiction. They are anxious, however, in case the British books do not do the work of anti-*Tom* novels, especially if the validity of these texts should be translated into a similar respect for Stowe's. A Southern gentleman writes a letter to the Stafford House ladies that generously surmises that they have been misled by the accuracy of British writers into believing *Uncle Tom's Cabin*: "You know that your Bulwer, and Dickens, and Warren, and Kingsley, your late Chancellor of the Exchequer, and such writers, have not overdrawn the horrible pictures of crime, and poverty, and degradation, and oppression, in your own country; and it is therefore not strange, but natural, that you should receive as true to nature, Mrs. Stowe's paler pictures of suffering among our Southern slaves."[75]

Yet although these texts use British writers liberally, they contain undercurrents of literary resentment, begrudging their own acknowledgments of transatlantic cultural traffic. Chase is disparaging about British literature, as his hero argues that contemporary writers are overrated, and only uncritical fashion binds us "to admire . . . James' 'solitary horsemen,' Bulwer's resounding periods, Scott's rhymes, and Dickens' ghosts."[76] Southwood actually gives another novelist, Disraeli, a role in her novel, making a jibe both at his *Coningsby* and his Jewishness in her character Sidonius Palestinus.[77]

Nevertheless, despite their apparent contempt for British writers, Chase and Southwood compounded their debts to the British social problem novel by borrowing their tone and subject-matter. There is more than a trace of *Oliver Twist* in Southwood's plot: Southwood's sweep risks roasting and smothering his charges in chimneys, like Dickens's sweep Gamfield, who is reputed to have "bruised three or four boys to death."[78] Not only that, but a boy in Southwood's novel is kidnapped by a criminal who, like Dickens's Fagin, is an anti-Semitic caricature and threatens to teach him "lying, thieving and drinking."[79]

Chase was especially indebted to Dickens. It is difficult not to see the reflection of Dickens's callous industrialist in *Hard Times*, Thomas Gradgrind, in Chase's Solomon Greasebeans. Greasebeans is attacked for attempting to send Britain's "surplus population" to America, using the Malthusian term that Dickens had also satirized, putting it in Scrooge's mouth in *A Christmas*

Carol. Greasebeans's association with Malthus similarly links him to Grad-grind, who has a son named after the economist.[80] Elsewhere Dickens is quoted approvingly (his comments on slavery in *Household Words*), and one of Chase's characters settles debts "after the fashion of Wilkins Micawber."[81]

Yet the preoccupation in these novels with the Duchess of Sutherland and the titled signatories of the Stafford House Address distinguishes their polit-ical analysis from that of their British models. Not only did the anti-*Tom* books displace race and gender—Stowe's points of campaign—with class, but they projected the main source of suffering in Britain not onto industrial cap-italists but onto the aristocracy. Unlike Disraeli, Dickens, Kingsley, and Mrs. Gaskell, Chase and Southwood focused very little on conditions in mills, fac-tories, and sweatshops. The plight of the sweeps in *Tit for Tat* is laid at the door of the aristocracy, who ignore the law, deliberately install chimneys that can only be cleaned by children, and then, as magistrates, turn a blind eye in court to abuses. The very pointedly named Lord Hardheart is taught the con-sequences of this behavior when his son is stolen by an aggrieved tenant and then sold to a sweep. To drive the lesson home, Hardheart finally realizes his son's fate just as a boy is at that very moment being scorched to death in his own chimneys.

Chase's complicated plot similarly opposes the aristocracy and the labor-ing classes. It tracks two supposed brothers, Christie and Robert Kane, who are persecuted by an unfeeling duke. Christie, a tenant farmer, is evicted, while Robert is taken by the press-gang in London. Robert is cruelly treated by his captors (he is whipped with a cat-o'-nine-tails while a clergyman stands idly by), but his family fares worse: his unprotected wife is evicted and raped in his absence and hemorrhages to death in a snowy street. Robert's son Harry is beaten and worked to an early grave at the weaving business of Solomon Greasebeans, who is in league with the Duchess of Sunderland and is himself a Pharisaical abolitionist, with "two consciences, one for American slavery, and the other for English serfdom."[82]

Although both sides of the *Uncle Tom* debate implicated the British aris-tocracy in the "appropriation" of the English people, it was not the major fo-cus of concern for British reform novelists. *Mary Barton* and *Hard Times* were concerned with factory workers in Manchester, while in *Sybil* it is an aristocrat who joins forces with a working-class radical. Disraeli evokes the wage slave metaphor, but he charges the middle class with causing the la-borer's misery: "It is that the Capitalist has found a slave that has supplanted the labour and ingenuity of man. Once he was an artizan: at the best, he now

only watches machines; and even that occupation slips from his grasp. . . .
The capitalist flourishes, he amasses immense wealth; we sink, lower and
lower."[83]

Apart from its strategic purpose in the *Uncle Tom* controversy, the British
aristocracy might thus seem an odd sort of target for Southwood and Chase,
at what François Bédarida calls the beginning of "a golden age of the bourgeoisie." And yet, as Bédarida also points out, the nobility were still inordi-
nately powerful and wealthy in the 1850s.[84] As Lord Shaftesbury discovered
when he succeeded to his title and estates in 1851, they were still neglecting
their rural tenants: after campaigning for housing reform in Parliament,
Shaftesbury found he had inherited an estate in which tenants lived in "filthy,
close, indecent, unwholesome" accommodation. The legacy included the responsibility for this state of affairs but not the cash to improve matters.[85]
David Cannadine argues that this class still contained "the most wealthy, the
most powerful, and the most glamorous people in the country" as late as the
1870s and that the idea of the rising bourgeoisie in this period, though much
discussed, was still largely just an idea: "[I]f the middle class arose as anything
during these years, it was largely as a new *rhetorical* formation."[86] The American satirists were missing the preoccupation with the capitalist classes in
British reform discourse: the aristocracy may not have been undeserving targets for their critique, but for British writers concerned with the condition of
England the middle class had already supplanted the aristocracy as a source
of anxiety about social injustice.

The emphasis on the upper rather than the middle classes was, of course,
necessary for Americans seeking to champion republican institutions at the
expense of Britain's highly class stratified monarchy. Southwood not only accused the English nobility of cruelty to the poor, she invoked the conspiracy
theory about British antipathy to American democracy. The upper crust in
England entertained "an inert hatred of America," while among the middle
classes of both countries "there exists the very best of feeling." She attributed
this phenomenon to an idea that the republican example of the United States
threatened the aristocrats' privileges.[87] Chase elaborated on this, asserting
that the whole antislavery campaign was part of a devious plot to disunite the
states and reduce America to chaos. This was entirely driven by an alliance
between industrialists like Greasebeans and aristocrats working to prevent
the notion of equality crossing the Atlantic: "[W]e intend to destroy republican institutions under the specious banner of liberty."[88]

This recurrent harping on the relationship of abolitionists and the British aristocracy meant that although Chase, like *Uncle Tom's Crib*, parodied British abolitionism, his representation lacked that satire's blackface fun at the expense of middle-class pomposity. Chase's scene in Dexeter Hall, where canting hypocrites weep over American slaves and ignore the starving British urchins in their midst, plants an American in the audience, an eloquent gentleman who explains that the British "founded" slavery in America and argues that American slaves are better cared for than British "serfs."[89] Chase's is not a working-class view of philanthropic posturing: his American orator is simply a better bourgeois whose arguments trounce those of the Dexeter Hall habitués.

As a tactic, Southwood's and Chase's attacks on the British aristocracy produced several ironies. For a start, Southwood's choice of victim, the chimney sweep, was not ideal for indicting the associates of Stafford House. One of the climbing boys' most passionate advocates was the very author of the Stafford House Address, Lord Shaftesbury. He had supported the regulation of chimney sweeps in 1840, was chairman of a Climbing Boys Society, and had introduced parliamentary bills (unsuccessfully) in 1853, 1854, and 1855. He remained active on their behalf until an act of Parliament was finally passed in 1875.[90] Southwood actually borrows some of the statistics for her novel from one of Shaftesbury's speeches.[91] Southwood and Chase ignored Shaftesbury's relation to the Stafford House Address. But one Southern editor, unaware of Shaftesbury's change of title from Viscount Ashley in 1851, mistakenly compared the author of the address to his younger self: "And who is this Lord Shaftesbury? Some unknown lordling; one of your modern philanthropists suddenly started up to take part in a passing agitation. It is a pity he does not look at home. Where was he when Lord Ashley was so notably fighting for the Factory Bill and pleading the cause of the English slave? We never even heard the name of Lord Shaftesbury *then*."[92]

Moreover, Southwood missed a chance to highlight a real inconsistency. It was apparently British women who were most opposed to the replacement of climbing boys with sweeping machines.[93] In directing her ire at the aristocrats, Southwood ignored the irony of the special appeal to women made by the Stafford House Address and of the Southern women's replies. Despite Louisa McCord's conviction, sometimes women were "on the side of the oppressor."

The process of fictionalizing the proslavery argument also introduced structural flaws. Neither novel entirely succeeded in making class politics look as miserably determinist as Stowe makes slavery. Both plots sacrifice total condemnation for a happy ending and in so doing contradict their attacks on the nobility. In Southwood's triumphant denouement the true identity of Hardheart's lost son is revealed, and he inherits both the estate and permission to marry his beautiful cousin. *English Serfdom*'s hero, Christie Kane, also turns out to be an aristocrat, the son of the Duke and Duchess of Sunderland. He too wins his girl, the daughter of an earl. In this the two novels replicate the anomalies critics have identified in the British social problem fiction from which they were borrowing. In *Oliver Twist* the orphan is saved from destitution by discovering respectable (bourgeois) relatives; Sybil Gerard in Disraeli's novel turns out to be a noble and marries a lord. Neither case suggests a solution for the exploitation of the working classes, and both could be interpreted as reaffirming the superior rights of, respectively, the middle and upper classes. Raymond Williams famously identified these novels' failure to translate sympathy into radicalism in *Culture and Society*, and many critics have been similarly disappointed.[94] In Chase's novel the about-face is even more inexplicable. *English Serfdom* makes the Duke and Duchess of Sunderland stand for the hypocrisies of Stowe's aristocratic friends, yet the novel rewards its hero with the very wealth and title it sets out to condemn.

When Chase reveals that heroic Christie Kane has been a lord all along while the vicious Montague is really a plebeian, he makes the noble by nature one in name also. In a literary parallel of some irony, Chase's babies-swapped-at-birth plot device was later adopted by Mark Twain for his anti-slavery story *Pudd'nhead Wilson*. In Twain's use too it produced a logical flaw: by making the "real black" man a brute while the "white" man raised in slavery is a natural gentleman, the novella confirms racist ideology even as it argues the arbitrariness of racial division.[95] In the same way Chase, like Southwood, fails to make his attack on the aristocracy conclusive when he rewards his hero by elevating him to the peerage: he is exploiting the class inequality his novel condemns.

These novelistic outcomes could be seen as weak concessions to the expectations of nineteenth-century readers, and, where such indifferent writers as Chase and Southwood are concerned, unsatisfactory meshings of plot and propaganda are less surprising than in Dickens or Disraeli. But the ideological contradictions the two anti-*Tom* novels create in their endings constantly overshadow their arguments. Elaine Hadley has defended the end of *Oliver Twist* in its context as part of a "melodramatic" view of society that sought to recuperate a social role for the aristocracy and harked back to the preindustrial model of society as a patriarchal family.[96] The similarity of this vision to that of Southern planter paternalism is hard to escape. That such narrative resolutions were attractive for apologists for slavery, with suitable racial adjustments, is clear from the number of anti-*Tom* novels set in the United States that see indigent white heroines accede to wealth by means of a judicious marriage.

Yet Chase and Southwood try valiantly to avert the comparison between old-fashioned European feudalism and its contemporary variant in the American South. The proslavery view of society was precisely "melodramatic" in Hadley's sense, but it conflicted with ideas of Americanness as democratic and republican. It is not just that Chase's and Southwood's critiques of British hierarchy falter when their novels whisk away the problems of individual characters, but they remind us that the defense of slavery usually accompanies the promotion of a Southern aristocracy. American newspaper attacks on the Duchess of Sutherland asserted the parallel social eminence of ladies like Julia Gardiner Tyler, and yet they also drew attention to the exploitation that lay behind the duchess's status: they condemned the snobbery that made her opinion important and yet tried to counteract it with their own. In the same way, lurking behind Chase's and Southwood's excoriations of injustice across the Atlantic was a yearning for respectable British society to recognize its kinship with the slave-owning South.

The role Chase seems to be envisaging for the British ruling class is not dissimilar from Tyler's picture of the responsibilities of a Southern matron. Chase demonstrates what his version of noblesse oblige might look like by having the Duchess of Sunderland neglect her duties. She evicts a tenant, saying, "What have we to do with their hardships? . . . We have claims upon their services instead of being under obligations to them." Read with the satirical twist Chase intends, her attitude reveals that she does have obligations and that the British nobility are responsible for the well-being of their dependents. The similarity of this thinking to the paternalist defense of slavery mobilized by writers such as Tyler is not lost on Chase. In fact, in another conspiracy placed in the mouth of one of his villains, he spells out how closely the planter lifestyle can be seen to resemble that of the British aristocrats. Greasebeans is explaining to his henchman how abolition will destabilize America, retailing the methods that will be used to turn Northern states against Southern ones: "We shall covertly arouse their jealousy and envy against their southern brethren, because they live without work. We shall say that to live in idleness is bringing down to too late a period the aristocratic habits of the cavaliers who settled the southern states. *We shall contrast their own industrious habits with those of the gassy, starchy, aristocracy of the*

South."[97] Despite its place in Greasebeans's conspiracy, this speech voices
some of the deepest contradictions in Chase's attack on British oppressions,
undermining both the representation of America as a haven of equality and
the contrast between aristocracy and slave owning. Drawing attention to the
"aristocratic habits" of some slave owners is a strange rhetorical move for
Chase, and it makes some of the tensions of his proslavery-but-antiaristocracy
stance explicit. The popular association of the Southern planters' lifestyle
with an "aristocratic" one could serve, in the writings of someone like Louisa
McCord, to illustrate the superior welfare of a slave workforce to a free one.
It could also attract some of the same accusations Southwood and Chase lev-
eled at the British upper classes—that their way of life was dated and unsus-
tainably exploitative.

These contradictions in the novels' critique—the tension between aspiration and rejection in their attitudes to British society—derive from the transatlantic dialogues about national manners that predated *Uncle Tom's Cabin.*
Chase and Southwood were not just engaging with the slavery question; their
novels resonate with the older quarrels produced by British travelers like
Trollope. They were about more than the condition of British society; they
were even about more than slavery. Such novels were also counterstrikes on
behalf of the American culture so many British critics had traduced.

National pride was as much at stake in these texts as slavery or its portrayal
in a novel. Both writers fomented a perceived cultural rivalry between America and England and delivered attacks not only on English social institutions
but also on English culture. They read here less like responses to the condition of England novels than to British visitors like Dickens and Trollope.

Domestic Manners had attacked the arts in America, describing theater audiences as noisy and inattentive and reinforcing European prejudices that
"the character of American literature" was lackluster. Trollope attributed this
inferiority to flaws in American education, blaming a lack of "acquirement of
Latin and Greek," with which "an extremely small proportion of the higher
classes in America possess [a] familiar acquaintance."[98] Southwood refuted
this and challenged Trollope's view of British schools. For once Stowe was
her ally: she had argued that the British public schools' emphasis on "the ancient classics has lain like a dead weight on all modern art and literature. . . .
[T]here would have been more variety and originality without them."[99]
Southwood agreed, dismissing Trollope's claims about the benefits of a clas-
sical education: "They go to Eton to learn a vast amount of slang. They go
to college and incur a great amount of debt, with a little smattering in one or

two dead languages; and they have the impudence to think that that is sufficient to put them on a par with the men whose lives are spent at hard work,
acquiring information and knowledge on every possible subject."[100] Southwood also went further, asserting that "learning, education, and knowledge
are despised and ignored" in England, and (echoing another British com-
plaint about American society) she argued that the veneration of money took
precedence there over culture.

Chase responded to the contradictory British claim that American women
were too intellectual, reversing Dickens's portrait of American women as radical bluestockings. He charged Stowe's British supporters with feminism,
describing an advocate of woman's rights who has "a decided predilection to
certain garments that have hitherto belonged to the male sex." She not only
sports bloomers but is something more sinister, being "hermaphroditish . . . in
[her] proclivities" and, from the "masculine direction of [her] thoughts[,] . . .
not [a] proper associate of the female sex."[101] Where the Southern reviews of
the Stafford House Address charged that British ladies had "strayed" from domestic concerns, and *Punch* had reiterated the point with some humor, Chase
predicted they would lead to a dire collapse of gender distinction.

In a more important attack even than that on antislavery feminists, Chase's
anti-*Tom* novel struck at the heart of the issue that made *Uncle Tom*'s progress
in Britain most galling. It responded to the arrogance of European attitudes
to American literature and the cultural domination of the United States by its
former colonial power. Ironically, for this Chase echoed Dickens by railing
against American publishing houses that unpatriotically reprinted British
books rather than paying American authors.[102] But Chase ignored the fact
that *Uncle Tom's Cabin,* itself stolen by a dozen British publishers, had
dramatically reversed the usual flow in pirated books across the Atlantic. Although he was keen to champion American literature in a society that venerated European writers, for Chase Stowe's outstanding example was, paradoxically, a national scandal. *Uncle Tom's Cabin* had become one of the most
internationally powerful representations of America, but for proslavery writers like Chase this could not be a cultural triumph for the United States but
only another sign of Britain's undiminished enmity.

ANSWERING THE "ANSWERS": "TOM" MANIA AND STOWE'S "DRED"

IN LIFE ORGANIZED AS IT IS AT THE SOUTH, THERE ARE TWO CURRENTS;– ONE, THE CURRENT OF THE MASTER'S FORTUNES, FEELINGS, AND HOPES; THE OTHER, THAT OF THE SLAVE'S.

Harriet Beecher Stowe, *Dred; A Tale of the Great Dismal Swamp*

Just like the parodists, playwrights, and proslavery novelists who responded to her text, Stowe herself could not resist reinterpreting it. And as with the other instances of *Tom* mania, Stowe's own versions of *Uncle Tom* were shaped by both ideology and genre. The dramatic adaptation, *The Christian Slave*, was necessarily more sensational than the documentary, *The Key to Uncle Tom's Cabin*. *Sunny Memories* was both a product and a record of *Tom* mania, but it was also primarily a travelogue. *Dred* ostensibly marked a return to the genre of *Uncle Tom's Cabin*, the sentimental novel, but by 1856 Stowe had changed both her textual and her political bearings. Although she blended in it some of the same structures as in the first book (the plantation novel, minstrelsy, and sentimental fiction), *Dred* brimmed with other influences, alluding to dozens of texts: it deepened *Uncle Tom*'s debts to Stowe's childhood favorites, Byron and Scott, but also referred to abolitionist tracts, slave narratives, and scenes from Frances Trollope and C. H. Wiley. Above all, *Dred* responded to the arguments, imagery, and characterization that had been generated by *Uncle Tom*: it was both a contribution to and a quarrel with *Tom* mania.

In political terms *Dred* engaged with texts from across the spectrum of debate, taking up both abolitionist and proslavery documents, both black activists and their writing, and also anti-*Tom* novels. It pointed to the futility of the answers' attempts to silence black voices and paid its respects to black authors, dramatizing the conflict between black and white (proslavery) utterances in the public arena. The paradox of a white author's championing of black testimony, itself a variant on blackface's simultaneous attraction to and ventriloquizing for black speakers, was played out in *Dred*'s own homages to the minstrel show. The novel was at times oblivious to the crudity of the devices it borrowed from blackface and at others acutely self-conscious, offering a more clearly realized—and feminized—minstrel show than *Uncle Tom*.

Many of *Dred*'s antecedents have already been pointed out. George Eliot had long ago noticed that Stowe had adapted the theme of the "conflict of races" from Scott.[1] Alice Crozier has observed that Dred is "more Byronic than Biblical," a reference the novel itself signals when one character is explicitly called "Byronic."[2] Crozier also located this novel, with *Uncle Tom*, in the "tradition" not only of Scott but also of "his American followers, Cooper, Simms,

Kennedy, Cooke."[3] Judie Newman adds biblical prophets and Robin Hood to
the list of *Dred*'s literary ancestors (*Dred*, 22). Like Crozier, Francis Pendleton Gaines included *Dred* unproblematically in the tradition of the plantation
novel, as did Richard Beale Davis, who claimed that Stowe used "the same or
similar scenes and even characters" as Kennedy and Cooke.[4] John Adams
traced the migration of a number of characters from *Uncle Tom* to *Dred*:
George Harris to Harry Gordon, little Harry to Tomtit, Miss Ophelia to Aunt
Nesbit, and Uncle Tom to Old Tiff. He also noted that Tom Gordon functions
in *Dred* as Legree does in the earlier novel, and he asserted that the minor
slave characters in both are near duplicates.[5] However, Davis rejected these
comparisons: Tiff is "entirely different," while Harry Gordon's situation is
"more subtle and more dangerous" than that of George Harris.[6]

Several of *Dred*'s reviewers commented on the fact that *Uncle Tom*'s success would also inevitably color readings of the new book. *Blackwoods*, for
instance, while listing many "defects" in it, especially that of repetitiveness,
admitted that, "sustained by our respect for Mrs Stowe[,] ... we have listened—twice, thrice, four times over often—to every word which she was
pleased to say."[7] Others suspected that it would be judged harshly, "since the
interest of novelty which attached so passionately to the first vivid picture of
American slavery ... has been largely satiated, and 'Dred' must pay the pen-
alty of his predecessor's success."[8] Either way, *Dred* could not lack for critical interest.

Yet though its first readers strained to make comparisons with *Uncle Tom's
Cabin*, *Dred*'s politics were noticeably more radical. Stowe had hinted in 1853
that *Uncle Tom* could be read too leniently: "In fictitious writing, it is possible
to find refuge from the hard and the terrible" in "those scenes which are
made bright by the generosity and kindness of masters and mistresses."[9]
There were still such slave owners in *Dred*, but the book was in other respects
much harsher on Southern society than *Uncle Tom's Cabin*. During its composition the slavery question had become incendiary, as the Kansas-Nebraska
Act of 1854 ratcheted up sectional tensions and precipitated the violent clashes
of Bleeding Kansas, while in May 1856 Stowe's acquaintance Charles Sumner was physically attacked in the Senate by Preston Brooks.

Also, Stowe's views on slavery had grown less conciliatory between 1851
and *Dred*'s publication in 1856. *Uncle Tom's Cabin* had made Stowe an antislavery activist in her readers' imaginations; to a certain extent she was required to become a real one in its aftermath. She had been forced to defend

herself against proslavery critics in *Key*; she was hailed as an ally by British and American abolitionists, had met Frederick Douglass and William Lloyd Garrison, and had organized an antislavery lecture series in Boston with the latter.[10] She had even been drawn into campaigning, collecting signatures in 1854 for two petitions to Congress against Stephen Douglas's Nebraska bill and publishing on the lines of the Stafford House Address "An Appeal to the Women of the Free States of America, on the Present Crisis in Our Country."[11]

The weight of these developments rubbed away the Christian pacifism of *Uncle Tom's Cabin*. *Dred*'s protagonist is not a domestic "uncle" but a runaway and would-be rebel, his name coincidentally echoing that of Dred Scott, whose legal struggle would make him the living answer to the claims of proslavery novelists. The homonym of "dread" also reflected the terror invested in the idea of slave insurgency in the 1850s.[12] In this fugitive plotting a revolution in the swamps Stowe invoked a nightmare, deliberately reviving memories of rebellions like those of Nat Turner and Denmark Vesey (*Dred*, 219, 405). The novel explores the mentality of slave resistance, not only recognizing slaves' right to freedom but guessing at their desire and their ability to take it for themselves. Her contemporaries represented rebels as monsters: in Thomas Gray's account Nat Turner is a "gloomy fanatic" leading a "band of savages" with "flinty bosoms."[13] Like Gray, Stowe endowed Dred with an unusual psychological state, but she dignified it with a reference to "a twilight-ground between the boundaries of the sane and insane, which the old Greeks and Romans regarded with a peculiar veneration" (*Dred*, 353).

Eric Sundquist dismissed Stowe's representation of "black resistance" in this novel as a "species of insanity," but *Dred*'s "twilight ground" precisely refuses to pronounce on Dred's mental condition.[14] Stowe's inability to commit Dred to insanity or otherwise signals not a rejection of black revolution but indecision. Stowe could not follow the British dramatizations of *Uncle Tom* so far as to paint a full-scale insurrection, but she was willing to raise the possibility. In the end there is no rebellion in this novel, which the *Blackwoods* reviewer asserted led to "ludicrous" bathos, as if in *Julius Caesar* "the conspirators, being met for the assassination[,] . . . received a message that he was not coming."[15] Nevertheless, since some of Dred's other prophecies, such as Nina's death by cholera, are fulfilled, the text encourages us to take his predictions of bloodshed seriously. By declaring that the Greeks and Romans "venerated" men such as Dred, Stowe was no doubt mystifying her own fence-sitting, but she also made her character magical rather than mad. Dred's special powers are endorsed in the novel not only in this historical parallel but also in the terms of nineteenth-century psychic research, declaring his "peculiar temperament" especially fit "for . . . mesmeric phenomena" (*Dred*, 354).

The extensive criticism of the novel's structure—its proliferation of plots and what Crozier saw as its disfigurement by an abrupt change of style and direction—could also be read as symptomatic of this indecision at *Dred*'s heart.[16] The novel is even uncertain about whether to focus on the black characters or on the white ones. *Dred*'s opening stars a plantation mistress, and Stowe seems first to capitulate to the expectations of the traditional plantation novel, including the romantic theme whose absence critics had commented on in *Uncle Tom*. Nina is initially the focus: coquettish and irresponsible, she seems to augur a plot of light bildungsroman in which she grows up to marry her fiancé, the enlightened planter Clayton. Although this mood is underpinned by the revelation that Nina's servant Harry is her half-brother, Dred himself does not appear until the final chapter of the first volume. As the slavery issue intensifies, the love interest wanes, so that Nina dies of cholera two thirds of the way through the novel, barely achieving her moral redemption before she slips away.

Thus the structure of the plantation novel is eventually abandoned, defying generic convention and thwarting the hopes *Dred* initially raises in the reader of a marriage at the end. Yet although Stowe herself eventually placed the slave character at the heart of this story, both in its creation and in its reception attention vacillated between Dred and the white characters. The plantation genre continued to haunt the book's publication history: one of Stowe's preliminary titles was *Canema*, the name of Nina's estate, and a postbellum edition restored that focus, renaming it *Nina Gordon*.[17]

Dred's shifts of emphasis in character and plot may be a reflection of the diversity of texts Stowe was drawing on and responding to. For a start, it made liberal reference to the sources amassed for *The Key to Uncle Tom's Cabin*. Ostensibly, *Key* presented "the original facts and documents upon which [*Uncle Tom*] is founded," yet Stowe acquired many of these after she had written her first novel. Many blackface performers claimed specific black sources for their acts, claims that were often both spurious and revealing about the exploitative processes the form involved. Stowe now similarly claimed that slave narratives and other black testimony lay behind *Uncle Tom's Cabin*.[18] Yet, as Newman points out, *Key* "might properly be described as the key to *Dred*."[19] The "mountain of materials" Stowe incorporated into *Key* included a special emphasis on the complicity of the courts and the majority of

churches with slavery that also became central to *Dred*.[20] One reverend
threatens to tar and feather Northern abolitionists with the same phrase *Key*
quotes from "William S. Plummer" (William Plumer) of Richmond: "If they
will set the country in a blaze, they ought to be the first ones to be warmed at
the fire" (*Dred*, 535).[21] *Dred* was thus in some ways a redramatization: *Key*
sought to guarantee *Uncle Tom* with facts; *Dred* laid over *Key* the glamour of
fiction.

Stowe's research for *Key* and her increasing contact with abolitionist individuals and groups after 1852 also contributed to the powerful presence in
Dred of abolitionist history. The book alludes to Amos Dresser, publicly
whipped in Nashville in 1835 for possessing abolitionist material, and Elijah
Lovejoy, murdered by a Mississippi mob in 1837. Men who read the *National
Era* in *Dred* are run out of town, while Clayton is struck with a cane in a
pointed reference to the Sumner incident: Tom Gordon proves "his eligibil-
ity for Congress by beating his defenceless acquaintance on the head, after
the fashion of the chivalry of South Carolina" (*Dred*, 613).

This identification with recent events in *Dred* is matched by Stowe's explicit evocation of slave narratives. Robert Levine has demonstrated the extent of Stowe's contacts with major African American figures in the years
between 1852 and 1856 and has drawn attention to the number of quotations
from slave narratives in *Key*. These, he argues, had a "major impact on the
racial politics of *Dred*," which he calls "an African American–inspired revision of *Uncle Tom's Cabin*." As Levine notes, the book refers to a number of
these new influences, including a sympathetic account of Denmark Vesey's
uprising and a character recognizable from Stowe's later portrait as Sojourner
Truth, whose exchange with Frederick Douglass over the merits of violent
resistance is also dramatized in *Dred*.[22] Stowe's great innovation in *Uncle Tom*
had been to direct the spotlight at slaves, as even the anti-*Tom* novels had implicitly recognized by developing their own slave characters. In *Dred* she underlined the importance of evidence provided by slaves themselves with an
acknowledgment that white Americans, however sympathetic, must defer to
those with firsthand knowledge: "[W]e shall never have all the materials for
absolute truth on this subject, till we take into account, with our own views
and reasonings, the views and reasonings of those who have bowed down to
the yoke, and felt the iron enter into their souls. We all console ourselves too
easily for the sorrows of others" (*Dred*, 556). She also recognizes the temptation for whites to be complacent: "[W]e talk and reason coolly of that which,
did we feel it ourselves, would take away all our power of composure and self-

control" (*Dred*, 556). Stowe's empathy here suggests she has moved some way from her alarm at George Harris's violent resentment of his fate in *Uncle Tom's Cabin*. Levine, who also quotes part of this passage, argues that, "[m]ore deeply and more thoroughly than most other whites of the time, Stowe paid regard to what African Americans had to say about slavery."[23]

The sentence that follows this passage in *Dred* indicates where Stowe had grasped her understanding of the gulf between the perceptions of enslaved people and free ones. Frederick Douglass's slave narrative prefaces his fight with the slave driver Covey—a real moment of violent resistance such as the ones George Harris contemplates—with the chiastic phrase "You have seen how a man was made a slave; you shall see how a slave was made a man."[24] Stowe echoes it with reference to a community plotting even more extensive rebellion: "[W]e have seen how the masters feel and reason. . . . [W]e must add, also, to our estimate, the feelings and reasonings of the slave" (*Dred*, 556). *Dred* also nods to Douglass's request that abolitionists refrain from publicizing the means of previous slave escapes because "we owe something to slaves south of the line as well as to those north of it," for which reason Dred omits details of his final flight from the South (*Dred*, 138, 143). *Dred* duly makes a mystery of the journey of one party of fugitives who travel "by ways and means which, as they may be wanted for others in like circumstances, we shall not further particularize" (*Dred*, 670).

Stowe's book also shared a major theme with that of many slave narratives: their interest in literacy was matched in *Dred* by a running concern with education. This was, of course, a long-standing obsession in Stowe's family.[25] Her own involvement with her sister Catharine Beecher's projects for teaching girls emerges in *Dred* as a passion for the moral cultivation not only of slaves but also of women, so that Clayton's experimental school for the slaves on his plantation is paralleled by the moral education of his fiancée, Nina. Stowe decries the fashionable schooling for girls that develops "the talent of shirking lessons, and evading rules, with a taste for side-walk flirtation[,] . . . a hatred of books, and a general dread of literary culture" and recommends something "stronger and more like a man's" (*Dred*, 48, 374). Education as a theme in the novel links classes and races, so that Nina's efforts at self-improvement resonate with the slave Tiff's anxieties that the white children he cares for should learn to read, and discussions of the inadequate school provision for poor whites is mirrored by disputes over Clayton's teaching of slaves on his plantation. The concern with education thus illustrates the interrelatedness of all Southern society, which in the novel means that the malign effects of slavery touch everyone, even the most privileged.

These discussions of schooling in the United States dovetail in *Dred* with its references to the slave narrative. *The Key to Uncle Tom's Cabin* extracted the now famous scene from Frederick Douglass's *Narrative* in which his mistress begins to teach him to read and his master forbids it on the grounds that the slave will become dissatisfied: "'[H]e would at once become unmanageable, and of no value to his master. . . . It would make him discontented and unhappy.'"[26] In *Dred* Stowe has an unscrupulous lawyer voice almost the same thoughts: "'You begin to let people think, and they won't stop where you want them to. . . . [T]he more you give, the more you may give'" (*Dred*, 218).[27] A slave in *Dred* also imitates Douglass by teaching himself to read in secret, using a Bible, a copy of *Robinson Crusoe*, and a Northern newspaper, an eclectic collection like the *Columbian Orator*, which Douglass ingeniously used as a primer (*Dred*, 638–39).[28] Douglass's description of his desperate efforts to learn to read and write and his image of enforced illiteracy as being "shut up in mental darkness" had clearly impressed Stowe, who advised her readers that "those who have always had books about them more than they could or would read know nothing about the passionate eagerness with which a repressed and starved intellect devours in secret its stolen food" (*Dred*, 638–39).[29] *Dred*'s concentration on the fugitive slave thus reveals a powerful sympathy not only for abolition but for the people Stowe recognized as its most authoritative advocates: the former slaves themselves. Yet although *Dred* both argued for the power of their texts and demonstrated it with sincere flattery, it was also acutely aware of the opposition. The book was designed to answer proslavery critics of *Uncle Tom* as much as it showcased black antislavery argument: a significant proportion of *Dred* is devoted to answering the answers to *Uncle Tom's Cabin*.

Dred's range of reference situates it between the two extremes of antislavery debate in the 1850s. Stowe's homages to the slave narrative acknowledge the power and urgency of black textual claims to freedom, but they also represent a powerful riposte to the central premise of the anti-*Tom* novels. In effect, they challenge those books' attempt to ventriloquize black voices and to claim both that black characters were contented and that they were ridiculous. *Dred* exposes the proslavery camp's exercises in racial image making in Tom Gordon's attempts to slander Harry by calling him impudent. When Nina protests, "'He is always gentlemanly. Everybody remarks it,'" Tom reveals the importance of representation: "'What a fool you are to encourage the use of that word in connection with any of your niggers!'" (*Dred*, 192). Admit that slaves can be "gentlemanly," and the proslavery argument is lost.

Stowe summons a variety of the devices of the anti-*Tom* novel, reclaiming the slave cabin as an antislavery symbol in the Clayton plantation's "cluster of neat cottages, each one of which had its little vegetable garden, and its plot carefully tended with flowers," and satirizing their arguments: "'[T]he best way to get along with negroes . . . is to make them happy; give them plenty to eat and drink and wear, and keep them amused and excited, and don't work them too hard'" (*Dred*, 403, 401). In *Dred* Harry answers that contention: lamenting "'the brutal violence of a vile and wicked man,'" he exclaims, "'Do they think broadcloth coats and gold watches can comfort a man for all this?'" (*Dred*, 434). Similarly, when Mr. Jekyl intones the view that "'[s]lavery is a great missionary enterprise for civilising and christianising the degraded African,'" Harry answers him: "'Wait till you see Tom Gordon's management of this plantation. . . . Sodom and Gomorrah don't equal some of these plantations, where nobody is anybody's husband or wife in particular!'" (*Dred*, 488). One of Stowe's complacent clerics takes the line that abolitionists have inflamed public opinion and thus prevented reform being effected quietly, but this view is undercut by the description of the behavior of one of his fellows: "During all the time that father Dickson and Clayton had been [putting the antislavery case], Dr. Calker had been making minutes with a pencil on a small piece of paper, for future use. It was always disagreeable to him to hear of slave-coffles and the internal slave-trade; and, therefore, when anything was ever said on these topics, he would generally employ himself in some other way than listening" (*Dred*, 529). This moment suggests that, rather than paying too much attention to abolitionist speakers, people find ways not to listen to them. Stirred neither by abolitionist fervor nor to a hot-headed defense of the institution, Calker, like the hypocritical institutions he represents, occupies himself with pointless minutiae.

Many of the answers to *Uncle Tom's Cabin* had defined themselves as apologias for the South as much as for slavery. *Dred* too concerned itself with Southernness, both challenging and reinforcing the anti-*Tom* novels' assertions of Southern uniqueness and sociocultural specificity. It refashioned, for an antislavery sensibility, their comments on the Southern landscape, differing social temperaments, and attitudes to alcohol.

A number of anti-*Tom* novels explored regional differences, identifying specifically Southern qualities but not necessarily idealizing them at the expense of Northern ones. Caroline Lee Hentz, brought up in Massachusetts but long resident in the South, attributed virtues to both sides in *The Planter's Northern Bride*. In it Northern and Southern dwelling places have different but equal charms: the New England cottage is a "neat, modest looking dwelling," while "Southern climes" harbor "the graceful verandah,–the pillared piazza." Descriptions of flora demonstrate Southern natural abundance, on the one hand, and the Northern work ethic, on the other: "'If you want beautiful flowers you must come to the South. . . . All that you cultivate here with so much care, grows wild in our forests,'" and the planter of the title appreciates the efforts of his hosts: "'I admire . . . your rich, blooming clover fields and cultivated plains . . . as a proof of the energy and industry of the sons of New England.'"[30]

This praise for Northern industriousness touched on the contemporary image of white Southerners as prone to lassitude. In *Uncle Tom's Cabin* Stowe had beautifully typified the two in Miss Ophelia's disgust at the "shiftless" state of the Southern kitchen and Marie St. Clare's hypochondriac inactivity. Perhaps surprisingly, Southerner Maria McIntosh's *The Lofty and the Lowly* also seemed at first to concede to the stereotype: its first two hundred pages contrast various aspects of Southern and "Yankee" prejudices in relation to work, and while a Northern manufacturer's son labors to clear his father's debts, the Southern planter's boy loses his inheritance by gambling. Yet McIntosh does not deem such behavior inevitable. After seeing examples of Northern industry, a Southern woman prefigures the pedagogical plantation mistresses in *Dred* by starting a Sunday school for slaves.[31] More accusingly, Martha Haines Butt invented a Northern visitor who initially refuses to allow slaves to run personal errands for her but after a few weeks is "too much fatigued" to take off her own shoes.[32]

In comparison to these texts *Dred* seems rather ungenerous, abandoning *Uncle Tom's* attempts to conciliate Southern readers. Like Hentz, Stowe contrasted the landscapes north and south of the Mason-Dixon Line, and her heroine's description of the topography and the industry of New Hampshire is very similar to the New England of *The Planter's Northern Bride*: "'[I]t's dreadfully poor, barren country; nothing but stony hills, and poor soil. And yet the people there seem to be so well off! They live in such nice, tight, clean-looking white houses.'"[33] Stowe's South, by contrast, is not a paradise but an environment in decline: "'[E]verything seems to be going to destruction. . . . [I]t seems as if everything had stopped growing, and was going backwards'" (*Dred*, 206). While Hentz praised the industry of New Englanders,

Stowe dwelled on Southern sloth, which of course she blamed on slavery: "[S]lave labor, of all others the most worthless and profitless, had exhausted the first vigor of the soil, and the proprietors gradually degenerated from those habits of energy which were called forth by the necessities of the first settlers" (*Dred*, 67).

These perceived differences in regional attitudes extended to that other symbol of moral probity or degeneration in midcentury New England—alcohol. In the anti-*Tom* novel campaigning against alcohol is represented as fanatical and of a piece with Northern extremism. If drink is a problem, it is largely so for slaves. The aptly named Bacchus in *Aunt Phillis's Cabin* troubles his owner with his capacity for spirits, even though his wife forbids them in their cabin. The last time Bacchus's master let him go to a camp meeting he was brought home in a cart. Yet although slaves in this novel "ain't like white people, no how, they can't 'sist temptation," temperance is regarded as an extremist movement associated with faddish Northern concerns like woman's rights. In *Aunt Phillis* a Southern army officer's wife rescues an ex-slave from deceiving abolitionists; the Northern reform community retaliates by associating the slave power with the demon drink. As revenge for the slight on abolitionism, they cook up a campaign to ostracize army folk in that town for the sin of putting wine in their pudding sauce.[34] Temperance and abolition, in other words, are linked conspiracies against the South.

Dred could only have fuelled such paranoia. It bears out with a vengeance Eastman's equation of antislavery activity with temperance fanaticism, since, as Cynthia Hamilton has pointed out, it associates the worst excesses of slavery with drunkenness, "operating within the double framework of antislavery and temperance," reinforcing the widespread Southern perception that abstinence was akin to abolitionism. Stowe was already connected with the alcohol controversy. Her father, Lyman Beecher, had helped launch the temperance movement, she herself had linked slavery and alcohol in *Uncle Tom* in the excesses of Simon Legree, and her son Fred became an alcoholic in his teens, a problem his mother blamed on the bad influence of Southern friends.[35] There were other *Uncle Tom* links with the movement: before their success with Aiken's *Uncle Tom's Cabin*, the Howard family had a hit at the Boston Museum in 1844 with the temperance play *The Drunkard*, and Aiken's drama helped slavery to join temperance as a fit subject for reform melodrama.[36] Whereas in *Aunt Phillis's Cabin* it is slaves who incapacitate themselves with liquor, in *Dred* alcoholic delirium is most likely to exhibit itself alongside the violent and irrational defense of slavery. Tom Gordon drowns the last whispers of his soul with alcohol; it further brutalizes the inadequate husband and father Cripps, and lynch mobs run on it.

Dred's most significant challenge to the anti-*Tom* novels was to address their contradictory claims about fugitive slaves. In Dred himself Stowe provides a character as unthinkable as a minstrel as her Uncle Tom, though his Christianity is militant rather than meek. Stowe also illuminates the phenomenon that the anti-*Tom* novels so consistently denied: at the center of *Dred* is a runaway community directed not by abolitionists but by a desperate desire for freedom. Like those books, *Dred* is full of fugitives; but it offers us slaves who opt to run away without prompting from Northerners or even abolitionists. In Dred himself it has at its heart an escaped slave who is a powerful visionary, not a misguided dupe. Rather than playing second fiddle to some white ideologue, Dred shelters vulnerable whites, accepting the children Tiff brings to the swamps to get away from poverty and their brutal father and saving Clayton from a lynch party. *Dred's* white people recuperate and are restored in the black community, a total rejection of the anti-*Tom* novels' assertions that blacks were necessarily and irredeemably dependent.

Several times *Dred* reverses the most common trope of the proslavery novels, the ungrateful escape of a slave brought by his master to the Free States. Harry's sister has been taken to Ohio by her owner, has been freed, and has married. A clever lawyer overturns both her Mississippi deed of emancipation and the act of freeing her "just [by] taking her into Ohio" (*Dred*, 222) so that she and her children can be reenslaved for Tom Gordon's benefit. Stowe's story here seems to mirror several of the fugitive causes célèbres of the 1850s—the failure of Harry's sister's claim to freedom on the grounds of former residence in a Free State matches the case of Elisha Brazealle's family, which Stowe had documented in *Key*.[37] It also echoes that of Dred Scott and that of the New Albany family of uncertain racial status: "'[S]he is so near white . . . the people round there, actually, some of them . . . didn't know but what she was a white woman from Ohio'" (*Dred*, 222). Eventually, Cora kills her children, like Cassy in *Uncle Tom* and also like another infamous fugitive, Margaret Garner, who fled Kentucky for Cincinnati in January 1856 and killed a child rather than see her recaptured.[38] This tale is echoed again by one of Dred's rescued slaves who "got free once, and got clear up to New York, and got me a little bit of a house, and a wife and two children, with a little money beforehand," and then was recaptured and sold (*Dred*, 358). These vignettes in *Dred*, like the slave narratives and the contemporary sensations over returned fugitive slaves, contest the assertions of the answers to *Uncle Tom's*

Cabin that escapes were orchestrated by Northern whites to the detriment of both masters and slaves. In contrast, they insist that running away was an act of desperation, independently conceived and executed, and that Northerners conspired most often with slave owners. The scandal lay not in slave escapes but in the frequency of their enforced returns to bondage.

There is one example in *Dred* of the idea that so proliferated in anti-*Tom* novels, of the abolitionist advising slaves to flee, and Stowe uses it to suggest that Southern paranoia about this phenomenon is dangerously misplaced. After Dred has been killed defending another slave, Clayton notices "a perilous degree of excitement" among his band, "which, unless some escape-valve were opened, might lead to most fatal results" (*Dred*, 642). Clayton advises the people hidden in the Dismal Swamp to try "flight to the Free States" to prevent violence. One critic has condemned this aspect of the novel as a species of Colonizationism, akin to George Harris's removal to Liberia at the end of *Uncle Tom's Cabin*: "[It is] an inability to imagine a future America in which blacks have any legitimate place."[39] This judgment wrongly assumes that Clayton directs the slaves out of the country and ignores the hypersensitivity of the fugitive question in the 1850s; this episode touched on a powerful fear in the proslavery imagination. Stowe was not advising black people to leave America but invoking a patriotic shock at the situation British *Tom* plays had so loved: that the monarchical British lion was protecting fugitives from the so-called land of the free.

The white slave owner's extraordinary part in this situation was itself proof against such simple interpretations as Stowe's intention to expel African Americans from the United States. As a vindication of the proslavery charge that abolitionists were responsible for slave escapes, this aspect of the novel also necessitated some defensiveness. Stowe spells out the forces that are ranged against Clayton's even contemplating such action, let alone taking it: "One can scarcely appreciate the moral resolution and force of character which could make a person in Clayton's position in society—himself sustaining, in the eyes of the law, the legal relation of a slave-holder—give advice of this kind" (*Dred*, 642). She makes this a sign of extraordinary intellectual and moral qualities in her hero rather than, as with the villains of the anti-*Tom* novels, a symptom of depravity: "It was . . . only by the discerning power of a mind sufficiently clear and strong to see its way through the mists of educational association, that Clayton could feel himself to be doing right in thus violating the laws and customs of the social state under which he was born" (*Dred*, 643). There are two justifications for this course of action, neither of which is evident in the *Tom* novels. The first is also apparent to the slave narrators ("his belief in the inalienable right of every man to liberty"), but the second is Stowe's own: "[H]e had at this time a firm conviction that nothing but the removal of some of these minds from the oppressions which were goading them could prevent a development of bloody insurrection" (*Dred*, 643). Stowe offers both the slaves' perspective—it is their right to be free—and a warning to those who cannot share it: "[T]he underground railroad . . . has removed many a danger from their dwellings" (*Dred*, 643).

To a significant degree, then, *Dred* is designed to be a radical text, deferring to black writers and defending precisely the subversive activity of the Underground Railroad, which the anti-*Tom* novels had obsessively fictionalized and simultaneously sought to deny. Positioning itself against the answers to *Uncle Tom*, creating, in fact, an anti-anti-*Tom*, *Dred* both affirmed black experience, as Stowe had encountered it, and acknowledged slaves' agency in their acts of resistance. The book staged an encounter between opposing ends of the slavery debate, pitting the insights of the slave narrative against proslavery fantasy. Like the anti-*Tom* novels, it invented black characters to speak for black people. Unlike them, it also asserted the value of black speakers and writers.

Yet there are puzzling equivocations in *Dred*. Clayton, whose constant battles with the legal and clerical avatars of slavery and whose eventual freeing of his own slaves and support of the fugitives signal his ideological correctness in the novel, writes to Harry that he does not believe the slaves are fully ready for freedom. He accepts their entitlement to the American ideal ("'I admit your right, and that of all men, to life, liberty and the pursuit of happiness'"), but his support does not extend to revolution because he does not believe black people are ready for the franchise: "'[I]f I believed that [black people] were capable of obtaining and supporting a government, I should believe in their right to take . . . means to gain it. But I do not, at present'" (*Dred*, 553).

This is one of the reasons why education is such a critical theme in the novel: it allows Stowe, like Clayton, to argue for emancipation without relinquishing anxieties about black people. In one description of Dred Stowe seems to associate in one image *Sunny Memories*' awed descriptions of European antiquities and its lament over Elizabeth Greenfield: "[W]hat a loss to art is the enslaving of a race which might produce so much musical talent."[40] Clayton imagines Dred as "one of those old rude Gothic doorways, so frequent in European cathedrals, where scriptural images, carved in rough granite, mingle themselves with a thousand wayward, fantastic freaks of architecture" (*Dred*, 632). This vision suggests to Clayton the wasted potential Dred embodies: "[H]e thought, with a sigh, how much might have been accomplished by a soul so ardent and a frame so energetic, had they been enlightened and guided" (*Dred*, 632). Had Dred been "enlightened and guided," had Greenfield "had culture equal to her voice and ear," what might have been accomplished!

Dred's uncultivated ability signals the extent to which the school on the Clayton plantation represented both Stowe's faith in black people and her distrust, hence her accusations of black irresponsibility and childishness, which mirrored the beliefs of many of her opponents. Clayton's determination in the novel to "educate and fit ... for freedom" (*Dred*, 51) his four hundred slaves fictionally calls Louisa McCord's bluff: her public letter to the Duchess of Sutherland had asked her to pay for the emancipation of McCord's own labor force.[41] Yet *Dred* also managed to endorse the assertion made by McCord, Tyler, and others that the ownership of slaves was a burden. In her anti-*Tom* novel Caroline Rush insisted that "the greatest slave on a plantation is the mistress. She is like the mother of an immense family.... [T]hey are the most improvident race in the world, and must have a superior mind to guide them."[42] Stowe, who at times took pains to refute such claims about African Americans and slavery, nevertheless reproduced this one exactly in *Dred* even down to its maternal imagery: "The duties of a southern housekeeper, on a plantation, are onerous beyond any amount of northern conception.... For the most part, the servants are only grown-up children, without consideration, forethought, or self-control" (*Dred*, 64). In this *Dred* rehearses the proslavery argument that the peculiar institution was a responsibility rather than a privilege, and it also borrows the underpinning racial theory that justified perpetual bondage.

Stowe's identification with the slave mistress is probably an unconscious reflection of the fact noted by Joan Hedrick, that Stowe's conception of the "negro character" was initially based on "her position as white mistress to black servants." What Hedrick calls Stowe's "contradictory consciousness," in which "she overidentified with [her servants] as women, [while] she distanced herself from their race and class," is reflected in *Dred*'s cheerful endorsement of the institution of domestic service.[43] The novel ends with Old Tiff, now technically free in New York, still devotedly tending the offspring, now the second generation, of his long-dead mistress. Hamilton has observed that "Tiff's escape poses little threat to white supremacy"; it is also no challenge to class relations.[44] Liberated he may be, but he is still a servant, and enthusiastically so. His persona chimes with a myth that would persist after the Civil War: with his white hair and glasses, Tiff resembles later stage presentations of Uncle Tom as a kindly old retainer or even of Joel Chandler Harris's Uncle Remus.[45] Stowe's view is expressed in Clayton's letter to Harry: "'I see no reason why the relation of master and servants may not be continued through our states, and the servants yet be free men'" (*Dred*, 553). Although *Dred* advocates education for all, it cannot envisage an alternative to the social stratification in which some are waited upon while others wait. As in *Sunny Memories*, where she attributed (implicitly middle-class) Englishwomen's superior complexions to the abundance and loyalty of their servants, Stowe unthinkingly positioned herself, in this aspect of the novel, among those who profited from this arrangement of society. Slaveholders in the anti-*Tom* novels often referred to their slaves as servants, and of course the two words are etymologically connected.[46] The preface to *Key* had compared the "picturesque . . . family attachment of old servants" in slavery and on an English estate, yet there was no acknowledgment of the link in *Dred*.[47]

The conflicting racial impulses in the novel—the move to champion black potential while underplaying black achievement—thus had a class dimension. Class is a central theme in *Dred*, which allows Stowe to respond to critiques of *Uncle Tom* in both the plantation novel and the British anti-*Tom*s. *Dred* takes up the cause of the poor white Southerner as a counterpart to the impoverished Britons her critics had ranged against *Uncle Tom*'s slaves. In Europe as in the United States a common response to *Uncle Tom* mania had been, "*Look at your own lower classes.*" Stowe's reply had been a chapter in *The Key to Uncle Tom's Cabin* entitled "Poor White Trash." She argued that the institution of slavery had produced "a poor white population as degraded and brutal as ever existed in any of the most crowded districts of Europe."[48] The argument is spelled out in *Dred* by Clayton: "'I don't believe there's any country in old, despotic, Europe where the poor are more miserable, vicious, and degraded, than they are in our slave states'" (*Dred*, 580). He too argues that slavery is responsible: "'[I]t prevents general education of the whites, and keeps the poorer classes down to the lowest point, while it enriches a few'" (*Dred*, 207).

Few anti-*Tom* novels featured white Southerners outside the planter class, but Hentz's *The Planter's Northern Bride* made the plain-living but industrious yeoman family indicative of the health of Southern society. Hentz described this family in great detail, including their log cabin, dress, appearance, food, and sleeping arrangements. The text is, on the whole, approving of their "primitive habits," rustic manners, and unrefined lifestyle: they are "clean and tidy, though rough and uncouth," and manifest "homely good sense, contentment and appreciation of each other." Again Hentz strives to be fair to both regions. Compared to indigent families in the North, this one seems slightly worse off: their cabin is like a New England cottage, only that would have glass windows, and the teenage girls are still uneducated, putting the heroine in mind of "'the superior advantages of the children of New England, where the blessings of education are as diffusive as the sunbeams of heaven, gilding the poor and lowly as well as the rich.'" However, the planter predicts that the energy with which the family is setting about cultivation will soon bring in "'money enough to purchase some negroes,'" while the children "'will be rich, and be associated with the magnates of the land.'"[49]

Hentz's concerns in this chapter are, of course, very similar to Stowe's, and the interest in the girls' education is especially suggestive, but *Dred* offers no portraits of contented small farmers, although there were many in nineteenth-century North Carolina.[50] *Dred* is preoccupied with what Stowe sees as the hopeless poor, the squatters and loafers on the margins of society. Like Hentz, she pays particular attention to their lack of learning and contrasts this situation with the facilities available in the North, but her verdict is damning. Cripps's wife's dying wish is that her children should be taught to read; he, on the other hand, is suspicious of literacy because he "'always got cheated by them damn reading, writing Yankees, whenever I've traded with 'em'" (*Dred*, 139–40). Nina complains that "'there isn't any school where they could send their children, if they wanted to learn,'" and wishes the legislature would institute some "'as they do up in New York State'" (*Dred*, 150, 176). Unlike Hentz's yeoman, Cripps will never be rich, as he is "constantly buying what he could not sell, and losing on all that he did sell" (*Dred*, 132).

Cripps also drinks his assets away, and his shiftlessness and dipsomania suggest the limitations of Stowe's concern for him. The book represents the condition of the white poor as deplorable, both morally and materially, but it is ambivalent about extending to them the sympathy it expends on slaves. Drink in *Dred* is both a lower-class indulgence and a sign of other failings.[51] Cripps leaves his sick wife and small children to be fed by means of Tiff's ingenuity and eats their food himself when "he had drank up his last quarter of a dollar at the tavern" (*Dred*, 133). He makes a second marriage to "a bundle of tawdry, dirty finery . . . so far gone in intoxication as scarcely to be sensible of what she was doing": she is the daughter of Abijah Skinflint the whiskey seller. Skinflint himself lives in a log cabin with a wife who drinks immoderately and a brood of "forward, dirty and ill-mannered" children (*Dred*, 301, 503). The Skinflints exemplify "the lowest of that class of poor whites whose wretched condition is not among the least of the evils of slavery" (*Dred*, 503). The mob who waylay good Father Dickson after Tom Gordon has plied them with whiskey unite the "wretched" mores of this social group, the depredations of alcohol, and proslavery violence. They are "surly, wolfish-looking" men who spit tobacco quids and preach anarchy in "rough" slang: "'Now old cock, you may as well know fust as last, that we don't care a cuss for the civil authorities, as you call them'" (*Dred*, 596, 598).

Dred exacerbates the condition of the Southern poor with a contrasting vision of the North as a near-classless society. In New Hampshire Nina observes that "'the Governers of the State are farmers, sometimes, and work with their own men. The brain and the hand go together, in each one—not one great brain to fifty pair of hands. . . . There are no high and low *classes* there'" (*Dred*, 287). Nevertheless, even as she praised the classlessness of New England, Stowe contradicted her egalitarian rhetoric with the antirevolutionary suggestion that social reform in the South could take the limited course it had taken in England. Clayton asserts that, unlike its European counterparts, England's aristocracy has resisted revolution "'because it knew when to *yield*; because it never confined discussion; because it gave way gracefully before the growing force of the people'" (*Dred*, 586). His friend Russel's reply directly equates slave owners with British duchesses: "'[Y]ou won't make *our* aristocracy believe it'" (*Dred*, 586). Stowe is torn between her admiration for the British nobility and an awareness that their privilege is not so different from that of the plantocracy she denounces, simultaneously blaming and excusing both in her declaration that the "aristocratic nature of society at the South so completely segregates people of a certain position in life" from their inferiors that "the most fearful things may be transacting in their vicinity unknown or unnoticed" (*Dred*, 361).

Stowe's inconsistency here is part of a deeper resemblance between *Dred* and the anti-*Tom* novels set in London, which could not make up their minds whether to damn noblemen or to aspire to be them. In *Dred* as in *English Serfdom* it is not enough to show that the poor are oppressed; the suffering of the hero must be special because his manners and morals mark him out from his impoverished fellows. The victims in *Tit for Tat* and *English Serfdom* are revealed to be displaced aristocrats themselves; in *Dred* Cripps's children are not only "pretty-looking" and "genteel" (like their betters in appearance) but are descended maternally "from a distant branch of one of the most celebrated families in Virginia" (*Dred*, 367, 131). As in the novels that sought to answer *Uncle Tom's Cabin*, as in the British condition of England novels on which they were modeled, the victims of the class system in *Dred* come from the upper classes all along.

The congenial poor whites in *Dred* are poor by accident rather than breeding. Tiff is the mouthpiece for this sense of natural "quality" when he advises his young mistress how to behave like a lady: "'[Y]ou's got it in you; you was born to it, honey. It's in de blood'" (*Dred*, 298). Tiff's instruction implies that class is biologically determined, since his mistress's is her birthright, and "'if you was one of dese yer por white folks, dere be no use of your trying; cause dat ar 'scription o' people couldn't never be ladies'" (*Dred*, 298). Just like Dickens and Disraeli, Chase and Southwood, Stowe asks her readers to sympathize with what she portrays as an oppressed class but not to identify with it. It is only by imagining the genteel reduced that readers can be expected to understand the desperation of poverty.

This gentility is also closely bound up with femininity. Several anti-*Tom* novels had preempted *Dred*'s concern about Tiff's mistress with heroines who were unaccustomed to the work circumstances forced them to undertake. In Rush's *North and South* a Northern white family is driven by financial ruin to the extremity of seeking paid employment, whereupon "poor Lily's hands [were] so toughened by hard work . . . that she felt, in handling the needle, as if her fingers were all thumbs."[52] In Hentz's novel the planter worries lest the heroine's butter making has impaired her hands and is relieved to see that they are "fair and symmetrical." Hentz even describes the beauty routine that has preserved her from signs of labor: she sews in gloves with truncated fingers, "ingeniously adapted for such a purpose," and has "been taught, as a regular duty, to draw on a pair of thick woollen mittens before she wielded the broom and exercised the duster."[53] In *Dred* Tiff protects his little mistress with the advice that ladies "'don't demean demselves with sweeping and scrubbing.'" Instead, "'dey sews, and dey knits'" (*Dred*, 297–98). *Dred*'s conflicting signals about class are summed up in Anne Clayton's paradoxical defense of her "levelling doctrine" about the universal right to education, conscripting her Southern aristocratic credentials in the promotion of social equality: "'Let it level, then! . . . I don't care! I come from the old Virginia cavalier blood, and am not afraid of anything'" (*Dred*, 405). In *Dred* as in all its predecessors, only the most wellborn can afford to obliterate social distinctions.

The poor whites in *Dred* are thus appealing only if they conform to middle-class and feminine social codes. Those who eschew bourgeois refinements of habit, speech, and manner are presumed anathema to the reader's genteel sensibilities. There is an acute contrast here with the tradition of southwestern humor, which celebrated the very character types *Dred* demonizes. In those texts they furnish a kind of warmhearted honesty and frontier authenticity, and their vernacular bluntness is prized.[54] Despite this apparent antipathy, *Dred* also contains echoes of this genre. William Gilmore Simms's *The Sword and the Distaff* and C. H. Wiley's *Life at the South: A Companion to "Uncle Tom's Cabin"* both posed as anti-*Tom* novels, although, as I have argued, in neither case with much credibility. Yet although they are not much linked with the concerns of Stowe's first novel, both prefigure *Dred* in startling ways, suggesting that Stowe was indebted to, although deeply distrustful of, this strain of writing about the Southern frontier.

Simms's *The Sword and the Distaff* is set "at the close of the Revolution" and pits a Falstaffian American, Captain Porgy, against a traitor who is scheming to steal his land and his slaves. The picaresque plot features gory battle scenes and frequent gambling and drinking—even the heroes are fond of Jamaica rum. Where Stowe stamps these masculine pursuits with disapproval, Simms enjoys them. At one point Porgy's overseer invokes the classic frontier boast to insult the sheriff's man, calling him "'hafe man, hafe horse, and two parts alligator,'" and at another Porgy employs the same trick Twain's Huckleberry Finn plays on Jim, pretending that an alarm in the night never happened so that his companion will assume he has been dreaming.[55] Yet in Twain the incident has an instructive purpose: Huck pretends to Jim that his memory of being separated in the night by fog was all a nightmare; Jim's rebuke makes Huck see that he has behaved like "trash."[56] As Eric Lott points out, Twain uses "the pathos that minstrel shows in the 1840s and 1850s had begun to pin to the slaves to make his case" (and one might add *Uncle Tom's Cabin* into this cultural inheritance too).[57] Porgy similarly convinces Sergeant Millhouse that his impression that reinforcements appeared in the night was the result of too heavy a supper, but here the black character—Porgy's cook, Tom—is in on the ruse.[58] Simms's use of the trick does not leaven the comedy with sentiment, and this is in keeping with the tenor of the book, which consistently privileges masculinity over femininity.[59]

In one of Simms's villains we see a more striking resemblance to *Dred*, for Simms almost seems to have provided the precursor of Stowe's Cripps. Bostwick, too, is a squatter. He lives in a "decayed" wigwam, "one of the meanest sort of log-houses" in the swamps. He takes off every penny earned by his "thin, frail, pale-faced" wife, who resembles Cripps's consumptive one.[60] Bostwick's children, like Cripps's, are most unlike their father—one daughter reads the Bible, just as in *Dred* Tiff hopes Cripps's children will learn to do.

While *The Sword and the Distaff* prefigures one of *Dred*'s characters, Wiley's *Life at the South* is uncanny in its resemblances to Stowe's novel: it could almost have supplied both plot and protagonist. Wiley was also, like Stowe, interested in education: he founded the North Carolina public school system in the 1850s and wrote a textbook, *The North-Carolina Reader*, but *Life at the South* is far from earnest.[61] Rather, it borders on the surreal (it opens with some frontier types trading wives for goods, and the minstrel figures Zip Coon and Dan Tucker both feature as [white] characters), but it contains a runaway slave who lives in North Carolina's Great Dismal Swamp and who heads a band of outlaws. Wild Bill, as he is called, calls on God to avenge the sufferings of slaves, has read "'all the books of my master's son,'" and has also "been, for years past, *a reader of nature* and a thinker." Wild Bill, like Dred, is both wild and strangely impressive, and he too has the ability to vanish in and out of the woods without warning. Stowe's official model for Dred, Nat Turner, was hanged, and so eventually is Bill, and before he dies he too leaves a manuscript history of his life, like the one Turner is supposed to have dictated to his white amanuensis. Yet the book's delight in "low bred and vulgar people" and their pastimes, its tall tales (a man captures an enemy who turns out to be a bear who dares him to a "wrastle"), and its comic amorality signal its place in the tradition of southwestern writing.[62] If Stowe did borrow from Wiley, she spring-cleaned his text's morals and manners for *Dred*.

The camp meeting is one example of a scene in *Life at the South* that gets a very different spin in *Dred*. Several minstrel show *Uncle Toms* had featured camp meetings, Sanford's and Christy and Wood's proslavery productions reducing the religious power of Stowe's *Tom* to this simple reference to a rustic institution. Moore and Burgess's antislavery *Uncle Tom* had also featured a camp meeting scene and treated it more respectfully, but it still marked the camp meeting's brand of piety, and therefore Tom's, as peculiarly black by offering a pseudospiritual as "The Song of the Camp Meeting":

> So it's wait for de chariot dat to take us dere am coming;
> Wait for it, chillun, at de corner ob de road;
> In de midnight, in de silence we may hear dem wheels a-humming,
> Wait for it chillun, at de corner ob de road.[63]

But if the minstrel show camp meeting represented black culture, in both Wiley and Stowe it had significance for white characters too.

In both novels major plot developments occur at the camp meeting. Dred interrupts the camp meeting in Stowe's text with a mysterious pronouncement, and a black servant breaks into the preaching in Wiley's with an extraordinary cry. Dred begins his exhortation with "Woe unto you that desire the day of the Lord"; the preacher in *Life at the South* declaims, "'Wo, wo, to you, hell bound sinners!'" Virtually the only difference between the two camp meetings lies in the tone in which they are treated. Wiley's is comic—his character Job crashes through on horseback with a prisoner, both screaming, and chaos ensues: "[T]he furious riders were now roaring and bellowing in the outskirts of the camp. . . . [W]omen fainted, men clung by their elders and preachers, children screamed, and all ran to and fro, wailing and wringing their hands."[64] In Stowe's book the interruption is an exhibition of Dred's prophetic powers that sobers his listeners rather than provoking hysteria: "[W]hen the sound ceased, men drew in their breath, and looked on each other, and the crowd began slowly to disperse, whispering in low voices to each other" (*Dred*, 340). A scene that in Wiley is comic is thus transformed in *Dred* into something deadly serious, an apocalyptic warning about ignoring the spiritual consequences of sin and particularly of slavery.

There may have been another literary reference in the staging of Stowe's and Wiley's camp meetings. Both had a famous precursor in Frances Trollope's *Domestic Manners of the Americans*. *Domestic Manners* provides us with a context for the camp meeting as a species of peculiarly American religious expression and as one of the experiences of the American frontier that an English visitor "had long wished for . . . the opportunity . . . of attending," even though the prospect of camping in "the back woods of Indiana was by no means agreeable."[65] Trollope's camp meeting is a crucial part of her condemnation of American culture: the occasion provoked in her "horror and disgust." She admired the effect of moonbeams on rapt young faces and "the lurid glare thrown by the altar-fires on the woods beyond" but was revolted by the extreme manifestations of religious emotion: "hysterical sobbings, convulsive groans, shrieks and screams the most appalling." One of these was almost the same phrase used in Wiley, "'Woe! woe to the backsliders!'"[66]

Dred, which, like Trollope, judges the event with eyes of ladylike fastidiousness, revises her verdict. Whereas Wiley reclaimed the camp meeting as a site for peculiarly American comedy, Stowe pays her respects to its powerful evocations of religious emotion. The genteel party from Nina Gordon's plantation are not implicated in any potential vulgarity because they have come merely out of "curiosity," but not only Nina but her aunt Maria, Anne Clayton, and even her puritan aunt Nesbit attend (*Dred*, 314). These worthy feminine judges, like Trollope, ponder the spiritual benefit of such occasions, but they are more tolerant. While Anne Clayton is appalled, stating, "'[R]eligion is a sacred thing with me, and I don't like to see it travestied,'" Nina argues that a "'good laugh at its oddities'" is "'healthy,'" and Clayton adds masculine approbation, declaring that he has "'known real conversions to take place under just these excitements'" (*Dred*, 316, 317).

Trollope also claimed that the preachers took advantage of young girls under the guise of comforting them and described the exploitation of one pretty woman's fervor: "I saw her, ere I left the ground, with her hand fast locked, and her head supported by a man who looked very much as Don Juan might, when sent back to earth as too bad for the regions below."[67] Like *Domestic Manners*, *Dred* links the camp meeting with licentiousness and unscrupulous preying on women. In *Dred*, however, the association is used not to damn the religious meeting but for an antislavery purpose. Religion here, as elsewhere in the novel, is perverted by slavery, as a trader tries to sell a woman to Father Bonnie right in the midst of the meeting. And Stowe's exploited girl is a victim not of lecherous ministers but of slavery: as Father Dickson sings hymns over her, seventeen-year-old Emily dies. There may be a sexual element to her ruin (her mistress "'used to say I was a wild girl, and laughed too loud'"), but Emily has been sold for trying to run away to her mother (*Dred*, 343). Thus the horror Trollope feels at the camp meeting is displaced in *Dred* onto the slave trading that goes on alongside it, while the scenes that Wiley evokes for comic purposes are powerfully contrasted in Stowe by the warning Dred issues, so like the rhetoric of the camp meeting preachers yet for once rightfully dire—not a formulaic prompt to hysteria but true prophecy.

Blackface, of course, was designed to explore the connections of class with contradictory racial feelings. Yet while *Dred* borrows several elements from the minstrel tradition, the ironies and ambiguities of the stage are not always apparent in the novel. For example, Anne Clayton pays her slaves a backhanded compliment on their intellectual curiosity that repeats the patronizing equation of black people with children and repeats a staple tenet of minstrel humor, that black speakers habitually misuse the English language: "'[T]he negroes are sometimes laughed at for mispronouncing words, which they will do in a very droll manner; but it's only because they are so taken with the sounds of words that they will try to pronounce beyond the sphere of their understanding, like bright children'" (*Dred*, 420). These mispronunciations are "very droll," like blackface ones, but Anne Clayton cannot allow them to contain any parodic or subversive aspects. Her assumption lacks the potential complexity of the stage stump speech, in which the performer could collude with a white audience to ridicule an alien high culture or slyly implicate the audience in contentious sentiments. Anne Clayton accepts the premise that "black" language is flawed but ignores the paradoxical use to which it was often put on the stage: she plays the device for sympathy not irony.

Elsewhere, too, *Dred* adopts blackface's racial characterizations literally, without any compensating sense of play. For example, in Old Hundred, the coachman with a thousand excuses for staying in the stable, Stowe re-creates *Uncle Tom*'s Sam as a lazy man rather than a mischievous one. In that novel Mrs. Shelby knows as well as Sam does that his utterances are tongue-in-cheek and his delay in saddling the horses is only mock foolishness, with a secret, vital purpose. But Old Hundred compounds laziness with lies in frustrating Nina's attempts to send a message: "'Course I couldn't tell her I *wouldn't* take de critturs out; so I just trots out scuse'" (*Dred*, 115).

Dred's reworking of Topsy similarly divests the character of complexity: Stowe seems not to have recognized that gender politics had played a large part in Topsy's special appeal. In *Dred* there is a similar scamp, Tomtit, who also performs somersaults and pirouettes, sings in "a very high key," and is fiendishly naughty, but Tomtit is male. Tomtit's repertoire includes "Camptown Races" and even the misplaced rhetoric of blackface, punning on a biblical text: "'We's unprofitable servants, all on us. Lord's marcy that we an't 'sumed!'" (*Dred*, 79, 80). His catchphrase, a parallel with Topsy's "nebber was born," is adapted to the novel's educational motif and also echoes that of Dickens's Jo in *Bleak House*: "'Don't know nothing at all—never can'" (*Dred*, 80).[68] Like Topsy, Tomtit has a straitlaced spinster to torment, and he upsets Aunt Nesbit's attempts at religious instruction as Topsy parodied Ophelia's. However, if Topsy was a female Jim Crow, Tomtit is Topsy in trousers. As I mentioned, Adams compares him with *Uncle Tom*'s Harry, whom Mr. Shelby nicknames Jim Crow, but Tomtit's Jim Crow act is also a remasculating mimicry of Topsy's.[69]

Yet although *Dred*'s blackface sometimes lacks the signifying complexity of the stage or its uses in *Uncle Tom*, Stowe still employed it purposefully in the novel. In the chapter "The Troubadour" Stowe not only conjures up a sentimental vision of the minstrel show, once again challenging its traditional

gender affiliations, but attacks its uses in proslavery fiction. The concert on
the Clayton plantation rewrites the numerous occasions in anti-*Tom* novels
when performing slaves provide amusement for onlooking whites. Not only
that, the scene seems to be a specific reference to a minor tradition, in which
slaves are imagined creating impromptu verses commenting upon the love
lives of their masters. In Robert Criswell's *"Uncle Tom's Cabin" Contrasted
with Buckingham Hall* the servant Jerry sings about the Englishman ("'Good
ole Doctor from de Nort'") who has come to marry Miss Cora.[70] Similarly, in
James Hungerford's *The Old Plantation* the slave Clothilda sings her own
compositions, which comment on the love affairs of the white folks.[71] J. Kennard Jr. had supplied a version of it in 1845, when he imagined a slave called
Sambo putting on a show for his master's family during which he improvises
topical rhymes, disclosing that the master is running for Congress, the mistress has a new gold watch, and the young mistress has a new beau. Kennard
claimed that "thousands at the South would recognise the foregoing as a
faithful sketch of a not infrequent scene."[72] Certainly, any reader of *Dred*
would recognize it, for in an almost identical scene Clayton's slave Dulcimer
twits Nina about Clayton's courting:

> "Oh, mas'r is often absent—do you know where he goes?
> He goes to North Carolina, for de North Carolina rose." (*Dred*, 417)

Although commonplace in one sense, however, *Dred*'s take on this trope does
have some special qualities. For a start, it takes place in the context of what
is a self-conscious performance. This is not an impromptu scene of slave exuberance but an elaborately arranged occasion to which invitations have
been issued. It takes place on a carefully constructed stage: "[L]amps had
been hung up in the trees, twinkling on the glossy foliage. A sort of booth or
arbor was built of flowers and leaves at one end, to which the party was marshaled in great state. Between two magnolia-trees a white curtain was hung
up" (*Dred*, 415). As the decoration suggests, this show is not of the rowdy
variety typical of minstrelsy but is a genteel, even feminized spectacle. In a
flattering reversal of concert-hall practice, the singers throw bouquets of
flowers at the audience, directing a wreath of orange blossoms at Nina in a
decorative allusion to her likely marriage.

In part this feminization of the minstrel show is an extension of Stowe's
uses of it in *Uncle Tom*, where she had placed middle-class women in the interlocutor role and let Jim Crow anarchy into the girlish realms of needlework and housekeeping. Yet in terms of blackface iconography it is signifi-

cant that Dulcimer has achieved and not merely aspired to elegance in his arrangements. There is no suggestion of the minstrel stump speaker here, imitating the customs of his betters but unwittingly off-key. Yes, the whole event is a mockery of upper-class entertainments, right down to the formality of the invitation: "The Magnolia Grove troubadours request the presence of Mr. and Miss Clayton and Miss Gordon at an operatic performance, which will be given this evening, at eight o'clock, in the grove" (*Dred*, 412).

But the white characters in *Dred* are being treated to a sophisticated parody of their own culture, orchestrated by a slave who has "lounged around the lobbies of many an opera-house" (*Dred*, 412). This parodic element has its own place in minstrelsy, of course. It is present in the Kennard sketch, where the slave's invitation is in blackface "dialect": "'Sambo sends compliments to massa and Misse, and de young gemmon and ladies, and say he gwine to gib musical entertainment to company dis evening.'"[73] But very little of blackface's emphasis on undermining high culture is in evidence in *Dred*. Instead, this episode chimes with Stowe's assertion throughout the novel that, with education, African Americans can be successfully assimilated into white society. Dulcimer and his fellows are not merely having fun at the expense of their betters, they are demonstrating that they can master the codes of this elite genre. Anne Clayton remarks of her "versifying" slave Lettice that "'if I chose to encourage and push her on, she might turn out a second Phillis Wheatly [*sic*],'" naming the former slave who astonished eighteenth-century society by producing accomplished neoclassical verses (*Dred*, 419). The comparison would be especially apt if we accepted Vernon Loggins's dismissal of Wheatley's work as "noteworthy as an accomplishment in imitation . . . [containing] nothing which marks it as the work of a member of the African race."[74]

The concert at Magnolia Grove is intended by its author to demonstrate, as Clayton puts it, that "'if ever [the African race] . . . become highly civilised, they will excel in music, dancing and elocution'" (*Dred*, 420). Stowe thus exploits a minstrel scenario for her own purposes, inverting the usual premise of the blackface scene—that black speakers comically mistake and mangle white culture—to show off the success with which they can appropriate it. Dulcimer and his fellows are not the comic failures of blackface convention, condemned always to shadow white culture but never to equal its achievements. Stowe was allowing her fictional characters to do what Frank Webb hoped his wife would do in her performances of *The Christian Slave*: demonstrate black genius.

Elsewhere in the novel Stowe does put blackface to traditionally double-edged uses, employing a maneuver that both revels in irony and exposes its workings. Tom Gordon's valet keeps in with his master by exhibiting "the licensed audacity of a court buffoon," but for all his punning and clowning, Stowe allows him to explain that he has the same needs and desires as his fellow men. Although he begins his speech with the stump sermon address ("'Fac' is, bredren'"), Jim's problem is deadly serious: "'I never's going to have a wife till I can get one dat'll belong to myself.'" It is as if Sam in *Uncle Tom's Cabin* has grown up and is now claiming the dignity of an adult (*Dred*, 646). Jim, in fact, is very like Sam, regularly making "burlesque imitations" of prayer meetings (*Dred*, 647). The difference is that Jim uses his performative skills to defeat his master—he wins himself an hour in the woods to conspire with the would-be fugitives by pleasing them with minstrelsy: "He sang, he danced, he mimicked sermons, carried on mock meetings" (*Dred*, 647). His efforts would sum up the content of many blackface shows and indeed the tone (he "seemed to whip all things sacred and profane together"), but in this text they are life-saving (*Dred*, 647). When Tom catches Jim on his return, the slave is forced to throw himself into the character of the irresponsible scamp so beloved of proslavery rhetoric ("'Why, laws, mas'r, honey, chile, 'fore my heavenly mas'r, I done forgot every word you said!'"), and it works: "[T]he ludicrous grimace and tone, and attitude of affected contrition, with which all this was said, rather amused Tom" (*Dred*, 648).

This is virtually the same as Sam's act with Mrs. Shelby in *Uncle Tom* (willful but winning disobedience), but here it is played out for a bad master, and its effect is emancipating. The white man is trapped by his own limited expectations of Jim and blinded by his refusal to believe in the black man's basic humanity. His suspicion about Jim's absence is allayed, and Jim, who will run off that night, slathers his final performance in an irony Tom is too blinkered to read. When asked to repeat the text of the sermon he has supposedly attended in the woods, Jim says, "'Ye shall sarch fur me in de mornin and ye won't find me.'" As he declares, "'Dat ars' a mighty solemn text, mas'r, and ye ought to be 'flecting on 't'" (*Dred*, 649).

This devastating critique of the worst assumptions of minstrelsy is reinforced in the novel by its association with lynch mobs: Tom Gordon's vigilante group is called "THE ASSOCIATE BANDS OF THE GLORIOUS IMMORTAL COONS," making the connection between the blackface character Zip Coon and the folk practice of "raising Cain," which W. T. Lhamon has shown has very close associations with minstrelsy. Tom Gordon's henchmen illustrate what is meant by the phrase perfectly, parading "with barbarous and dissonant sounds, such as the beating of tin pans, the braying of horns, and shouts of savage merriment" (*Dred*, 663).

In a still more complex manifestation of blackface processes the mob are only defeated by a kind of whiteface class cross-dressing. Clayton's friend Russel distracts the rioters by posing as one of them in an incongruous motley: "a shaggy old great coat, . . . a red bandanna silk handkerchief, . . . a very fiery and dashing tie, and . . . an old hat which had belonged to one of the servants" (*Dred*, 664). He gives them a rousing speech, literally from a tree stump, "in that peculiar slang dialect, which was vernacular with them," and leads them off to get drunk (*Dred*, 664). If real white mobs could use Jim Crow costumes and stump speeches to assail genteel abolitionists, Stowe's antislavery sympathizers could reciprocate. In keeping with the novel's contempt for the "lower class of whites" and its ambivalence about blackface, the upper classes do the mocking and without the mediation of minstrelsy, since Frank Russel's impersonation is of other whites, parodying not "black" dress but that of the rioters themselves (*Dred*, 664). Stowe's most telling response to the anti-*Tom* novels was to turn their tactics back on them, ventriloquizing the supporters of slavery just as they had invented black figures to parrot their condemnations of her book. Like them, Stowe returned to minstrel caricature to make her argument, but in *Dred*, unlike *Uncle Tom's Cabin*, she made the end men white.

EPILOGUE

Although this book is concerned with *Uncle Tom's Cabin* at the height of its fame, *Tom* mania was by no means exhausted when Stowe published *Dred* in 1856. The majority of plays and sketches were performed in 1852 and 1853, and most of the copycat novels had been written by 1854, but there were still revivals of the *Tom* plays throughout the 1850s, while *The Black Gauntlet*, *Ellen*, and *The Slaveholder Abroad* were all published in 1860. The second life of Aiken's dramatization in the 1870s, when the sheer number of traveling tent shows provided enough work for employment agencies specifically devoted to *Tom* show actors, could provide material for a book in itself, not to mention *Uncle Tom*'s leap into celluloid in the early years of the film industry, when the *Tom* shows supplied the actors and the material for almost a dozen of the first moving picture reels.[1]

It is beyond the scope of this study to do so, but it would be worth tracking *Uncle Tom*'s life after emancipation, when the text's association with slavery became a less urgent consideration, and yet its status as a cultural wonder or as a major national phenomenon had by no means diminished. As its political significance shifted, *Uncle Tom*'s meanings evolved yet again. By the turn of the century *Tom* plays were being advertised as "interesting to the rising generation" on the grounds of their "historical scenes and the clear pictures of life in the South before the war," while in 1934 a playbill declared that "*Uncle Tom's Cabin* is not simply an amusement, it is a drama of our country, and the only one that is a part of our Nation's History."[2] These suggest that *Uncle Tom* still had political connotations, but that now it could stand not only for slavery or even for the Civil War but also for antebellum nostalgia ("the South before the war") and the national literature ("a drama of our country") as well as history. The Lincoln legend held that *Uncle Tom* had caused the Civil War, yet the playbills cheerfully conflated Stowe's text with the world that war destroyed.

Ironically but perhaps inevitably, given the intensity of Southern feeling about *Uncle Tom* in the 1850s, *Uncle Tom's Cabin* remained a powerful symbol in the South. As Thomas Riggio has argued, patriotic Southern fiction turned to *Uncle Tom's Cabin* as a prototype and an antagonist through the Reconstruction and beyond.[3] Most obviously, Thomas Dixon's racist novel *The Leopard's Spots* was written in reaction to a dramatic performance of *Uncle Tom's Cabin* and burlesqued Stowe's characters. Similarly, Margaret Mitchell intended *Gone with the Wind* to refute Stowe's view of the South.[4] The *Tom* mania of the 1850s lingered in such texts in the long afterlives of the racist caricatures developed in proslavery minstrels shows and anti-*Tom* novels.

Paradoxically, *Uncle Tom's Cabin* has also remained a significant memory in African American literature and culture. However, whereas Southern literature has evoked a relatively consistent vision of *Uncle Tom* and continued to see Stowe as an enemy of the South, the *Uncle Tom's Cabin* remembered in African American literature has changed almost out of all recognition. Stowe has been repeatedly, almost obsessively, rewritten ever since the 1850s. *Dred's* self-contradicting stress on the importance of black voices, while its author once again took up her pen as the (white) champion of the slaves, perhaps suggests why Stowe's novels have so often proved a spur for African American writers. As I have suggested, black people were directly affected by the book in the 1850s: the imagery of the novel and the conventions of stage *Uncle Toms* were more than influential, they were sometimes conscripted to force racial caricature on actual persons and events. Yet many contemporaries saw *Uncle Tom's Cabin* as the liberator of the slaves, and, as we have seen, some black writers publicly hailed it as a friend, even if they also expressed irritation with it in private.

Consequently, the book has remained a powerful—and problematic—reference for writing about race in America. In 1874 the young Charles Chesnutt recorded in his diary that he had just reread the first volume of *Uncle Tom's Cabin*, commenting, "It was no ways old to me, although I have read it before," and when he later expressed an ambition to write an exposé of race relations in the South, he set out to compete with Stowe's book, which he saw as one of the two giants in the field.[5] As I have noted elsewhere, Chesnutt's 1899 short story "The Passing of Grandison" also offers a sharp commentary on the 1850s anti-*Tom* novels' obsession with fugitive slaves, and it overturns the premise of Stowe's own 1853 sketch on a similar theme, *Uncle Sam's Emancipation.*[6]

Chesnutt's dream was a symptom of the novel's undiminished significance for representations of African Americans, and African American writing has continued to allude to *Uncle Tom's Cabin*. Recognizing the persistence of its myths, black writers have nevertheless increasingly exposed, rejected, and eventually begun to parody them. Early in the twentieth century the hero of James Weldon Johnson's *Autobiography of an Ex-Colored Man* gave a cautious approval to Stowe's "panorama of slavery" and credited it moreover with the life-changing revelation of his racial identity: "[I]t opened my eyes as to who and what I was and what my country considered me." However, other writers have quarreled with Stowe, and with increasing vigor: Wallace Thurman's "Topsy" figure, for instance, in *The Blacker the Berry* linked Stowe's character with subservient clowning and internalized self-hatred. With the title of his short story collection, *Uncle Tom's Children*, Richard Wright nodded ironically toward Stowe's claim to represent black people and also signaled his rejection of her sentimentality, but of course he also necessarily evoked her text yet again in connection with fictions of race and the South. Later LeRoi Jones created an "Alternate Ending" to *Uncle Tom's Cabin* that barely seems to relate to the novel at all, itself perhaps a refutation of Stowe's story and her right to tell it. Ishmael Reed made the book and its author (and even her legend) surreal in *Flight to Canada*. Robert Alexander produced a coruscating take on the *Tom* play in *I Ain't Yo' Uncle*, while the dancer Bill T. Jones's parodic, disturbing, and sometimes affectionate piece "Last Supper at Uncle Tom's Cabin/The Promised Land" was designed, he claims, to reflect a reading of the novel that found it "hokum, misinformation[,] . . . moving, infuriating, beautiful, embarrassing, and important."[7]

These ongoing challenges to *Uncle Tom* represent the lingering power not only of Stowe's representations but also of the accretions to the novel deposited by other texts. Wright was defying the " 'Uncle Tom' which denoted . . . the cringing type who knew his place before white folk," a creature long separated from the powerful and principled Christian of Stowe's imaginings.[8] Wright's image may even have been traceable back to minstrelsy, to the proslavery dramatizations whose Uncle Toms were happy in slavery, or to the sentimental "Uncles" of Stephen Foster's songs.

Blackface had partly enabled the adaptability of *Uncle Tom's Cabin*, and it continued to leave traces in the popular idea of the text, but it is noticeable that twentieth-century versions of *Uncle Tom's Cabin* treat it primarily as a tale of regional or racial significance. The sense of the book's national and especially its international impact has receded. Given the relative world power of the United States in the twenty-first century, it can seem extraordinary now to remember that moment in the 1850s when America was so sensitive to what other nations thought of its institutions and its literature; *Uncle Tom's*

Cabin could almost be seen as a harbinger of the successful later exports of American cultural products all over the world. Blackface and then *Tom* mania proved to be only the first of many crazes that traveled east across the Atlantic, but the case of *Uncle Tom's Cabin* should remind us that these processes can be unpredictable: the meanings of texts, like performances, can mutate as they move.

NOTES

Introduction

1. "Aunt Phillis's Cabin"; "Aunt Phillis's Cabin Again"; "A New Thing"; "Uncle Tom in England"; "Uncle Tom's Cabin"; "Uncle Tom's Cabin As It Is."

2. See, for instance, *Liberator*, 26 March, 9 April, 7 May, 11 June, 9 July, 6 August, 20 August, 10 September, 17 September, and 10 December 1852; and 25 March, 27 May, 3 June, 26 August, 9 September, and 16 December 1853.

3. "The Theatres," 1160.

4. Mott, *Golden Multitudes*, 118, 119; Wilson, *Crusader in Crinoline*, 182, 197, 200; Gossett, *Uncle Tom's Cabin and American Culture*, 164; Lorimer, "Bibles," 39.

5. Gilroy, *The Black Atlantic*; other useful examinations of race and culture in a transatlantic context include Roach, *Cities of the Dead*, and Brody, *Impossible Purities*.

6. For an exposition of these connections see Thistlethwaite, *The Anglo-American Connection*.

7. See Bolt, *The Anti-Slavery Movement*; Fladeland, *Men and Brothers*; Blackett, *Building an Antislavery Wall*; Taylor, *British and American Abolitionists*; Ripley, ed., *The Black Abolitionist Papers*.

8. Stowe, *Sunny Memories*.

9. See, for instance, Lease, *Anglo-American Encounters*; Weisbuch, *Atlantic Double-Cross*; Gravil, *Romantic Dialogues*; Giles, *Transatlantic Insurrections*.

10. Gohdes, *American Literature in Nineteenth-Century England*.

11. "Uncle Tom's Cabin," *Times* (London), 3 September 1852, 5.

12. Wilson, *Crusader in Crinoline*, 151; Gossett, *Uncle Tom's Cabin and American Culture*, 88; Adams, *Harriet Beecher Stowe*, 36.

13. Mott, *A History of American Magazines*, 142; Mott, *Golden Multitudes*, 116–17.

14. Mott, *Golden Multitudes*, 125–26; Baker, "Introduction," 21; McFeely, *Frederick Douglass*, 119–45.

15. See, for instance, Search, "From Our London Correspondent"; "Novels and Their Influences," 93; and "The Uncle Tom Epidemic," 355.

16. "Uncle Tom in Europe," 69; Garrison, "*Uncle Tom's Cabin*," 50.

17. Zboray, "Antebellum Reading," 67, 73, 76.

18. Hedrick, *Harriet Beecher Stowe*, 225.

19. Wilson, *Crusader in Crinoline*, 182; Hedrick, *Harriet Beecher Stowe*, 225–30.

20. Hedrick, *Harriet Beecher Stowe*, 224.

21. Brodhead, "Veiled Ladies," 277.

22. What was actually said at their meeting in 1862 was not recorded in Stowe's letters. Lincoln is supposed, of course, to have called her "the little woman who wrote the book that started this great war" (Hedrick, *Harriet Beecher Stowe*, 306).

23. Daumier, "Actualités." The text reads in full: "1er Bas Bleu—Profitons de l'occasion, . . . L'Oncle Tom est à la mode . . . hâtons-nous d'écrire un roman intitule La Tante Tom. 2me Bas Bleu—ça me botte!"

24. Foucault, "What Is an Author," 19.

25. Paul Lauter, "Teaching Nineteenth-Century Women Writers," in Lauter, *Canons and Contexts*, 114–32, 118.

26. Baker and Sarbin, *The Lasting of the Mohicans*, 9.

27. Stoneman, *Brontë Transformations*, 5; see also Widdowson, *Hardy in History*.

28. Bennett, *Readers and Reading*, 2.

29. Iser, *The Act of Reading*, 169; on the reader-response critics' interest in the textual construction of readers see Machor, ed., *Readers in History*, viii; Bennett, *Readers and Reading*, 3–4.

30. Iser, *The Act of Reading*, 107; Certeau, "Reading as Poaching," 155; Glavin, *After Dickens*, 2.

31. The phrase "cultural conversation" is borrowed from Mailloux, "Misreading as a Historical Act," 9.

32. Price, *The Anthology*, 12.

33. The phrase "intracultural translation" and the various definitions of translation supplied above come from Bassnett and Lefevere, eds., *Translation*, 8, 6.

34. See chapter 5; Guillory, *Cultural Capital*.

35. Toll, *Blacking Up*, v.

36. Cantwell, *Bluegrass Breakdown*, 255.

37. Cockrell, *Demons of Disorder*.

38. Wittke, *Tambo and Bones*; Toll, *Blacking Up*; Boskin, *Sambo*.

39. Lott, *Love and Theft*, 5.

40. See Saxton, "Blackface Minstrelsy," and *The Rise and Fall of the White Republic*; Roediger, *The Wages of Whiteness*.

41. Lhamon, *Raising Cain*.

42. See Sundquist, *To Wake the Nations*, 276–94.

43. See especially Lott, *Love and Theft*; Lhamon, *Raising Cain*; Roediger, *The Wages of Whiteness*.

44. On Stowe and sentimental literature see Brown, *The Sentimental Novel*; Papashvily, *All the Happy Endings*; Baym, *Woman's Fiction*. On Stowe and mothers see Ammons, "Stowe's Dream."

45. Brown, *Domestic Individualism*, 40. Brown attributes these contradictions largely to the individualist values promoted by Stowe's sentimental vision; I argue that they are more likely to be derived from blackface. It is also, of course, more accurate to describe Stowe's politics in *Uncle Tom* as antislavery than as strictly abolitionist.

46. Bolt, *Victorian Attitudes to Race*, 30.

47. Fredrickson, *The Black Image*, 102.

48. Lorimer, "Bibles," 35, 39.

49. Toll, *Blacking Up*, 31.

50. See Lott, *Love and Theft*, 45; and [Charles Mathews], *Mr. Mathews at Home*, (London, 1824), quoted in Marshall and Stock, *Ira Aldridge*, 40. See also the 1821 version printed by J. Duncombe, reprinted in 1979 as Mathews, *Mr Mathews at Home*, 98–117.

51. On British and Irish minstrelsy see Bratton, "English Ethiopians"; Pickering, "White Skin, Black Masks"; Anthony, "Early Nigger Minstrel Acts"; Riach, "Blacks and Blackface." My discussion of these developments in chapter 5 draws on my argument in "Competing Representations."

52. See Marshall and Stock, *Ira Aldridge*.

CHAPTER 1. Topsy and the End Man: Blackface in *Uncle Tom's Cabin*

1. *"The White Slave"*; "Uncle Tom's Cabin," quoted from the *New York Independent* in "Uncle Tom's Cabin As It Is."

2. Briggs, "Uncle Tomitudes," 101.

3. Melville, "Bartleby the Scrivener," 59.

4. Weisbuch, *Atlantic Double-Cross*, 45.

5. "American Slavery"; Briggs, "Uncle Tomitudes," 101.

6. "Literature of Slavery," 607.

7. "The Uncle Tom Epidemic," 355–58, 357. See also the review *"Uncle Tom's Cabin*, by Harriet Beecher Stowe."

8. "American Slavery."

9. Wilson, "From Our Brooklyn Correspondent."

10. Birdoff, *The World's Greatest Hit*, 23.

11. Lott, *Love and Theft*, 212.

12. Hawthorne, *House of the Seven Gables*, 36, 50–51.

13. Fishkin discusses this episode in some detail in *Was Huck Black?* 112–13.

14. Walters, *Stephen Foster*, 51. See Wilson on the Lane Scandal, on the originals of George and Eliza, and on the Underground Railroad (*Crusader in Crinoline*, 79–81, 86–87, 107); see Hedrick on Lane and abolition in Cincinnati (*Harriet Beecher Stowe*, 102–9).

15. Emerson, *Doo-Dah!* 116–20; Hedrick, *Harriet Beecher Stowe*, 67.

16. Walters, *Stephen Foster*, 60–61. For a detailed account of this period in Stowe's life see Hedrick, *Harriet Beecher Stowe*, 67–217.

17. Nevin, "Stephen C. Foster," 608.

18. For accounts of this period in Foster's life see Walters, *Stephen Foster*, and Emerson, *Doo-Dah!* 116–48.

19. In fact, minstrel audiences varied significantly over time and according to venue and location. Always largely white and predominantly male, they did include

women and children at the larger, more respectable minstrel halls in big cities. Minstrelsy may have been largely working class, but gentlemen also attended. See Butsch, *The Making of American Audiences*, 87–93.

20. Winans, "Early Minstrel Show Music," 83; Tawa, *Sweet Songs*, 91.

21. Hamm, *Yesterdays*, 137.

22. See Dennison, *Scandalize My Name*, 114–15; Hamm, *Yesterdays*, 137.

23. See Winans, "Early Minstrel Show Music," 83, 91, 93; Tawa, *Sweet Songs*, 89, 97. Finson suggests that the frequency with which the press attacked genteel amateurs for singing minstrel songs indicates that middle-class interest in blackface predated the more "respectable" forms (*The Voices That Are Gone*, 222).

24. See Butsch, *The Making of American Audiences*, 89–93.

25. Scott, *The Singing Bourgeois*, 92.

26. Scott, *The Singing Bourgeois*, 85; Winans, "Early Minstrel Show Music," 80; Emerson, *Doo-Dah!* 75. On the Hutchinsons see Hamm, *Yesterdays*, 141–61, and Hamm's comments on this in chapter 4 of *Putting Popular Music in Its Place*, 98–100. See also Jordan, *Singin' Yankees*; Mosely, "The Hutchinson Family."

27. Scott, *The Singing Bourgeois*, 83–84.

28. A number of these may be found in Eaklor, *American Antislavery Songs*. See, for instance, the adaptation of "Old Dan Tucker" written for an antislavery picnic at Danvers from 1845 (163–64) or Justitia's 1858 rendition of "Lucy Neal" (221–22). See also Dennison, *Scandalize My Name*, 159.

29. Printed in the *Liberator*, 8 August 1845, reprinted in Eaklor, *American Antislavery Songs*, 163–64, 163.

30. Jesse Hutchinson, "Get off the Track," reprinted in Eaklor, *American Antislavery Songs*, 254–55. In one of a number of stage references, the Hutchinsons' 1844 number "The Old Granite State" was parodied by the Ethiopian Serenaders as "The Old Virginny State" (Odell, *Annals of the New York Stage*, 5:56).

31. Jesse Hutchinson, "Get off the Track," quoted in Dennison, *Scandalize My Name*, 168; program note, "Georgia Champions," 1845, quoted in Winans, "Early Minstrel Show Music," 90.

32. Lhamon, *Raising Cain*, 90–98, on Stowe see 97–98.

33. Dennison, *Scandalize My Name*, 170–71.

34. Toll, *Blacking Up*, 68; "Virginia Minstrels," program, Dublin, 1844, quoted in Toll, *Blacking Up*, 34.

35. Kennard Jr., "Who Are Our National Poets?" 333–34. Both the songs are from minstrel shows. "Jenny Get Your Hoe-cake Done" was a popular hit dating from at least 1840 and was sung by Sweeney and Whitlock. See the playbills in Moreau, *Negro Minstrelsy in New York*, 1:717–18, and in Dennison, *Scandalize My Name*. The other, ironically, was later widely adapted and sung by blacks well into the twentieth century. See also Levine, *Black Culture and Black Consciousness*, 192–93.

36. Kennard Jr., "Who Are Our National Poets?"

37. Stowe, *Uncle Tom's Cabin*, 17, 19 (hereafter cited in text as *UTC*).

38. Kennard Jr., "Who Are Our National Poets?"

39. In a different version of the same joke, Mark Twain claimed to have convinced

his mother and Aunt Betsey Smith that the Christy Minstrel Troupe were African missionaries (Twain, *Autobiography*, 62).

40. Toll, *Blacking Up*, 80–82, 86.

41. Sundquist, "Slavery, Revolution," 18.

42. On Stowe and sentimental or domestic literature see Brown, *The Sentimental Novel*; Papashvily, *All the Happy Endings*; Baym, *Woman's Fiction*; Ryan, *The Empire of the Mother*; Kelley, *Private Woman, Public Stage*. On Stowe and heroines see Ammons, "Stowe's Dream." Douglas attacks Stowe, along with the other sentimentalists, in *The Feminization of American Culture*. Tompkins champions them in *Sensational Designs*. There are more critical readings of Stowe's sentimental politics in Bowlby, "Breakfast in America"; Brown, *Domestic Individualism*; Samuels, ed., *The Culture of Sentiment*.

43. Several critics have noted that some of Stowe's characters fit blackface types. I argue that minstrelsy provided Stowe with much more than techniques of characterization. Davis argued that "many of Stowe's people of color owe something of their comic characters to the minstrel show" ("Mrs. Stowe's Characters-in-Situations," 114). Fiedler asserted that there were "standard minstrel-show types among the astonishing array of Afro-American characters . . . comic darkies brought on for comic relief" (*What Was Literature*, 167). Lott surmises that Uncle Tom, Topsy, and Adolph "are surely inheritances from the minstrel show" (*Love and Theft*, 222). Lhamon argues that Stowe "sluiced into abolitionist tableaus some of the power of minstrel conventions" (*Raising Cain*, 96, 140–45).

44. Lhamon, *Raising Cain*, 96–97.

45. See Cockrell, *Demons of Disorder*, 85, and Lhamon, *Raising Cain*, 19, on the early blackface milieu.

46. Zanger, "The Minstrel Show," 34. On the structure of the minstrel show and on this part of the act see Toll, *Blacking Up*, 52–57.

47. I would not dispute Davis's argument that Sam's "hilarious fun-loving semi-roguery" here is "kin" to that of servant figures in Walter Scott and his disciples, James Fenimore Cooper and William Gilmore Simms, but the dialectical structure of this dialogue is more specifically derived from the stage ("Mrs. Stowe's Characters-in-Situations," 114).

48. See Roediger, *The Wages of Whiteness*, 61–81; also Saxton, *The Rise and Fall of the White Republic*, 165–82. Lhamon also comments on the blackface aspects of Topsy's "raising Cain" (*Raising Cain*, 144).

49. Cockrell, *Demons of Disorder*, 94.

50. For examples of blackface stump speeches see Toll, *Blacking Up*, 55; Holmberg and Schneider, "Daniel Decatur Emmett's Stump Sermons."

51. Lhamon, *Raising Cain*, 190.

52. Holmberg and Schneider, "Daniel Decatur Emmett's Stump Sermons," 34.

53. See Lhamon, *Raising Cain*, 1–55.

54. Zanger, "The Minstrel Show," 35.

55. See Holmberg and Schneider, "Daniel Decatur Emmett's Stump Sermons," 32. Dillard, discussing the attribution of this phenomenon primarily to black speakers,

points out that to speakers of black varieties of English apparent malapropisms may actually be the correct usage for that variety and may only seem to be mistakes to the standard English listener (*Black English*, 107).

56. Brown, *Domestic Individualism*, 45.

57. Cockrell, *Demons of Disorder*, 180 n. 97.

58. Cockrell, *Demons of Disorder*, 147. On this point I differ from Lhamon, who does connect Topsy with the wench (*Raising Cain*, 142).

59. Lott discusses the wench role in general and "Lucy Long" in particular (*Love and Theft*, 160–68, 160–61).

60. Lhamon also identifies this scene as an end man–interlocutor exchange (*Raising Cain*, 145).

61. Hawthorne, *The Scarlet Letter*, 134.

62. "Blackberrying," 486–87.

63. Davis, "Mrs. Stowe's Characters-in-Situations," 114.

64. In 1855 the Howard family announced a new song for their *Uncle Tom* at the National Theatre, "Oh! I'se So Wicked," while in the Moore and Burgess minstrel version the other slaves sang "She's the Wickedest Critter in the World." See "Testimonial to Manager A. H. Purdy"; Moore and Burgess Minstrels, *Uncle Tom's Cabin*.

65. See Hedrick, *Harriet Beecher Stowe*, esp. 125, 173–85.

66. "Blackberrying," 486.

67. These jokes resemble what one commentator called "the insoluble conundrum and the indigestible jest" blackface had borrowed from the circus ("American Popular Ballads," *Round Table*, 6 February 1864, quoted in Emerson, *Doo-Dah!* 92). See also the lyrics to Stephen Foster's 1847 hit "Oh! Susanna": "It rained all night de day I left, / De wedder it was dry; / The sun so hot I froze to def," and so on (quoted in Emerson, *Doo-Dah!* 127).

68. The classic example is the opening of Douglass, *Narrative*.

69. On the blackface dandy see Cockrell, *Demons of Disorder*, 92–109; Lott, *Love and Theft*, 131–35; Bank, *Theatre Culture*, 160–62.

70. Sambo and Quimbo may in their names have brought to mind grotesque and degrading portraits, and their appearances in the novel would have reinforced them. "Sambo" was, at the time Stowe wrote, a clichéd generic name for a black male; although it was probably derived from West African names, it would have brought to mind hostile representations of blacks (Dillard, *Black English*, 131, 130).

71. On songs in the novel see Austin, "*Susanna*," 229–32.

72. As Austin points out, Stowe seems by this to echo Frederick Douglass's famous description of slave songs, which contain a coded desperation only the initiated can hear: the song is not only not "unmeaning," it has two meanings for its listeners (Austin, "*Susanna*," 231; Douglass, *Narrative*, 58).

73. Stowe, *The Key to Uncle Tom's Cabin*, 95.

74. Lott, *Love and Theft*, 124.

75. Burnett, *The One I Knew*, 51.

76. Burnett, *The One I Knew*, 49.

77. Burnett, *The One I Knew*, 51.

78. Mcdowell, "In the First Place," 203.

79. Franchot, "The Punishment of Esther," 143.

80. Shirley Samuels, "Introduction," in Samuels, ed., *The Culture of Sentiment*, 6.

81. Butsch, *The Making of American Audiences*, 85. For different interpretations of this paradox see Lott, *Love and Theft*; Cockrell, *Demons of Disorder*; Lhamon, *Raising Cain*; Zanger, "The Minstrel Show," 33–38.

82. Cockrell traces the absorption of European folk rituals into black traditions in the New World and the reappearance of both in early blackface in *Demons of Disorder*. Lhamon, *Raising Cain*, shows that in the financially impoverished and racially mixed district of New York's Catherine Market black "charisma" and performative traditions were prominent in the interplay of cultures that produced blackface. Both these writers stress the differences between early minstrelsy and its incarnations after the 1840s: as middle-class audiences took to blackface, it lost its satirical bite and ambiguities and became more clearly derogatory. The minstrelsy with which *Uncle Tom* was associated, in other words, was more likely than earlier forms to be read explicitly as racial portraiture and tended in its content to be more hostile to African Americans (Cockrell, *Demons of Disorder*, 147; Lhamon, *Raising Cain*, 45).

83. "Jim Crow" was attributed variously to a Kentucky stable boy, a Cincinnati stage driver, and a porter from Pittsburgh; other writers provided more fanciful ideas about supposed black authors. See C.L., "An Old Actor's Memories"; Nevin, "Stephen C. Foster," 608–9; Kennard Jr., "Who Are Our National Poets?" 334–41; Nathanson, "Negro Minstrelsy." For a fuller list and a discussion of some of these myths of origin see Lott, *Love and Theft*, 59–62.

84. Constance Rourke, "Traditions for a Negro Literature," in Rourke, *The Roots of American Culture*, 262–74, 265–66. The insensitivity of this claim has sometimes blinded readers to the subtlety of Rourke's commentary, however, which was alert to blackface's cultural fusions and qualities of travesty.

85. Green, "'Jim Crow,' 'Zip Coon'"; Toll, *Blacking Up*; Saxton, "Blackface Minstrelsy," 3–28, and *The Rise and Fall of the White Republic*; Roediger, *The Wages of Whiteness*; Lott, *Love and Theft*. Other accounts of minstrelsy include Boskin, *Sambo*; Hutton, "The Negro on the Stage"; Jackson, "The Minstrel Mode"; Matthews, "The Rise and Fall of Minstrelsy"; Minnigerode, *The Fabulous Forties*; Nathan, *Dan Emmett*; Rourke, *American Humor*, 3–28; Wittke, *Tambo and Bones*.

86. "American Slavery."

87. Eliot, review of *Dred*, 43, emphasis in original.

88. Yarborough, "Strategies of Black Characterization," 72.

89. Quoted in Wilson, *Crusader in Crinoline*, 70.

90. On Bodichon see Hirsch, *Barbara Leigh Smith Bodichon*; Herstein, *A Mid-Victorian Feminist*.

91. See Bodichon, *An American Diary*.

92. Bodichon, *An American Diary*, 130, 62.

93. Bodichon, *An American Diary*, 77. On Bodichon's dress see Hirsch, *Barbara*

Leigh Smith Bodichon, 154. Bodichon also scandalously eschewed corsets (Herstein, *A Mid-Victorian Feminist*, 57).

94. Bodichon, *An American Diary*, 77.

CHAPTER 2. Minstrel Variations: *Uncle Toms* in the Minstrel Show

1. Toll, *Blacking Up*, 88; see also Cockrell, *Demons of Disorder*, 154.

2. On Foster see Nevin, "Stephen C. Foster"; Walters, *Stephen Foster*; Austin, "*Susanna*"; Emerson, *Doo-Dah!* (hereafter cited in text). For collections of his songs see, for example, Jackson, ed., *Stephen Foster Song Book*, and Foster, *Stephen Foster*.

3. Hamm illustrates this with the verse from "Away down Souf" that elaborates on "My lub she hab a very large mouf" (*Yesterdays*, 210).

4. Stephen Foster, "Old Uncle Ned," reproduction of an 1848 Milletts Songster, in Jackson, ed., *Stephen Foster Song Book*, 104–7.

5. Stephen Foster, "Old Folks at Home," 1851, quoted in Austin, "*Susanna*," 246.

6. For evidence that the argument was being made as early as 1867 see Nevin, "Stephen C. Foster."

7. L. V. H. Crosby, "The Slave Mother" (Boston, 1853), quoted in Tawa, *Sweet Songs*, 90.

8. For a detailed account of this period in Foster's life see Walters, *Stephen Foster*, and Emerson, *Doo-Dah!* 116–48; on Stowe see Hedrick, *Harriet Beecher Stowe*, 67–217.

9. Hamm, *Yesterdays*, 225.

10. Many of these songs are reprinted in Eaklor, *American Antislavery Songs*.

11. Hamm, *Yesterdays*, 217.

12. On "home songs" see Austin, "*Susanna*," 123–62.

13. "Musical Review," *Dwight's Journal*, 31 July 1852, quoted in Tawa, *Sweet Songs*, 114.

14. Quoted in Austin, "*Susanna*," 233, and Emerson, *Doo-Dah!* 193.

15. Sanford's Opera House, playbill.

16. Moore, *G. W. Moore's Ethiopian Anecdotes*, vi.

17. Dumont, *The Witmark Amateur Minstrel Guide*, 37.

18. Dumont, *The Witmark Amateur Minstrel Guide*, 15.

19. Dumont, *The Witmark Amateur Minstrel Guide*, 60. On the cakewalk see Sundquist, *To Wake the Nations*, 276–94.

20. "Dat's What's de Matter," in Scott, ed., *Brudder Bones*, 82. The lecture is recorded as "written expressly for Harry Pell, by John F. Poole."

21. "Benefit of Frank Brower"; George Christy and Woods Minstrels, playbill.

22. Wood and Sedgwick, "Poor Uncle Tom, Song and Chorus."

23. See Toll, *Blacking Up*, 94–97; Lott, *Love and Theft*, 228–29.

24. "Dat's What's de Matter," in Scott, ed., *Brudder Bones*, 84.

25. Toll, *Blacking Up*, 94.

26. Birdoff, *The World's Greatest Hit*, 141.

27. *Uncle Tom: An Ethiopian Interlude.*

28. Frank Brower, "Happy Uncle Tom: A Celebrated Plantation Scene," in Scott, ed., *Brudder Bones*, 149–52, 151.

29. C. H. White, "Old Dad's Cabin: A Negro Farce in one act and one scene. Written and arranged by C. White. 25 minutes," in *Darkey Plays*, 5–16.

30. Sable Harmonists, playbill.

31. Toll, *Blacking Up*, 71.

32. Sam Sharpley's Minstrels, program; Sanford's Opera House, playbill.

33. Toll, *Blacking Up*, 93.

34. George Christy and Woods Minstrels, playbill.

35. Birdoff, *The World's Greatest Hit*, 141.

36. Sanford's Opera House, playbill.

37. Sanford's Opera House, playbill.

38. George Christy and Woods Minstrels, playbill; Sanford's Opera House, playbill.

39. *Our Day*, 2, 4.

40. Roppolo, "Uncle Tom in New Orleans," 219 n. 17.

41. *Our Day*, 4.

42. "Repetition of the New Southern Drama."

43. "Repetition of the New Southern Drama."

44. Birdoff, *The World's Greatest Hit*, 139.

45. Soran and Hewitt, "Aunt Harriet Becha Stowe."

46. See, for instance, Alexander's "Tom," who offers to "stoop, shuffle, and bend over backwards with a smile for every white person I meet" (in Alexander, *I Ain't Yo' Uncle*, 25). Major defines "Uncle Tom" as a "derogatory term for African American; a servile 'Negro'; a black person who is culturally disloyal; a black person who does not practice racial or cultural loyalty; a pejorative term for any African-American perceived to be 'middle-class,' to own property and to have money in the bank" (*Juba to Jive*, 492). The journalist Darcus Howe characterized Stowe's Tom in a similar fashion on a British television debate about the novel (*The Talk Show*, shown on BBC4 [London], 20 March 2002).

47. Wetmore, "Uncle Tom's Cabin Song."

48. Dan Rice, "Uncle Tom's Cabin," in *Dan Rice's Original Comic and Sentimental Poetic Effusions* (Philadelphia, 1860), quoted in Dennison, *Scandalize My Name*, 179.

49. Dennison gives examples of a number of these songs (*Scandalize My Name*, 146–47). Also see "The Other Side of Jordan," in Moreau, *Negro Minstrelsy in New York*, 2:197–202, which I discuss in chapter 6.

50. "Jordan," *Ettla No. 1*, 97, quoted in Dennison, *Scandalize My Name*, 145.

51. "Pop Goes the Weasel" by S. T. Gordon (1859), reprinted in Jackson, ed., *Popular Songs*, 179; Jackson also discusses its origins and variants (279). See also Finson, *The Voices That Are Gone*, 192.

52. Hill, "The Ghost of Uncle Tom." For a discussion of these songs see Riis, "The Music and Musicians," 272–73.

53. Hutchinson, "Little Topsy's Song."

54. Ordway's Aeolians, playbill.

55. The *OED* cites a reference from 1874 that describes the kind of effect that could be produced with a chromatrope: "Phantasmagoric representation, dissolving views" (*Oxford English Dictionary*, s.v. "chromatrope").

56. Ordway's Aeolians, playbill.

57. Ordway's Aeolians, playbill.

58. Moore, *G. W. Moore's Ethiopian Anecdotes*, dust jacket; Moore and Burgess Minstrels, *Uncle Tom's Cabin*.

59. Moore and Burgess Minstrels, *Uncle Tom's Cabin*.

60. Sanford's Opera House, playbill; "Repetition of the New Southern Drama."

61. E. P. Christy, "Pompey's Trip to New York," in Christy, *Christy's Plantation Melodies*, 3:19. In this variant Stowe appears as Aunty Sarah Rowe.

62. E. P. Christy, "Uncle Tom's Gone to Rest," in Christy, *Christy's Plantation Melodies*, 3:20–21.

63. Wood and Sedgwick, "Poor Uncle Tom, Song and Chorus."

64. Frederick Douglass, *North Star*, 27 October 1848, quoted in Lott, *Love and Theft*, 15; Frederick Douglass, "Gavitt's Original Ethiopian Serenaders," in Douglass, *The Life and Writings*, 5:141; and Douglass, "The Anti-Slavery Movement."

65. Douglass, "The Anti-Slavery Movement," 2.

66. "Repetition of the New Southern Drama."

67. Birdoff, *The World's Greatest Hit*, 139; *American National Biography*, s.v. "Brownlow, William Gannaway."

68. "Repetition of the New Southern Drama."

CHAPTER 3. Copycat Critics: The Anti-*Tom* Novel and the Fugitive Slave

1. Holmes, "Uncle Tom's Cabin," 727; "Novels and Their Influences."

2. Grayson's poem *The Hireling and the Slave* is usually classed with these novels (Grayson, *The Hireling and the Slave*). See Gaines, *The Southern Plantation*, 46–47; Gardiner, "Proslavery Propaganda"; Gossett, *Uncle Tom's Cabin and American Culture*, 430–31. Gardiner and Gossett produce slightly different lists but total thirty-one titles between them. See also Tandy, "Pro-Slavery Propaganda"; Hayne, "Yankee in the Patriarchy"; Hildreth, *Harriet Beecher Stowe*; Gardiner, "The Assault upon Uncle Tom"; Peterson, "Aunt Phillis's Cabin." This chapter deals with *The Olive-Branch*; [Brown], *The Planter*; Butt, *Antifanaticism*; Cowdin, *Ellen*; Criswell, *"Uncle Tom's Cabin" Contrasted with Buckingham Hall*; Eastman, *Aunt Phillis's Cabin*; Flanders, *The Ebony Idol*; Hall, *Frank Freeman's Barber's Shop*; Hentz, *The Planter's Northern Bride*; Herndon, *Louise Elton*; McIntosh, *The Lofty and the Lowly*; Page, *Uncle Robin's Cabin*; [Peterson], *The Cabin and Parlor*; Rush, *North and South*; Schoolcraft, *The Black Gauntlet*; Smith, *Uncle Tom's Cabin As It Is*; [Smythe], *Ethel Somers*; [Thorpe], *The Master's House*; [Townsend], *The Brother Clerks*; "Vidi," *Mr. Frank*.

3. Gossett, *Uncle Tom's Cabin and American Culture*, 430–31.

4. Rhoda Coleman Ellison, introduction to Hentz, *The Planter's Northern Bride*, viii.

5. "Aunt Phillis's Cabin Again." The review takes the line that Eastman's book is "so low and vulgar" that it discredits the proslavery camp.

6. "Vidi," *Mr. Frank*, 234.

7. [Thorpe], *The Master's House*. Hayne discusses the ambivalences of this text in detail in "Yankee in the Patriarchy."

8. Hall, *Frank Freeman's Barber's Shop*, 84–86.

9. I'm referring, of course, to slave narrators such as Frederick Douglass, William Wells Brown, Solomon Northup, William and Ellen Craft, Henry "Box" Brown, and so on.

10. Flanders, *The Ebony Idol*, 88, 129; Lott, *Love and Theft*, 29, 132.

11. On the influence of these folk practices see Lhamon, *Raising Cain*; Cockrell, *Demons of Disorder*.

12. [Brown], *The Planter*; Grayson, *The Hireling and the Slave*; [Peterson], *The Cabin and Parlor*; Criswell, *"Uncle Tom's Cabin" Contrasted with Buckingham Hall*; Rush, *North and South*; Butt, *Antifanaticism*; Schoolcraft, *The Black Gauntlet*; Hentz, *The Planter's Northern Bride*; Eastman, *Aunt Phillis's Cabin*.

13. Criswell, *"Uncle Tom's Cabin" Contrasted with Buckingham Hall*, 139–40; Eastman, *Aunt Phillis's Cabin*, 265–80.

14. Cowdin, *Ellen*; Herndon, *Louise Elton*; "Vidi," *Mr. Frank*.

15. [Smythe], *Ethel Somers*, 3.

16. Wiley, *Life at the South*; earlier published as Wiley, *The Adventures of Old Dan Tucker*; first published as *Roanoke: or, Where Is Utopia*.

17. Advertisement appended to the back of the English edition of Smith, *Uncle Tom's Cabin As It Is*.

18. Gaines, *The Southern Plantation*, 46; publicity material appended by the publishers to the back of Smith, *Uncle Tom's Cabin As It Is*, 1. See also [Thorpe], *The Master's House*. John Cassell of London also published it that year, and Gossett cites a third edition (New York: J. C. Derby, 1855).

19. Advertisements pasted in the flyleaf of Stowe, *The Key to Uncle Tom's Cabin*.

20. On Lippincott's and T. B. Peterson see Madison, *Book Publishing in America*, 13–14, 36, 85–86; Tebbel, *Between Covers*, 47–48, 71–72; Keely, "Lippincott, Joshua Ballinger." See Eastman, *Aunt Phillis's Cabin*; Butt, *Antifanaticism*; "Vidi," *Mr. Frank*; Herndon, *Louise Elton*; Schoolcraft, *The Black Gauntlet*; *The Olive-Branch*; Starnes, *The Slaveholder Abroad*.

21. *Cheap Book Newspaper*, 6. On T. B. Peterson's publication of his brother see "American Literary Publishing Houses," 49:360.

22. *Cheap Book Newspaper*, 8. "Cabin and Parlor" from *McMakin's Model American Courier*, 23 October 1852, reprinted in *Cheap Book Newspaper*, 6.

23. [Peterson], *The Cabin and Parlor*, 6.

24. "Cabin and Parlor."

25. Noted in the diary of Charles William Holbrook, reprinted in Hall, "A Yankee Tutor," 89.

26. Weller argues that even in journals like the *Southern Literary Messenger* and the *Southern Quarterly Review* reviewers often paid more attention to Stowe than to the anti-*Tom* novels and for the most part praised her book in comparison to theirs ("'Written with a Mrs Stowe's Feeling'").

Notes to Chapter 3

27. "American Slavery and Uncle Tom's Cabin" (this article also dealt with "Slavery in the Southern States, by a Carolinian"); "Black Letters"; "Literature of Slavery."

28. See, for example, "Aunt Phillis's Cabin"; "Aunt Phillis's Cabin Again"; "Uncle Tom's Cabin As It Is"; "The Cabin and the Parlor"; [Hildreth], *Archie Moore*.

29. "Black Letters," 209, 210, 212–13.

30. "Uncle Tom's Cabin As It Is."

31. Butt, *Antifanaticism*, vii, 266.

32. "Uncle Tom," *New Orleans Weekly Picayune*, 30 August 1852, reprinted in "American Slavery and Uncle Tom's Cabin," 237–38.

33. Louisa McCord, "*Uncle Tom's Cabin*," *Southern Quarterly Review* (January 1853), reprinted in McCord, *Louisa S. McCord*, 273.

34. McCord, *Louisa S. McCord*, 256, 270.

35. Butt, *Antifanaticism*, v.

36. Rush, *North and South*, 30; [Peterson], *The Cabin and Parlor*, 90; Smith, *Uncle Tom's Cabin As It Is*, 181; Page, *Uncle Robin's Cabin*, 106–19.

37. On antebellum plantation fiction see Gaines, *The Southern Plantation*; Taylor, *Cavalier and Yankee*; Ridgely, *Nineteenth Century Southern Literature*; Wimsatt, "Antebellum Fiction."

38. Burnett, *The One I Knew*, 211.

39. "Literature of Slavery," 594.

40. See Handlin, *The American Home*, 17.

41. [Peterson], *The Cabin and Parlor*, 24.

42. Eastman, *Aunt Phillis's Cabin*, 103.

43. Criswell, "*Uncle Tom's Cabin*" *Contrasted with Buckingham Hall*, 55.

44. Hentz, *The Planter's Northern Bride*, 129–30.

45. "American Slavery and Uncle Tom's Cabin," 236.

46. Hentz, *The Planter's Northern Bride*, 206.

47. Davis, "Mrs. Stowe's Characters-in-Situations," 109.

48. Ridgely accepted that it was an "answer" in "*Woodcraft*" and in *William Gilmore Simms*, but Hetherington has used the dates to argue against that conclusion ("William Gilmore Simm's Captain Porgy," in Hetherington, ed., *Cavalier of Old South Carolina*, 38–40).

49. Simms to James Henry Hammond, 15 December 1852, in Simms, *The Letters*, 3:222.

50. [Peterson], *The Cabin and Parlor*, 39.

51. Simms, *The Sword and the Distaff*, 124. It was reissued as *Woodcraft* in 1854. For a more detailed reading of the novel see Gray, *Writing the South*, 52–57.

52. "Black Letters," 213.

53. Stowe, *The Key to Uncle Tom's Cabin*, 41. One of Stowe's professed models for Tom is discussed in Hovet, "Mrs. Thomas C. Upham's 'Happy Phebe.'"

54. Eastman, *Aunt Phillis's Cabin*, 137.

55. Page, *Uncle Robin's Cabin*, 22; McIntosh, *The Lofty and the Lowly*, 207.

56. [Peterson], *The Cabin and Parlor*, 42, 25, 156–57.

57. Page, *Uncle Robin's Cabin*, 263.

58. Eastman, *Aunt Phillis's Cabin*, 194–95; quote from Page, *Uncle Robin's Cabin*, 290.

59. Butt, *Antifanaticism*, 14.

60. *The Olive-Branch*, 309; Hall, *Frank Freeman's Barber's Shop*, 86, 88; Butt, *Antifanaticism*, 20; [Peterson], *The Cabin and Parlor*, 9–11; Smith, *Uncle Tom's Cabin As It Is*, 24, 83, 84.

61. Criswell, *"Uncle Tom's Cabin" Contrasted with Buckingham Hall*, 77.

62. Criswell, *"Uncle Tom's Cabin" Contrasted with Buckingham Hall*, 149–50.

63. "Vidi," *Mr. Frank*, 225.

64. W. E. B. Du Bois, "Of the Sorrow Songs," in Du Bois, *The Souls of Black Folk*, 204–16; Douglass, *Narrative*, 57–58.

65. Douglass, *Narrative*, 58.

66. [Brown], *The Planter*, 80.

67. [Peterson], *The Cabin and Parlor*, 78, 79.

68. Hall, *Frank Freeman's Barber's Shop*, 12.

69. Page, *Uncle Robin's Cabin*, 19.

70. Hentz, *The Planter's Northern Bride*, 337.

71. [Peterson], *The Cabin and Parlor*, 9–11, 322.

72. Criswell, *"Uncle Tom's Cabin" Contrasted with Buckingham Hall*, illustrations: "Sing Darkeys Sing," 64–65, "The Festival," 112–13, 66, 67, 69, 114, 123, 149–50.

73. Eastman, *Aunt Phillis's Cabin*, 122.

74. Page, *Uncle Robin's Cabin*, 22.

75. Criswell, *"Uncle Tom's Cabin" Contrasted with Buckingham Hall*, 66.

76. Kennard Jr., "Who Are Our National Poets?" 338.

77. Page, *Uncle Robin's Cabin*, 194.

78. [Peterson], *The Cabin and Parlor*, 139.

79. "Vidi," *Mr. Frank*, 169.

80. In his 1901 novel, *The Marrow of Tradition*, Charles Chesnutt satirizes Northerners on a fact-finding mission to the South by having them mistake a cakewalk performed in blackface by a white character for the real thing. Their convenient conclusion is that "[s]urely a people who made no complaints could not be very much oppressed" (565).

81. J. W. McAndrews is supposed not only to have copied his Watermelon Man act from a Savannah vendor he saw in 1856 but to have bought the man's clothes, cart, and donkey as well (Toll, *Blacking Up*, 45). For accounts of the origin of Jim Crow see C.L., "An Old Actor's Memories," 10, and Nevin, "Stephen C. Foster," 608. These legends have been much commented upon, as they seem to symbolize the patterns of appropriation and exploitation that are apparent in minstrelsy, though they were not always produced by blackface performers themselves. See Lott, *Love and Theft*, 19; Lhamon, *Raising Cain*, 185; Cockrell, *Demons of Disorder*, 63. Lhamon and Cockrell in particular demonstrate how little the legends owed to history and how much to fantasy.

82. "Vidi," *Mr. Frank*, 174.

83. *The Olive-Branch*, 309.

84. Eastman, *Aunt Phillis's Cabin*, 138–39.

85. Butt, *Antifanaticism*, 16.

86. The issue crops up in Flanders, *The Ebony Idol*; Rush, *North and South*; "Vidi," *Mr. Frank*; McIntosh, *The Lofty and the Lowly*; Herndon, *Louise Elton*; [Townsend], *The Brother Clerks*; Criswell, *"Uncle Tom's Cabin" Contrasted with Buckingham Hall*; Cowdin, *Ellen*; Hall, *Frank Freeman's Barber's Shop*; [Thorpe], *The Master's House*; Page, *Uncle Robin's Cabin*; Smith, *Uncle Tom's Cabin As It Is*; Hentz, *The Planter's Northern Bride*; Eastman, *Aunt Phillis's Cabin*; Butt, *Antifanaticism*. According to Hayne's and Gossett's classification, five of these writers were Southerners, five were Northerners, two (Hentz and Thorpe) were Northerners long transplanted to the South, and two were unknown (Hayne, "Yankee in the Patriarchy," 180–81; Gossett, *Uncle Tom's Cabin and American Culture*, 430–31).

87. Stampp, *The Peculiar Institution*, 137.

88. Page, *Uncle Robin's Cabin*, 77, 20.

89. "Vidi," *Mr. Frank*, 39.

90. Butt, *Antifanaticism*, 38.

91. Smith, *Uncle Tom's Cabin As It Is*, 165, 141.

92. Cowdin, *Ellen*, 32.

93. Herndon, *Louise Elton*, 397; Hentz, *The Planter's Northern Bride*, 14; Criswell, *"Uncle Tom's Cabin" Contrasted with Buckingham Hall*, 151.

94. Hentz, *The Planter's Northern Bride*, 197, 281.

95. Hall, *Frank Freeman's Barber's Shop*, 220.

96. McIntosh, *The Lofty and the Lowly*, 168.

97. Cowdin, *Ellen*, 17.

98. Hentz, *The Planter's Northern Bride*, 281.

99. Page, *Uncle Robin's Cabin*, 39–40.

100. "Vidi," *Mr. Frank*, 51; Eastman, *Aunt Phillis's Cabin*, 57.

101. Smith, *Uncle Tom's Cabin As It Is*, 181.

102. Hentz, *The Planter's Northern Bride*, 391.

103. Eastman, *Aunt Phillis's Cabin*, 61; "Vidi," *Mr. Frank*, 39; McIntosh, *The Lofty and the Lowly*, 69.

104. McIntosh, *The Lofty and the Lowly*, 70.

105. Cowdin, *Ellen*, 24; Hall, *Frank Freeman's Barber's Shop*, 30; Hentz, *The Planter's Northern Bride*, 450.

106. Criswell, *"Uncle Tom's Cabin" Contrasted with Buckingham Hall*, 58.

107. Page, *Uncle Robin's Cabin*, 38, 45.

108. Eastman, *Aunt Phillis's Cabin*, 215–26.

109. Page, *Uncle Robin's Cabin*, 66.

110. Eastman, *Aunt Phillis's Cabin*, 218.

111. "Vidi," *Mr. Frank*, 38; *The Olive-Branch*, 143.

112. [Peterson], *The Cabin and Parlor*, 324; Cowdin, *Ellen*, 187; Eastman, *Aunt Phillis's Cabin*, 260; Criswell, *"Uncle Tom's Cabin" Contrasted with Buckingham Hall*, 10, 150; Smith, *Uncle Tom's Cabin As It Is*, 19; "Vidi," *Mr. Frank*, 214.

113. Quoted in "The 'Senior Editor.'"

114. Stampp, *The Peculiar Institution,* 110, 118.

115. Quarles, *Black Abolitionists,* 149, 144.

116. Harrold, *American Abolitionists,* 67.

117. Birney quoted in Quarles, "Freedom's Black Vanguard," 181.

118. Quarles, "Freedom's Black Vanguard," 185; Litwack, *North of Slavery,* 248; Stewart, *Holy Warriors,* 124; Campbell, *The Slave Catchers.*

119. Stowe, "Antislavery Literature."

120. "American Slavery and Uncle Tom's Cabin," 249.

121. Stampp, *The Peculiar Institution,* 110.

122. Cartwright quoted in Stampp, *The Peculiar Institution,* 109; Frederickson, *The Black Image,* 57.

123. Quarles, "Freedom's Black Vanguard," 175.

124. Quarles, *Black Abolitionists,* 163.

125. Wood, *Blind Memory,* 78, 84.

126. Stowe, *The Key to Uncle Tom's Cabin,* 346–63, 306–30. For a detailed description of the case see Harrold, *The Abolitionists,* 70.

127. Aiken, *The Key to Uncle Tom's Cabin.*

128. On slave narratives see Andrews, *To Tell a Free Story;* Foster, *Witnessing Slavery;* Smith, *Where I'm Bound;* Starling, *The Slave Narrative.*

129. [Thorpe], *The Master's House,* 54, 55.

130. According to Campbell, 191 slaves were claimed in federal courts between 1850 and 1860, and in the majority of cases their return to slavery was enforced. Campbell asserts that more than two hundred alleged fugitives were arrested and only twelve successfully defended their claims to freedom (*Slave Catchers,* 167, 249).

131. Campbell, *Slave Catchers,* 87; Harrold, *The Abolitionists,* 64 and passim.

132. Harrold, *American Abolitionists,* 80; Quarles, "Freedom's Black Vanguard," 185–87.

133. Quarles, "Freedom's Black Vanguard," 186.

134. Famous examples include Frederick Douglass, William and Ellen Craft, and William Wells Brown (Litwack, *North of Slavery,* 249).

135. I have relied for this account on Finkelman, *An Imperfect Union,* and his *Dred Scott v. Sandford,* 1–52.

136. Finkelman, *Dred Scott v. Sandford,* 50.

137. After failing to secure it in the courts, the Blows purchased Scott's freedom in May 1857 (Finkelman, *Dred Scott v. Sandford,* 229).

138. Stowe, *The Key to Uncle Tom's Cabin,* 346, 349.

139. Eastman, *Aunt Phillis's Cabin,* 229.

140. Hentz, *The Planter's Northern Bride,* 203.

141. "Vidi," *Mr. Frank,* 28.

142. Stowe, *The Key to Uncle Tom's Cabin,* 364.

143. Hall, *Frank Freeman's Barber's Shop,* 128–29.

144. "The Wrong Negro," in *Our Day,* 3.

145. The case is described in Campbell, *Slave Catchers,* 115–16.

CHAPTER 4. Minstrelsy, Melodrama, and Reform Drama:
Uncle Tom Plays in New York

1. Some of these other versions are listed in Mason, *Melodrama*, 210 n. 6. See also Roppolo, "Uncle Tom in New Orleans"; Toll, *Blacking Up*, 88–97; Gossett, *Uncle Tom's Cabin and American Culture*, 260–83; and Birdoff, *The World's Greatest Hit*, passim. Mason, *Melodrama*, includes Kunkel's troupe's version, which I have characterized as a minstrel piece; in practice, as I have suggested, it is sometimes hard to distinguish minstrel productions from "straight" theater.

2. Birdoff, *The World's Greatest Hit*, 141; "Benefit of Frank Brower."

3. Dumont, *The Witmark Amateur Minstrel*, 36–37. On doubles and mammoths see Birdoff, *The World's Greatest Hit*, 320.

4. See Riis, "The Music and Musicians," 280.

5. Hamm, *Yesterdays*, 215; Austin, "Susanna," 235.

6. Aiken, *Uncle Tom's Cabin* (hereafter cited in text); Austin, "Susanna," 235; "Repetition of the New Southern Drama."

7. Stowe, *The Christian Slave* (Boston), 3, 6.

8. Austin, "Susanna," 235; Riis, "The Music and Musicians," 272.

9. See McConachie, *Melodramatic Formations*, 175, 158.

10. Aiken's lasted ten weeks in Troy, followed by further success in Albany; Conway's managed thirteen weeks in Boston. See Birdoff, *The World's Greatest Hit*, 54; Adams, *E Pluribus Barnum*, 131, 138.

11. Birdoff, *The World's Greatest Hit*, 54; Lott, *Love and Theft*, 214.

12. On the 1870s rage for "Tomming" see Birdoff, *The World's Greatest Hit*, 257, and Davis, "Tom Shows." On the Thorne family's touring with Conway see Birdoff, *The World's Greatest Hit*, 251. The promptbook copy of Conway's play housed in the Harry Ransom Humanities Research Center, University of Texas at Austin, dates from a Boston Museum revival of 1876. It is hereafter cited in the text.

13. Advertisement, quoted in Birdoff, *The World's Greatest Hit*, 89. Lott sees the "small war" between the productions as "surprising and significant" (*Love and Theft*, 223–24).

14. Birdoff, *The World's Greatest Hit*, 90–96; *Liberator*, 16 December 1853, quoted in Birdoff, *The World's Greatest Hit*, 88.

15. Letter from William Lloyd Garrison to Helen Garrison, 5 September 1853, quoted in Mason, *Melodrama*, 97.

16. Darkening house lights during the performance was only beginning to emerge as a practice in the midcentury. See McConachie, *Melodramatic Formations*, 160; Booth, *Theatre in the Victorian Age*, 83–84.

17. "Uncle Tom Dramatized."

18. Hadley, *Melodramatic Tactics*, 101.

19. Birdoff, *The World's Greatest Hit*, 51–52.

20. Pillsbury, "'Uncle Tom's Cabin' at a Boston Theatre."

21. "Uncle Tom Among the Bowery Boys"; *New York Atlas*, 16 October 1853, quoted in Lott, *Love and Theft*, 227.

22. "'Uncle Tom' on the Stage."

23. *New York Tribune*, 8 August 1853, quoted in Lott, *Love and Theft*, 227.

24. "Uncle Tom Dramatized."

25. "Uncle Tom Among the Bowery Boys."

26. *New York Tribune*, 8 August 1853, quoted in Lott, *Love and Theft*, 227.

27. On melodrama in general see Rahill, *The World of Melodrama*; Booth, *English Melodrama*; Booth, *Victorian Spectacular Theatre*; Redmond, ed., *Melodrama*; Meisel, *Realisations*; Bratton, Cook, and Gledhill, eds., *Melodrama*. On American melodrama see Grimstead, *Melodrama Unveiled*; Nye, *The Unembarrassed Muse*; Mason, *Melodrama*; McConachie, *Melodramatic Formations*; Butsch, *The Making of American Audiences*.

28. Hamblin, *Nick of the Woods*. The script was based on the 1837 novel by Robert Montgomery Bird.

29. Hamblin, *Nick of the Woods*, 2.4.

30. Booth, "Melodrama and the Working Class," 100.

31. Rahill, *The World of Melodrama*, xvii.

32. Mason, *Melodrama*, 12.

33. See McConachie, *Melodramatic Formations*, esp. pt. 3, "Business-Class Theatre for the Respectable, 1845–1870"; Halttunen, *Confidence Men and Painted Women*, esp. 192–96; Douglas, *The Feminization of American Culture*; Butsch, *The Making of American Audiences*, 66–80.

34. Smith, *The Drunkard*, 5.1.

35. Birdoff, for instance, attributes "respectable" audiences and theatrical practices like the matinee performance to *Uncle Tom's Cabin* (*The World's Greatest Hit*, 53, 72–73).

36. Davis, "Tom Shows," 350.

37. McConachie, *Melodramatic Formations*, 165.

38. McConachie, "Out of the Kitchen," 23–24. On women in the audiences see McConachie, *Melodramatic Formations*, 165.

39. McConachie, "Out of the Kitchen," 5. He concedes that "both adaptations were anti-slavery, though Aiken's version was much closer to Garrisonian abolitionism than Conway's."

40. Adams, *E Pluribus Barnum*, 131.

41. Grimstead, *Melodrama Unveiled*, 241; see also McConachie, "Out of the Kitchen," 215.

42. Bank, *Theatre Culture*, 141.

43. "H. J. Conway's *Uncle Tom's Cabin*," program.

44. McConachie, *Melodramatic Formations*, 194.

45. McConachie, *Melodramatic Formations*, 158; Birdoff, *The World's Greatest Hit*, 100.

46. "H. J. Conway's *Uncle Tom's Cabin*," playbill.

47. Ann Douglas, "The Domestication of Death," in Douglas, *The Feminization of American Culture*, 200–226.

48. *New Orleans Daily Delta*, 29 January 1854, quoted in Hirsch, "Uncle Tomi-

tudes," 325. On this production see Brown, *A History of the New York Stage*, 1:130. Stevens himself died on 9 February from injuries received in a wrestling match.

49. "Uncle Tom's Cabin," playbill, Bowery Theatre, New York.

50. "Uncle Tom Among the Bowery Boys."

51. Birdoff contends that the play ran from 23 August to 4 September 1852, but a playbill survives for 10 September 1852 (*The World's Greatest Hit*, 24). See also "National Theatre—A. H. Purdy," playbill.

52. "National Theatre—A. H. Purdy," playbill.

53. The "maniac" in *The Drunkard* helps unmask its villain. "Uncle Tom's Cabin," *New York Herald*, 3 September 1852, reprinted in Moses and Brown, eds., *The American Theatre*, 72–75, 74.

54. Moses and Brown, eds., *The American Theatre*, 74.

55. Mason remarks that they "could be revised [with very few changes] into a fairly conventional series of melodramatic episodes involving a young mother and her child running away from any villain's evil clutches" (*Melodrama*, 119).

56. See also, for instance, the 1860s playbill that promises "Escape of Eliza on the floating ice, and the Baffled Pursuers. Thrilling Tableau!" "Uncle Tom's Cabin," playbill, Academy of Music in Chelsea, New York.

57. "Uncle Tom's Cabin," playbill, Bowery Theatre, New York.

58. "H. J. Conway's *Uncle Tom's Cabin*," playbill.

59. Hamblin, *Nick of the Woods*, 2.4. On "braggart scenes" and the figure of the "ring-tailed roarer" or screamer see Hauck, *Crockett*, 77; Reynolds, *Beneath the American Renaissance*, 449–57.

60. She introduces her song and dance with the exclamation "I 'spects I'se de wickedest critter in de world" (Aiken, *Uncle Tom's Cabin*, 2.4).

61. McConachie, "Out of the Kitchen," 10; see also Lott, *Love and Theft*, 226.

62. "Uncle Tom Dramatized."

63. H. J. Conway to Moses Kimball, 1 June 1852, quoted in McConachie, "H. J. Conway's Dramatization," 151.

64. Birdoff, *The World's Greatest Hit*, 42; *New York Daily Times*, 27 July 1853, quoted in Lott, *Love and Theft*, 217.

65. "National Theatre—A. H. Purdy," playbill.

66. Quoted in McConachie, "H. J. Conway's Dramatization," 150.

67. Lott, *Love and Theft*, 218. Lott's observations about Conway's Topsy and his recognition of the end man and the interlocutor in the Sam and Andy scene with Mrs. Shelby seem to me to be equally applicable to the novel, as I have suggested in chapter 1.

68. On Japan see the *Oxford English Dictionary*: "a varnish of exceptional hardness, which originally came from Japan. The name is now extended to other varnishes of a like sort *esp.* to (a) a black varnish obtained by cooking asphaltum with linseed oil, used for producing a black gloss on metal and other materials." A different joke depending on Day and Martin's manufacture of blacking can be found in Dickens, *Our Mutual Friend*, 23.

69. Stewart, *Holy Warriors*, 70.

70. Kerber, "Abolitionists and Amalgamators."

71. Lapsansky, "Graphic Discord," 225, 227.

72. Kerber, "Abolitionists and Amalgamators," 35.

73. Minute Book of the Western Anti-Slavery Society, 17 August 1848, quoted in Gara, "The Professional Fugitive," 198.

74. Quoted in McConachie, "H. J. Conway's Dramatization," 150, emphasis in original.

75. Brody, *Impossible Purities*.

76. Brody, *Impossible Purities*, 8.

CHAPTER 5. *Uncle Tom* in London: British Dramatizations

1. "Uncle Tom's Cabin," letter to *Times* (London).

2. "The Theatres," 1160.

3. *Eclectic Review*, December 1852, quoted in Rezé, "L'accueil," 419.

4. Fitzball, *Thirty-five Years*, 260–61.

5. These productions are documented in Nicoll, *History of the English Drama*; Mullin, *Victorian Plays*. The Lord Chamberlain's Collection at the British Library holds many of these scripts, and reviews in the *Theatrical Journal* and the *Dramatic Review* suggest further examples.

6. Speight, *The Juvenile Drama: A Union Catalogue*, 33. See also his *The Juvenile Drama: The History of the English Toy Theatre*; *Uncle Tom's Cabin: A Story of Negro Slavery*.

7. "Westminster Theatre."

8. Fitzball, *Thirty-five Years*, 261.

9. "Metropolitan Theatres," *Theatrical Journal* (London), 8 December 1852.

10. Fitzball, *Thirty-five Years*, 262.

11. "Metropolitan Theatres," *Theatrical Journal* (London), 29 September 1852; "Drama, Public Amusements & c.," *Critic* (London), 1 October 1852.

12. "Drama, Public Amusements & c.," *Critic* (London), 1 December 1852.

13. "Mr J. C. Carpenter's Entertainment."

14. "Metropolitan Theatres," *Theatrical Journal* (London), 11 December 1852.

15. *The Tyrant!* 1.1. On burlesques see Baddeley, *The Burlesque Tradition*.

16. *The Tyrant!* 1.1.

17. Birdoff comments on the extended length of the play, on its innovation in "black" roles, and on its attraction of "new" respectable audiences (*The World's Greatest Hit*, 48, 42, 51–52).

18. An advertisement in the *Era* (London) of 12 September 1852 indicates that the *Uncle Tom* at the Standard appeared with "'Living Marionettes,' the Tableaux of Madame Warton and Troupe, a Ballet Divertissement, and a Drama called 'The King, the Farmer, the Court'" (Advertisement, 1). "Metropolitan Theatres," *Theatrical Jour-*

nal (London), 15 September 1852, describes Madame Warton's accompaniment as "Poses Plastiques."

19. *Uncle Tom's Cabin: A Story of Negro Slavery*, 2.3, 2.4; *Uncle Tom's Cabin–or the Negro Slave*, 2.3; [Courtney], *Uncle Tom's Cabin*, 3.5; [Fitzball], *Uncle Tom's Cabin*, 2.5; *Uncle Tom's Cabin; or, the Fugitive Slave!* 2.7; *The Slave Hunt!* 2.7.

20. [Young], *Equestrian Version*, 1.1, 1.2, 1.3, 1.7, 1.8

21. [Fitzball], *Uncle Tom's Cabin*, 2.4.

22. *The Slave Hunt!* 1.1, 2.5.

23. Lemon and Taylor, *Slave Life*.

24. Birdoff, *The World's Greatest Hit*, 161–62; Saxon, *P. T. Barnum*, 200.

25. Webster's edition of Lemon and Taylor's *Slave Life* indicates on its title page that it was sold in Boston; "Mr. B. Young Respectfully Announces His Benefit," play-bill.

26. [Fitzball], *Uncle Tom's Cabin*, 2.2.

27. See Stephens, *The Censorship*, esp. 92–101; Stephens, "William Bodham Donne"; Foulkes, *Church and Stage*.

28. "The Theatres."

29. "Music and the Drama."

30. *Uncle Tom's Cabin* (City of London), 3.1.

31. *Uncle Tom's Cabin*, Webb's Juvenile Drama, 1.4.

32. *Uncle Tom's Cabin* (City of London), 3.1.

33. Fitzball, *Uncle Tom's Cabin*, 3.4.

34. [Courtney], *Uncle Tom's Cabin*, 3.5.

35. "Uncle Tom's Cabin," letter to *Times* (London).

36. "The Uncle Tom's Cabin Mania."

37. *The Tyrant!* 1.1.

38. Rezé, "L'accueil," 425.

39. Doyle, "The Land of Liberty."

40. Pitt, *Uncle Tom's Cabin*, 1.1; *Uncle Tom's Crib!* 1.2.

41. [Courtney], *Uncle Tom's Cabin*, 2.1; *Uncle Tom's Cabin* (City of London), 1.1; [Young], *Equestrian Version*, 1.1; *Uncle Tom's Cabin* (operatic version), 1.1; *Uncle Tom's Cabin: A Story of Negro Slavery*, 2.4.

42. *Uncle Tom's Cabin–or the Negro Slave*, 2.3; [Courtney], *Uncle Tom's Cabin*, 2.2. Douglass, "What to the Slave."

43. *Characters and Scenes in Uncle Tom's Cabin*, Webb's Juvenile Drama, Pollock's Toy Museum, set piece.

44. "Adelphi."

45. "*Uncle Tom* at the Paris Ambigu-Comique."

46. Lemon and Taylor, *Slave Life*, 1.3, 1.2, 2.3.

47. "Metropolitan Theatres," *Theatrical Journal* (London), 29 September 1852.

48. Fitzball, *Uncle Tom's Cabin*, 1.1, 1.3, 1.4.

49. Lemon and Taylor, *Slave Life*, 2.3; *Uncle Tom's Cabin–or the Negro Slave*, 2.3; *Uncle Tom's Cabin* (City of London), 2.2.

50. [Fitzball], *Uncle Tom's Cabin*, 1.3; Fitzball, *Uncle Tom's Cabin*, 1.1. Black pud-

ding is a Lancashire specialty made with pig blood and pork fat. See Grigson, *English Food*, 169.

51. Birdoff, *The World's Greatest Hit*, 152.

52. *Uncle Tom's Cabin; or, the Fugitive Slave!* 1.1.

53. Mayhew, *London Labour*, 36–37, 43.

54. The *Times* quoted in Wilson, *East End Entertainment*, 204.

55. See also [Courtney], *Uncle Tom's Cabin*, 3.1.

56. Fisch, *American Slaves*, 12.

57. "The Theatres," 1160; "Drama, Public Amusements & c.," *Critic* (London), 1 December 1852, 632; "Music and the Drama"; "The Theatres," 1160; "Adelphi," 385; "Drama, Public Amusements & c.," *Critic* (London), 1 October 1852; and "Drama."

58. *The Tyrant!* 1.1.

59. Powell, *Women and the Victorian Theatre*, 109; [Fitzball], *Uncle Tom's Cabin*, 1.4.

60. [Fitzball], *Uncle Tom's Cabin*, 1.2.

61. [Courtney], *Uncle Tom's Cabin*, 2.5; *Uncle Tom's Cabin—or the Negro Slave*, 1.4.

62. *Uncle Tom's Cabin* (City of London), 2.4; *Uncle Tom's Cabin; or, the Fugitive Slave!* 1.4, 2.7.

63. [Courtney], *Uncle Tom's Cabin*, 1.4.

64. Lemon and Taylor, *Slave Life*, 1.2, 1.4, 2.1, 2.3, 3.2, 3.3.

65. "Olympic."

66. "The Theatres," 1160; "Drama, Public Amusements & c.," *Critic* (London), 1 December 1852, 631; "Drama." The *Era* is quoted in Birdoff, *The World's Greatest Hit*, 162–63.

67. Fitzball, *Uncle Tom's Cabin*, 1.1.

68. *Uncle Tom's Cabin—or the Negro Slave*, 1.4, 2.1.

69. *Uncle Tom's Cabin; or, the Fugitive Slave!* 1.4.

70. *Uncle Tom's Cabin* (City of London), 3.2, 2.1.

71. Lemon and Taylor, *Slave Life*, 3.2.

72. Pitt, *Uncle Tom's Cabin*, 1.1. See Brody, *Impossible Purities*, 76–77 for another reading of this scene.

73. *Uncle Tom's Cabin; or, the Fugitive Slave!* 1.2.

74. *Uncle Tom's Cabin: A Story of Negro Slavery*, 2.1.

75. *Uncle Tom's Cabin—or the Negro Slave*, 1.1.

76. *Uncle Tom's Cabin—or the Negro Slave*, 1.1, 1.2.

77. Lemon and Taylor, *Slave Life*, 1.1.

78. *The Slave Hunt!* 2.7.

79. This claim is made, for example, by Lott, who declares that Mathews's caricatures of black Americans were "the first popular antecedents of blackface acts" (*Love and Theft*, 45).

80. "To Mr James Smith, February 3, 1823," letter quoted in Mathews, *The Life and Correspondence*, 289.

81. See Reynolds, *Minstrel Memories*.

82. Pickering, "White Skin, Black Masks"; Anthony, "Early Nigger Minstrel Acts."

83. Riach, "Blacks and Blackface," 231.

84. Pickering, "White Skin, Black Masks," 74; Anthony, "Early Nigger Minstrel Acts," 120; Meer, "Competing Representations."

85. Wilson, *To the Finland Station*, 220.

86. Pickering, "White Skin, Black Masks," 74, 76.

87. Moore, *G. W. Moore's Ethiopian Anecdotes*, dust jacket; Moore and Burgess Minstrels, *Uncle Tom's Cabin*.

88. Pickering, "White Skin, Black Masks," 72.

89. Rehin, "Blackface Street Minstrels"; Rehin, "Harlequin Jim Crow," 688.

90. Pickering, "White Skin, Black Masks," 83; Rehin, "Blackface Street Minstrels," 22.

91. On British minstrelsy see Pickering, "Mock Blacks."

92. Bratton, "English Ethiopians," 135–36.

93. Pickering, "White Skin, Black Masks," 75.

94. Rehin, "Blackface Street Minstrels," 20.

95. Bratton, "English Ethiopians," 128; Pickering, "White Skin, Black Masks," 83; Meer, "Competing Representations," 149.

96. See Bratton, "English Ethiopians," 128–29.

97. Pickering, "White Skin, Black Masks," 84.

98. "The Ethiopian Serenaders." See chapter 3 and also my discussion of Kennard's article in chapter 1. See also "Uncle Tom's Cabin," *Nonconformist*, 708.

99. Bratton, "English Ethiopians," 128.

100. Rehin, "Blackface Street Minstrels," 31.

101. Pickering, "White Skin, Black Masks," 76; Pickering, "Mock Blacks," 212.

102. See Meer, "Competing Representations," 155–60.

103. "Grand Combination of Talent."

104. Bratton, "English Ethiopians," 132.

105. Rehin, "Harlequin Jim Crow," 689.

106. "Juba at Vauxhall."

107. See Blackett, "Cracks in the Antislavery Wall," 192.

108. [Fitzball], *Uncle Tom's Cabin*, 1.1.

109. Fitzball, *Uncle Tom's Cabin*, 1.1; *Uncle Tom's Cabin*, Webb's Juvenile Drama, 1.1.

110. Dickens, *American Notes*, 138. The *Illustrated London News* of 1847 is quoted in the notes for that edition (343). Lane was one of the first black performers to tour with minstrel shows (Southern, *The Music of Black Americans*, 94–95).

111. *The Tyrant!* 1.1.

112. "Nelly Bly," in Jeffreys, ed., *Songs Sung*, 1.

113. Fitzball, *Uncle Tom's Cabin*; Pitt, *Uncle Tom's Cabin*; Lemon and Taylor, *Slave Life*; *The Slave Hunt!*

114. Neale, *Uncle Tom's Cabin*.

115. "Uncle Tom's Cabin," playbill, Royal Lyceum, Toronto.

116. *Uncle Tom's Cabin—or the Negro Slave*, 1.1.

117. [Fitzball], *Uncle Tom's Cabin*, 2.1.

118. *The Slave Hunt!* 2.2.

119. [Fitzball], *Uncle Tom's Cabin*, 1.1. See also *Uncle Tom's Cabin; or, the Fugitive Slave!* 1.1.

120. Lemon and Taylor, *Slave Life*, 1.1.

121. *Uncle Tom's Cabin*, Webb's Juvenile Drama, 3.12.

122. [Young], *Equestrian Version*, 1.2.

123. *Uncle Tom's Cabin—or the Negro Slave*, 1.2; *Uncle Tom's Cabin* (City of London), 1.3.

124. Jeffreys, "Far Away from Old Kentucky."

125. Lemon and Taylor, *Slave Life*, 2.3.

126. Lemon and Taylor, *Slave Life*, 2.3. On "wench," or drag, roles in minstrelsy see Lott, *Love and Theft*, 159–68.

127. Lemon and Taylor, *Slave Life*, 2.3, 3.1.

128. *Uncle Tom's Cabin—or the Negro Slave*; Pitt, *Uncle Tom's Cabin*; *Uncle Tom's Cabin; or, the Fugitive Slave!*

129. Lemon and Taylor, *Slave Life*, 3.2, 2.3.

130. *Uncle Tom's Crib!* 1.1.

131. *Uncle Tom's Crib!* 1.1.

132. See Fisch, *American Slaves*, 69–90.

133. Scobie, *Black Britannia*, 24; Walvin, *Black and White*, 189; Mayhew, *London Labour*, 260.

134. On this see Ripley, ed., *The Black Abolitionist Papers*; Blackett, *Building an Antislavery Wall*; Fisch, *American Slaves*.

135. Brown, *The American Fugitive in Europe*, 203–7.

136. Jessie S. F. C. Taylor, *A Memory Sketch of My Husband, Genius and Musician, Samuel Coleridge-Taylor* (1943), quoted in Lorimer, *Colour, Class and the Victorians*, 67.

137. "Olympic."

CHAPTER 6. *Tom* Mania in Britain: The Stafford House Address and "Real Uncle Toms"

1. "*Uncle Tom's Cabin*," *Southern Literary Messenger*, 638.

2. For a discussion of British periodical reviews of the novel see Lorimer, *Colour, Class and the Victorians*, 83–85; and Fisch's chapter "'Exhibiting Uncle Tom in some shape or other': The Commercialization and Reception of *Uncle Tom's Cabin* in England," in *American Slaves*, 11–32.

3. Shepperson, "Harriet Beecher Stowe and Scotland," 40.

4. See Bolt, *The Anti-Slavery Movement*; Fladeland, *Men and Brothers*; Blackett, *Building an Antislavery Wall*; Taylor, ed., *British and American Abolitionists*; Ripley, ed., *The Black Abolitionist Papers*.

5. Blackett, *Building an Antislavery Wall*, 26.

6. Fladeland, *Men and Brothers*, 356. There is conflicting evidence about the purpose of this fund, some sources suggesting that it was collected for slaves, others to
compensate Stowe for revenue lost through the piracy of British publishers. The dis-
crepancies may account for the lingering accusations that Stowe misappropriated
funds or muddled her accounts. See Fladeland, *Men and Brothers*, 356; Wilson, *Crusader in Crinoline*, 233; Hedrick, *Harriet Beecher Stowe*, 246–48.

7. Fladeland, *Men and Brothers*, 357, 353; Midgley, *Women Against Slavery*, 146;
Taylor, *Women of the Antislavery Movement*, 83. Rice argues against this view that
"the active abolitionist impulse weaken[ed]" in the "emotive forms of antislavery enthusiasm" that Stowe called forth ("Literary Sources," 146).

8. Brodhead, "Veiled Ladies," 273–93, 277.

9. Wilson, *Crusader in Crinoline*, 232. Wilson also suggests that the Queen con-
trived an apparently accidental meeting during Stowe's second visit in 1856 (248–50).

10. On Stowe's visit to Britain see Wilson, *Crusader in Crinoline*, 207–33; Hedrick,
Harriet Beecher Stowe, 233–50; Stowe, *Sunny Memories*.

11. Mulvey, *Transatlantic Manners*, 144, and on this phenomenon in American visitors generally see 132–46.

12. Stowe, *Sunny Memories*, 175.

13. Quoted in Hedrick, *Harriet Beecher Stowe*, 264.

14. *Dictionary of National Biography*, s.v. "Cooper, Antony Ashley, Seventh Earl of
Shaftesbury"; Battiscombe, *Shaftesbury*; Finlayson, *The Seventh Earl*.

15. Finlayson, *The Seventh Earl*, 343; "The Affectionate and Christian Address of
Many Thousands of the Women of England," 3F. The document was soon popularly
known as the Stafford House Address, after the residence of the Duchess of Sutherland, who promoted it.

16. Reported in "Slavery in the United States."

17. Fladeland, *Men and Brothers*, 352; Wilson, *Crusader in Crinoline*, 205–7; Finlayson, *The Seventh Earl*, 343–45; Hedrick, *Harriet Beecher Stowe*, 244–46.

18. The full text is quoted in Wilson, *Crusader in Crinoline*, 207.

19. On this event see Stewart, *Holy Warriors*, 88–98.

20. On other British addresses see Midgley, *Women Against Slavery*, 128, 132, 199;
on American petitions see Stewart, *Holy Warriors*, 82; Deborah Bingham Van Broek-
hoven, "'Let Your Names Be Enrolled': Method and Ideology in Women's Antislavery
Petitioning," in Yellin and Van Horne, eds., *The Abolitionist Sisterhood*, 179–99.

21. Ruth Bogin and Jean Fagan Yellin, introduction to Yellin and Van Horne, eds.,
The Abolitionist Sisterhood, 1–19, 8. Stewart also contends that the supplicating biblical terms common to such documents helped women signatories see petitions as part
of their traditional gendered "sphere" (*Holy Warriors*, 82).

22. *Proceedings of the Anti-Slavery Conventions of American Women ... 1837*,
quoted in Amy Swerdlow, "Abolition's Conservative Sisters: The Ladies' New York
City Anti-Slavery Societies, 1834–1840," in Yellin and Van Horne, eds., *The Abolitionist Sisterhood*, 31–44, 40–41.

23. See Midgley, *Women Against Slavery*, 148.

24. Despite public perception, the Duchess of Sutherland's interest in slavery long predated Stowe's book; for instance, she entertained delegates to the World Anti-Slavery Conference in 1840. See Pugh, "Women and Slavery," 188; Fladeland, *Men and Brothers*, 356; Midgley, *Women Against Slavery*, 126. Midgley argues that British sympathy partly transcended class because it was "racially based" (*Women Against Slavery*, 146).

25. The extent of working-class involvement is a matter of debate. For an outline of this discussion see Fladeland, *Abolitionists*, vii.

26. Fisch, *American Slaves*, 11–32.

27. The duchess had been among the ladies Victoria refused to part with during the "Bedchamber Crisis" of 1839. See *Dictionary of National Biography*, s.v. "Leveson-Gower, Harriet Elizabeth."

28. "American Abolitionists and the London Times," *National Anti-Slavery Standard*, 9 December 1852, quoted in Pugh, "Women and Slavery," 191.

29. Klingberg, "Harriet Beecher Stowe," 545.

30. "The Lady Abolitionists," 1164.

31. "The Lady Abolitionists," 1164.

32. Finlayson, *The Seventh Earl*, 344–45; "The Lady Abolitionists," 1164; Academicus, "To the Editor of *The Times*"; R.G.D., "To the Editor of *The Times*"; Shuttleworth, "To the Editor of *The Times*." Some of these replies are discussed in Pugh, "Women and Slavery," 191.

33. See Richards, *A History of the Highland Clearances*, esp. 1:212–14, 230, 284–315. See also Grimble's introduction to MacLeod, *Gloomy Memories*, 24–30. Newman condemns Stowe's blindness on this issue in "Stowe's Sunny Memories."

34. *New York Daily Tribune*, 9 February 1853, quoted in Shepperson, "Harriet Beecher Stowe and Scotland," 42.

35. MacLeod, *Gloomy Memories in the Highlands of Scotland*.

36. Stowe, *Sunny Memories*, 219–28.

37. William Cobbett, "Slave Trade," *Cobbett's Weekly Political Register* 7 (1805), quoted in Gallagher, *The Industrial Reformation*, 8.

38. Gallagher, *The Industrial Reformation*, 5.

39. See Butsch, *The Making of American Audiences*, 52–55. On the relation of the riot to minstrelsy see Lott, *Love and Theft*, 66–67.

40. Birdoff, *The World's Greatest Hit*, 121.

41. "Take Care of Number One. As Sung by Julius Von Bonhorst, of Sanford's Opera House, with great applause," in *Dixey's Essence of Burnt Cork*, 64–65.

42. "The Other Side of Jordan," reprinted in Paskman and Spaeth, eds., *"Gentlemen, Be Seated!"* 201. For another version of this see chapter 2.

43. "Pop Goes the Weasel," published by S. T. Gordon in 1859, reprinted in Jackson, ed., *Popular Songs*, 179. See also Finson, *The Voices That Are Gone*, 192.

44. *Times* (London), 3 September 1853; *Reynolds's Newspaper* (London), 15 May 1853, 1A; Reynolds, "Black Slavery Abroad"; *Northern Ensign and Weekly Gazette for the Counties of Caithness, Ross, Sutherland, Orkney, and Zetland* (Scotland), 25 September 1853; *Leader* (London), 18 September 1852, 900; *Star of Freedom* (London),

24 September 1852, 105. These and other articles making the comparison are discussed in Lorimer, *Colour, Class and the Victorians*, 93–100, and Klingberg, "Harriet Beecher Stowe," 548.

45. "An Affectionate and Christian Address of Many Thousands of the Women of the United States," 3; *John Bull* (London), 15 January 1853, 37.

46. "The Earl of Shaftesbury's Rejoinder"; Lorimer, *Colour, Class and the Victorians*, 100.

47. Eacker makes this argument for Louisa McCord and the Grimké sisters in "A 'Dangerous Inmate' of the South," 27.

48. See Ginzberg, *Women and the Work of Benevolence*, 67.

49. "The Lady Abolitionists," 1164.

50. "To the Editor of *The Times*."

51. "To the Earl of Shaftesbury."

52. Academicus, "To the Editor of *The Times*."

53. *Times* (London), 15 February 1853; Pugh, "Women and Slavery," 193–94; Seager II, *And Tyler Too*, 404–5.

54. "To the Duchess of Sutherland," 120. The essay was also reprinted elsewhere, including in the *New York Daily Times*, 5 February 1853.

55. Headnote to Louisa S. McCord, "British Philanthropy and American Slavery: An Affectionate Response to the Ladies of England, etc., from the Ladies of the Southern United States," *De Bows Review* (March 1853), reprinted in McCord, *Louisa S. McCord*, 281. On Louisa McCord see Thorpe, *Female Persuasion*; Fox-Genovese, *Within the Plantation Household*, 242–89; and the notes, chronology, and O'Brien's introduction to McCord, *Louisa S. McCord*.

56. Midgley, *Women Against Slavery*, 149.

57. Tyler, "Address," 122.

58. McCord, *Louisa S. McCord*, 281.

59. "Woman's True Mission," 303; Tyler, "Address," 120.

60. Duvall commented on the "obtuseness" of commentators who used the domestic metaphor against Stowe, which he argued she had refuted in the novel ("*Uncle Tom's Cabin*: The Sinister Side," 16). The home was associated with the nation in many places in the 1850s: Frederika Bremer's 1853 account of her travels in the United States was called *Homes of the New World*, while a series of biographical profiles of American presidents framed their achievements in terms of residences. The portraits of Lincoln (*From Pioneer Home to White House*), George Washington (*From Farm House to White House*), and later James Garfield (*From Log Cabin to White House*) condensed the American dream into a series of house removals (Handlin, *The American Home*, 21).

61. Louisa McCord, "A Letter to the Duchess of Sutherland, from a Lady of South Carolina," *Charleston Mercury*, 10 August 1853, reprinted in McCord, *Louisa S. McCord*, 351. She makes the same argument in "British Philanthropy" (285).

62. Quoted in Gossett, *Uncle Tom's Cabin and American Culture*, 191.

63. McCord, *Louisa S. McCord*, 359; "Charity Which Does Not Begin at Home,"

Southern Literary Messenger (April 1853), reprinted in McCord, *Louisa S. McCord*, 347.

64. "Woman's True Mission," 303.

65. Tyler, "Address," 120.

66. Fox-Genovese, *Within the Plantation Household*, 202–3.

67. Pugh, "Women and Slavery," 186.

68. McCord, "British Philanthropy," 293. On the relevance of these gestures to Southern ideas of honor see Greenberg, *Honor and Slavery*. On women's relationship to these codes see Fox-Genovese, *Within the Plantation Household*, 49.

69. Fox-Genovese, *Within the Plantation Household*, 63, 195.

70. McCord, *Louisa S. McCord*, 357–58.

71. Stowe, *Sunny Memories*, 175. Mulvey notes the similarity between the system Stowe praises and Southern defenses of the plantation (*Transatlantic Manners*, 143).

72. "The Patriot Julia."

73. *Times* (London), 15 February 1853, 4B.

74. "A Talk with Mrs. Tyler."

75. "The Patriot Julia."

76. "The Ladies of the Creation," v–xvi.

77. Pugh, "Women and Slavery," 194.

78. "Sisters and Slavery." *Punch* also mimics the address in "Logic for the Legrees," which argues that the intransigence shown by its critics will lead to slave rebellion.

79. "The Ladies' Battle."

80. *Frederick Douglass' Paper*, 8 April 1852; William G. Allen, letter to *Frederick Douglass' Paper*, 20 May 1852; Martin Delaney, letter to *Frederick Douglass' Paper*, 1 April 1853, quoted in Levine, "*Uncle Tom's Cabin* in *Frederick Douglass' Paper*," 73–74, 75, 81. See also Banks, "Uncle Tom's Cabin and Antebellum Black Response," 209–27; Yarborough, "Strategies of Black Characterization"; Stepto, "Sharing the Thunder."

81. Douglass, "The Anti-Slavery Movement."

82. See Winks, "The Making of a Fugitive Slave Narrative."

83. John Brown, *Slave Life in Georgia* (1855), quoted in Innes, *A History of Black and Asian Writing*, 92.

84. Craft, *Running a Thousand Miles*, 39, 49, 53.

85. Northup, *Twelve Years*. On the debt to Stowe see Stepto, "Sharing the Thunder," 135–36; on the dedication see Andrews, *To Tell a Free Story*, 181, and Stowe, *The Key to Uncle Tom's Cabin*, 342.

86. Northup, *Twelve Years*, 379.

87. Northup, *Twelve Years*, 338, my emphasis. McIntosh referred to "Life Among the Lowly" in the title of *The Lofty and the Lowly*. Northup's narrative repeats the phrase in its final sentence, in which he hopes "henceforward to lead an upright though lowly life, and rest at last in the church yard where my father sleeps" (*Twelve Years*, 406).

88. Northup, *Twelve Years*, 349.

89. Andrews, *To Tell a Free Story*, 179–87. Stepto argues that "The Heroic Slave" rejects the subservience of Uncle Tom ("Sharing the Thunder," 145–52). See Douglass, "The Heroic Slave."

90. Douglass, *My Bondage*.

91. Douglass, *Narrative*, 48; Stowe, *The Key to Uncle Tom's Cabin*, 24. For a more detailed comparison of the three texts discussed here see Meer, "Sentimentality."

92. Douglass, *My Bondage*, 57.

93. William Wells Brown to William Lloyd Garrison, 17 May 1853, *Liberator*, 3 June 1853, reprinted in Ripley, ed., *The Black Abolitionist Papers*, 1:344–46, 345.

94. William Wells Brown, speech delivered at Manchester Town Hall, 1 August 1854, reprinted in Ripley, ed., *The Black Abolitionist Papers*, 1:398–406, 400.

95. Quoted in "Opinions of the British Press," in Brown, *The Travels*, 229–32. The *Narrative of William Wells Brown, a Fugitive Slave*, first published in Boston in 1847, came out in four English editions between 1849 and 1853. See Paul Jefferson, "Introduction," in Brown, *The Travels*, 16.

96. Barbara McCaskill, "Introduction," in Craft, *Running a Thousand Miles*, xvii.

97. Douglass, *Life and Times*, 271–79.

98. William G. Allen, speech delivered at the Stock Exchange, Leeds, 29 November 1853, reprinted in Ripley, ed., *The Black Abolitionist Papers*, 1:367–70, 370. See also Innes, *A History of Black and Asian Writing*, 114.

99. Sarah Remond, speech delivered at the Athenaeum, Manchester, 14 September 1859, reprinted in Ripley, ed., *The Black Abolitionist Papers*, 1:457–61, 458; William Craft, letter to the editor of the *Morning Advertiser* (London) (September 1852), reprinted in Ripley, ed., *The Black Abolitionist Papers*, 1:316–23, 317; see also William Craft, speech delivered at Spitalfields Chapel, 14 October 1859, reprinted in Ripley, ed., *The Black Abolitionist Papers*, 1:465–68.

100. Stowe, *Sunny Memories*, 312.

101. William G. Allen to William Lloyd Garrison, London, 20 June 1853, in Ripley, ed., *The Black Abolitionist Papers*, 1:355–58, 357.

102. On Ward see Ripley, ed., *The Black Abolitionist Papers*, 1:300–301.

103. Stowe, *Sunny Memories*, 309, 312. On Ellen Craft see McCaskill, "'Yours Very Truly.'"

104. Stowe, *Sunny Memories*, 232.

105. "Uncle Tom on His Travels." Dandy Jim suggests the minstrel song "Dandy Jim of Caroline."

106. *A Popular Selection of Ethiopian Melodies*, 33.

107. *Black Diamonds*, 347.

108. *Black Diamonds*, 353–56. The book also comments on Greenfield (34).

109. Starnes, *The Slaveholder Abroad*. I discuss this further in the next chapter.

110. Starnes, *The Slaveholder Abroad*, 49–52.

111. Starnes, *The Slaveholder Abroad*, 63–67.

112. Starnes, *The Slaveholder Abroad*, 67.

113. Starnes, *The Slaveholder Abroad*, 67. This argument is rehearsed, for in-

stance, by Louisa McCord in "Diversity of the Races; Its Bearing upon Negro Slavery," *Southern Quarterly Review* (April 1851), and "Negro-mania," *De Bow's Review* (May 1852), both reprinted in McCord, *Louisa S. McCord,*, 159–86, 184.

114. McCord, *Louisa S. McCord*, 183.

115. Pickering, "'A Jet Ornament to Society,'" 29; Trotter, *Music and Some Highly Musical People*, 66–87; Stowe, *Sunny Memories*, 207, 307–10, 335.

116. The blackface sketch collection *Black Diamonds* makes a further joke with Greenfield's reputation, calling her the "black . . . goose" (34).

117. Johnston, "Miss Elizabeth T. Greenfield."

118. Stowe, *Sunny Memories*, 308, 335.

119. The term originates in Frederickson, *The Black Image*. Frederickson links Stowe's thinking to the lectures of Alexander Kinmont and others who ascribed special religious, artistic, and musical qualities to black people (*Black Image*, 97–129).

120. Stowe records Greenfield performing it twice (*Sunny Memories*, 208, 309).

121. Southwood, *Tit for Tat*, ii. I discuss this and Chase's novel, below, further in the next chapter.

122. Chase, *English Serfdom*, vii–viii, 172.

123. Lapsansky, "Afro-Americana"; Gardner, "Stowe Takes the Stage"; Clark, "Solo Black Performance."

124. Webb, "Biographical Sketch," i–iii. Quotations from the play are taken from Stowe, *The Christian Slave* (Boston).

125. "Stafford House," *Daily News*; "Mrs Mary E. Webb." The *Daily News* review was partially reproduced, alongside a portrait of Webb reading, in the *Illustrated London News* (London), 2 August 1856, 121–22.

126. "Stafford House," advertisement.

127. Stowe, *The Christian Slave* (Boston), 3.1, 2.12.

128. Clark, "Solo Black Performance," 346.

129. Stowe, *The Christian Slave* (Boston), 3.6.

130. Stowe, *The Christian Slave* (London).

131. Stowe, *The Christian Slave* (Boston), 1.11, 1.2, 2.4.

132. "Stafford House," *Daily News*.

133. "Stafford House," *Daily News*.

134. Webb shared this treatment not only with Greenfield but with other antislavery lecturers and exotics "exhibited" for entertainment in nineteenth-century Britain. See Fisch, *American Slaves*, 69–90; Altick, *The Shows of London*, 274–75, 276–79; McCaskill, "'Yours Very Truly,'" 509–29; Meer, "Competing Representations."

135. Gardner, "Stowe Takes the Stage," 80. Sarah Siddons was a great English tragic actress of the late eighteenth century.

136. "Stafford House," *Daily News*.

137. "Mrs Mary E. Webb."

138. "Stafford House," *Daily News*.

139. Brodhead, "Veiled Ladies." See also Kelley, *Private Woman, Public Stage*, esp. vii.

140. By way of comparison, other concerts and entertainments advertised in the

same place ranged from between one shilling and seven shillings and sixpence, while the weekly salary of a London clerk was about a guinea and a half. Advertisements (for Crystal Palace Illustrations/Display of Fountains, Jullien's Concert at the Royal Surrey Gardens), *Daily News* (London), 25 July 1856, 4. See also Altick, "English Publishing," 146.

141. Wilson, *Crusader in Crinoline*, 209; Hedrick, *Harriet Beecher Stowe*, 241.

142. "Stafford House," *Daily News*.

143. See Lorimer, *Colour, Class and the Victorians*, esp. "Black Gentlemen and the Mid-Victorians," 45–68; and Fisch's analysis of the receptions of Sarah Remond and Henry "Box" Brown (*American Slaves*, 69–90).

144. *Warrington Guardian*, quoted in Fisch, *American Slaves*, 88.

145. See "Uncle Tom's Cabin," letter to *Times* (London), discussed in chapter 5 and in Fisch, *American Slaves*, 22–23. On Brown see Fisch, *American Slaves*, 73–83.

146. Stowe, *Sunny Memories*, 307–8.

147. *Illustrated London News* (London), 2 August 1856, 121.

148. "Stafford House," *Daily News*; "Mrs Mary E. Webb."

149. "Stafford House," *Daily News*.

150. Martin Delaney, letter to *Frederick Douglass' Paper*, 1 April 1853; Levine, "*Uncle Tom's Cabin* in *Frederick Douglass' Paper*," 81.

151. Gardner, "Stowe Takes the Stage," 80.

152. "Mrs Mary E. Webb."

153. "Stafford House," *Daily News*.

154. Letter to Mr. and Mrs. Edward Baines, quoted in Clark, "Solo Black Performance," 342.

155. Webb, "Biographical Sketch," iii.

CHAPTER 7. Foreign Manners and Memories:
Tom Mania and Transatlantic Literature

1. Weisbuch, *Atlantic Double-Cross*, xviii.

2. Quoted in C. E. Stowe's preface to Stowe, *Sunny Memories*, 1:xxxvii.

3. Sydney Smith, *Edinburgh Review* (1820), reprinted in Ruland, ed., *The Native Muse*, 156–57.

4. Lease, *Anglo-American Encounters*, 27, 38; Weisbuch, *Atlantic Double-Cross*, 12.

5. Letter quoted in Gilbertson, *Harriet Beecher Stowe*, 161.

6. Gohdes, *American Literature in Nineteenth-Century England*, 128.

7. The American apologies include J. K. Paulding's *The United States and England* (1815) and *John Bull in America* (1824); Robert Walsh's *Appeal for the Judgments of Great Britain* (1824); James Fenimore Cooper's *Notions of the Americans* (1828); and Washington Irving's "English Writers on America," in *The Sketchbook* (1819–20). Examples of American advocates of independence in literature include Henry Wadsworth Longfellow, "Graduation Address" (1832); Evert Duyckink in the *New York Literary World* (1847); Herman Melville's "Hawthorne and His Mosses," *New York Literary World* (1850); and Ralph Waldo Emerson's "The American Scholar" (1837)

and "The Poet" (1844). These and many others are reprinted in Ruland, ed., *The Native Muse*. See also Hawthorne, *Our Old Home* (1863).

8. Lease, *Anglo-American Encounters*, 88 and passim.

9. On Stowe's childhood reading see Wagenknecht, *Harriet Beecher Stowe*, 144; on the gifts to luminaries see Gilbertson, *Harriet Beecher Stowe*, 159; on these literary pilgrimages see Lease, *Anglo-American Encounters*, and also their respective accounts in Irving's *Sketchbook* (1819–20), Emerson's *English Traits* (1856), and Stowe's *Sunny Memories*.

10. Stowe, *Sunny Memories*, 35–36.

11. On Eliot see Hughes, *George Eliot*, 429, and Hedrick, *Harriet Beecher Stowe*, 383; on Mrs. Gaskell see Uglow, *Elizabeth Gaskell*, 353, 423, 436. Sabiston suggests that there are structural similarities between Mrs. Gaskell's *Mary Barton* (1848) and *Uncle Tom's Cabin* ("Anglo-American Connections").

12. Stowe, *Sunny Memories*, 212, 200–201.

13. Other famous examples include Alexis de Tocqueville's *De la démocratie en Amérique* (1835) and Frederika Bremer's *Homes of the New World* (1853).

14. See Mesick, *The English Traveller in America*; Nevins, ed., *American Social History*; Mulvey, *Transatlantic Manners*; John S. Whitley and Arnold Goldman, introduction to Dickens, *American Notes*.

15. Marryat quoted in introduction to Dickens, *American Notes*, 15.

16. Trollope, *Domestic Manners*; Dickens, *American Notes*.

17. Trollope, *Domestic Manners*, 314.

18. Mulvey, *Transatlantic Manners*, 78.

19. Trollope, *Domestic Manners*, 185–99.

20. Dickens, *American Notes*, 269–84, 284.

21. Stowe, *Sunny Memories*, 21.

22. "Mrs. H. B. Stowe at Stafford House."

23. See Wilson, *Crusader in Crinoline*, 229; Brown, letter to William Lloyd Garrison.

24. See Ransom, *Fanny Trollope*, 78; Neville-Sington, *Fanny Trollope*, 173–74.

25. Grayson, *The Hireling and the Slave*, 40.

26. Dickens, *American Notes*; Dickens, *Martin Chuzzlewit*. On the American response to *American Notes* see Kaplan, *Dickens*, 152–53.

27. Letter quoted in Stone, "Charles Dickens and Harriet Beecher Stowe," 193.

28. On Dickens's suspicion and Stowe's reading see Wagenknecht, *Harriet Beecher Stowe*, 144. Tillotson noted that "to put a child at the centre of a novel for adults was virtually unknown when Dickens wrote *Oliver Twist* and *The Old Curiosity Shop*" ("Introductory," 19).

29. Gerson, *Harriet Beecher Stowe*, 70; Stowe, *Sunny Memories*, 322. John and Dot are characters from *The Cricket on the Hearth* (1845), Charlie is from *Bleak House* (1853), and the rest refer to *Nicholas Nickleby* (1838–39).

30. For Justice Talfourd's toast see Stowe, *Sunny Memories*, 190; for Dickens's thanks see C. E. Stowe's preface to Stowe, *Sunny Memories*, 1:xli.

31. Stowe, *Sunny Memories*, 14; Meckier, *Innocent Abroad*, 6, 7.

32. Stowe, *Sunny Memories*, 194.

33. Meckier, *Innocent Abroad*, 39, 43.

34. "'Uncle Bull's Cribbing' *Published by Everybody and Co.*"

35. Stowe, *Sunny Memories*, x.

36. Dickens, *Martin Chuzzlewit*, 346, 347.

37. Dickens, *Martin Chuzzlewit*, 336, 357.

38. Dickens, *Bleak House*, 123.

39. The first installment was published in March 1852. See Louisa S. McCord, "Carey on the Slave Trade," *Southern Quarterly Review* (January 1854), reprinted in McCord, *Louisa S. McCord*, 415.

40. Rush, *North and South*, 20.

41. Schoolcraft, *The Black Gauntlet*, 216, 511.

42. Denman, *Uncle Tom's Cabin*, 7. Altick gives both their sales figures: *Bleak House* sold about 35,000 copies in 1852–53, while Stowe's British and colonial sales at that time were in the region of 1.5 million (*The English Common Reader*, 301, 384).

43. Charles Dickens to Mrs. Cropper, December 1852, quoted in Stone, "Charles Dickens and Harriet Beecher Stowe," 194.

44. Dickens, *Bleak House*, 53.

45. On Emerson's disappointment see Weisbuch, *Atlantic Double-Cross*, 3–4.

46. Trollope, *Domestic Manners*, 45.

47. Stowe, *Sunny Memories*, 28, 251.

48. Weisbuch, *Atlantic Double-Cross*, xviii.

49. See Cunliffe, *Chattel Slavery*; Gallagher, *The Industrial Reformation*, 4–33.

50. Gallagher, *The Industrial Reformation*, 4.

51. O'Brien, *Conjectures of Order*, 2:952.

52. "American Slavery and Uncle Tom's Cabin," 255.

53. The Earl of Carlisle is quoted in Gilbertson, *Harriet Beecher Stowe*, 160.

54. Neville-Sington, *Fanny Trollope*, 167–70.

55. *Times*, 15 February 1853, 4b–c.

56. *American and English Oppression, and British and American Abolitionists: A Letter Addressed to R. D. Webb, Esq., by an American, in His Fatherland* (London, 1853), quoted in Bolt, *The Anti-Slavery Movement*, 12.

57. "The Effect of Uncle Tom in Europe."

58. David James McCord, "American Institutions—the Monroe Doctrine—Intervention—etc.," *De Bow's Review* (December 1853), quoted in McCord, *Louisa S. McCord*, 352.

59. "The Effect of Uncle Tom in Europe," 70. The argument was repeated in "Uncle Tom's Cabin," *New York Observer*.

60. *Uncle Tom in England: or, A Proof that Black's White.* Fisch discusses this text in detail (*American Slaves*, 33–51).

61. Reade, *It Is Never Too Late to Mend*, 166, 210.

62. Dickens, *American Notes*, 146.

63. Grayson, *The Hireling and the Slave*; [Brown], *The Planter*; Southwood, *Tit for Tat*; Chase, *English Serfdom*; Starnes, *The Slaveholder Abroad*.

64. [Brown], *The Planter*, 5, 10.

65. Starnes, *The Slaveholder Abroad.*

66. Chase, *English Serfdom*, 214, 254.

67. Southwood, *Tit for Tat*, i, ii, 196.

68. Wilson, *Crusader in Crinoline*, 229; Finlayson, *The Seventh Earl*, 344; Chase, *English Serfdom*, 77.

69. These books have also been dubbed "industrial" novels, although, as Guy points out, they were not recognized as a genre until the 1950s (*The Victorian Social-Problem Novel*, 3). See also Klingberg, "Harriet Beecher Stowe," 543.

70. Elizabeth Gaskell, *Mary Barton* (1848) and *North and South* (1855); Charles Dickens, *Hard Times* (1854); Benjamin Disraeli, *Sybil: or, The Two Nations* (1845); Charles Kingsley, *Alton Locke, Tailor and Poet* (1850). Also usually included in this group, though it is too late for this discussion, is George Eliot, *Felix Holt, the Radical* (1866).

71. James Kirk Paulding had advanced this argument as early as 1822 in his *Sketch of Old England*. See Tise, *Proslavery*, 47.

72. Louisa S. McCord, "Negro and White Slavery—Wherein Do They Differ?" *Southern Quarterly Review* (July 1851), and "*Uncle Tom's Cabin*," *Southern Quarterly Review* (January 1853), both in McCord, *Louisa S. McCord*, 188, 246.

73. McCord, *Louisa S. McCord*, 190.

74. Southwood, *Tit for Tat*, 43.

75. [Brown], *The Planter*, 11, 145, 147, 29.

76. Chase, *English Serfdom*, 179. He is referring to G. P. R. James (1799?–1860), "the doyen of hack historical novelists," famous for rehashing openings involving "two horsemen"; Edward George Earle Lytton Bulwer-Lytton (1803–73); Sir Walter Scott; and Charles Dickens. See Sutherland, ed., *Longman Companion to Victorian Fiction.*

77. Southwood, *Tit for Tat*, 53–54. Sidonia is a character, sometimes supposed to represent Disraeli's own opinion, in *Coningsby* (1844) and *Tancred* (1847). See Braun, "Introduction," 20.

78. Dickens, *Oliver Twist*, 62.

79. Southwood, *Tit for Tat*, 70; the peddler has a "Jew's accent" (81). On Dickens and anti-Semitism see Schlicke, ed., *Oxford Reader's Companion to Dickens*, 309.

80. Chase, *English Serfdom*, 87; Dickens, *A Christmas Carol*, 51; Dickens, *Hard Times.*

81. Chase, *English Serfdom*, 201, 227. The reference is, of course, to the character in Dickens's *David Copperfield* (1849–50).

82. Chase, *English Serfdom*, 178.

83. Disraeli, *Sybil*, 151.

84. Bédarida, *A Social History of England*, 48, and see 2–72.

85. Quoted in Finlayson, *The Seventh Earl*, 331–33.

86. Cannadine, *The Decline and Fall*, 2, and *Class in Britain*, 72.

87. Southwood, *Tit for Tat*, 195.

88. Chase, *English Serfdom*, 109.

89. Chase, *English Serfdom*, 77–87.

90. Finlayson, *The Seventh Earl*, 350, 351, 549.

91. Southwood, *Tit for Tat*, 37.

92. Quoted in Finlayson, *The Seventh Earl*, 345.

93. Battiscombe, *Shaftesbury*, 127.

94. Williams, *Culture and Society*, 87–109. On critical responses to the social problem novels see Guy, *The Victorian Social-Problem Novel*, 13–63.

95. Twain, *Pudd'nhead Wilson*.

96. Hadley, *Melodramatic Tactics*, 127.

97. Chase, *English Serfdom*, 17, 110, my emphasis.

98. Trollope, *Domestic Manners*, 242, 243.

99. Stowe, *Sunny Memories*, 244.

100. Southwood, *Tit for Tat*, 13, 110.

101. Chase, *English Serfdom*, 232.

102. Chase, *English Serfdom*, 124.

CHAPTER 8. Answering the "Answers": *Tom* Mania and Stowe's *Dred*

1. Eliot, review of *Dred*, 43. Adams asserted that "Dred is himself[,] . . . except for a detail of pigmentation, a hero from Scottish literature, a wild chieftain fleeing to an inaccessible stronghold from which he has sallied forth to confound the oppressors of his people" (*Harriet Beecher Stowe*, 42).

2. Crozier, *The Novels*, 206; Stowe, *Dred*, 34 (hereafter cited in text).

3. Crozier, *The Novels*, 55.

4. Gaines, *The Southern Plantation*, 40; Davis, "Mrs. Stowe's Characters-in-Situations," 109.

5. Adams, *Harriet Beecher Stowe*, 43.

6. Davis, "Mrs. Stowe's Characters-in-Situations," 115–16.

7. "Dred," 695.

8. "*Dred* and *American Slavery*," 324; "The Political Crisis," 565.

9. Stowe, *The Key to Uncle Tom's Cabin*, v–vi, 5.

10. Hedrick, *Harriet Beecher Stowe*, 236, 252.

11. Hedrick, *Harriet Beecher Stowe*, 256; reprinted in Hedrick, ed., *The Oxford Harriet Beecher Stowe Reader*, 452–56.

12. Gerson claims that an early version of the title was indeed *Dread* (*Harriet Beecher Stowe*, 105).

13. Thomas Gray, "Nat Turner's Confessions," first published in 1831, extracted in appendix 1 of Stowe, *Dred*, 679–91, 680–81.

14. Sundquist, *To Wake the Nations*, 79. Sundquist's conclusion is echoed by Grüner in "Stowe's *Dred*." Levine, *Martin Delany*, 169–70, reads the novel as an endorsement of Dred's mind-set, arguing that Dred's violent propositions "retain a privileged place in the novel" despite their being pitted against Milly's pacifism. He opposes the "critical consensus" represented by Mabee and Mabee Newhouse, *Sojourner Truth*, 89; Hedrick, *Harriet Beecher Stowe*, 259; and Foster, *The Rungless Ladder*, 85.

15. "Dred," 701.

16. Crozier, *The Novels*, 38–39. The *Blackwoods* reviewer called the novel "a series of imperfectly developed plots" ("Dred," 695).

17. Hedrick, *Harriet Beecher Stowe*, 258; Grüner, "Stowe's *Dred*," 8.

18. It has been claimed that there were black muses behind the songs of Billy Whitlock, Ben Cotton, E. P. Christy, Stephen Foster, and Dan Emmett; there is a variety of stories testifying that Jim Crow was stolen from a black person or persons; and songs were adapted from the New Orleans acts of the black singers Picayune Butler and Old Corn Meal. See Cantwell, *Bluegrass Breakdown*, 262; Toll, *Blacking Up*, 45.

19. Newman, "Was Tom White?"

20. Stowe's use of legal material is discussed in Crane, "Dangerous Sentiments"; and Grüner, "Stowe's *Dred*," 1–37. *Dred*'s three appendices consist of evidence drawn from *The Key to Uncle Tom's Cabin* on legal and clerical matters and the "confessions" of Nat Turner, including the court certificate of judgment upon him (Stowe, *Dred*, 678–726).

21. Plumer's version reads, "If abolitionists will set the country in a blaze, it is but fair that they should receive the first warning [*sic*] at the fire" (from a letter to the chairman of the Committee of Correspondence, Richmond Presbyterian Church, quoted in Stowe, *The Key to Uncle Tom's Cabin*, 400).

22. Levine, *Martin Delany*, 146, 161, 168. On Vesey see Stowe, *Dred*, 268, 273. Compare the description of Milly (*Dred*, 82–85), her story (*Dred*, 227–44), and her clash with Dred (*Dred*, 575–77) with Stowe's "Sojourner Truth, the Libyan Sibyl." Stowe's article was first published long after *Dred* in the *Atlantic Monthly* of April 1863. Yellin argues that Stowe makes Truth "passive" and a "mutilate," a reading I find perverse, since although the portrait is marred by condescension on Stowe's part and Truth is represented speaking in exaggerated dialect, Stowe cannot obscure Truth's extraordinary dynamism and vitality, and, as Levine observes, the article clearly indicates that she took control of the meeting. See Yellin, *Women and Sisters*, 81–82; and Levine, *Martin Delany*, 153.

23. Levine, *Martin Delany*, 147. See also his "In and Out of the Parlor."

24. Douglass, *Narrative*, 107.

25. Stowe's sister Catharine had founded and run two schools, the Hartford Female Seminary and the Western Female Institute; Stowe had studied at Hartford and taught at both. Catharine had campaigned for women to be trained as teachers and sent to schoolchildren in the West, and Stowe had written a geography textbook for schools. See Beecher, *The Evils Suffered by American Women*; and Hedrick, *Harriet Beecher Stowe*, 58–66 and passim.

26. Stowe, *The Key to Uncle Tom's Cabin*, 25.

27. See also *The Key to Uncle Tom's Cabin*, 25. Jekyl here paraphrases Douglass's master, Hugh Auld, who says, "If you give a nigger an inch he will take an ell" (Douglass, *Narrative*, 78).

28. Douglass, *Narrative*, 83.

29. Douglass, *Narrative*, 81.

30. Hentz, *The Planter's Northern Bride*, 94, 63.

31. McIntosh, *The Lofty and the Lowly*, 207.

32. Butt, *Antifanaticism*, 179–87, 187.

33. Hentz, *The Planter's Northern Bride*, 206.

34. Eastman, *Aunt Phillis's Cabin*, 33, 32, 63.

35. Hamilton, "*Dred*: Intemperate Slavery," 264, 261.

36. Birdoff, *The World's Greatest Hit*, 30.

37. Stowe, *The Key to Uncle Tom's Cabin*, 220–22.

38. Yanuck, "The Garner Fugitive Slave Case"; Campbell, *The Slave Catchers*, 144–47.

39. Grüner, "Stowe's *Dred*," 11.

40. Stowe, *Sunny Memories*, 335.

41. McCord, *Louisa S. McCord*, 330–60, 357–58.

42. Rush, *North and South*, 226.

43. Hedrick, *Harriet Beecher Stowe*, 209.

44. Hamilton, "*Dred*: Intemperate Slavery," 265.

45. Harris, *Nights with Uncle Remus*.

46. Both derive from the Latin *servus*. See the *Oxford English Dictionary*.

47. Stowe, *The Key to Uncle Tom's Cabin*, v.

48. Stowe, *The Key to Uncle Tom's Cabin*, 365, emphasis in the original.

49. Hentz, *The Planter's Northern Bride*, 324, 322, 326.

50. McIlwaine, *The Southern Poor-White*, 36.

51. McIlwaine notes several examples of grog-selling poor whites in antislavery fiction (*The Southern Poor-White*, 35–36).

52. Rush, *North and South*, 304.

53. Hentz, *The Planter's Northern Bride*, 64, 65.

54. On southwestern humor see Rourke, *American Humor*; Blair and Meine, eds., *Half Horse Half Alligator*; James M. Cox, "Humor of the Old South West," in Rubin Jr., ed., *The Comic Imagination*, 101–12; Hauck, *Crockett*; Gray, *Writing the South*; Reynolds, *Beneath the American Renaissance*.

55. Hauck points out the frequency with which this boast has been evoked, from the Crockett stories through Twain's *Life on the Mississippi* and into the television age (*Crockett*, 77); it is obviously also the reference in the title to Blair and Meine's *Half Horse Half Alligator*. Twain's debt to the southwestern tradition has long been acknowledged, while Newman has further drawn out the connections between Twain and Stowe in "Was Tom White?"

56. Twain, *Adventures of Huckleberry Finn*, 70–72.

57. Lott, "Mr Clemens and Jim Crow," 138–39.

58. Simms, *The Sword and the Distaff*, 316.

59. This is related to Mackethan's argument that Widow Eveleigh is an answer to Stowe's powerful women ("Domesticity in Dixie") and Weller's that Simms masculinizes feminine roles to "redefine sentimentality as an expression of male sensibilities" ("'Written with a Mrs Stowe's Feeling,'" 158–59).

60. Simms, *The Sword and the Distaff*, 240.

61. Wiley, *The North-Carolina Reader*. On Wiley see O'Brien, *Conjectures of Order*, 1:346–50.

62. Wiley, *Life at the South*, 82, my emphasis, 124, 106–7.

63. Moore and Burgess Minstrels, *Uncle Tom's Cabin*.

64. Wiley, *Life at the South*, 108.

65. Trollope, *Domestic Manners*, 126.

66. Trollope, *Domestic Manners*, 130–31. Compare with Wiley, *Life at the South*, 108.

67. Trollope, *Domestic Manners*, 131.

68. Jo proclaims, "I don't know nothink" (Dickens, *Bleak House*, 313).

69. Adams, *Harriet Beecher Stowe*, 43. It is also worth comparing Tomtit with the child Stowe depicts in her portrait of Sojourner Truth (Stowe, "Sojourner Truth, the Libyan Sibyl").

70. Criswell, *"Uncle Tom's Cabin" Contrasted with Buckingham Hall*, 149.

71. Hungerford, *The Old Plantation*, 101.

72. Kennard Jr., "Who Are Our National Poets?" 336–37.

73. Kennard Jr., "Who Are Our National Poets?" 336.

74. Loggins, *The Negro Author*, 16.

Epilogue

1. This period is dealt with most comprehensively in Birdoff, *The World's Greatest Hit*. See also Leonard, *Masquerade in Black*, 185.

2. "Uncle Tom's Cabin," playbill, n.p., n.d. (probably early 1900s); "Uncle Tom's Cabin," playbill, Warren, New Hampshire.

3. Riggio, "Uncle Tom Reconstructed"; see also Weller, "'Written with a Mrs Stowe's Feeling.'"

4. Fiedler, *What Was Literature?*

5. The other was Albion Tourgée's *A Fool's Errand*. See Chesnutt, *The Journals*, 50, 125.

6. Charles Chesnutt, "The Passing of Grandison," in Chesnutt, *The Collected Stories*, originally published in *The Wife of His Youth* (1899). See Meer, "The Passing of Charles Chesnutt."

7. Johnson, *The Autobiography of an Ex-Colored Man*, 35; Thurman, *The Blacker the Berry*, 40; Wright, *Uncle Tom's Children*; Jones, *Uncle Tom's Cabin: Alternate Ending*; Reed, *Flight to Canada*; Alexander, *I Ain't Yo' Uncle*; Jones, *Last Night on Earth*, 205.

8. Wright, *Uncle Tom's Children*, xxx.

BIBLIOGRAPHY

ABBREVIATION

LCC   The Lord Chamberlain's Collection, The British Library

PLAYS IN MANUSCRIPT COLLECTIONS

Aiken, George L. *The Key to Uncle Tom's Cabin.* 1853. G. C. Howard Collection, Harry Ransom Humanities Research Center, University of Texas at Austin.

——. *Uncle Tom's Cabin.* Undated prompt copy with manuscript additions to unattributed printed source. G. C. Howard Collection, Harry Ransom Humanities Research Center, University of Texas at Austin.

Conway, H. J. *Uncle Tom's Cabin.* Boston Museum, 1876. Harry Ransom Humanities Research Center, University of Texas at Austin.

[Courtney, John.] *Uncle Tom's Cabin.* First performed at the Royal Surrey, 1 November 1852. LCC.

Fitzball, Edward. *Uncle Tom's Cabin.* First performed at Drury Lane, December 1852. LCC.

[Fitzball, Edward.] *Uncle Tom's Cabin.* First performed at the Royal Olympic, 20 September 1852. LCC.

Pitt, G. D. *Uncle Tom's Cabin: A Nigger Drama.* First performed at the Pavilion Theatre, 9 October 1852. LCC.

The Slave Hunt! or, St. Clare and the Happy Days of Uncle Tom. First performed at the Victoria, 21 February 1853. LCC.

Uncle Tom's Cabin. First performed at the City of London theatre, January 1853. LCC.

Uncle Tom's Cabin. Operatic version, first performed October 1852. LCC.

Uncle Tom's Cabin; or, the Fugitive Slave! First performed at the Victoria, 20 September 1852. LCC.

Uncle Tom's Cabin—or the Negro Slave. First performed at the Standard, 13 September 1852. LCC.

Uncle Tom's Crib! or Nigger Life in London!! First performed at the Strand, 14 October 1852. LCC.

[Young, H.] *Equestrian Version of Uncle Tom's Cabin.* First performed at Astley's Amphitheatre, 22 November 1852. LCC.

PRINTED PRIMARY SOURCES

Academicus. "To the Editor of *The Times*." *Times* (London). 1 December 1852, 8B.

"Adelphi." *Theatrical Journal* (London). 8 December 1852, 385.

Advertisement. *Era* (London). 12 September 1852, 1.

"The Affectionate and Christian Address of Many Thousands of the Women of England to Their Sisters, the Women of the United States of America." *Times* (London). 9 November 1852, 3F.

"An Affectionate and Christian Address of Many Thousands of the Women of the United States of America to Their Sisters, the Women of England." *Times* (London). 13 January 1853, 3.

Aiken, George L. *Uncle Tom's Cabin*. In *Dramas from the American Theatre, 1762–1909*. Edited by Richard Moody, 360–96. Boston: Houghton Mifflin, 1970.

Alexander, Robert. *I Ain't Yo' Uncle: The New Jack Revisionist "Uncle Tom's Cabin."* In *Colored Contradictions: An Anthology of Contemporary African American Plays*. Edited by Harry J. Elam Jr. and Robert Alexander. New York: Plume/Penguin, 1996.

"American Slavery." *Times* (London). 3 September 1852. Reprinted in *New York Daily Times*. 18 September 1852, 5.

"American Slavery and Uncle Tom's Cabin." *North British Review* (November 1852): 235–58.

"Aunt Phillis's Cabin." *Liberator*. 8 October 1852, 163.

"Aunt Phillis's Cabin Again." *Liberator*. 8 October 1852, 163.

Beecher, Catharine. *The Evils Suffered by American Women and American Children: The Causes and the Remedy*. New York: Harper and Brothers, 1846.

"Benefit of Frank Brower." Playbill. Sanford's Opera House, Philadelphia, 23 September 1859. Harvard Theatre Collection.

"Blackberrying." In *Dramas from the American Theatre, 1762–1909*. Edited by Richard Moody, 486–87. Boston: Houghton Mifflin, 1970.

Black Diamonds by "Professor Julius Cesar Hannibal" of the New York Picayune. New York: A. Romney, 1855.

"Black Letters: or Uncle Tom-Foolery in Literature." *Graham's Magazine* (February 1853): 209–15.

Bodichon, Barbara Leigh Smith. *An American Diary 1857–8*. Edited by Joseph W. Reed Jr. London: Routledge and Kegan Paul, 1972.

Bremer, Frederika. *Homes of the New World*. London: Arthur Hall, 1853.

Briggs, Charles. "Uncle Tomitudes." *Putnam's Monthly* (January 1853): 97–102.

[Brown, David.] *The Planter; or, Thirteen Years in the South*. Philadelphia: H. Hooker, 1853.

Brown, William Wells. *The American Fugitive in Europe: Sketches of Places and People Abroad*. 1855. Reprinted as *The Travels of William Wells Brown*. Edited by Paul Jefferson. New York: Markus Wiener, 1991.

——. Letter to William Lloyd Garrison. London, 17 May 1853. Reprinted in *Journal of Negro History* 10 (1925): 544–45.

Burnett, Frances Hodgson. *The One I Knew the Best of All*. London: Frederick Warne, 1893.

Butt, Martha Haines. *Antifanaticism: A Tale of the South*. Philadelphia: Lippincott Grambo, 1853.

"Cabin and Parlor." *Southern Literary Messenger* (November 1852): 703.

"The Cabin and the Parlor." *Liberator*. 7 January 1853, 2.

Characters and Scenes in Uncle Tom's Cabin. Webb's Juvenile Drama. London: Webb, n.d.

Chase, Lucien B. *English Serfdom and American Slavery: Or Ourselves As Others See Us*. New York: H. Long, 1854.

Cheap Book Newspaper and Magazine Establishment of T. B. Peterson. Catalog. Philadelphia: T. B. Peterson, 1852.

Chesnutt, Charles W. *The Collected Stories of Charles W. Chesnutt*. Edited by William L. Andrews. New York: Mentor, 1992.

——. *The Journals of Charles W. Chesnutt*. Edited by Richard H. Brodhead. Durham, NC: Duke University Press, 1993.

——. *The Marrow of Tradition*. In *Three Classic African-American Novels*. Edited by Henry Louis Gates Jr. New York: Vintage Classics, 1990.

Christy, E. P. *Christy's Plantation Melodies*. 3 vols. Baltimore, MD: Fisher and Brothers, 1854.

C.L. "An Old Actor's Memories: What Mr Edmon S. Conner Recalls about His Career." *New York Times*. 5 June 1881, 10.

Cowdin, Mrs. V. G. *Ellen; or, The Fanatic's Daughter*. Mobile: S. H. Goetzel, 1860.

Craft, William and Ellen. *Running a Thousand Miles for Freedom: The Escape of William and Ellen Craft from Slavery*. Edited by Barbara McCaskill. Athens: Brown Thrasher Books, University of Georgia Press, 1999.

Criswell, Robert. *"Uncle Tom's Cabin" Contrasted with Buckingham Hall, the Planter's Home; or, A Fair View of the Slavery Question*. New York: Fanshaw, 1852.

Darkey Plays: A Collection of Ethiopian Dramas, Farces, Interludes, Burlesque Operas, Extravaganzas, Comicalities, Whimsicalities, Etc., Etc. New York: Happy Hours Company, n.d.

Daumier, Honoré. "Actualités." *Le Charivari* (Paris). 18 November 1852, 3.

Denman, Lord. *Uncle Tom's Cabin, Bleak House, Slavery and the Slave Trade: Six Articles by Lord Denman Reprinted from the Standard*. London: Longman, Brown, Green and Longmans, 1853.

Dickens, Charles. *American Notes for General Circulation*. 1842. Edited by John S. Whitley and Arnold Goldman. London: Penguin Classics, 1985.

——. *Bleak House*. 1853. Edited by Nicola Bradbury. Harmondsworth: Penguin, 1996.

——. *A Christmas Carol*. 1843. In *The Christmas Books*. Vol. 1. Edited by Michael Slater. London: Penguin Classics, 1985.

——. *Hard Times*. 1854. Edited by David Craig. London: Penguin Classics, 1985.

——. "The Lazy Tour of Two Idle Apprentices in Five Chapters: Chapter the First." *Household Words*. 3 October 1857. In *"Gone Astray" and Other Papers from Household Words*. Edited by Michael Slater, 420–28. London: J. M. Dent, 1998.

——. *Martin Chuzzlewit.* 1844. London: Penguin Classics, 1986.

——. *Oliver Twist.* 1837–39. Harmondsworth: Penguin, 1985.

——. *Our Mutual Friend.* 1865. Harmondsworth: Penguin, 1997.

Disraeli, Benjamin. *Coningsby, or the New Generation.* 1844. Edited by Thom Braun. Harmondsworth: Penguin, 1989.

——. *Sybil, or the Two Nations.* 1845. Edited by Thom Braun. London: Penguin Classics, 1985.

Dixey's Essence of Burnt Cork. Philadelphia: Winch, 1859.

Douglass, Frederick. "The Anti-Slavery Movement. A Lecture by Frederick Douglass before the Rochester Ladies' Anti-Slavery Society." *Frederick Douglass' Paper.* 23 March 1855, 2.

——. "The Heroic Slave." In *Autographs for Freedom.* Edited by Julia Griffiths. Boston: J. P. Jewett, 1853.

——. *Life and Times of Frederick Douglass, His Early Life as a Slave, His Escape from Bondage, and His Complete History: An Autobiography.* 1881. New York: Gramercy Books, 1993.

——. *The Life and Writings of Frederick Douglass.* Edited by Philip S. Foner. New York: International Publishers, 1975.

——. *My Bondage and My Freedom.* 1855. New York: Dover, 1969.

——. *Narrative of the Life of Frederick Douglass, an American Slave.* 1845. Edited by Houston A. Baker. London: Penguin, 1986.

——. "What to the Slave Is the Fourth of July?" Speech given in Rochester, New York, 5 July 1852. Reprinted in Frederick Douglass, *The Frederick Douglass Papers.* Series 1, *Speeches, Debates, and Interviews.* 5 vols. Edited by John W. Blassingame, 2:359–88. New Haven, CT: Yale University Press, 1982.

Doyle, Richard. "The Land of Liberty." *Punch: or, the London Charivari* (London) (1847): 215.

"Drama." *Critic* (London). 1 January 1853, 27.

"Drama, Public Amusements & c." *Critic* (London). 1 October 1852, 521.

"Drama, Public Amusements & c." *Critic* (London). 1 December 1852, 631–32.

"Dred." *Blackwoods Edinburgh Magazine* (Edinburgh) (December 1856): 693–714.

"*Dred* and *American Slavery.*" *Quarterly Review* (London) (January–April 1857): 324–52.

Du Bois, W. E. B. *The Souls of Black Folk.* 1903. Edited by Donald Gibson. London: Penguin, 1989.

Dumont, Frank. *The Witmark Amateur Minstrel Guide and Burnt Cork Encylopaedia.* Chicago: M. Witmark, 1899.

"The Earl of Shaftesbury's Rejoinder." *Globe* (London). 26 January 1853, 1.

Eastman, Mary H. *Aunt Phillis's Cabin.* Philadelphia: Lippincott Grambo, 1852.

"The Effect of Uncle Tom in Europe." *New York Independent.* 5 May 1852, 69–70.

Eliot, George. Review of *Dred: A Tale of the Great Dismal Swamp* by Harriet Beecher Stowe. In *Critical Essays on Harriet Beecher Stowe.* Edited by Elizabeth Ammons, 43–44. Boston: Hall, 1980.

"The Ethiopian Serenaders." *Illustrated London News.* 24 January 1846, 61.

"Ethiopian Serenaders—St James's Theatre." *Daily News* (London). 18 March 1846, 4.

Fitzball, Edward. *Thirty-five Years of a Dramatic Author's Life*. London: Newby, 1859.

Flanders, Mrs. G. M. *The Ebony Idol*. New York: Appleton, 1860.

Foster, Stephen. *Stephen Foster: Minstrel Show Songs*. New York: Da Capo Press, 1980.

Garrison, William Lloyd. *"Uncle Tom's Cabin: or, Life Among the Lowly." Liberator*. 26 March 1852, 50.

George Christy and Woods Minstrels. Playbill. New York, 10 April 1854. Harvard Theatre Collection.

"Grand Combination of Talent." *Punch: or, the London Charivari* (London) (1847): 153.

Grayson, William J. *The Hireling and the Slave, Chicora and Other Poems*. Charleston, SC: McCarter, 1856.

"H. J. Conway's *Uncle Tom's Cabin*." Program. Boston, 15 November 1852. Boston Museum. Harvard Theatre Collection.

"H. J. Conway's *Uncle Tom's Cabin* at the Boston Museum." Playbill. Boston, 15 November 1852. Harvard Theatre Collection.

Hale, Sarah Josepha. *Liberia; or, Mr Peyton's Experiments*. New York: Harper & Brothers, 1853.

Hall, Rev. Bayard R. *Frank Freeman's Barber's Shop*. New York: Charles Scribner, 1852.

Hamblin, Louisa. *Nick of the Woods*. 1837. In *Victorian Melodramas*. Edited by James L. Smith. London: Dent, 1976.

Harris, Joel Chandler. *Nights with Uncle Remus: Myths and Legends of the Old Plantation*. Boston: Houghton Mifflin, 1881.

Hawthorne, Nathaniel. *House of the Seven Gables*. 1851. Harmondsworth: Penguin American Classics, 1986.

———. *The Scarlet Letter*. 1850. Edited by Nina Baym. Harmondsworth: Penguin, 1986.

Hentz, Caroline Lee. *The Planter's Northern Bride*. 1854. Edited by Rhoda Ellison. Chapel Hill: University of North Carolina Press, 1970.

Herndon, Mary E. *Louise Elton; or, Things Seen and Heard*. Philadelphia: Lippincott, Grambo, 1853.

[Hildreth, Richard]. *Archie Moore, the White Slave; or, Memoirs of a Fugitive*. 1836. Boston: Tappan and Whittemore, 1852.

Hill, Martha. "The Ghost of Uncle Tom, Composed by Miss Martha Hill, and Sung by the Hutchinson Family at Their Concerts throughout the Union." New York: Horace Waters, [1854]. American Antiquarian Society.

Holmes, George Frederick. "Uncle Tom's Cabin. A Review." *Southern Literary Messenger* (December 1852): 721–31.

Hungerford, James. *The Old Plantation and What I Gathered There in an Autumn Month*. New York: Harper and Brothers, 1859.

Hutchinson, Asa. "Little Topsy's Song." Words by Miss Eliza Cook. Composed and Affectionately Dedicated to His Mother by Asa Hutchinson. As sung at the Concerts of the Hutchinson Family. Boston: Oliver Ditson, 1853. American Antiquarian Society.

Hutton, Laurence. "The Negro on the Stage." *Harper's New Monthly Magazine* 79 (1889): 131–45.

Jackson, Richard, ed. *Stephen Foster Song Book*. New York: Dover, 1974.

Jeffreys, Charles. "Far Away from Old Kentucky." Music by J. H. Tully. London: Jeffreys, 1852.

——, ed. *Songs Sung at the Adelphi Theatre in "Slave Life."* London: C. Jeffreys, n.d.

Johnson, James Weldon. *The Autobiography of an Ex-Colored Man*. 1912. London: X Press, 1995.

Johnston, J. R. "Miss Elizabeth T. Greenfield–'The Black Swan.'" *Frederick Douglass' Paper*. 26 February 1852, 3.

Jones, Bill T. *Last Night on Earth*. New York: Pantheon, 1995.

Jones, LeRoi. *Uncle Tom's Cabin: Alternate Ending*. In *The Fiction of LeRoi Jones/Amiri Baraka*. Chicago: Lawrence Hill, 2000.

"Juba at Vauxhall." *Illustrated London News*. 5 August 1848, 77.

Kennard, J., Jr. "Who Are Our National Poets?" *Knickerbocker; or, New York Monthly Magazine* (October 1845): 334–41.

"The Ladies' Battle." *Punch* (London) (1853): 83.

"The Ladies of the Creation, or, How I Was Cured of Being a Strong-Minded Woman." *Punch* (London) (1853): v–xvi.

"The Lady Abolitionists." *Spectator* (London). 4 December 1852, 1163–64.

Lemon, Mark, and Tom Taylor. *Slave Life; or, Uncle Tom's Cabin*. London: Webster, n.d.

"Literature of Slavery." *New Englander* (November 1852): 588–613.

"Logic for the Legrees." *Punch* (London) (1853): 52.

MacLeod, Donald. *Gloomy Memories in the Highlands of Scotland versus Mrs. Harriet Beecher Stowe's Sunny Memories in (England) a Foreign Land: or a Faithful Picture of the Extirpation of the Celtic Race from the Highlands of Scotland*. 1856. Glasgow: Archibald Sinclair, 1892.

Mathews, Charles. *Mr Mathews at Home*. 1821. Edited by Richard L. Klepac. London: Society for Theatre Research, 1979.

Mathews, Mrs. Charles. *The Life and Correspondence of Charles Mathews, the Elder*. Edited by Edmund Yates. London: Routledge, Warne and Routledge, 1860.

Mayhew, Henry. *London Labour and the London Poor*. London: Penguin, 1985.

McCord, Louisa S. *Louisa S. McCord: Political and Social Essays*. Edited by Richard Lounsbury. Charlottesville: University Press of Virginia, 1995.

McIntosh, Maria Jane. *The Lofty and the Lowly; or, Good in All and None All-good*. New York: Appleton, 1853.

Melville, Herman. "Bartleby the Scrivener." 1853. In *Billy Budd and Other Stories*. Edited by Harold Beaver. Harmondsworth: Penguin, 1985.

"Metropolitan Theatres." *Theatrical Journal* (London). 15 September 1852, 291.

"Metropolitan Theatres." *Theatrical Journal* (London). 29 September 1852, 307.

"Metropolitan Theatres." *Theatrical Journal* (London). 8 December 1852, 386.

"Metropolitan Theatres." *Theatrical Journal* (London). 11 December 1852, 378.

Moody, Richard, ed. *Dramas from the American Theatre 1762–1909*. Boston: Houghton Mifflin, 1966.

Moore, G. W. *G. W. Moore's Ethiopian Anecdotes and Goakes*. London: Clarke, 1869.

Moore and Burgess Minstrels. *Uncle Tom's Cabin Told in Musical Tableaux Vivants by George R. Sims*. Music by Ivan Caryll. London: J. Miles & Co., n.d.

Moreau, Charles C., ed. *Negro Minstrelsy in New York*. 2 vols. New York: N.p., 1891.

"Mr. B. Young Respectfully Announces His Benefit." Playbill. Philadelphia, 24 May 1864. Library Company of Philadelphia.

"Mr. J. C. Carpenter's Entertainment." *Theatrical Journal* (London). 5 January 1853, 7.

"Mrs. H. B. Stowe at Stafford House." *Illustrated London News*. 14 May 1853, 374.

"Mrs Mary E. Webb." *Morning Herald* (London). 29 July 1856, 5E.

"Music and the Drama." *Athenaeum* (London). 25 September 1852, 1039.

Nathanson, Y. S. "Negro Minstrelsy, Ancient and Modern." *Putnam's Monthly Magazine* (January 1855): 72–79.

"National Theatre–A. H. Purdy." Playbill. New York, 10 September 1852.

Neale, Frederick. *Uncle Tom's Cabin: or, Harlequin and Lucy Neal*. Juvenile version adapted by J. K. Green. London: Green, n.d.

Nevin, Robert P. "Stephen C. Foster and Negro Minstrelsy." *Atlantic Monthly* (November 1867): 608–16.

"A New Thing." *Liberator*. 8 October 1852, 163.

Northup, Solomon. *Twelve Years a Slave: Narrative of Solomon Northup*. 1853. In *Puttin' on Ole Massa: The Narratives of Henry Bibb, William Wells Brown, and Solomon Northup*. Edited by Gilbert Osofsky, 225–406. New York: Harper and Row, 1969.

"Novels and Their Influences." *Pennsylvanian*. Reprinted in *Liberator*. 11 June 1852.

The Olive-Branch; or, White Oak Farm. Philadelphia: J. B. Lippincott, 1857.

"Olympic." *Theatrical Journal* (London). 29 September 1852, 307.

Ordway's Aeolians. Playbill. Ordway Hall, Washington St., Boston, 20 January 1853.

Our Day. Devoted to Choice Literature, Business, the News, Commerce. Pamphlet advertising Sanford's Opera House for the 1860–61 season. Philadelphia: Sanford's Opera House, 1861. Harvard Theatre Collection.

Page, John W. *Uncle Robin's Cabin in Virginia and Tom Without One in Boston*. Richmond: J. W. Randolph, 1853.

"The Patriot Julia." Reprinted in *Liberator*. 18 February 1853, 28.

[Peterson, Charles Jacobs.] Pseud. J. T. Randolph. *The Cabin and Parlor; or, Slaves and Masters*. Philadelphia: T. B. Peterson, 1852.

Pillsbury, Parker. "'Uncle Tom's Cabin' at a Boston Theatre." *Ohio Antislavery Bugle*. 16 November 1852. Reprinted in *Liberator*. 24 December 1852, 205.

"The Political Crisis in the United States." *Edinburgh Review* (Edinburgh) (July–October 1856): 561–97.

A Popular Selection of Ethiopian Melodies As Sung at Sanford's American Opera House, (Eleventh St. above Chesnut) by His Unrivaled Troupe. Philadelphia: McLaughlin Brothers, 1855.

Reade, Charles. *It Is Never Too Late to Mend: A Matter-of-Fact Romance*. 1856. London: James Nisbet, n.d.

Reed, Ishmael. *Flight to Canada*. 1976. New York: Scribner's, 1998.

"Repetition of the New Southern Drama of the Old Plantation. The Real Uncle Tom by Mr. G. W. Jamison." Playbill. Bowery Theatre, New York, 7 March 1860. Harvard Theatre Collection.

Reynolds, George W. M. "Black Slavery Abroad and White Slavery at Home." *Reynolds's Newspaper* (London). 10 April 1853, 8C.

R.G.D. "To the Editor of *The Times*." *Times* (London). 1 December 1852, 8B.

Rush, Caroline E. *North and South, or, Slavery and Its Contrasts. A Tale of Real Life*. Philadelphia: Crissy and Markley, 1852.

Sable Harmonists. Playbill. Boston, 24 March (no year). Harvard Theatre Collection.

Sam Sharpley's Minstrels. Program. Philadelphia, n.d. Harvard Theatre Collection.

Sanford's Opera House. Playbill. Philadelphia, 15 August 1861. Harvard Theatre Collection.

Schoolcraft, Mrs. Henry R. *The Black Gauntlet: A Tale of Plantation Life in South Carolina*. Philadelphia: J. B. Lippincott, 1860.

Scott, John F., ed. *Brudder Bones Book of Stump Speeches and Burlesque Orations*. New York: Dick & Fitzgerald, 1868.

Search, Edward. "From Our London Correspondent." *Liberator*. 20 May 1853.

"The 'Senior Editor' against Uncle Tom's Cabin." *New York Independent*. 16 June 1852.

Shuttleworth, Janet Kay. "To the Editor of *The Times*." *Times* (London). 1 December 1852, 8C.

Simms, William Gilmore. *The Letters of William Gilmore Simms*. 3 vols. Edited by Mary C. Simms Oliphant, Alfred Taylor Odell, and T. C. Duncan Eaves. Columbia: University of South Carolina Press, 1954.

——. *The Sword and the Distaff: or "Fair, Fat and Forty" a Story of the South at the Close of the Revolution*. Charleston: Walker, Richards, 1852.

"Sisters and Slavery." *Punch* (London) (1853): 37.

"Slavery in the United States." *Times* (London). 29 November 1852, 8C.

Smith, W. L. G. *Uncle Tom's Cabin As It Is; or, Life at the South: Being Narratives, Scenes, and Incidents in the Real "Life of the Lowly."* London: W. Tegg, n.d.

Smith, William Henry. *The Drunkard*. 1837. In *Victorian Melodramas*. Edited by James L. Smith. London: Dent, 1976.

[Smythe, James M.] *Ethel Somers: or, the Fate of the Union*. Augusta: H. D. Howell, 1857.

Soran, Charles, and John H. Hewitt. "Aunt Harriet Becha Stowe." Baltimore, MD: Henry McCaffrey; New Orleans: H. D. Hewitt, 1853.

Southwood, Marian. *Tit for Tat: A Novel by a Lady of New Orleans*. New York: Garret; London: Clarke, Beeton, 1856.

"Stafford House." Advertisement. *Daily News* (London). 25 and 26 July 1856, 4.

"Stafford House: Dramatic Readings by a Coloured Native of Philadelphia." *Daily News* (London). 29 July 1856, 5.

"Stafford House: Dramatic Readings by a Coloured Native of Philadelphia." *Illustrated London News* (London). 2 August 1856, 121–22.

Starnes, Ebenezer. *The Slaveholder Abroad: or, Billy Buck's Visit, with His Master, to England*. Philadelphia: J. B. Lippincott, 1860.

Stowe, C. E. "Preface." In *Sunny Memories of Foreign Lands* by Harriet Beecher Stowe. 2 vols. 1:i–xli. Boston: Phillips, Sampson; New York: J. C. Derby, 1854.

Stowe, Harriet Beecher. "Antislavery Literature." *New York Independent*. 21 February 1856.

——. *The Christian Slave: A Drama Founded on a Portion of "Uncle Tom's Cabin."* Boston: Phillips, Sampson, 1855.

——. *The Christian Slave: A Drama Founded on a Portion of "Uncle Tom's Cabin."* London: Sampson Low, 1856.

——. *Dred; A Tale of the Great Dismal Swamp*. 1856. Edited by Judie Newman. Halifax: Ryburn BAAS American Library, 1992.

——. *The Key to Uncle Tom's Cabin*. London: Clarke, Beeton, 1853.

——. "Sojourner Truth, the Libyan Sibyl." In *Narrative of Sojourner Truth: A Bondswoman of Olden Time, with a History of Her Labors and Correspondence Drawn from Her "Book of Life."* 1878. Edited by Jeffrey C. Stewart. New York: Oxford University Press, 1991.

——. *Sunny Memories of Foreign Lands*. Author's ed. with illustrations. 1 vol. London: Sampson Low, 1854.

——. *Sunny Memories of Foreign Lands*. 2 vols. Boston: Phillips, Sampson; New York: J. C. Derby, 1854.

——. *Uncle Tom's Cabin*. 1852. Edited by Elizabeth Ammons. New York: W. W. Norton, 1994.

"A Talk with Mrs. Tyler." *Punch* (London) (1853): 89.

"Testimonial to Manager A. H. Purdy." Playbill. Purdy's National Theatre, New York, 1855. Harvard Theatre Collection.

"The Theatres." *Spectator* (London). 4 December 1852, 1159–60.

[Thorpe, T. B.] *The Master's House: A Tale of Southern Life*. New York: McElrath, 1854.

Thurman, Wallace. *The Blacker the Berry*. 1929. London: X Press, 1994.

["Tom-mania."] *Spectator* (London). 4 December 1852, 1160.

"To the Duchess of Sutherland and the Ladies of England." *Southern Literary Messenger* 19 (February 1853): 120–26.

"To the Earl of Shaftesbury." *Times* (London). 1 December 1852, 8B.

[Townsend, Mrs. Gideon.] *The Brother Clerks: A Tale of New Orleans*. New York: Derby & Jackson, 1857.

Trollope, Frances. *Domestic Manners of the Americans*. 1832. Edited by Pamela Neville-Sington. Harmondsworth: Penguin, 1997.

Trotter, James M. *Music and Some Highly Musical People*. 1878. Chicago: Afro-Am Press, 1969.

Twain, Mark. *Adventures of Huckleberry Finn*. 1884. Edited by Sculley Bradley et al. New York: W. W. Norton, 1977.

——. *Autobiography of Mark Twain*. London: Chatto and Windus, 1960.

——. *Pudd'nhead Wilson.* 1894. Harmondsworth: Penguin Classics, 1986.

Tyler, Julia Gardiner. "Address 'To the Duchess of Sutherland and the Ladies of England.'" *Southern Literary Messenger.* 19 February 1853, 120–26.

The Tyrant! The Slave!! The Victim!!! & The Tar!!!! London: Thomas Hailes Lacy, [1864].

"'Uncle Bull's Cribbing' Published by Everybody and Co." *Punch* (London) (1852): 135.

"Uncle Tom Among the Bowery Boys." *New York Daily Times.* 27 July 1853.

Uncle Tom: An Ethiopian Interlude in One Scene. New York: Happy Hours Company, 1874. In *Nineteenth-Century American Drama.* New Canaan, CT: Readex, 1980. Microfiche.

"*Uncle Tom* at the Paris Ambigu-Comique." *Spectator* (London). 22 January 1853, 79.

"Uncle Tom Dramatized." *New York Daily Tribune.* 8 August 1853. Reprinted in playbill. National Theatre, New York, September 1853. Harvard Theatre Collection.

"Uncle Tom Dramatized." *New York Herald.* 23 July 1853.

"The Uncle Tom Epidemic." *Literary World.* 4 December 1852, 355–58.

"Uncle Tom in England." *Liberator.* 8 October 1852, 163.

Uncle Tom in England: or, A Proof that Black's White. London: Houlston and Stoneman; New York: A. D. Failing, 1852.

"Uncle Tom in Europe." *New York Independent.* 5 May 1852, 69.

"Uncle Tom on His Travels." *New York Tribune.* Reprinted in *Liberator.* 4 March 1853, 33.

"'Uncle Tom' on the Stage." *Liberator.* 9 September 1853, 142.

"Uncle Tom's Cabin." Letter to *Times* (London). 7 September 1852. Reprinted in *Liberator.* 22 October 1852, 170.

"Uncle Tom's Cabin." *Liberator.* 8 October 1852, 163.

"Uncle Tom's Cabin." *New York Observer.* 26 May 1853, 1666.

"Uncle Tom's Cabin." *Nonconformist* (London). 8 September 1852, 707–9.

"Uncle Tom's Cabin." Playbill. Academy of Music in Chelsea, New York, [1860s]. Harvard Theatre Collection.

"Uncle Tom's Cabin." Playbill. Bowery Theatre, New York, 10 February 1854. Harvard Theatre Collection.

"Uncle Tom's Cabin." Playbill. N.p., n.d. Harvard Theatre Collection.

"Uncle Tom's Cabin." Playbill. People's Hall, Montpelier, [1880s]. Harvard Theatre Collection.

"Uncle Tom's Cabin." Playbill. Royal Lyceum, Toronto, 6 February 1857. Harvard Theatre Collection.

"Uncle Tom's Cabin." Playbill. Warren, New Hampshire, 1934. Harvard Theatre Collection.

"*Uncle Tom's Cabin.*" *Southern Literary Messenger* (October 1852): 630–38.

"Uncle Tom's Cabin." *Times* (London). 3 September 1852, 5.

"Uncle Tom's Cabin." *Times* (London). 7 September 1852. Reprinted in *Liberator.* 22 October 1852, 170.

Uncle Tom's Cabin. Webb's Juvenile Drama. London: H. J. Webb, n.d.

"Uncle Tom's Cabin As It Is." *Liberator.* 8 October 1852, 163.

Uncle Tom's Cabin: A Story of Negro Slavery. Pictorial Plays. London: G. Purkess, n.d.

"*Uncle Tom's Cabin*, by Harriet Beecher Stowe." *Literary World.* 24 April 1852, 291–92.

"The Uncle Tom's Cabin Mania." *British Army Despatch.* Reprinted in *Liberator.* 21 January 1853, 9.

"Vidi." *Mr. Frank: The Underground Mail-Agent.* Philadelphia: Lippincott, Grambo, 1853.

Webb, Frank. "Biographical Sketch." In *The Christian Slave: A Drama Founded on a Portion of "Uncle Tom's Cabin"* by Harriet Beecher Stowe, i–iii. London: Sampson Low, 1856.

"Westminster Theatre: The Political Topsy." *Punch, or the London Charivari.* 23 October 1852, 178–79.

Wetmore, W. J. "Uncle Tom's Cabin Song, Duette and Quartette, As Sung by the National Vocalists, also by New Orleans Serenaders." Song sheet. New York: Millett's Music Saloon, 1852.

"*The White Slave: or, Memoirs of a Fugitive.*" *National Era.* 5 August 1852, 126.

Wiley, Calvin Henderson. *The Adventures of Old Dan Tucker, and His Son Walter: A Tale of North Carolina.* London: Willoughby, 1851.

——. *Life at the South: A Companion to "Uncle Tom's Cabin."* Philadelphia: T. B. Peterson, 1852.

——. *The North-Carolina Reader.* Philadelphia: Lippincott, Grambo, 1851.

——. *Roanoke: or, Where Is Utopia.* In *Sartains Union Magazine of Literature and Art* (1849).

Wilson, William J. "From Our Brooklyn Correspondent." *Frederick Douglass' Paper.* 17 June 1852, 3.

"Woman's True Mission, or 'The Noble Ladies of England.'" *Southern Literary Messenger* (May 1853): 303–6.

Wood, Henry, and Alfred Sedgwick. "Poor Uncle Tom, Song and Chorus." Song sheet. American Antiquarian Society.

Wright, Richard. *Uncle Tom's Children.* 1940. New York: Harper Perennial, 1993.

SECONDARY SOURCES

Adams, Bluford. *E Pluribus Barnum: The Great Showman and the Making of U.S. Popular Culture.* Minneapolis: University of Minnesota Press, 1997.

Adams, John R. *Harriet Beecher Stowe.* Boston: Twayne, 1989.

Altick, Richard. *The English Common Reader: A Social History of the Mass Reading Public, 1800–1900.* Chicago: University of Chicago Press, 1957.

——. "English Publishing and the Mass Audience in 1852." In *Writers, Readers and Occasions: Selected Essays on Victorian Literature and Life.* Edited by Richard Altick. Columbus: Ohio State University Press, 1989.

——. *The Shows of London.* Cambridge, MA: Harvard University Press, 1978.

"American Literary Publishing Houses, 1638–1899 Part 2 N–Z." In *Dictionary of Lit-*

erary Biography. Edited by Peter Dzwonkoski, 49:360–65. Detroit: Gale Research, 1986.

Ammons, Elizabeth, ed. *Critical Essays on Harriet Beecher Stowe*. Boston: Hall, 1980.

——. "Stowe's Dream of the Mother-Savior: *Uncle Tom's Cabin* and American Women Writers before the 1920s." In *New Essays on Uncle Tom's Cabin*. Edited by Eric J. Sundquist, 155–95. Cambridge: Cambridge University Press, 1986.

Andrews, William L. *To Tell a Free Story: The First Century of Afro-American Autobiography, 1760–1865*. Urbana: University of Illinois Press, 1986.

Anthony, Barry. "Early Nigger Minstrel Acts in Britain." *Music Hall* 12 (1980): 118–23.

Austin, William W. *"Susanna," "Jeannie," and "The Old Folks at Home": The Songs of Stephen C. Foster from His Time to Ours*. New York: Macmillan, 1975.

Baddeley, V. C. Clinton. *The Burlesque Tradition in the English Theatre after 1660*. London: Methuen, 1952.

Baker, Houston A. "Introduction." In *Narrative of the Life of Frederick Douglass, an American Slave* by Frederick Douglass. London: Penguin, 1986.

Baker, Martin, and Roger Sarbin. *The Lasting of the Mohicans: The History of an American Myth*. Jackson: University Press of Mississippi, 1995.

Bank, Rosemarie K. *Theatre Culture in America, 1825–1860*. Cambridge: Cambridge University Press, 1997.

Banks, Marva. "Uncle Tom's Cabin and Antebellum Black Response." In *Readers in History: Nineteenth-Century American Literature and the Contexts of Response*. Edited by James L. Machor, 209–27. Baltimore, MD: Johns Hopkins University Press, 1993.

Bassnett, Susan, and André Lefevere, eds. *Translation, History and Culture*. London: Pinter, 1990.

Battiscombe, Georgiana. *Shaftesbury: A Biography of the Seventh Earl: 1801–1885*. London: Constable, 1974.

Baym, Nina. *Woman's Fiction: A Guide to Novels by and about Women in America, 1820–1870*. Ithaca, NY: Cornell University Press, 1978.

Bédarida, François. *A Social History of England, 1851–1990*. Translated by A. S. Forster and Jeffrey Hodgkinson. London: Routledge, 1991.

Bennett, Andrew, ed. *Readers and Reading*. London: Longman, 1995.

Birdoff, Harry. *The World's Greatest Hit: Uncle Tom's Cabin*. New York: S. F. Vanni, 1947.

Blackett, Richard. *Building an Antislavery Wall: Black Americans in the Atlantic Abolitionist Movement, 1830–1860*. Baton Rouge: Louisiana State University Press, 1983.

——. "Cracks in the Antislavery Wall: Frederick Douglass's Second Visit to England (1859–1860) and the Coming of the Civil War." In *Liberating Sojourn: Frederick Douglass and Transatlantic Reform*. Edited by Martin Crawford and Alan Rice, 187–206. Athens: University of Georgia Press, 1999.

Blair, Walter, and Franklin J. Meine, eds. *Half Horse Half Alligator: The Growth of the Mike Fink Legend*. Chicago: University of Chicago Press, 1956.

Bolt, Christine. *The Anti-Slavery Movement and Reconstruction: A Study of Anglo-American Co-operation 1833–1877*. London: Oxford University Press, 1969.

——. *Victorian Attitudes to Race*. London: Routledge and Kegan Paul, 1971.

Booth, Michael R. *English Melodrama*. London: Herbert Jenkins, 1965.

——. "Melodrama and the Working Class." In *Dramatic Dickens*. Edited by Carol Hanbery Mackay, 96–109. London: Macmillan, 1989.

——. *Theatre in the Victorian Age*. Cambridge: Cambridge University Press, 1991.

——. *Victorian Spectacular Theatre 1850–1910*. Boston: Routledge and Kegan Paul, 1981.

Boskin, Joseph. *Sambo: The Rise and Demise of an American Jester*. New York: Oxford University Press, 1986.

Bowlby, Rachel. "Breakfast in America—*Uncle Tom*'s Cultural Histories." In *Nation and Narration*. Edited by Homi K. Bhabha, 197–212. London: Routledge, 1990.

Bratton, J. S. "English Ethiopians: British Audiences and Black-face Acts, 1835–65." *Yearbook of English Studies* 2 (1981): 126–42.

Bratton, J. S., Jim Cook, and Christine Gledhill, eds. *Melodrama: Stage, Picture, Screen*. London: British Film Institute, 1994.

Braun, Thom. "Introduction." In *Coningsby, or the New Generation* by Benjamin Disraeli, 7–21. Harmondsworth: Penguin, 1989.

Brodhead, Richard H. "Veiled Ladies: Toward a History of Antebellum Entertainment." *American Literary History* 1 (1989): 273–93.

Brody, Jennifer DeVere. *Impossible Purities: Blackness, Femininity and Victorian Culture*. Durham, NC: Duke University Press, 1998.

Brown, Gillian. *Domestic Individualism: Imagining Self in Nineteenth-Century America*. Berkeley: University of California Press, 1990.

Brown, Herbert Ross. *The Sentimental Novel in America 1789–1860*. Durham, NC: Duke University Press, 1940.

Brown, T. Allston. *A History of the New York Stage from the First Performance in 1732 to 1901*. 1903. New York: Benjamin Blom, 1964.

"Brownlow, William Gannaway." In *American National Biography*.

Butsch, Richard. *The Making of American Audiences from Stage to Television, 1750–1990*. Cambridge: Cambridge University Press, 2000.

Campbell, Stanley W. *The Slave Catchers: Enforcement of the Fugitive Slave Law, 1850–1860*. Chapel Hill: University of North Carolina Press, 1968.

Cannadine, David. *Class in Britain*. New Haven, CT: Yale University Press, 1998.

——. *The Decline and Fall of the British Aristocracy*. New Haven, CT: Yale University Press, 1990.

Cantwell, Robert. *Bluegrass Breakdown: The Making of the Old Southern Sound*. Urbana: University of Illinois Press, 1984.

Certeau, Michel de. "Reading as Poaching." Reprinted from *The Practice of Everyday Life*. Translated by Steven Rendall. In *Readers and Reading*. Edited by Andrew Bennett, 155. London: Longman, 1995.

Clark, Susan F. "Solo Black Performance before the Civil War: Mrs. Stowe, Mrs. Webb, and 'The Christian Slave.'" *New Theatre Quarterly* 13 (1997): 339–48.

Cockrell, Dale. *Demons of Disorder: Early Blackface Minstrels and Their World*. Cambridge: Cambridge University Press, 1997.

"Cooper, Antony Ashley, Seventh Earl of Shaftesbury." In *Dictionary of National Biography*.

Crane, Gregg D. "Dangerous Sentiments: Sympathy, Rights and Revolution in Stowe's Antislavery Novels." *Nineteenth-Century Literature* 51 (1996): 176–204.

Crozier, Alice C. *The Novels of Harriet Beecher Stowe*. New York: Oxford University Press, 1969.

Cunliffe, Marcus. *Chattel Slavery and Wage Slavery: The Anglo-American Context 1830–1850*. Athens: University of Georgia Press, 1979.

Davis, J. Frank. "Tom Shows." *Scribner's Magazine* 67 (1925): 355–60.

Davis, Richard Beale. "Mrs. Stowe's Characters-in-Situations and a Southern Literary Tradition." In *Essays on American Literature in Honor of Jay B. Hubbell*. Edited by Clarence Gohdes, 108–25. Durham, NC: Duke University Press, 1967.

Dennison, Sam. *Scandalize My Name: Black Imagery in American Popular Music*. New York: Garland, 1982.

Dillard, J. L. *Black English: Its History and Usage in the United States*. New York: Random House, 1972.

Douglas, Ann. *The Feminization of American Culture*. New York: Alfred A. Knopf, 1977.

Duvall, Severn. "*Uncle Tom's Cabin*: The Sinister Side of the Patriarchy." *New England Quarterly* 36 (1963): 3–22.

Eacker, Susan. "A 'Dangerous Inmate' of the South: Louisa McCord on Gender and Slavery." In *Southern Writers and Their Worlds*. Edited by Christopher Morris and Steven G. Reinhardt, 27–40. Arlington: Texas A&M University Press, 1996.

Eaklor, Vicki L. *American Antislavery Songs: A Collection and Analysis*. New York: Greenwood, 1988.

Emerson, Ken. *Doo-Dah! Stephen Foster and the Rise of American Popular Culture*. New York: Da Capo Press, 1988.

Fiedler, Leslie. *What Was Literature? Class Culture and Mass Society*. New York: Simon and Schuster, 1982.

Finkelman, Paul. *Dred Scott v. Sandford: A Brief History with Documents*. Boston: Bedford Books, 1997.

——. *An Imperfect Union: Slavery, Federalism, and Comity*. Chapel Hill: University of North Carolina Press, 1981.

Finlayson, Geoffrey B. A. M. *The Seventh Earl of Shaftesbury*. London: Eyre Methuen, 1981.

Finson, Jon. *The Voices That Are Gone: Themes in Nineteenth Century American Popular Song*. New York: Oxford University Press, 1994.

Fisch, Audrey. *American Slaves in Victorian England*. Cambridge: Cambridge University Press, 2000.

Fishkin, Shelley Fisher. *Was Huck Black? Mark Twain and African American Voices*. New York: Oxford University Press, 1993.

Fladeland, Betty. *Abolitionists and Working-Class Problems in the Age of Industrialization*. Baton Rouge: Louisiana State University Press, 1984.

———. *Men and Brothers: Anglo-American Antislavery Cooperation.* Urbana: University of Illinois Press, 1972.

Foster, Charles H. *The Rungless Ladder: Harriet Beecher Stowe and New England Puritanism.* Durham, NC: Duke University Press, 1954.

Foster, Frances Smith. *Witnessing Slavery: The Development of Ante-Bellum Slave Narratives.* Westport, CT: Greenwood, 1979.

Foucault, Michel. "What Is an Author?" Translated by Donald F. Bouchard. *Screen* 20 (1979): 13–29.

Foulkes, Richard. *Church and Stage in Victorian England.* Cambridge: Cambridge University Press, 1997.

Fox-Genovese, Elizabeth. *Within the Plantation Household: Black and White Women of the Old South.* Chapel Hill: University of North Carolina Press, 1988.

Franchot, Jenny. "The Punishment of Esther: Frederick Douglass and the Construction of the Feminine." In *Frederick Douglass: New Literary and Historical Essays.* Edited by Eric J. Sundquist, 141–65. Cambridge: Cambridge University Press, 1990.

Fredrickson, George M. *The Black Image in the White Mind: The Debate on Afro-American Character and Destiny, 1817–1914.* New York: Harper and Row, 1971.

Gaines, Francis Pendleton. *The Southern Plantation: A Study in the Development and Accuracy of a Tradition.* New York: Columbia University Press, 1924.

Gallagher, Catherine. *The Industrial Reformation of English Fiction: Social Discourse and Narrative Form, 1832–1867.* Chicago: University of Chicago Press, 1985.

Gara, Larry. "The Professional Fugitive in the Abolition Movement." *Wisconsin Magazine of History* 48 (1964): 196–204.

Gardiner, Jane. "The Assault upon Uncle Tom: Attempts of Pro-Slavery Novelists to Answer *Uncle Tom's Cabin*, 1852–60." *Southern Humanities Review* 12 (1978): 313–24.

———. "Proslavery Propaganda in Fiction Written in Answer to *Uncle Tom's Cabin*, 1852–61: An Annotated Checklist." *Resources for American Literary Study* 7 (1977): 201–9.

Gardner, Eric. "Stowe Takes the Stage: Harriet Beecher Stowe's *The Christian Slave.*" *Legacy* 15 (1998): 78–84.

Gerson, Noel. *Harriet Beecher Stowe: A Biography.* New York: Praeger, 1976.

Gilbertson, Catherine. *Harriet Beecher Stowe.* New York: D. Appleton–Century, 1937.

Giles, Paul. *Transatlantic Insurrections: British Culture and the Formation of American Literature, 1730–1860.* Philadelphia: University of Pennsylvania Press, 2001.

Gilroy, Paul. *The Black Atlantic: Modernity and Double Consciousness.* London: Verso, 1993.

Ginzberg, Lori D. *Women and the Work of Benevolence: Morality, Politics and Class in the Nineteenth-Century United States.* New Haven, CT: Yale University Press, 1990.

Glavin, John. *After Dickens: Reading, Adaptation and Performance.* Cambridge: Cambridge University Press, 1999.

Gohdes, Clarence. *American Literature in Nineteenth-Century England.* New York: Columbia University Press, 1944.

Gossett, Thomas F. *Uncle Tom's Cabin and American Culture*. Dallas: Southern Methodist University Press, 1985.

Gravil, Richard. *Romantic Dialogues: Anglo-American Continuities, 1776–1862*. Houndsmills: Macmillan, 2000.

Gray, Richard. *Writing the South: Ideas of an American Region*. Cambridge: Cambridge University Press, 1986.

Green, Alan W. C. "'Jim Crow,' 'Zip Coon': The Northern Origins of Negro Minstrelsy." *Massachusetts Review* 11 (1970): 385–97.

Greenberg, Kenneth S. *Honor and Slavery*. Princeton, NJ: Princeton University Press, 1996.

Grigson, Jane. *English Food*. 1974. London: Penguin, 1992.

Grimble, Ian. "Introduction." In *Gloomy Memories: The Highland Clearances of Strathnaver* by Donald MacLeod, 24–30. Bettyhill: Strathnaver Museum, 1996.

Grimstead, David. *Melodrama Unveiled: American Theater and Culture 1800–1850*. Chicago: University of Chicago Press, 1968.

Grüner, Mark Randall. "Stowe's *Dred*: Literary Domesticity and the Law of Slavery." *Prospects* 20 (1995): 1–37.

Guillory, John. *Cultural Capital: The Problem of Literary Canon Formation*. Chicago: University of Chicago Press, 1993.

Guy, Josephine M. *The Victorian Social-Problem Novel*. Houndsmills: Macmillan, 1996.

Hadley, Elaine. *Melodramatic Tactics: Theatricalized Dissent in the English Marketplace, 1800–1885*. Stanford, CA: Stanford University Press, 1995.

Hall, D. D. "A Yankee Tutor in the Old South." *New England Quarterly* 33 (1960): 82–91.

Halttunen, Karen. *Confidence Men and Painted Women: A Study of Middle-Class Culture in America, 1830–1870*. New Haven, CT: Yale University Press, 1982.

Hamilton, Cynthia S. "*Dred*: Intemperate Slavery." *Journal of American Studies* 34 (2000): 257–77.

Hamm, Charles. *Putting Popular Music in Its Place*. Cambridge: Cambridge University Press, 1995.

——. *Yesterdays: Popular Song in America*. New York: Norton, 1979.

Handlin, David P. *The American Home: Architecture and Society, 1815–1915*. Boston: Little, Brown, 1979.

Harrold, Stanley. *The Abolitionists and the South, 1831–1861*. Lexington: University Press of Kentucky, 1995.

——. *American Abolitionists*. Harlow: Longman, 2001.

Hauck, Richard Boyd. *Crockett: A Bio-Bibliography*. Westport, CT: Greenwood, 1982.

Hayne, Barrie. "Yankee in the Patriarchy: T. B. Thorpe's Reply to *Uncle Tom's Cabin*." *American Quarterly* 20 (1968): 180–95.

Hedrick, Joan. *Harriet Beecher Stowe: A Life*. New York: Oxford University Press, 1994.

——, ed. *The Oxford Harriet Beecher Stowe Reader*. New York: Oxford University Press, 1999.

Herstein, Sheila R. *A Mid-Victorian Feminist, Barbara Leigh Smith Bodichon*. New Haven, CT: Yale University Press, 1985.

Hetherington, Hugh W., ed. *Cavalier of Old South Carolina: William Gilmore Simms*. Chapel Hill: University of North Carolina Press, 1966.

Hildreth, Margaret Holbrook. *Harriet Beecher Stowe: A Bibliography*. Hamden, CT: Shoestring Press, 1976.

Hirsch, Pam. *Barbara Leigh Smith Bodichon: Feminist, Artist and Rebel*. 1998. London: Pimlico, 1999.

Hirsch, Stephen A. "Uncle Tomitudes, the Popular Reaction to *Uncle Tom's Cabin*." In *Studies in the American Renaissance*. Edited by Joel Myerson, 303–30. Boston: Twayne, 1978.

Holmberg, Carl Bryan, and Gilbert D. Schneider. "Daniel Decatur Emmett's Stump Sermons: Genuine Afro-American Culture, Language and Rhetoric in the Negro Minstrel Show." *Journal of Popular Culture* 19 (Spring 1986): 27–38.

Hovet, Theodore R. "Mrs. Thomas C. Upham's 'Happy Phebe': A Feminine Source of Uncle Tom." *American Literature* 51 (1979): 267–70.

Hughes, Kathryn. *George Eliot: The Last Victorian*. London: Fourth Estate, 1999.

Innes, C. L. *A History of Black and Asian Writing in Britain, 1700–2000*. Cambridge: Cambridge University Press, 2002.

Iser, Wolfgang. *The Act of Reading: A Theory of Aesthetic Response*. Translated by David Henry Wilson. Baltimore, MD: Johns Hopkins University Press, 1978.

Jackson, Blyden. "The Minstrel Mode." In *The Comic Imagination in American Literature*. Edited by Louis D. Rubin Jr., 149–56. New Brunswick, NJ: Rutgers University Press, 1973.

Jackson, Richard, ed. *Popular Songs of Nineteenth-Century America*. New York: Dover, 1976.

Jordan, Philip D. *Singin' Yankees*. Minneapolis: University of Minnesota Press, 1947.

Kaplan, Fred. *Dickens: A Biography*. Baltimore, MD: Johns Hopkins University Press, 1988.

Keely, Karen A. "Lippincott, Joshua Ballinger." In *American National Biography*. Edited by John A. Garraty and Mark C. Carnes, 17:722–23. New York: Oxford University Press, 1999.

Kelley, Mary. *Private Woman, Public Stage: Literary Domesticity in Nineteenth Century America*. New York: Oxford University Press, 1984.

Kerber, Linda K. "Abolitionists and Amalgamators: The New York City Race Riots of 1834." *New York History* 48 (1967): 28–39.

Klingberg, Frank J. "Harriet Beecher Stowe and Social Reform in England." *American Historical Review* 43 (1938): 542–52.

Lapsansky, Phillip S. "Afro-Americana: Frank J. Webb and His Friends." *Annual Report of the Library Company of Philadelphia for 1990* (1991): 27–43.

——. "Graphic Discord: Abolitionist and Antiabolitionist Images." In *The Abolitionist Sisterhood: Women's Political Culture in Antebellum America*. Edited by Jean Fagan Yellin and John C. Van Horne, 201–30. Ithaca, NY: Cornell University Press in Cooperation with the Library Company of Philadelphia, 1994.

Lauter, Paul. *Canons and Contexts*. New York: Oxford University Press, 1991.

Lease, Benjamin. *Anglo-American Encounters: England and the Rise of American Literature*. Cambridge: Cambridge University Press, 1981.

Leonard, William Talbot. *Masquerade in Black*. Metuchen, NJ: Scarecrow Press, 1986.

"Leveson-Gower, Harriet Elizabeth." In *Dictionary of National Biography*.

Levine, Lawrence W. *Black Culture and Black Consciousness: Afro-American Folk Thought from Slavery to Freedom*. New York: Oxford University Press, 1977.

Levine, Robert S. "In and Out of the Parlor." *American Literary History* 7 (1995): 669–80.

——. *Martin Delany, Frederick Douglass and the Politics of Representative Identity*. Chapel Hill: University of North Carolina Press, 1997.

——. "*Uncle Tom's Cabin* in *Frederick Douglass' Paper*: An Analysis of Reception." *American Literature* 64 (1992): 71–93.

Lhamon, W. T., Jr. *Raising Cain: Blackface Performance from Jim Crow to Hip Hop*. Cambridge, MA: Harvard University Press, 1998.

Litwack, Leon. *North of Slavery*. Chicago: University of Chicago Press, 1961.

Loggins, Vernon. *The Negro Author: His Development in America*. New York: Columbia University Press, 1931.

Lorimer, Douglass A. "Bibles, Banjoes and Bones: Images of the Negro in the Popular Culture of Victorian England." In *In Search of the Visible Past: History Lectures at Wilfrid Laurier University, 1973–4*. Edited by Barry M. Gough, 31–50. Waterloo, Ontario: Wilfrid Laurier University Press, 1975.

——. *Colour, Class and the Victorians: English Attitudes to the Negro in the Mid-Nineteenth Century*. Leicester: Leicester University Press, 1978.

Lott, Eric. *Love and Theft: Blackface Minstrelsy and the American Working Class*. New York: Oxford University Press, 1993.

——. "Mr Clemens and Jim Crow: Twain, Race, and Blackface." In *The Cambridge Companion to Mark Twain*. Edited by Forrest G. Robinson, 129–52. Cambridge: Cambridge University Press, 1995.

Mabee, Carleton, and Susan Mabee Newhouse. *Sojourner Truth: Slave, Prophet, Legend*. New York: New York University Press, 1993.

Machor, James L., ed. *Readers in History: Nineteenth Century American Literature and the Contexts of Response*. Baltimore, MD: Johns Hopkins University Press, 1993.

Mackethan, Lucinda H. "Domesticity in Dixie: The Plantation Novel and *Uncle Tom's Cabin*." In *Haunted Bodies: Gender and Southern Texts*. Edited by Anne Goodwyn Jones and Susan V. Donaldson. Charlottesville: University of Virginia Press, 1997.

Madison, Charles A. *Book Publishing in America*. New York: McGraw-Hill, 1966.

Mailloux, Steven. "Misreading as a Historical Act: Cultural Rhetoric, Bible Politics, and Fuller's 1845 Review of Douglass's *Narrative*." In *Readers in History: Nineteenth Century American Literature and the Contexts of Response*. Edited by James L. Machor, 3–31. Baltimore, MD: Johns Hopkins University Press, 1993.

Major, Clarence. *Juba to Jive: A Dictionary of African American Slang*. 1970. New York: Penguin, 1994.

Marshall, Herbert, and Mildred Stock. *Ira Aldridge, the Negro Tragedian*. London: Rockliff, 1958.

Mason, Jeffrey D. *Melodrama and the Myth of America*. Bloomington: Indiana University Press, 1993.

Matthews, Brander. "The Rise and Fall of Minstrelsy." *Scribner's Magazine* 57 (1915): 754–59.

McCaskill, Barbara. "'Yours Very Truly': Ellen Craft—The Fugitive as Text and Artifact." *African American Review* 28 (1994): 509–29.

McConachie, Bruce A. "H. J. Conway's Dramatization of *Uncle Tom's Cabin*: A Previously Unpublished Letter." *Theatre Journal* 34 (1982): 149–54.

——. *Melodramatic Formations: American Theatre and Society, 1820–1970*. Iowa City: University of Iowa Press, 1992.

——. "Out of the Kitchen and into the Marketplace: Normalizing *Uncle Tom's Cabin* for the Antebellum Stage." *Journal of American Drama and Theatre* 3 (1991): 5–28.

Mcdowell, Deborah E. "In the First Place: Making Frederick Douglass and the Afro-American Tradition." In *Critical Essays on Frederick Douglass*. Edited by William L. Andrews, 192–213. Boston: Hall, 1991.

McFeely, William S. *Frederick Douglass*. New York: Norton, 1991.

McIlwaine, Shields. *The Southern Poor-White from Lubberland to Tobacco Road*. New York: Cooper Square, 1970.

Meckier, Jerome. *Innocent Abroad: Charles Dickens's American Engagements*. Lexington: University Press of Kentucky, 1990.

Meer, Sarah. "Competing Representations: Douglass, the Ethiopian Serenaders and Ethnic Exhibition in London." In *Liberating Sojourn: Frederick Douglass and Transatlantic Reform*. Edited by Martin Crawford and Alan Rice, 141–65. Athens: University of Georgia Press, 1999.

——. "The Passing of Charles Chesnutt: Mining the White Tradition." *Wasafiri* 27 (1998): 5–10.

——. "Sentimentality and the Slave Narrative: Frederick Douglass's *My Bondage and My Freedom*." In *The Uses of Autobiography*. Edited by Julia Swindells, 89–97. London: Taylor and Francis, 1995.

Meisel, Martin. *Realisations: Narrative, Pictorial, and Theatrical Arts in Nineteenth-Century England*. Princeton, NJ: Princeton University Press, 1983.

Mesick, Jane Louise. *The English Traveller in America 1785–1885*. New York: Columbia University Press, 1922.

Midgley, Clare. *Women Against Slavery: The British Campaigns, 1780–1870*. London: Routledge, 1992.

Minnigerode, Meade. *The Fabulous Forties: 1840–1850*. New York: Putnam, 1924.

Mosely, Caroline. "The Hutchinson Family: The Function of Their Song in Ante-Bellum America." *Journal of American Culture* 1 (1978): 713–23.

Moses, Montrose, and John Mason Brown, eds. *The American Theatre as Seen by Its Critics, 1752–1934*. New York: Cooper Square, 1967.

Mott, Frank Luther. *Golden Multitudes: The Story of Best Sellers in the United States*. New York: Bowker, 1947.

——. *A History of American Magazines, 1850–1865*. Cambridge, MA: Harvard University Press, 1938.

Mullin, Donald. *Victorian Plays: A Record of Significant Productions on the London Stage, 1837–1901*. New York: Greenwood Press, 1987.

Mulvey, Christopher. *Transatlantic Manners: Social Patterns in Nineteenth-Century Anglo-American Travel Literature*. Cambridge: Cambridge University Press, 1990.

Nathan, Hans. *Dan Emmett and the Rise of Negro Minstrelsy*. Norman: University of Oklahoma Press, 1962.

Neville-Sington, Pamela. *Fanny Trollope: The Life and Adventures of a Clever Woman*. London: Viking, 1997.

Nevins, Allan, ed. *American Social History as Recorded by British Travellers*. 1923. New York: Augustus M. Kelley, 1969.

Newman, Judie. "Introduction." In *Dred: A Tale of the Great Dismal Swamp*, by Harriet Beecher Stowe, edited by Judie Newman. Halifax: Ryburn BAAS American Library, 1992.

——. "Stowe's Sunny Memories of Highland Slavery." In *Special Relationships: Anglo-American Affinities and Antagonisms, 1854–1936*. Edited by Janet Beer and Bridget Bennett, 28–41. Manchester: Manchester University Press, 2002.

——. "Was Tom White? Stowe's *Dred* and Twain's *Pudd'nhead Wilson*." *Slavery and Abolition* 20 (1999): 125–36.

Nicoll, Allardyce. *History of the English Drama 1660–1900*. Vol. 6. Cambridge: Cambridge University Press, 1959.

Nye, Russel. *The Unembarrassed Muse: The Popular Arts in America*. New York: Dial Press, 1970.

O'Brien, Michael. *Conjectures of Order: Intellectual Life and the American South, 1810–1860*. 2 vols. Chapel Hill: University of North Carolina Press, 2004.

Odell, George C. *Annals of the New York Stage*. New York: Columbia University Press, 1928.

Papashvily, Helen Waite. *All the Happy Endings: A Study of the Domestic Novel in America, the Women Who Wrote It, the Women Who Read It, in the Nineteenth Century*. Port Washington, NY: Kennikat Press, 1972.

Paskman, Dailey, and Sigmund Spaeth, eds. *"Gentlemen, Be Seated!" A Parade of the Old-Time Minstrels*. Garden City, NY: Doubleday Doran, 1928.

Peterson, Beverly. "Aunt Phillis's Cabin: One Reply to Uncle Tom." *Southern Quarterly* 33 (1994): 97–112.

Pickering, Michael. "'A Jet Ornament to Society': Black Music in Nineteenth-Century Britain." In *Black Music in Britain: Essays on the Afro-Asian Contribution to Popular Music*. Edited by Paul Oliver, 16–33. Milton Keynes: Open University Press, 1990.

——. "Mock Blacks and Racial Mockery: The 'Nigger' Minstrel and British Imperialism." In *Acts of Supremacy: The British Empire and the Stage, 1790–1930*. Edited by J. S. Bratton, 179–236. Manchester: Manchester University Press, 1991.

——. "White Skin, Black Masks: 'Nigger' Minstrelsy in Victorian England." In *Music Hall Performance and Style*. Edited by J. S. Bratton, 70–91. Milton Keynes: Open University Press, 1986.

Powell, Kerry. *Women and the Victorian Theatre*. Cambridge: Cambridge University Press, 1997.

Price, Leah. *The Anthology and the Rise of the Novel: From Richardson to George Eliot*. Cambridge: Cambridge University Press, 2000.

Pugh, Evelyn. "Women and Slavery: Julia Gardiner Tyler and the Duchess of Sutherland." *Virginia Magazine of History and Biography* 188 (1980): 186–202.

Quarles, Benjamin. *Black Abolitionists*. Oxford: Oxford University Press, 1969.

——. "Freedom's Black Vanguard." In *New Issues in the African American Renaissance*. Edited by Nathan I. Huggins, Martin Kilson, and Daniel M. Fox, 1:174–90. New York: Harcourt Brace Jovanovich, 1971.

Rahill, Frank. *The World of Melodrama*. University Park: Pennsylvania State University Press, 1967.

Ransom, Teresa. *Fanny Trollope: A Remarkable Life*. London: Alan Sutton, 1995.

Redmond, James, ed. *Melodrama*. Cambridge: Cambridge University Press, 1992.

Rehin, George F. "Blackface Street Minstrels in Victorian London and Its Resorts: Popular Culture and Its Racial Connotations as Revealed in Polite Opinion." *Journal of Popular Culture* 15 (1981): 19–38.

——. "Harlequin Jim Crow: Continuity and Convergence in Blackface Clowning." *Journal of Popular Culture* 9 (1975): 682–701.

Reynolds, David S. *Beneath the American Renaissance: The Subversive Imagination in the Age of Emerson and Melville*. Cambridge, MA: Harvard University Press, 1988.

Reynolds, Harry. *Minstrel Memories: The Story of Burnt Cork Minstrelsy in Great Britain from 1836 to 1927*. London: Alston Rivers, 1928.

Rezé, Michel. "L'accueil fait à la case de l'Oncle Tom en Angleterre en 1852." *Études Anglaises* 24 (1971): 415–30.

Riach, Douglas. "Blacks and Blackface on the Irish Stage, 1830–60." *Journal of American Studies* 7 (1973): 231–41.

Rice, C. Duncan. "Literary Sources and British Attitudes to Slavery." In *Anti-Slavery, Religion, and Reform: Essays in Memory of Roger Anstey*. Edited by Christine Bolt and Seymour Drescher, 319–34. Folkeston: Dawson, Archon, 1980.

Richards, Eric. *A History of the Highland Clearances: Agrarian Transformation and the Evictions, 1746–1886*. 2 vols. London: Croom Helm, 1982.

Ridgely, J. V. *Nineteenth-Century Southern Literature*. Lexington: University Press of Kentucky, 1980.

——. *William Gilmore Simms*. New York: Twayne, 1962.

——. "*Woodcraft*: Simm's First Answer to *Uncle Tom's Cabin*." *American Literature* 31 (1959–60): 421–33.

Riggio, Thomas P. "Uncle Tom Reconstructed: A Neglected Chapter in the History of a Book." *American Quarterly* 28 (1976): 56–60.

Riis, Thomas L. "The Music and Musicians in Nineteenth-Century Productions of *Uncle Tom's Cabin*." *American Music* 4 (1986): 268–86.

Ripley, C. Peter, ed. *The Black Abolitionist Papers*. Vol. 1, *The British Isles, 1830–1865*. Chapel Hill: University of North Carolina Press, 1985.

Roach, Joseph. *Cities of the Dead: Circum-Atlantic Performance*. New York: Columbia University Press, 1996.

Roediger, David. *The Wages of Whiteness: Race and the Making of the American Working Class*. London: Verso, 1991.

Roppolo, Joseph P. "Uncle Tom in New Orleans: Three Lost Plays." *New England Quarterly* 27 (1954): 213–26.

Rourke, Constance. *American Humor: A Study of the National Character*. 1931. Garden City, NY: Doubleday Anchor Books, 1953.

———. *The Roots of American Culture and Other Essays*. New York: Harcourt Brace, 1942.

Rubin, Louis D., Jr., ed. *The Comic Imagination in American Literature*. New Brunswick, NJ: Rutgers University Press, 1973.

———, ed. *The History of Southern Literature*. Baton Rouge: Louisiana State University Press, 1985.

Ruland, Richard, ed. *The Native Muse: Theories of American Literature from Bradford to Whitman*. 1972. New York: E. P. Dutton, 1976.

Ryan, Mary P. *The Empire of the Mother: American Writing about Domesticity, 1830–1860*. New York: Haworth Press, 1982.

Sabiston, Elizabeth Jean. "Anglo-American Connections: Elizabeth Gaskell, Harriet Beecher Stowe and the 'Iron of Slavery.' " In *The Discourse of Slavery: Aphra Behn to Toni Morrison*. Edited by Carl Plasa and Betty J. Ring, 94–117. London: Routledge, 1994.

Samuels, Shirley, ed. *The Culture of Sentiment: Race, Gender and Sentimentality in Nineteenth-Century America*. New York: Oxford University Press, 1992.

Saxon, A. H. P. T. *Barnum: The Legend and the Man*. New York: Columbia University Press, 1989.

Saxton, Alexander. "Blackface Minstrelsy and Jacksonian Ideology." *American Quarterly* 27 (1975): 3–28.

———. *The Rise and Fall of the White Republic: Class Politics and Mass Culture in Nineteenth Century America*. London: Verso, 1990.

Schlicke, Paul, ed. *Oxford Reader's Companion to Dickens*. Oxford: Oxford University Press, 2000.

Scobie, Edward. *Black Britannia: A History of Blacks in Britain*. Chicago: Johnson, 1972.

Scott, Derek B. *The Singing Bourgeois: Songs of the Victorian Drawing Room and Parlour*. Milton Keynes: Open University Press, 1989.

Seager, Robert, II. *And Tyler Too: A Biography of John & Julia Gardiner Tyler*. New York: McGraw-Hill, 1963.

Shepperson, George. "Harriet Beecher Stowe and Scotland." *Scottish Historical Review* 32 (1953): 40–46.

Smith, Sidonie. *Where I'm Bound: Patterns of Slavery and Freedom in Black American Autobiography*. Westport, CT: Greenwood Press, 1974.

Southern, Eileen. *The Music of Black Americans: A History*. 1971. 2nd ed., with a new foreword, New York: Norton, 1983.

Speight, George. *The Juvenile Drama: A Union Catalogue*. London: Society for Theatre Research, 1999.

——. *The Juvenile Drama: The History of the English Toy Theatre*. London: Macdonald, 1946.

Stampp, Kenneth M. *The Peculiar Institution: Slavery in the Antebellum South*. New York: Vintage, 1956.

Starling, Marion Wilson. *The Slave Narrative: Its Place in American History*. Boston: G. K. Hall, 1982.

Stephens, John Russell. *The Censorship of English Drama 1824–1901*. Cambridge: Cambridge University Press, 1980.

——. "William Bodham Donne: Some Aspects of His Later Career as Examiner of Plays." *Theatre Notebook* 25 (1970): 25–32.

Stepto, Robert B. "Sharing the Thunder: The Literary Exchanges of Harriet Beecher Stowe, Henry Bibb, and Frederick Douglass." In *New Essays on Uncle Tom's Cabin*. Edited by Eric J. Sundquist, 135–53. Cambridge: Cambridge University Press, 1986.

Stewart, James Brewer. *Holy Warriors: The Abolitionists and American Slavery*. 1976. Revised ed., New York: Hill and Wang, 1996.

Stone, Harry. "Charles Dickens and Harriet Beecher Stowe." *Nineteenth Century Fiction* 12 (1957): 188–202.

Stoneman, Patsy. *Brontë Transformations: The Cultural Dissemination of Jane Eyre and Wuthering Heights*. Hemel Hempstead: Prentice Hall/Harvester Wheatsheaf, 1996.

Sundquist, Eric J., ed. *New Essays on Uncle Tom's Cabin*. Cambridge: Cambridge University Press, 1986.

——. "Slavery, Revolution, and the American Renaissance." In *The American Renaissance Reconsidered*. Edited by Walter Benn Michaels and Donald E. Pease, 1–33. Baltimore, MD: Johns Hopkins University Press, 1985.

——. *To Wake the Nations: Race in the Making of American Literature*. Cambridge, MA: Harvard University Press, 1993.

Sutherland, John, ed. *Longman Companion to Victorian Fiction*. Harlow: Longman, 1988.

Tandy, Jeanette Reid. "Pro-Slavery Propaganda in American Fiction of the 'Fifties.'" *South Atlantic Quarterly* 21 (January and April 1922): 41–51, 170–79.

Tawa, Nicholas E. *Sweet Songs for Gentle Americans: The Parlor Song in America, 1790–1860*. Bowling Green, OH: Bowling Green University Popular Press, 1980.

Taylor, Clare. *Women of the Antislavery Movement: The Weston Sisters*. New York: St. Martin's Press, 1995.

——, ed. *British and American Abolitionists: An Episode in Transatlantic Understanding*. Edinburgh: Edinburgh University Press, 1974.

Taylor, William R. *Cavalier and Yankee: The Old South and American National Character*. London: W. H. Allen, 1963.

Tebbel, John. *Between Covers: The Rise and Transformation of Book Publishing in America*. New York: Oxford University Press, 1987.

Thistlethwaite, Frank. *The Anglo-American Connection in the Early Nineteenth Century*. Philadelphia: University of Pennsylvania Press, 1959.

Thorpe, Margaret Farrand. *Female Persuasion: Six Strong-Minded Women.* New Haven, CT: Yale University Press, 1949.

Tillotson, Kathleen. "Introductory." In *Novels of the 1840s.* First published in 1954. Reprinted in *The Victorian Novel: Model Essays in Criticism.* Edited by Ian Watt, 3–26. London: Oxford University Press, 1971.

Tise, Larry E. *Proslavery: A History of the Defense of Slavery in America, 1701–1840.* Athens: University of Georgia Press, 1987.

Toll, Robert. *Blacking Up: The Minstrel Show in Nineteenth Century America.* New York: Oxford University Press, 1974.

Tompkins, Jane. *Sensational Designs: The Cultural Work of American Fiction 1790–1860.* New York: Oxford University Press, 1985.

Uglow, Jenny. *Elizabeth Gaskell.* London: Faber and Faber, 1993.

Wagenknecht, Edward. *Harriet Beecher Stowe: The Known and the Unknown.* New York: Oxford University Press, 1965.

Walters, Raymond. *Stephen Foster: Youth's Golden Gleam.* Princeton, NJ: Princeton University Press, 1936.

Walvin, James. *Black and White: The Negro and English Society 1555–1945.* London: Allen Lane, the Penguin Press, 1973.

Watt, Ian. *The Victorian Novel: Model Essays in Criticism.* London: Oxford University Press, 1971.

Weisbuch, Robert. *Atlantic Double-Cross: American Literature and British Influence in the Age of Emerson.* Chicago: University of Chicago Press, 1986.

Weller, Saranne. "'Written with a Mrs Stowe's Feeling': *Uncle Tom's Cabin* and the Paradigms of Southern Authorship in the Anti-Tom Tradition, 1852–1902." Ph.D. diss., University of Warwick, 2001.

Widdowson, Peter. *Hardy in History: A Study in Literary Sociology.* London: Routledge, 1989.

Williams, Raymond. *Culture and Society.* 1958. London: Hogarth, 1987.

Wilson, A. E. *East End Entertainment.* London: Arthur Barker, 1954.

Wilson, Edmund. *To the Finland Station: A Study in the Writing and Acting of History.* London: Secker and Warburg, 1942.

Wilson, Forrest. *Crusader in Crinoline: The Life of Harriet Beecher Stowe.* London: Hutchinson, 1942.

Wimsatt, Mary Ann. "Antebellum Fiction." In *The History of Southern Literature.* Edited by Louis D. Rubin Jr., 92–107. Baton Rouge: Louisiana State University Press, 1985.

Winans, Robert B. "Early Minstrel Show Music, 1843–1852." In *Musical Theatre in America: Papers and Proceedings of the Conference on the Musical Theatre in America.* Edited by Glenn Laney, 71–97. Westport, CT: Greenwood, 1984.

Winks, Robin W. "The Making of a Fugitive Slave Narrative: Josiah Henson and Uncle Tom: A Case Study." In *The Slave's Narrative.* Edited by Charles T. Davis and Henry Louis Gates Jr., 113–33. Oxford: Oxford University Press, 1985.

Wittke, Carl. *Tambo and Bones: A History of the American Minstrel Stage.* Durham, NC: Duke University Press, 1930.

Wood, Marcus. *Blind Memory: Visual Representations of Slavery in England and America, 1780–1865.* Manchester: Manchester University Press, 2000.

Yanuck, Julius. "The Garner Fugitive Slave Case." *Mississippi Valley Historical Review* 40 (1853): 47–66.

Yarborough, Richard. "Strategies of Black Characterization in *Uncle Tom's Cabin* and the Early Afro-American Novel." In *New Essays on Uncle Tom's Cabin.* Edited by Eric J. Sundquist, 45–84. Cambridge: Cambridge University Press, 1986.

Yellin, Jean Fagan. *Women and Sisters: The Antislavery Feminists in American Culture.* New Haven, CT: Yale University Press, 1989.

Yellin, Jean Fagan, and John C. Van Horne, eds. *The Abolitionist Sisterhood: Women's Political Culture in Antebellum America.* Ithaca, NY: Cornell University Press in Cooperation with the Library Company of Philadelphia, 1994.

Zanger, Jules. "The Minstrel Show as Theater of Misrule." *Quarterly Journal of Speech* 60 (1974): 33–38.

Zboray, Ronald. "Antebellum Reading and the Ironies of Technological Innovation." *American Quarterly* 40 (1988): 65–82.

GENERAL INDEX

INDEX OF CHARACTERS IN VERSIONS OF "UNCLE TOM'S CABIN"

Separate from or
independent of ...